Academic and Professional Publishing

CHANDOS
PUBLISHING SERIES

Chandos' new series of books is aimed at all those individuals interested in publishing. They have been specially commissioned to provide the reader with an authoritative view of current thinking. If you would like a full listing of current and forthcoming titles, please visit our website, www.chandospublishing.com, email wp@woodheadpublishing.com or telephone +44 (0) 1223 399140.

New authors: we are always pleased to receive ideas for new titles; if you would like to write a book for Chandos, please contact Dr Glyn Jones on email gjones@chandospublishing.com or telephone +44 (0) 1993 848726.

Bulk orders: some organisations buy a number of copies of our books. If you are interested in doing this, we would be pleased to discuss a discount. Please contact on email wp@woodheadpublishing.com or telephone +44(0) 1223 499140.

Academic and Professional Publishing

EDITED BY

ROBERT CAMPBELL, ED PENTZ AND IAN BORTHWICK

Oxford Cambridge New Delhi

Chandos Publishing
Hexagon House
Avenue 4
Station Lane
Witney
Oxford OX28 4BN
UK
Tel: +44 (0) 1993 848726
Email: info@chandospublishing.com
www.chandospublishing.com
www.chandospublishingonline.com

Chandos Publishing is an imprint of Woodhead Publishing Limited

Woodhead Publishing Limited
80 High Street
Sawston
Cambridge CB22 3HJ
UK
Tel: +44 (0) 1223 499140
Fax: +44 (0) 1223 832819
www.woodheadpublishing.com

First published in 2012

ISBN: 978-1-84334-669-2 (print)
ISBN: 978-1-78063-309-1 (online)

British Library Cataloguing-in-Publication Data.
A catalogue record for this book is available from the British Library.

Typeset by Domex e-Data Pvt. Ltd.
Printed in the UK and USA.

Contents

List of figures and tables

Figures

Tables

About the authors

Kent Anderson is the CEO/Publisher for the *Journal of Bone & Joint Surgery*. Prior to this, he was the Executive Director of Product Development for the *New England Journal of Medicine*, the Publishing Director for *NEJM*, and Director of Medical Journals at the American Academy of Pediatrics. He has worked in healthcare publishing for more than 20 years, and has been a writer, editor, designer, copy editor, managing editor and publisher. He has launched products, designed systems and created innovative services over the years, and has served on various advisory, professional and oversight boards. He is the Editor-in-Chief of the *Scholarly Kitchen*, writes fiction under his pen name Andrew Kent, and has degrees in English and business.

Caroline Black has worked in STM publishing for more than 25 years, holding senior positions at Current Science, Thomson Science, Lippincott Williams & Wilkins and Blackwell Publishing. After four years as Managing Director of Mac Keith Press, in September 2011 she took up the post of Managing Director of Portland Press Ltd and Group Head of Publishing of the Biochemical Society. Caroline has contributed as a tutor to the STM Intensive Course on Journal Publishing for the past four years and has chaired seminars for ALPSP and ISMTE. She also developed ALPSP's Introduction to Journals Publishing course and ran it until 2010.

Volker Böing is Director of the Process & Content Management Department at the scientific publisher Springer. He studied library and information science and computer science at the Humboldt University Berlin. During his professional career in the scientific publishing industry he worked as project manager, responsible for further development of workflow and content management IT systems and was manager of process and solution design teams.

Ian Borthwick is a Porfolio Development Manager at IET Standards Limited, part of the Institution of Engineering and Technology (IET), UK, where he develops standards-based professional products in energy, sustainability and technology. Ian previously worked as a Commissioning Editor at Woodhead Publishing, UK, where he set up a successful series of energy reference books. Ian is the Under-35 board member of the International Association of Scientific, Technical & Medical Publishers (STM) serving 2008–2014, where his interests lie not only in addressing industry developments and promoting best practices, but also in improving engagement with junior and middle managers in the publishing industry. He also served as Course Tutor on STM's 20th Intensive Course in Journal Publishing – Europe, 2010.

Robert Campbell is Senior Publisher at Wiley-Blackwell Publishing and is Chair of the Publishing Research Consortium (PRC); he is also a former Chair of the International Network for the Availability of Scientific Publications (INASP), the International Association of Scientific, Technical and Medical Publishers (STM) and CrossRef. He received an honorary doctorate from Oxford Brookes University in 2005 and in 2009 received an ALPSP Award for Contribution to Scholarly Publishing. He is the co-author or author of three books on publishing and over 60 articles.

Nick Canty is a lecturer in the Centre for Publishing at University College London, UK, where he teaches on the MA in Publishing programme. He worked in the publishing industry for almost 15 years as a commissioning editor and publisher at Pearson plc, Thomson Reuters and most recently ran a publishing division at a UK-based professional institution. He was a member of the Professional Development Committee of the Association of Learned and Professional Society Publishers (ALPSP) and is a member of the Association for Publishing Education (APE).

Todd Carpenter is Executive Director of the National Information Standards Organization (NISO), www.niso.org, a US-based non-profit membership association that fosters the development and maintenance of standards that facilitate the creation, persistent management and effective interchange of information used in publishing, research and education. In addition to his role at NISO, Mr Carpenter serves as the Secretary of ISO's Technical Committee on Information and Documentation, Subcommittee on Identification and Description (TC 46/SC 9). Prior to joining NISO, Mr Carpenter had been Director of Business Development with BioOne. He has also held management positions at The Johns Hopkins University Press, the Energy Intelligence Group and The Haworth Press. Todd is a graduate of Syracuse University and holds a masters degree in business from The Johns Hopkins University.

Michael Clarke is the Executive Vice President for Product and Market Development at Silverchair Information Systems. In this role he leads Silverchair's development of next-generation semantic tools and platforms for STM and scholarly publishers. Prior to joining Silverchair, he was the founder and principal of Clarke Publishing Group, a consultancy specialising in electronic publishing. Additionally, Michael has held positions at the American Medical Association, the American Academy of Pediatrics and the University of Chicago Press. He currently serves as a board member for both the Society for Scholarly Publishing and the Council of Science Editors. A graduate of the University of Chicago and the University of Colorado, Michael is a frequent contributor to the *Scholarly Kitchen.*

Rod Cookson has been Editorial Director for Earth, Biological and Environmental Science journals at Taylor & Francis since 2007, managing a portfolio of 180 journals. Prior to that, Rod was Geography Publisher at Routledge, and worked on Management and Finance journals for four years at Blackwell Publishing (now Wiley-Blackwell). In total, Rod has worked in Editorial roles for the past 16 years. He takes a keen interest in how technology can enrich and improve researchers' publishing and communication experience. Rod enjoys cycling, playing football, the catharsis provided by West Ham United's endless travails, watching cricket, reading crime fiction and educating his children on the delights of PG Wodehouse and the Marx Brothers.

Adam Finch is an analyst in Science Excellence with the Commonwealth Scientific and Industrial Research Organisation in Australia. His earlier work includes a critical review of author citation metrics appearing in the 2010 volume of *Bioessays*, the establishment of group-level impact metrics for the Cochrane Database of Systematic Reviews, and contribution to a paper for *British Journal of Urology* on the citation performance of British urology researchers. Prior to 2011, he was the Bibliometrics Analyst for Wiley-Blackwell, based in Oxford, UK, in which role he undertook citation analysis and strategic development for dozens of high-impact titles. Since moving to Australia, he has worked as a research performance analyst for Flinders University and a solutions consultant for Thomson Reuters. Competing interests: This chapter was written prior to the author taking on a role with Thomson Reuters Australia.

David Green is Global Journals Publishing Director for Taylor and Francis Group. He is responsible for 1650 journals published under the T&F, Routledge and Psychology Press imprints. He holds BA and MA degrees in Politics from Lancaster University, and a DPhil in international relations from the University of Sussex. David has over three decades of experience in journal publishing. He edited a number of policy journals for Butterworth Scientific in the 1970s and 1980s, before joining Carfax Publishing in 1987, which later was taken over by Routledge – itself acquired by the T&F Group in 1998. David has represented T&F on a number of scholarly publishing industry bodies, and is currently a member of the Steering Committee of the Publishing Research Consortium (PRC), established by the trade bodies to commission independent research on key issues for the industry (http://www.publishingresearch.net/). David enjoys France, Italy, walking, crosswords, historical buildings, art galleries, supporting his football team, watching cricket and music (especially jazz) when he is relaxing.

Irene Hames is an independent editorial consultant and adviser to the publishing, higher education and research sectors. She has a PhD in cell biology but has worked in scientific publishing on scholarly journals and books for over 30 years. She is frequently called upon to give talks and advise on editorial issues, has been a member of a number of working parties on peer review and was the specialist adviser to the UK House of Commons Science and Technology Committee for its inquiry into peer review in 2011. She is the author of the book *Peer Review and Manuscript Management in Scientific Journals: guidelines for good practice*, published by Wiley-Blackwell in association with ALPSP (the Association of Learned and Professional Society Publishers). Irene is a Council Member and Trustee of COPE (Committee on Publication Ethics) and also holds advisory roles with Sense About Science and the International Society of Managing and Technical Editors (ISMTE). In December 2011 she was made a Fellow of the Society of Biology.

John S. Haynes began his career as a research chemist with a PhD from the University of British Columbia, followed by a post-doctoral fellowship at the University of Oxford. He made the transition to scientific publishing in 1988 working for Taylor & Francis and then Academic Press. John spent 17 years at the UK's Institute of Physics

Publishing, serving from 1992 to 2001 as publisher of an impressive suite of physics journals, and from 2001 to 2007 as Head of Business Development, leading IOP's international partnerships in China and Japan. Subsequently, John spent almost two years as Editorial Director for Royal Society of Chemistry, where he put in place an ambitious growth plan. Along the way, he earned an MBA, led publishing workshops for organisations such as INASP and ALPSP, and is a lecturer on the STM Master Class. John joined AIP early in 2009 as Vice President Publishing. He is responsible for AIP's publishing programme, including flagship products and services such as Scitation, UniPHY, and market-leading journals such as *Applied Physics Letters*, *Journal of Applied Physics* and *AIP Advances*.

Michael Jubb is Director of the Research Information Network (RIN). He has held a variety of posts, as an academic historian; as an archivist at the Public Record Office; at the Department of Education and Science; as Deputy Secretary of the British Academy; and as Deputy Chief Executive of the Arts and Humanities Research Board (AHRB) from 1998 to 2005. Since then he has been Director of the RIN, a research and policy unit focusing on the changing needs and behaviours of the key players in the scholarly communications landscape: researchers (in all disciplines), research funders, publishers, libraries and universities. He has been responsible in the past five years for over 30 major reports on key aspects of the scholarly communications landscape, ranging from researchers' use of libraries and their services, through changes to cataloguing and discovery services, to analyses of the economics of scholarly communications, and how they are changing.

Michael Mabe is CEO of the International Association of Scientific, Technical and Medical Publishers (STM) and has over 30 years' experience of academic publishing. After reading chemistry and doing research at Oxford, he joined the scientific staff of OUP's *Oxford English Dictionary*. Since then, he has worked for the British Standards Institution and held a number of senior publishing and management positions at Pergamon Press and Elsevier. He is a Visiting Professor in Information Studies at University College London and at the University of Tennessee, Knoxville, USA. Since 2008 he has been Chair of the PEER Project, a major multi-stakeholder European Union-funded research study of the effects of systematic Green Open Access, which will report its results in 2012.

Tony O'Rourke is Commercial Director for the Royal College of Nursing Publishing. He completed his undergraduate education in 1984, having studied at the Fachhochschule Reutlingen (Dipl. FH. Europäisches Studienprogramm für Betriebwirtschaft), one of Germany's leading Business Schools, and Middlesex University (BA Hons. European Business Administration). Since graduating, Tony has spent his entire career in publishing, working in a wide variety of publishing areas which include trade press, directories, newsletters, reference and full-text datasets, online journals and databases. He has worked for VNU Business Publications (1984–1991), Chadwyck-Healey (1991–2000), now part of ProQuest, IOP Publishing (2000–2012) and RCN Publishing (2012–). In the late 1990s he helped to develop business models used to sell full text and reference works on the Web. He was appointed a Fellow of the Institute of Sales and Marketing Management in 2000. Tony is a Director (Non-Executive) and Member of Council for ALPSP, the Association of Learned and Professional Society Publishers. He has also served on the Serial Publishers Executive of the Publishers Association, UK, as well as on committees of other trade associations. When he is not working, he is Governor of a primary school in North Somerset and is an avid music collector. Tony is married with three children and lives just outside Bristol, UK.

Ed Pentz is the Executive Director of CrossRef, a not-for-profit membership association of publishers set up to provide a cross-publisher reference linking service. Ed was appointed as CrossRef's first Executive Director, and first employee, when the organisation was created in 2000. Prior to joining CrossRef Ed held electronic publishing, editorial and sales positions at Harcourt Brace in the US and UK and managed the launch of Academic Press' first online journal, the *Journal of Molecular Biology*, in 1995. Ed is on the board of directors of ORCID, Inc., the International DOI Foundation and UKSG. Ed has a degree in English Literature from Princeton University and current lives in Oxford, UK, where he enjoys poker, pub quizzes and coaching youth football (soccer).

Frances Pinter was the founding Publisher at Bloomsbury Academic, specialising in humanities and social sciences and pioneering the use of Creative Commons licensing for scholarly books. She is now working independently on developing a variety of open access business models for monographs. She is a Visiting Fellow at the London School of Economics where she conducts research in the area of intellectual property rights. Previously she was Publishing Director at the Soros Foundation

(Open Society Institute) working in 30 transition countries supporting publishing development after the fall of communism. Earlier in her career she founded Pinter Publishers that also owned Leicester University Press and established the imprint Belhaven Press. She has published in Logos and most recently with Hugh Look on 'Open Access and Monograph Publishing' in *New Review of Academic Librarianship*, 2010.

Mark Seeley has spent most of his professional career at Elsevier, the leading science and medical publisher. Mark is active in STM industry and public policy issues, and has contributed to a number of industry guidelines on copyright, permissions and data issues, through the STM trade association. Mark received his B.Ph. from Thomas Jefferson College (Grand Valley State, Michigan) and his J.D. from Suffolk University (Boston), and is admitted to practice in Massachusetts and New York.

Joy van Baren is a User Experience Portfolio Manager for Elsevier's User Centered Design (UCD) team. The UCD team is intimately involved in all phases of the product lifecycle to refine product and service definitions, work directly with customers to understand their needs, and conduct usability tests, all to achieve the ultimate goal to deliver products and interfaces that maximise efficiency for customers. Joy joined Elsevier in 2004, and played an instrumental role in the design and development of the all-science abstract and citation database Scopus. She currently oversees user research and design activities for Elsevier's SciVal suite of performance, planning and funding tools. She participates in large research initiatives such as the JISC-funded study 'Developing tools to inform the management of research and translating existing good practice' conducted by Imperial College London and Elsevier. Joy has an M.Sc. in Applied Cognitive Psychology from the University of Amsterdam and a Professional Doctorate in Engineering in User-System Interaction from Eindhoven University of Technology. Prior to joining Elsevier in 2004 Joy worked as an academic researcher at Eindhoven University of Technology and as Research Associate at Philips Research.

Elizabeth (Liz) Wager is a freelance publications consultant. After a zoology degree from the University of Oxford she worked for Blackwell Scientific Publications as an editor, for Janssen Cilag as a medical writer and then for Glaxo Wellcome as Head of International Medical Publications. Working in the pharmaceutical industry she developed an interest in publication ethics and led the development of Good Publication Practice for Pharmaceutical Companies and was involved in developing the European Medical Writers Association guidelines on the role of medical writers. In 2001, she set up her own company, Sideview, which provides writing, training and consultancy services for doctors, drug companies, publishers and universities. She has acted as a consultant to Wiley-Blackwell and helped to develop the company's Best Practice Guidelines on Publication Ethics. She is a member of the Ethics Committees of both the *BMJ* and the World Association of Medical Editors. She served on the World Health Organization's Scientific Advisory Group on trial registration. She has been a member of the Committee on Publication Ethics' (COPE) governing Council since 2006, serving as Chair from 2009 to 2012. She created the COPE flowcharts, helped to revise COPE's Code of Conduct for Editors and developed its ethical audit.

Lois F. Wasoff has a legal and consulting practice in Concord, Massachusetts, specialising in copyright law and publishing. In addition to her role as general counsel to Publishers International Linking Association, Inc. ('CrossRef'), she works with publishing companies, not-for-profit organisations, individuals and law firms. She was a member of the Section 108 Study Group, which examined the copyright exceptions in US law for libraries and archives, is a past Chairman of the Copyright Committee of the Association of American Publishers and was a Trustee and a member of the Executive Committee of the Copyright Society of the USA. She received her B.A. from Hofstra University (Hempstead, New York) and her J.D. from New York University School of Law, and is admitted to practice in New York and Massachusetts.

Anthony Watkinson is a senior lecturer in the Centre for Publishing at University College London, UK. He spent 40 years in academic and professional publishing with senior posts in Academic Press, Oxford University Press, Chapman & Hall, International Thomson Academic and Professional, Blackwell and Wiley mostly in editorial positions. He is a consultant to the UK Publishers Association and also works for the International Association of Scientific, Technical & Medical Publishers. His research field is scholarly communication and he has published books on how to choose a publisher (for learned societies) and on the management of journals.

Keith Webster is Vice-President and Director of Academic Relations and Strategy at John Wiley & Sons. Before joining Wiley in September 2011, Keith was Dean of Libraries and University Librarian at The University of Queensland in Australia. Previous posts include University Librarian at Victoria University of Wellington, New Zealand, Head of Information Policy at HM Treasury in London and Director of Information Services at the School of Oriental & African Studies, University of London. He has been an Adjunct Professor of Library Management at Victoria University of Wellington and Honorary Professor of Information Science at City University, London. Keith is a Chartered Fellow and an Honorary Fellow of the Chartered Institute of Library and Information Professionals. He has held a number of offices in professional bodies, including Chair of the Editorial Board, *Australian Library Journal*, Vice-President of the Library and Information Association of New Zealand Aotearoa, Honorary Treasurer of the Chartered Institute of Library and Information Professionals, membership of the UK Parliament's Advisory Council on Libraries and Honorary Secretary of the Institute of Information Scientists.

1

Introduction: overview of academic and professional publishing

Robert Campbell

Abstract: This introductory chapter presents the reader with an overview of the historical trends, current status and market developments in academic and professional publishing, and a dark cloud gathering over the industry. The chapter notes how these widespread changes are addressed throughout the book, with chapters providing insight into the integrated, innovative and multi-disciplinary approaches publishers are applying to adapt to the challenges facing the industry and take publishing forward. It also outlines what publishers do, how publishers add value and what the future may look like for the industry.

Key words: Industry trends, peer review, added value, journals, books, data, market development.

Introduction

The purpose of this book is to provide publishing professionals and interested stakeholders with a timely and comprehensive update on the widespread changes in academic and professional publishing and the integrated, innovative and multi-disciplinary approaches being applied to adapt to the challenges presented. While we attempt to cover books, journals and new models for scholarly communication in this work, the emphasis is on journals given their dominant position in the academic and professional publishing market. In several of the chapters, the authors look at recent developments to shape their views on how publishing may evolve. We all agree that we are in a period of rapid change and this has been the stimulus for our writing the book. We also cover what publishers do, how publishers add value and what the future may look like for the industry. This introductory chapter presents the reader with an overview of the historical and current trends and developments, a dark cloud gathering over the industry, and an outlook on the industry's exciting future.

Trends in journal publishing

Journal publishing is a success story, although it has its critics. The nature of this criticism has been fairly constant and is typified by the quotation below:

> 'Librarians are suffering because of the increasing volume of publications and rapidly rising prices. Of special concern is the much larger number of periodicals that are available and that members of the faculty consider essential to the successful conduct of their work. Many instances were found in which science departments were obliged to use all of their allotment for library purposes to purchase their periodical literature which was reported as necessary for the work of the department.'

This might have been published last week, but in fact it appeared in a report prepared for the Association of American Universities in 1927. One of the concerned institutions was Cornell University, where a list of 633 periodical subscriptions increased in price by 182 per cent between 1910 and 1925 (Okerson, 1986).

Such criticism – mainly around pricing, too much published, role and control – has led in the last decade to a much greater understanding of the field, partly gained through research into publishing, which is reflected throughout this book. As a core example, Michael Mabe (in Chapter 17) takes us back to the mid-17th century correspondence of Henry Oldenburg to outline the basic functions of a research journal: registration, certification, dissemination and archiving. This has proven to be a robust model with the number of titles growing steadily in an almost straight-line graph from the launch of *The Philosophical Transaction of the Royal Society* in 1665 to a total of around 23 000 journals (Mabe, 2003) and at least 27 000 in 2011 with the proliferation of pay-to-publish (Gold Road) Open Access titles. Although these basic functions remain the same, means such as pricing and technology continue to evolve as is discussed in several chapters in this book.

Mabe also identified the answer to the 'increasing volume of publishing' concerns, as he showed that journal growth simply reflects the growth in the research community. This trend also addresses another criticism, that peer review is unsustainable as reviewers can no longer be found to review the ever increasing number of articles submitted. The answer is that the growth in the research community and thus the availability of reviewers increases in line with the growth in articles produced (Vines *et al.*, 2010). There is also evidence that the number of articles produced per researcher per annum is dropping slightly, e.g. from 0.82 in 1984 to 0.78 in 1998, although the average number of authors per article is increasing, e.g. from 2.5 in 1980 to 3.8 in 2002 (Moed, 2005).

The four phases of the 'modern journal'

Journals were essentially national entities until the Second World War, published by societies, university presses or specialist academic publishing houses (particularly in Germany). The international research journal as a successful business model stems from the launch of *Biochimica et Biophysica Acta* in 1946. It lost money for several years but was seen by Robert Maxwell and others as the future. The investment in tertiary education and research ensured a well-funded market in the 1950s and 1960s. Mari Pijnenborg at Elsevier saw this as the 'discovery' phase in the four phases of development of the 'modern journal' (see Figure 1.1).

In the second phase, 'exploitation', commercial as well as not-for-profit publishers invested in launching new titles and growing them. Commercial publishers gained market share as they were able to publish more articles and charge accordingly as they were not constrained by needing to keep costs down for members. These subscription-based journals probably reached their peak in hard copy circulation around 1986, when the industry saw more restricted library budgets, cutbacks in holdings and talk of a 'serials crisis'. Publishers had to manage their journals more carefully in the third phase ('management'), seeking efficiencies through new technology (e.g. typesetting) and the economies of scale achieved through mergers and acquisitions.

By the early 1990s the loss in circulation was forcing prices up, leading to further cancellations and thereby reducing access to journal content. A symptom of this problem was the rise in document delivery activity. The British Library's document supply service was delivering over 3 million articles per annum. Publishers sought to collect compensatory

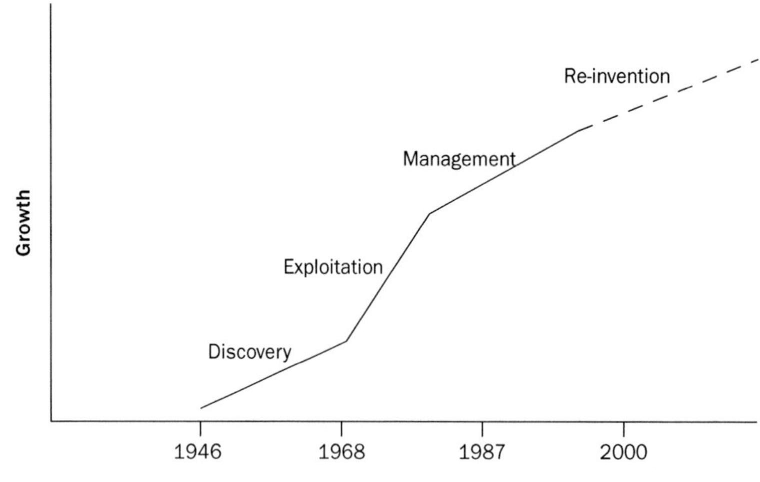

Figure 1.1 The four phases of the 'modern journal', based on an idea from Mari Pijnenborg. From Campbell and Wates (2009)

copyright income from photocopying either directly or through Reproduction Rights Organization (RROs) which grew with this increasing photocopying.

The impact of these difficult times was a driver in the development of the Open Access (OA) movement, although the situation has improved hugely since then. Just in time the Internet and related technology enabled publishers to develop new pricing models based on licences giving online access to much more content for little extra cost, epitomised by the so-called 'Big Deal' (see Chapter 12 by O'Rourke). The development of this transformative pricing model was actually state-funded. The original pilot was funded by the Higher Education Funding Council in the UK in 1996, with the aim of maintaining access to high-quality peer-reviewed journals in the face of rising print-on-paper costs and cancellations, and to reduce the unit cost of information.

We are now deep in the fourth phase, 're-invention', to which most of this book is devoted. Unlike the newspaper and music industries, journal publishing has survived the migration to the digital age stronger and more successful. Part of the explanation for this may be that newspapers and music sell largely to individuals while journals sell largely to institutions.

The role of institutional libraries is to provide access to the appropriate information for researchers and students. The peer-reviewed journal is an essential element and the library community has the responsibility for maintaining this. Librarians may criticise publishers at times, yet they have worked with publishers to see the journal through an extraordinary metamorphosis. The development of journals has depended on the relationship with the library community, although now that research funders have joined the publishing scene (with the aim of ensuring access to the outcome of the research they have funded, as discussed below) the system will most likely become more complex.

The rise, fall and rise in circulation

The circulation of a particular research journal (see Figure 1.2) since its launch in 1972 illustrates the recent history of journals publishing. The print circulation increased steadily reaching a peak in 1986. Despite the efforts of two exceptional editors in this case, and although the journal published more articles and thus became a more significant publication, the circulation fell slowly and steadily. It probably held up better as a life science title than other titles in other disciplines, e.g. chemistry and physics.

As in Mari Pijnenborg's model, 're-invention' for this journal was dramatic. The journal was made available online from 1996 and new pricing models came into play with the minimal extra cost per extra user, as exemplified by the 'Big Deal'. Circulation was also boosted by arrangements with organisations providing access in developing countries (e.g. International Network for the Availability of Scientific Publications – INASP; Access to Global Online Research in Agriculture – AGORA). With a higher rejection rate, higher Impact Factor, faster publication and greater

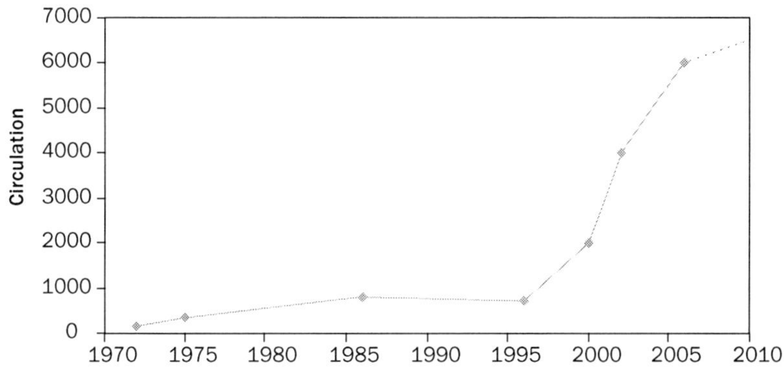

Figure 1.2 The rise, fall and rise in circulation of a research journal. From Campbell and Wates (2008)

circulation, this fairly specialised journal typifies what has been achieved since the mid-1990s (see Chapter 5 by Green and Cookson, and Chapter 6 by Haynes). With hard copy circulation down to 60, it is now effectively an e-journal (see Chapter 8 by Böing).

In contrast, the publication of monographs has seen an unremitting decline in circulation from the early 1970s when print-runs were often around 2500–3000 (see Chapter 5 by Green and Cookson). More titles are produced than ever before but print-runs are down to 300–500. What we saw happen 15 years ago in journals, however, is now happening for monographs as the e-book concept gets underway. There are even OA book publishers (see Chapter 7 by Pinter).

Current status

As discussed above, the journal has come through an initial phase of re-invention successfully, with digitisation of the model leading to much wider access at lower unit cost. However, as indicated in later chapters, after an investment of more than £2 billion since 2000 in digitising the publishing process, there is potential to do a lot more. Around 3500 publishers produce around 1.8 million peer-reviewed articles per year in 27 000 journals. The journal publishing industry employs (directly) 110 000 people globally and publishers return at least 10 per cent of their revenue to the academic community through support for editorial activity. The structure of the industry is presented in Figure 1.3. Many of the small publishers in the industry are self-publishing societies producing one or two titles. A number of journals are also published on behalf of societies by commercial and not-for-profit publishers. Currently there is some migration of titles from self-publishing societies to international publishers (Campbell, 2010).

In total around half of the 27 000 journals are owned and controlled by societies and in virtually all of these cases article peer review and journal policy are the responsibilities of independent academics rather than publishing staff. The false accusation that editorial policy is determined by 'big global businesses' seems to be one irritation that publishers have to put up with and is grossly unfair to the huge community of academics who devote so much time to editing.

What journal publishers do is outlined in Figure 1.4. It is dependent on publishers providing authors with a service first encapsulated by Oldenburg in his four functions. Why authors submit an article to a

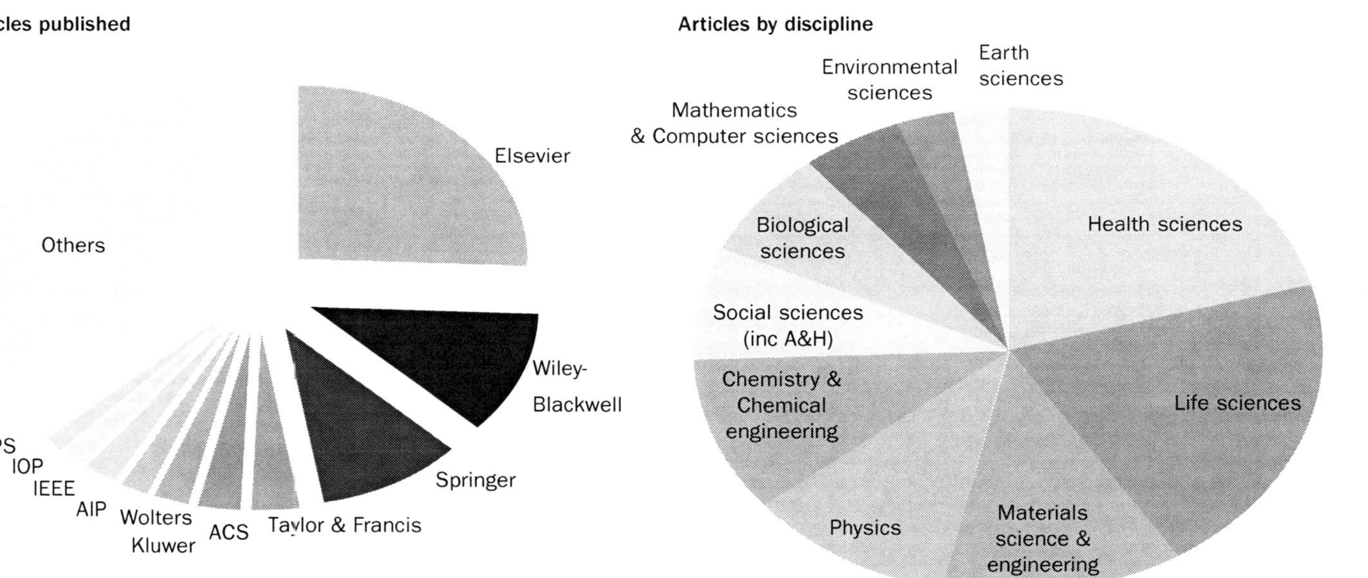

Figure 1.3 The journal publishing industry – From *Access to Research Outputs: a UK Success Story*. The Publishers Association, STM and ALPSP

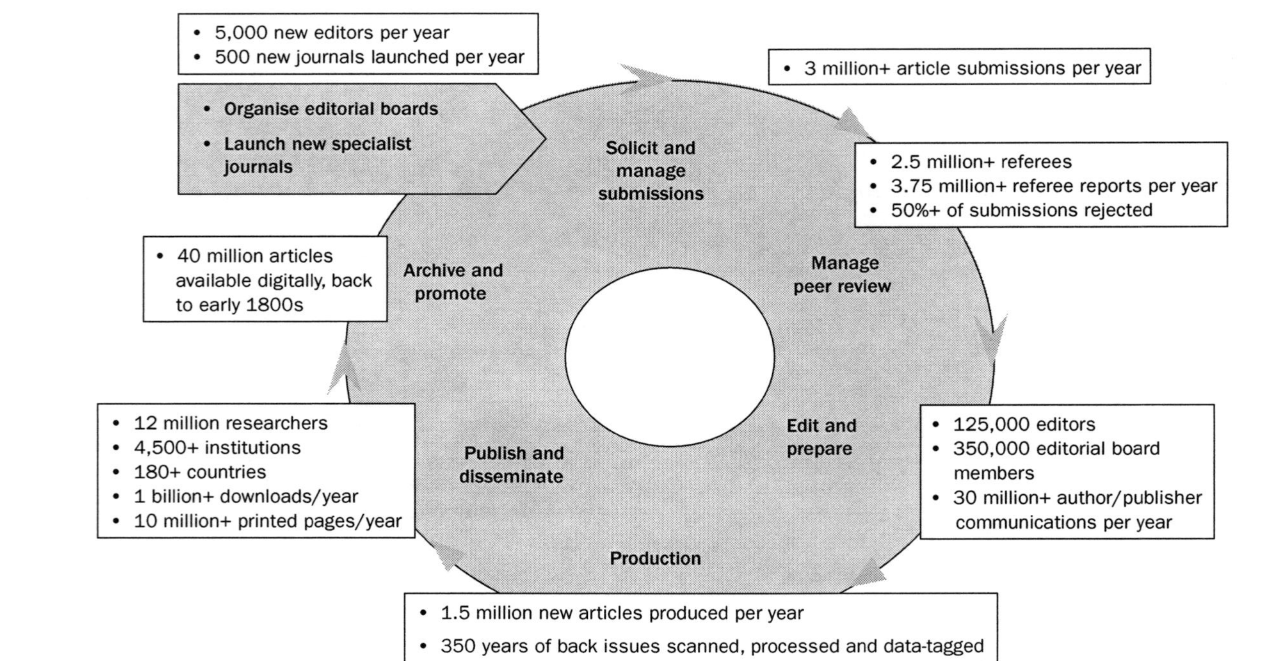
• 5,000 new editors per year
• 500 new journals launched per year
• Organise editorial boards
• Launch new specialist journals
• 3 million+ article submissions per year
Solicit and manage submissions
• 2.5 million+ referees
• 3.75 million+ referee reports per year
• 50%+ of submissions rejected
Manage peer review
• 40 million articles available digitally, back to early 1800s
Archive and promote
Edit and prepare
• 125,000 editors
• 350,000 editorial board members
• 30 million+ author/publisher communications per year
• 12 million researchers
• 4,500+ institutions
• 180+ countries
• 1 billion+ downloads/year
• 10 million+ printed pages/year
Publish and disseminate
Production
• 1.5 million new articles produced per year
• 350 years of back issues scanned, processed and data-tagged

Note: industry estimates based on known numbers for a subset of the industry that are then scaled to 100% based on the article share of the known subset.

Figure 1.4 What do publishers do? From *Access to Research Outputs: a UK Success Story*. The Publishers Association, STM and ALPSP

journal has been regularly surveyed since the 1980s. Reaching their peers and gaining recognition usually heads the list with concern over copyright at the bottom. The involvement of the academic community is massive: over 125 000 editors, 350 000 editorial board members, 2.5 million referees and 12 million researchers.

In a recent Outsell Report (Ware, 2011) a wider range of STM publishing is used (including workflow and geophysical markets) to reach a total estimated market size for 2011 of $26 billion as opposed to the widely used estimate of $5 billion for the library market for journals. Ten billion dollars might be a more accurate estimate for the journal market for 2011. The report lists the ways in which STM publishers and information providers add value:

- sorting and assessment of research outputs;
- publication of primary literature, supplementary data and patents;
- aggregation of content;
- distillation of evidence – reference works and meta-reviews;
- creating standards and consensus seeking;
- granularisation, tagging and prioritisation of content, identification, and application of rules;
- systems integration, data structure and exchange standards, content maintenance, and updating procedure;
- integration of content from multiple sources;
- creating and monitoring behaviour change;
- development of workflow analytics and best practice benchmarking at the level of the individual, department, institution and geopolitical entity.

As Mark Ware points out this list is evolving, driven by market demand (e.g. for just-in-time knowledge) and new technologies. For a more detailed description of what journal publishers do see Morris *et al.* (2013).

Electronic publishing

Most journals are still distributed as print on paper along with online access but the migration to e-only is inevitable and should hugely enhance the efficiency of the scholarly communications system and engender change. Indeed, e-only is already the basis of Gold OA, i.e. open access on publication funded by author-side payment via Article Processing Charges (APCs).

Along with the saving in publishing costs, an e-only environment enables new pricing models, and should allow for significant saving in library overheads. The development of appropriate pricing (see Chapter 12 by O'Rourke), perhaps based on usage and even citation status and other post-publication metrics, along with the reduction in library overheads, will require close co-operation between publishers and librarians. Universal access is the objective. One extreme approach might be a national site licence enabling access to all of a publisher's content across all users from Higher Education and industry to the general public.

A global survey in the UK (PRC, 2010) indicated 93 per cent of researchers reported 'very easy or fairly easy access' in universities, but it should be possible to do better provided that policy-makers realise not only that increasing funding of R&D will produce more articles, but also that the cost of publishing these articles has to be met. Alongside this, funders need to accept responsibility in managing the wider issue of the research data that is analysed and reported in journals, which should be properly curated and preserved to enable permanent access (Campbell and Meadows, 2011), more on which below.

It should be clear from this book that publishing in 2012 involves a range of investment and expertise scarcely imagined in the early 1990s, and yet library budgets that support the publication of journals have dropped steadily as a percentage of total university budgets.

Journals and data

Our current era of research was described by Jim Gray of Microsoft as being all about data exploration, unifying theory + experiment + simulation. It should offer tremendous opportunities for publishers. The journal has been described as the ultimate metadata for a researcher's data yet until recently the relationship between a journal article and the underlying data on which it is based has received little attention. As outlined by Efke Smit: 'data and publications belong together because publications make data discoverable; are the most thorough metadata of data; provide the author/research credits for the data; and gain depth by supplying data' (Smit *et al.*, 2011).

Again we are seeing policy driven by funders who have become more aware of the importance of improving access to the accelerating quantity of data their funding has generated. They have been supported by publishers in this; for example, see the declaration on Open Access to Data by the STM Association and ALPSP (STM/ALPSP websites, 2006).

Currently, funders' policies on data management are not well aligned with market needs, with policies varying by funder, type of research, university and discipline. The situation in publishing is also unclear. For example, in the Parse Insight 2009 survey, 71 per cent of the larger publishers stated that authors can submit their underlying digital research data yet 69 per cent of the larger publishers said they have no preservation arrangements for digital research data (Knipers and van der Hoeven, 2009). The accessibility of data lags behind the accessibility of journals. In the 2010 PRC survey only 38 per cent of researchers found it easy or fairly easy to access data sets and data models.

It seems likely that libraries and their repositories will take on much of the responsibility for managing data. Funders will require a plan for data management in any grant proposal and the researcher will usually go to their library colleagues to provide for and then implement this. Where librarians once employed subject specialists they will now recruit data managers. And we are seeing Oldenburg's four functions applied to data management. We could even see the later 'fifth function' – i.e. generating citation data used for measuring impact – operate for data as researchers will need to demonstrate the impact of their work. DataCite, a library-led organisation, is co-operating with CrossRef to provide DOIs for linking, which could create the necessary basis for research data metrics. A new community of data managers could forge a new and productive relationship with journal publishers, but it is early days. Alongside all the technical issues there is no clear business model.

A dark cloud

Many of the chapters in this book take a view on the future from the standpoint of the subject addressed, but sitting above like a dark cloud is the possible intervention by policy-makers and funders. Journal publishing has flourished through its independent yet close relationship with the academic community: researchers, teachers and librarians. Much of its value comes from this independence and the concomitant need to maintain high standards in an ever more competitive marketplace.

Driven by the slogan 'what is publicly paid for, should be publicly accessible', funders have added 'with free access to the outcome' to their mission to fund the best research. Led by the US National Institutes of

Health (NIH), some have introduced stipulations on how grantees should publish. The NIH request that grantees should archive for free access over the Internet made little impact, but when stiffened up to a mandate more researchers complied, especially when publishers posted for them. Damage was limited by an embargo of up to 12 months and a policy based on posting of the author's accepted version of the article although the final published version is preferred.

The problem with this so-called 'Green Road' approach to OA (often referred to as the 'no-one pays' model) is that if free access to versions of an article become commonplace then librarians are likely to cancel subscriptions (Beckett and Inger, 2007). It would also lead to a different article version (see NISO, 2008) being archived in different places, undermining one of the basic functions of the journal. The author's accepted version is inevitably inferior to the Version of Research maintained on the publisher's site (Wates and Campbell, 2007).

We could see further intervention from the European Commission. With Framework Programme 7 (FP7) there was a target of 20 per cent of the projects funded to follow a policy of Green OA. Compliance seems to have been limited, partly because publishers are not posting for authors. There was also vague support for Gold OA (which could be described as 'sustainable OA'), but the funding is unclear and will not apply to articles published after the end of the programme. There is talk, however, of a more comprehensive policy for the next research framework programme, Horizon 2020, which follows on from FP7 in 2014. For example, there could be a target of 100 per cent Green OA, funding for Gold OA but with a set maximum APC, or a model amendment to any publication agreement that the author might sign with the publisher to this end. It is not clear how researchers would react to restrictions on a basic right, freedom to publish how they choose (with potential implications for their autonomy as researchers).

One notable development in this area has been the announcement that the Wellcome Trust, the Howard Hughes Medical Institute and the Max Planck Institute are launching a Gold OA journal – *eLife* – aimed at competing with *Nature*, *Science* and *Cell*. It will be completely OA, i.e. no charge even to the author, for an initial period. Apparently the peer review policy will eliminate unnecessary requests for revision and cycles of revision. It will be interesting to see how any potential conflicts of interest are managed and whether other funders will also switch budgets from research to journal publishing. (At least it might create a new market for this book.)

Strangely the major funders in North America and Europe are silent on the role of research reports. Most funders expect grantees to produce a report at the end of their study. These could give the public free access to the outcome of the research they have funded (one of the drivers of the Open Access movement), yet clearly funders prefer to pick up the low-hanging fruit – the journal articles in which publishers have invested. At this stage, funders do not seem to be prepared to invest in properly organising the production of research reports to a sufficient standard for general access despite policy statements on public access and sharing data – such reports could be developed to act as an interface with the underlying research data.

Such influential newcomers and market developments could disrupt the system for a while, but in the long run publishing could emerge stronger, just as with OA publishing, which has been absorbed by the industry and is now represented on trade committees and in international organisations such as CrossRef. The understanding of publishing that funders might gain from direct involvement should shape their policy.

The future

The future of publishing is addressed throughout this book and particularly in the closing chapters (Chapter 17 by Mabe, Chapter 18 by Anderson and Chapter 19 by Pentz).

In the introduction to *Journal Publishing* (Page *et al.*, 1997), the section on the future concluded that no one model would be dominant over the next few years and that: 'Publishers may just have time to develop new systems to cope with even more research output alongside even more limited budgets'.

The race against time continues at a greater pace, as will be apparent in the book. Academic and professional publishing is an exciting place to be.

References

Beckett, C. and Inger, S. (2007) *Self-archiving and Journal Subscriptions: Co-existence or Competition?* PRC Summary, Papers 2.

Campbell, R. (2010) Publishing Partnerships can help society journal. *Research Information*, April/May.

Campbell, R. and Wates, E. (2008) *Subscription-Based Journal Publishing, in Open Access: Opportunities and Challenges. A Handbook*. European Commission, Brussels.

Campbell, R. and Wates, E. (2009) 'Journal Publishing: implications for a digital library policy', in D. Baker and W. Evans (eds). *Digital Library Economics: an Academic Perspective*. Oxford: Chandos.

Campbell, R. and Meadows, A. (2011) Scholarly journal publishing: where do we go from here? *Learned Publishing*, 24: 171–81.

Knipers, T. and van der Hoeven, J. (2009) *Insight into Digital Preservation of Research Output in Europe*. PARSE insight, European Commission.

Mabe, M. (2003) The growth and number of journals. *Serials: The Journal of the Serials Community*, 16:2.

Moed, H.F. (2005) *Citation Analysis in Research Evaluation*. Berlin: Springer.

Morris, S., Barnas, E., LaFrenier, D. and Reich, M. (2013) *The Handbook of Journal Publishing*. Cambridge: Cambridge University Press, in press.

NISO (2008) *Journal Article Versions (JAV)*: Recommendation of the NISO/ALPSP JAV Technical Working Group, NISO-RP-8-2008.

Okerson, A. (1986) Periodical Prices: a history and discussion. *Advances in Serials Management, JAI Press*, 1: 101–34.

Page, G., Campbell, R. and Meadows, J. (1997) *Journal Publishing*. Cambridge: Cambridge University Press.

Publishers Research Consortium (PRC) Report (2010) *Access vs Importance: a global study assessing the importance of and ease of access to professional and academic information*. http://www.publishingresearch.net/

Smit, E., van der Hoeven, J. and Giaretta, D. (2011) Avoiding a dark age for data. *Learned Publishing*, 24: 35–49.

Vines, T., Reiseberg, L. and Smith, H. (2010) No crisis in supply of peer reviewers. *Nature*, 468: 104.

Ware, M. (2011) *Scientific, Technical and Medical Information: 2011 Market Forecast and Trends Report*. Burlingame, CA: Outsell.

Wates, E. and Campbell, R. (2007) Author's version vs publisher's version; an analysis of the copy-editing function. *Learned Publishing*, 20: 121–9.

2

Peer review in a rapidly evolving publishing landscape

Irene Hames

Abstract: Pre-publication peer review has long been recognised as a cornerstone of scholarly publishing. Despite various criticisms and a number of shortcomings, this scrutiny and critical assessment by experts is still considered essential by many. This chapter describes the realistic expectations of peer review and what constitutes good practice, emphasising the important role of the editor. It also outlines the many ways traditional peer review is being adapted, the new models that are appearing, and the increasing emphasis on openness and transparency. Various problems are addressed, including difficulties in finding reviewers, the imbalance between publication output and participation in peer review worldwide, the 'wastage' of reviews that accompanies the often repeated submission of manuscripts to journal after journal after rejection, and the increasing pressure on researchers not only to publish but to publish in high-impact journals. All these are impacting the peer-review processes of journals and editorial workload. The recent innovation to concentrate only on the assessment of soundness of research methodology and reporting pre-publication is receiving acceptance from researchers keen to publish their work without undue delay, and is being adopted by an increasing number of publishers. In this model, the evaluation of interest, importance and potential impact is left for after publication. The possibilities for post-publication review and evaluation in an online world are many and varied, but there are also many challenges. It is clear that, nearly three and a half centuries on from the appearance of the first journals, the opportunities for innovation and experimentation in peer review are greater than ever before.

Key words: Peer review, scholarly publishing, manuscript management, reviewers, blinded review, open review, editors, editorial decision-making, post-publication review, peer-review models, ethics, transparency.

Introduction

Peer review in scholarly publishing is the process by which research output is subjected to scrutiny and critical assessment by individuals who are experts in those areas. Traditionally this process of 'editorial' peer review (to distinguish it from the peer review of grant applications) takes place before publication. Researchers prepare reports of their work (commonly referred to as manuscripts) and submit them to journals for consideration for publication. Such scrutiny by external experts has been used in journal publishing for nearly 300 years, going back to the early to mid-18th century when the Royal Societies of Edinburgh and London started to consult their members on publication decisions in a regulated way, calling on those most knowledgeable in the subject matter (Kronick, 1990; Spier, 2002). Peer review only became widespread, however, after the middle of the 20th century, when the numbers of articles being produced and their specialisation and complexity went beyond that which most editors could handle on their own or had the expertise necessary to carry out a critical assessment (Burnham, 1990). Today, the scale of the operation is enormous, with over 1.5 million articles being published each year in around 25 000 peer-reviewed journals (Ware and Mabe, 2009).

Peer review is considered by many to be a critical and key element in journal publishing. Not only by editors, who have long recognised and appreciated its value (e.g. Laine and Mulrow, 2003), but also by the research community. The overwhelming majority of researchers in the large international surveys carried out by Ware and Monkman (2008) and Sense About Science (2009) considered that peer review greatly helps scientific communication, without it there would be no control, and that the accuracy and quality of work that has not been peer reviewed cannot be trusted. Around 90 per cent of the respondents in both surveys felt that their own last accepted paper had been improved by peer review – an important element that is often overlooked. That is not to say that peer review is perfect – it isn't. Even though the two surveys found much support for peer review, there was a degree of dissatisfaction (12 and 9 per cent, respectively). Also, around a third in each survey did not agree that the current peer-review system is the best that can be achieved.

The shortcomings of peer review have been highlighted (Wager and Jefferson, 2001) and criticisms levelled on a number of fronts (Smith, 2006, 2010a): about its quality and fairness, that it is open to abuse and bias, that it is expensive, slow and lacks consistency, and that it is conservative. There are concerns about delays, both in the time taken for review and decision at individual journals, and in the time taken for a piece of work to be published because it sometimes has to go from journal to journal, being rejected a number of times before finally being accepted (a manuscript can only be sent to one journal at a time). This multiple reviewing of what might essentially be the same manuscript has led to growing concern about the 'wastage' in reviewer effort (see below).

There have also been criticisms that in some top journals the weight given to reviewer suggestions for additional experiments is too great, with escalating and unrealistic demands being made and insufficient critical editor intervention (Lawrence, 2003; Ploegh, 2011). This highlights the central importance of the editor in the peer-review process. As put so well by one respondent in the Ware and Monkman survey (2008, p. 4): '...[peer review] works as well as can be expected. The critical feature that makes the system work is the skill and insight of the editor. Astute editors can use the system well, the less able who follow reviewer comments uncritically bring the system into disrepute.'

A common misconception is that reviewers 'accept' and 'reject' manuscripts. They don't. They assess, advise and make recommendations, and it is editors who make the publication decisions for their journals. If extra experiments are being suggested, it is their role to decide whether they are required. It is always a fine balance, and there are many authors who have reason to be grateful to the editors who have prevented them from publishing prematurely and provided the feedback that has led to the eventual publication of good, sound work. But equally, most researchers can relate 'horror stories' about their experiences of having work reviewed by journals. It is a human activity and so prone to the usual failings. There are also editors who are not as good, thorough or impartial as they should be, and reviewers who are slow, biased or rarely return adequate reviews.

As peer review determines what is published and where it is published, it plays a central role in the career prospects and funding opportunities of researchers as these depend heavily on publication records. Because of the importance of peer review there have been attempts to find evidence for its effectiveness and contest the proposition that 'a faith based rather than an evidence based process lies at the heart of science' (Smith, 2010a, p. 1). Jefferson *et al.* (2002, 2007), for example, have carried out systematic reviews on studies of the peer-review process in biomedical journals. They found little empirical evidence in support of its use as a mechanism to ensure the quality of biomedical research, but cautioned that 'the absence of evidence on efficacy and effectiveness cannot be interpreted as evidence of their absence' (Jefferson *et al.*, 2007, p. 2).

They actually found very few well-designed studies that could be included in their reviews and concluded that a well-funded programme of research was urgently required, although they acknowledged that 'the methodological problems in studying peer review are many and complex' (Jefferson *et al.*, 2007, p. 2). There is ongoing research into peer review, but this comes mostly from the biomedical field. Many high-quality studies are presented at the International Congresses on Peer Review and Biomedical Publication, which have been held every four years since 1989 (see http://www.ama-assn.org/public/peer/peerhome.htm). A review has also been carried out of studies published between 1945 and 1997 on a wide range of aspects of editorial peer review and covering the scholarly literature spectrum (Weller, 2001).

Publishers of scholarly journals play an important role in peer review, having invested heavily in both the supporting technological infrastructure and management of the peer-review process. Development of web-based online systems for manuscript submission and peer review began in the mid-1990s, and by the late 1990s they were entering the mainstream (Tananbaum and Holmes, 2008). In the following decade, these systems were refined and increased in sophistication, and adoption grew as authors, reviewers, editors and publishers became keen to reap the many benefits (Ware, 2005). At the beginning of the second decade of the 21st century, the great majority of journals, especially in STM (Scientific, Technical and Medical) areas, have web-based online submission and review. Part of this rapid adoption has been due to the large investment by publishers in the implementation of online systems and in the provision of training and support to editors and editorial offices. The importance of training cannot be overestimated, both for the technological aspects and for induction into good and ethical practice. Online systems are a tool, and just knowing how to use them is not the same as operating peer review according to good practice.

One of the problems with peer review, and probably why there is a degree of dissatisfaction with it, is that the quality across journals is very variable. There is little standardisation, or even knowledge by some of what good practice is. The situation is exacerbated by the nature of editorial work, where most people learn 'on the job'. Editors are usually appointed on the basis of their research records, reputation and 'vision' for the journal. Often they will come to the role without much experience of the editorial side of research publication. They will inevitably have been authors and reviewers, perhaps have been on editorial boards, but taking responsibility for peer review and editorial decision-making may be new to them. Considering the great power that comes with being an editor and the effects the actions of editors can have on the careers, reputations and research-funding opportunities of researchers, it is essential that they are properly equipped to take on this important role. Publishers have large pools of expertise they can draw on, both in-house and in the editorial offices of their journals. They should have induction and training programmes for their new editors and editorial staff, refreshing this regularly, and providing updates on new developments. In addition to the high-quality information some publishers provide on their own websites, a number of excellent organisations exist where editors can find guidelines on various aspects of peer review. Publishers have a duty to make their editors aware of these and to provide guidance on which can be trusted as sources of good and reliable advice.

Peer review is currently the subject of intense debate, with sometimes quite extreme and polarised views being put forward, from the belief that 'the peer review system is breaking down' (Fox and Petchey, 2010) to the recommendation 'the time has come to move from a world of "filter then publish" to one of "publish then filter" ' (Smith, 2010b). Blog postings on peer review tend to become vigorous discussions, receiving numerous comments (see, for example, Grant, 2010; Neylon, 2010; Rohn, 2010). Sometimes there is confusion about basic issues. What needs to be made very clear is that good practice in peer review is system and business-model independent, i.e. it doesn't matter whether a paper-, email- or web-based system is used, or whether a journal is subscription based, open access, with author-side payment, or has a hybrid model. Good and bad examples exist in all, and global statements linking quality with one model cannot, and should not, be made. It would be naïve, however, to ignore the fact that author-side-payment models have presented the opportunity for abuse and unscrupulous business ventures where authors may be charged to have their work published in journals purporting to be peer reviewed, but without much, or even any, quality review taking place. Indeed, Davis (2009a) has reported the case of a 'nonsense' manuscript being submitted and accepted for publication after 'peer review' and being sent a request for payment of the publication fee.

There is another common misconception. It is often assumed that the larger and more important or high impact a journal is, the better is its quality of peer review. This is not necessarily so. The large established journals do have very experienced teams and sophisticated processes built up over many years, but there are also many small, specialist journals operating rigorous peer review, often led by dedicated and knowledgeable editors and their equally committed editorial teams.

Peer review as the foundation of the primary literature

Peer review in perspective

Peer review is widely thought to be the cornerstone of scholarly publishing. But why is it important for researchers to publish their work? There are two main reasons. The first is to add their findings to the scholarly record (the primary literature). This is a reporting function and it is here that peer review has a central and critical role, making sure that the 'minutes of science' (Velterop, 1995) are a sound basis for further research, checking that work has been reported correctly and clearly, preventing inclusion of studies with flawed design or methodology. The second reason researchers need to publish is linked to an assessment function. Researchers are judged by the journals in which they publish, and institutions are judged by the publication records of their researchers. There is currently a journal hierarchy based on Impact Factor (Garfield, 2006; and see Thomson Reuters, http://thomsonreuters.com/products_services/science/free/essays/impact_factor/) and this journal attribute is used, but not without considerable criticism (Lawrence, 2007; UK House of Commons Science and Technology Committee, 2011, paragraph 177), as a 'proxy' evaluation for the merits of articles and researchers. Decisions on appointment, promotion and grant funding are influenced very heavily by it. There is real concern that researchers are being put under increasing pressure not only to publish, but to publish in high-impact journals, many of which will accept only what they consider to be the most important and novel work (consequently some have rejection rates of over 90 per cent; McCook, 2006). The use by certain countries of cash incentives for publication in international journals, with very large payments for acceptance by journals with high Impact Factors (Fuyuno and Cyranoski, 2006; Shao and Shen, 2011), has also led to concerns that integrity may sometimes be compromised. The increased pressure to publish can have effects on journals and editorial offices, and their peer-review processes – greatly increased numbers of submissions, authors aiming too high in their choice of journal and being rejected (sometimes a number of times at different journals as they work their way down the journal pecking order), work being sliced too thinly so as to increase publication output ('salami' publishing), premature submission of research (with, again, consequent rejection) and decisions being contested more frequently because so much hinges on a positive outcome. There may also be ethical implications, with increasing levels of questionable behaviour and misconduct

(Martinson *et al.*, 2005; Fanelli, 2009). This is not the healthiest of situations for researchers, scholarly publishing or peer review (Lawrence, 2003).

A quote by Stephen Lock made in 1991 (p. xi), the year he retired as editor of the *British Medical Journal* (*BMJ*), still sums up the situation well: 'And underlying these worries was yet another: that scientific articles have been hijacked away from their primary role of communicating scientific discovery to one of demonstrating academic activity.'

Submissions to journals are set to go on increasing. Also, the number of submissions from countries such as China and India, where research activity is expanding rapidly, is growing, resulting in an increasing proportion of global publications (Adams *et al.*, 2009a,b). In materials science, China has already become the largest single-country producer, having overtaken both Japan and the USA, and it will soon surpass the combined output of the EU-15 (Adams and Pendlebury, 2011). It is predicted to become the largest producer of research papers in the next decade, possibly by as early as 2013 (Royal Society, 2011a). The quality of the work from China is improving, and is making up an increasing proportion of the papers in high-impact journals (*Nature*, 2011). Publication is therefore likely to become even more competitive, especially in high-impact journals. This change in the 'geography of publication' is also impacting submission–reviewing dynamics (see below).

Peer review is used by many journals as a tool for selection as well as a quality-control step to check on the soundness of research methodology, results and reporting, to help editors choose those articles most suitable for their journal readership, and to meet the standards that have been set by their journals for quality, novelty, breadth of interest and potential impact. This grouping of articles into a hierarchy of journals has been shown to be important to researchers (Tenopir *et al.*, 2010). It is, however, a very much more subjective activity than the screen for soundness. The two functions of peer review have traditionally gone hand-in-hand. There is now, however, a new model, where the two functions have been separated. In 2006, the journal *PLoS ONE* was launched by the Public Library of Science (PLoS), with the remit to publish all submitted scientific and medical research that was sound – the peer-review process would concentrate only on ensuring scientific rigour, and not on the novelty, importance, interest or potential impact of the work. The evaluation of that would be left for the post-publication phase. This would ensure publication of sound research wasn't delayed as a result of authors needing to go to more than one journal because of rejection on the grounds of insufficient novelty or impact. The *PLoS ONE* model is being emulated by a number of other publishers, who are producing their own similar journals (e.g. *BMJ Open*, *Sage Open*, *Scientific Reports* from Nature Publishing Group, *Biology Open* from the Company of Biologists, *AIP Advances* from the American Institute of Physics), and is attracting a lot of interest from both researchers and grant funders. It is leading to a series of 'repository-type' journals – large online, open-access collections of research articles, either multi-disciplinary or subject-specific, that have been peer reviewed for soundness but no evaluation made beyond that as a requirement for publication. This is a rapidly evolving area, closely tied to increasing moves to open access, concerns about the proxy use of publication in high-impact journals in research/researcher assessment, and the opportunities arising for post-publication evaluation in an online world.

What peer review can and can't do

Peer review is sometimes portrayed as an infallible gold standard. It isn't. But in the hands of an experienced and knowledgeable editor it is a powerful tool. What are the realistic expectations of peer review? Ideally, it should (adapted, with permission, from Hames, 2007, pp. 2–3):

1. prevent the publication of bad work – filter out studies that have been poorly conceived, designed or executed;
2. check as far as possible from the submitted material that the research reported has been carried out well and there are no flaws in the design or methodology;
3. ensure that the work is reported correctly and unambiguously, complying with reporting guidelines where appropriate, with acknowledgement to the existing body of work and due credit given to the findings and ideas of others;
4. ensure that the results presented have been interpreted correctly and all possible interpretations considered;
5. ensure that the results are not too preliminary or too speculative, but at the same time not block innovative new research and theories;
6. provide editors with evidence to make judgements as to whether articles meet the selection criteria for their particular publications, for example on the level of general interest, novelty or potential impact;
7. provide authors with quality and constructive feedback;
8. generally improve the quality and readability of articles;
9. help maintain the integrity of the scholarly record.

What is it unrealistic to expect of peer review? It is not a guarantor of absolute truth. It is not its role to police research integrity or to determine whether there has been misconduct. The peer-review process cannot, for example, detect fraud that has occurred in the laboratory, and if an author is set on presenting falsified or fabricated results this can only be determined at laboratory level. Research and publication misconduct do occur, as has been demonstrated by surveys (Martinson *et al.*, 2005; Fanelli, 2009) and as can be seen by viewing the case studies brought to organisations such as COPE (the Committee on Publication Ethics, http://www.publicationethics.org/cases) and the retractions highlighted almost daily on the *Retraction Watch* blog (http://retractionwatch.wordpress.com/). However, if suspicions or allegations of misconduct arise during the peer-review process, editors cannot ignore them and must investigate at journal level to see whether there is enough substance to pass them on for proper investigation (see Hames, 2007, pp. 173–99). It is the responsibility of the institutions to which the individuals suspected of misconduct belong to carry out investigations into whether misconduct has or has not occurred. COPE is an organisation editors can turn to for help and advice on all aspects of publication ethics. Besides the many resources available on its website (codes of conduct, flowcharts on how to handle ethical problems, and other guidance), it holds a quarterly forum where editors can bring cases of ethical concern for discussion and advice.

The peer-review process

Requirements of a good peer-review system

What are the requirements of a good peer-review system? It should:

- involve assessment by external reviewers (not just by editors or editorial staff – that isn't peer review);
- be fair and without bias, either positive or negative;
- be timely;
- be kept confidential for any aspect that isn't operating under open review (see below);
- have systems and guidance in place to allow reviewers to provide quality and constructive feedback for both the editor and the authors;

- have decision-making based solely on the merits of the work, not influenced by who the authors are or where they come from, and not dictated by commercial considerations.

Peer review should not be a one-way street, with the editor working autonomously and rigidly, disregarding the views of others. Rather, it should be considered a dialogue – between the authors and the editor, between the reviewers and the editor, and between the readers and the journal, with all parties acting ethically and treating one another with respect. It is, however, expected that reviewers do not generally communicate direct with the authors unless this is approved by the journal. Clarity is of the essence in all the interactions, and helps avoid delays, misunderstanding and disputes: authors need to know the scope and quality of work a journal is interested in receiving, reviewers need to know the parameters within which they are reviewing, and editors need to make their instructions and decisions clear.

Journals vary in size and so do editorial offices, ranging from ones where one person does everything to those where there are many staff. The editor him/herself may carry out all the roles, seeing all manuscripts on submission and steering them through the whole peer-review process. They may share responsibilities with members of an editorial board, with individual editors handling manuscripts in different subject areas or from different geographical regions. The principles of good practice are the same whatever the size or organisation of a journal.

Publishers vary in the type of editor they use for their journals. Some (e.g. *Nature* and the *BMJ*) appoint internal, 'professional', staff editors, who are usually individuals with relevant research or practitioner experience but no longer active in research or in practice. Others (the large majority of specialist journals) have editors who are active researchers (sometimes called 'academic' editors), based in either academia or industry, or practitioners in their fields. Some journals (such as *Science*) have a combination of the two, where external editors are used for their subject knowledge and research expertise, and the staff editors manage the peer-review process and make the decisions on acceptance.

In all journals, the workflows and procedures (which should all be documented) need to be evaluated regularly to ensure they are still optimal and up to date with new developments, and are not either superfluous or unduly cumbersome.

'Traditional' peer review

The 'traditional' model of peer review includes, irrespective of whether web-based, email or paper systems are used, the following steps:

- The author submits his or her manuscript, acting on behalf of his or her co-authors in multi-author papers. This author may also take on the role of 'corresponding author', being the author with whom the journal corresponds during the peer-review process, or another author may be nominated for this.
- Manuscript receipt is acknowledged and an identification number allocated (this happens automatically with most online systems).
- The manuscript goes through a 'triage' step, where it is (i) checked for completeness and adherence to journal policies and ethical guidelines (effectively a technical/administrative check), and (ii) assessed editorially by someone with editorial decision-making responsibility (i.e. staff or academic editors, acting alone or in consultation), for such things as topic, scope, quality and interest, to determine whether these fall within the areas and standards defined by editorial policy.
- If deficiencies are found in the technical check that are extensive enough to preclude further consideration by a journal, the manuscript is returned to the authors for improvement and resubmission. Some guidance may also be given as to the level of interest in seeing it come back so that authors do not embark on a substantial effort only to have the manuscript rejected on editorial grounds once it is resubmitted. In less severe cases the manuscript may be put on hold while the authors provide the missing items, and moved on in the editorial process once these are in (with usually a time limit set for compliance).
- If a manuscript is found to be unsuitable on editorial grounds, it is rejected without further review – this is an 'editorial rejection', i.e. it hasn't been subjected to peer review. Rejection rates at this stage vary from journal to journal, but can be very high (60–80 per cent) in the top, highly selective journals.
- Those manuscripts that pass the initial triage are then sent for external, 'peer', review.
- The experts to whom manuscripts are sent for external assessment are usually called 'reviewers' or 'referees' (although the latter rather implies that the person is acting as an umpire or arbitrator, whereas that is the role of the editor).

- An editorial decision is made on the basis of the reviewers' reports and all the other information that the editor has related to that submission, and communicated to the author.

With increasing awareness of the incidence of plagiarism, many publishers have adopted a new online service to help in its detection – CrossCheck (http://www.crossref.org/crosscheck/index.html), which can be integrated into online manuscript systems. This enables screening for textual duplication and similarity between submitted manuscripts and work that has already been published in one form or another (screening against articles submitted to other journals, to enable duplicate submission to be picked up, is not something that is currently available). Because of the large number of publishers of scholarly related content who have signed up to the initiative, and so allow DOI-identified content that is held behind pay walls to be added to the CrossCheck database and crawled by the iParadigms text-comparison software behind CrossCheck – iThenticate (http://www.ithenticate.com/) – it is a very powerful tool. Areas of textual duplication are highlighted, but it requires human intervention to determine whether plagiarism has occurred. Often specialist subject knowledge is required to make that assessment, along with a good understanding of the features and limitations of the system, and these should always be mixed with a healthy dose of common sense. Journals vary as to the stage at which the duplication check is done. Some scan all submissions, some only those selected for external review, some only those recommended for publication, prior to formal acceptance, others just a random selection or only when there is reason to suspect plagiarism. Journals also need to think about what they will do when they discover plagiarism and whether different circumstances, for example the type and extent of the plagiarism or the seniority of the authors involved, warrant different actions. COPE has prepared a discussion paper to address these sorts of issues (COPE, 2011a).

Screening for inappropriate digital image manipulation may also be carried out. Following the pioneering work by the *Journal of Cell Biology* in this area (Rossner and Yamada, 2004), other journals have introduced checks into their workflows.

The introduction of new technologies to help detect problems with submissions has been a great benefit to journals and the peer-review process. However, this has also brought issues that have to be addressed by journals and their publishers – the increased workload on editors and editorial staff, and the need to ensure that the expertise required, not only to use the new screening tools but also to interpret the results, is in place. Increasing detection of suspect cases is also leading to increased pressures on editors, in terms of both the time needed to look into them and knowing what to do if misconduct rather than honest error appears to have occurred. COPE has produced a number of flowcharts to help editors faced with cases of suspected misconduct.

Types of peer review

There are a number of types of peer review (see Table 2.1).

Single-blind review

In single-blind review, the reviewers know who the authors are but the authors do not know who the reviewers are. This has long been the traditional form used by the majority of STM journals. Reviewer anonymity is considered to enable reviewers to provide honest, critical appraisals and unfavourable reviews without fear of reprisal from authors, this being particularly so in the case of younger reviewers and more senior authors, who may at some time be involved in their future job applications and funding proposals. The argument against this

Table 2.1 The common forms of pre-publication peer review

	Authors' names known	Authors' names not known
Reviewers' names known	**'Open' review** Term 'open' may also include: (i) Reviewers' names being disclosed for published articles (ii) Reviewers' reports (with or without names) being included with published articles (iii) Editorial correspondence and/or all versions of the manuscript being included with published articles (iv) Community/public being able to comment during review (v) Combinations of the above	(unlikely that this system is in operation anywhere)
Reviewers' names not known	**'Single-blind' review** The most common form in scientific, technical and medical (STM) journals	**'Double-blind' review** The most common form in the humanities and social sciences

system is that there is a lack of accountability, providing unscrupulous reviewers with the opportunity to make unwarranted negative comments, to intentionally delay the peer-review process so that they or others with whom they are connected can get or keep a head start on similar work, or even to steal ideas from the authors. Unconscious bias may go unchallenged. Editors can also get away with not being as transparent as they should be, for example saying that an external reviewer has been used when they themselves have carried out the review.

Double-blind review

In double-blind review, which is the main form used in the humanities and social sciences, neither the reviewers nor the authors know one another's identities. The argument is that this removes the potential influence (either positive or negative) of who the authors are (such as their status, gender or relationship to the reviewer) or where they come from (e.g. organisation, institution or country). One problem is that it can involve considerable effort to ensure manuscripts are anonymised, and another is that reviewers can frequently identify who the authors are (van Rooyen *et al.*, 1998). Some organisations and journals (e.g. the American Economic Association and *Political Analysis*) that have traditionally used double-blind review are moving to single-blind review because they consider the effectiveness of the former has decreased in the age of online search engines, with reviewers being able to search for similar titles to that of the submitted manuscript and coming up with working papers, conference contributions and other items linked to the work submitted, and so the authors (see Jaschik, 2011).

Open review and 'transparent' approaches

In open review the authors know the identities of the reviewers and the reviewers know the identities of the authors. This is felt by some to be a much more transparent approach than blinded review, with greater accountability (Godlee, 2002), and has been used successfully by the *BMJ* since 1999. Open review has taken on a broader meaning in recent years (see Table 2.1), being extended to include, for example, publication of the reviewers' names or their names and reports with published articles, and open commenting, either from a restricted community or from anyone. Authors and reviewers need therefore to check carefully what 'open review' means when they submit or agree to review manuscripts and that they are happy with the degree of openness.

Release of reviewers' names, reviews and editorial correspondence extends only to cases where submissions are accepted for publication; these details, including that a submission has been made, are generally kept confidential for those manuscripts not accepted.

Some publishers and journals have gone further with open review to increase transparency. BioMed Central, for example, provides a link to a 'pre-publication history' for each article published in its *BMC* series medical journals. The named reviewers' reports, the authors' responses and all the versions of the manuscript are posted online with the published article. Another journal, *The EMBO Journal*, has introduced what it calls a 'transparent editorial process' (Pulverer, 2010). Since 2009 it has invited authors to have a 'peer review process file' included online with their published articles. Around 95 per cent do, and the files are apparently popular and reasonably accessed (Pulverer, 2010). Included in the file are the timeline and correspondence relevant to the processing of the manuscript: the reviewers' reports (but with the reviewers' identities kept anonymous), the authors' responses, the editorial decision letters, and other correspondence between the editor and authors. There are no confidential comments in the review forms, and reviewers who have any concerns, for example about ethical issues or data integrity, are asked to write direct to the editor. As well as making transparent the 'black box' of the editorial process (for articles accepted for publication), the journal sees the editorial information it is providing as an educative tool for researchers, and evidence that the peer-review process is usually constructive and effective. *BMJ Open* posts signed reviewers' reports and authors' responses in a 'peer review history' file attached to the articles it publishes, along with previous versions of the manuscript.

Reviewer selection and finding reviewers

Selection of the most appropriate reviewers for each manuscript is critical to quality peer review. A good editor will carefully match reviewers with manuscripts, basing selection on appropriate area and level of expertise, effectiveness as a reviewer, and absence of conflicting interests that might prevent a fair and unbiased appraisal. The calibre of the reviewers is also critical. The editor of the *Journal of the American College of Cardiology* (*JACC*) has made the pertinent observation that 'the reviewers themselves are the weakest (or strongest) links' in peer review (DeMaria, 2010). Good reviewers who respond quickly to communications and provide timely and constructive reviews without bias are invaluable; those who are always slow, regularly fail to submit their reviews or provide superficial or inadequate reviews are a liability to editors who want to earn and keep the respect of their communities and attract and retain good authors.

Potential reviewers are identified from a number of places: the journal's own database, the specialist editors, the manuscript bibliography, subject and publication databases and suggestions from the authors (many journals ask authors to provide these, as well offering them the opportunity to list, with reasons, individuals they feel should not be approached to review). They may come from academia, research institutions, professional practice or industry – wherever the best people for the job are. The journal's own database should become a powerful resource, with up-to-date information on all aspects of reviewer expertise and performance as well as contact details. It should also grow, with new names being added, especially as new research disciplines and geographical areas open up and develop.

Journals vary in the number of reviewers they assign to each manuscript, but most commonly two to three are used (ALPSP/EASE, 2000; ALPSP and Kaufman-Wills Group, 2005; Ware and Monkman, 2008). Many editors will, however, choose to send some manuscripts to a greater number than usual, for example those covering controversial topics or where widely held views are being overturned. Multidisciplinary research also presents challenges, and a number of reviewers will generally be chosen with expertise in one or more of the areas if it proves impossible to find reviewers with expertise across the whole paper. A trusted reviewer with more general expertise may also be brought in to provide a broad overview. Editor guidance is critical in the review of multidisciplinary work if quality reviews are to be obtained. Reviewers need to be directed to focus their efforts appropriately and so avoid wasting time struggling with parts that fall outside the areas they are competent to assess.

Is it getting harder to find reviewers? This is difficult to judge as few data exist. Informal conversations with editors and general comments suggest that some journals are finding it more difficult. There has been some speculation (Fox and Petchey, 2010, p. 325) that 'the peer review system is breaking down and will soon be in crisis' because of a 'tragedy of the reviewer commons', where individuals exploit the system by submitting manuscripts but have little incentive to review manuscripts from others. Fox and Petchey (2010) have proposed a new system where authors 'pay' for their submissions using a 'currency' called PubCreds, which they earn by carrying out reviews. A number of arguments have been put forward against this model (Davis, 2010), and it is difficult to see it working, but suggestions for innovation should always be welcomed for discussion. Petchey and Fox (2011) are, in collaboration with some ecology journals, accumulating data on reviewing. Editors at the journal *Molecular Ecology* have published some data (Vines *et al.*, 2010). They analysed the number of requests to review that had to be sent to get a review between 2001 and 2010. The mean number did increase (from 1.38 in 2001 to 2.03 in 2010), suggesting that it was harder to find reviewers in 2010 than in 2001. However, as the change occurred mostly in 2008, coinciding with the journal's move from an email-based editorial system to an automated one, the authors suggest that invitations from 2008 on might have been blocked by spam filters, with some invitations never reaching the intended recipients. They also found their reviewer pool increased in proportion to increased submissions, and there was no increase in the average number of reviews by individual reviewers. From their results they concluded that there is 'little evidence for the common belief that the peer-review system is overburdened by the rising tide of submissions', and that their reviewer pool is accommodating the increased submissions. Other editors have reported similar experiences (British Antarctic Survey, 2011).

One of the reasons some journals may be finding it harder to find reviewers is that there is currently an imbalance between where submissions are coming from and who is doing the reviewing. For example, the USA is producing about 20 per cent of papers globally but conducting about 32 per cent of the reviews, whereas China is producing about 12–15 per cent of the papers but probably doing only 4–5 per cent of the reviewing (Elsevier, 2011a). This is believed to be a temporary, transitionary situation, and likely to become better balanced as young researchers in the newly emerging scientific nations become more established and experienced in peer reviewing. Publishers and journals have a crucial role to play in providing training in reviewing and publication procedures and ethics in these areas of the world, and also the tools editors need to help them find reviewers. New author-identification and name-disambiguation initiatives such as Open Researcher & Contributor ID (ORCID; http://www.orcid.org/) will aid identification of specific reviewers from countries where many names are common. Training for all reviewers is something that is generally lacking, and 68 per cent of the researchers in the Sense About Science survey (2009) agreed that formal training would improve the quality of reviews. One of the key recommendations of a UK House of Commons Science and Technology Committee inquiry into peer review was that all early-career researchers should be given the option for training in peer review (UK House of Commons Science and Technology Committee, 2011, paragraph 119). The important role of publishers in training reviewers from countries which are not traditional scientific leaders was also stressed, with the comment that this should help alleviate the imbalance between publication output and participation in peer review (paragraph 130).

The whole peer-review process only works because enough willing and appropriately qualified reviewers can be found. Why do they agree to review? It seems that the reasons are more altruistic than self-promotional, with the main ones being to play a part as a member of the academic community and enjoying being able to improve papers (Ware and Monkman, 2008; Sense About Science, 2009). Peer review is also regarded as an integral part of the professional activity of researchers, although it is currently not generally acknowledged in any formal way that brings them professional credit (see below for ways reviewers are acknowledged).

It is courteous, and ultimately more effective and efficient, to check with reviewers whether or not they will review a manuscript rather than just sending it to them (see Hames, 2007, pp. 53–60). Before reviewers are approached, checks should be made to ensure there aren't any reasons why they shouldn't be used as reviewers: for example, they are already reviewing other manuscripts, they have indicated that they are not currently available for reviewing duties, their reviewing record is poor (for either timeliness or review quality), they are at the same institution(s) as the author(s) or have too close a relationship (professional or personal) to them, or there are other conflicting interests that might bias their evaluation.

Existence and recognition of bias and potentially conflicting interests

Godlee and Dickersin (2003) distinguish between 'good' and 'bad' biases, defining (p. 92) the former as 'those in favour of important, original, well-designed and well-reported science' and the latter as 'those that reflect a person's pre-existing views about the source of a manuscript (its authors, their institutions or countries of origin) or about the ideas or findings it presents'. It is probably impossible to eliminate all bad biases, but good editors and journals work hard to minimise them in their choice of reviewers and by the guidance they give them.

According to the ICMJE Uniform Requirements for Manuscripts (International Committee of Medical Journal Editors, http://www.icmje.org/): 'Conflict of interest exists when an author (or the author's institution), reviewer, or editor has financial or personal relationships that inappropriately influence (bias) his or her actions (such relationships are also known as dual commitments, competing interests, or competing loyalties)' (ICMJE, 2011). However, just because a potentially conflicting relationship exists doesn't mean that an individual shouldn't be chosen to review a manuscript – that decision is up to the editor. The crucial issue is disclosure of all potentially competing interests. Journals handle this differently, ranging from those with very explicit guidelines and where specific and detailed questions are asked (e.g. those using the ICMJE-recommended form, http://www.icmje.org/ethical_4conflicts.html) to those that have just a general statement asking that all relevant potential conflicts of interest be disclosed. How much disclosure is required usually depends on how much potential financial influence there is from large commercial organisations.

Bias and potential conflicting interests within a journal or editorial office have to be handled very stringently. For example, if one of the editors submits a manuscript to the journal they should not have any involvement with its processing or handling, or be able to access any of the details associated with its review or the decision process.

Monitoring the review process

It is important to monitor the progress of manuscripts through the review process. The status of manuscripts at all stages should be checked regularly to ensure that none is stuck anywhere for whatever reason. Online submission and review systems have made this task much easier, bringing up lists of submissions at various stages, highlighting where reviews are overdue or where responses and revisions are outstanding. They also allow complete records of activity and communications to be associated with manuscripts, making it easier to answer queries and make the checks required when working on a manuscript at the various stages. The importance of adding all relevant information to the system that isn't automatically recorded – such as information from phone calls and emails – should be stressed to editorial users, so that records are complete and present a true record and audit trail that all members of the editorial team can consult, not only at the present time but also in the future, for example if a submission needs to be revisited, perhaps as part of a misconduct investigation.

Reminder schedules need to be set up for all stages. Personally tailored emails are important at times because authors and reviewers can get frustrated at automatic requests that may be inappropriate or reminders that are too demanding or badly timed, especially when reviewers have, for example, made arrangements with the editor or editorial office to submit their reviews later. One of the keys to a successful journal is the good relationships it establishes with its community of authors and reviewers (who are, after all, mainly the same group) and the goodwill it builds up.

Evaluation and decision-making

When all the reviews for a manuscript are in from the external reviewers, a decision needs to be made on its fate. As stressed above, it is not the reviewers who make the decision on whether a manuscript should be published, but the editor. It is also the editor's role to advise the authors on what does or does not need to be done to make a manuscript acceptable for publication in their journal (and many offer advice that will be helpful to the authors even if the manuscript is going to be declined and will need to be submitted to another journal). Any editor who always says 'carry out the revisions recommended by the reviewers' isn't doing their job. Sometimes this direction will be applicable, but in many cases some intervention and direction by the editor are needed. There are hard and soft reviewers, some who ask for too much additional work, work that is better suited for a follow-up publication, some who may have missed an important point or not expressed themselves clearly. Some of their comments may even be wrong. When things like this are spotted by the editor it inspires confidence in authors that the editor has actually read their manuscript and carried out a critical appraisal of the reviewers' comments.

Making the decision and communicating it to the authors

The arrangements for decision-making vary from journal to journal, ranging from the situation in small ones where a single editor makes all the decisions to that in large journals where a number of editors may be involved. With multiple editors, each may have responsibility for making decisions independently, or there may be layers of editorial seniority, with recommendations from, for example, subject editors going to a more senior editor for approval and, probably, also editorial input.

Decision-making isn't a matter of 'counting votes', especially as different reviewers may have different strengths and expertise, and be focusing on different aspects of a single manuscript. Some may also not be too familiar with a journal or its policies and aspirations, particularly if they weren't provided with good guidance as part of the review process. It is the comments resulting from the critical appraisals from the reviewers that are important. An editor may decide that further review is needed before a decision can be made, in which case the manuscript will be sent to an additional reviewer (or reviewers), perhaps with special guidance, instructions and questions based on what is already in. Alternatively, some editors may want to have a conversation with the authors to get their responses to specific questions, or clarification on any areas of confusion before making a final decision – this is part of the 'dialogue' of quality and fair peer review.

Once the decision has been made, it needs to be communicated to the authors. It should be made absolutely clear what the decision is, and, if a revision is being invited, exactly what the conditions for acceptance are – such as, what extra work needs to be done, what missing controls should be provided, and which journal policy requirements need to be met and cannot be compromised on, for example regarding material and data availability and sharing. Authors may not, for a number of reasons, be able to fulfil these and they need to know this at the point of decision, not months later when they submit a new manuscript only to find they have wasted all that time because it is impossible for them to meet the requirements critical for acceptance. Authors shouldn't hesitate to get back to editors for clarification if they have any doubts or concerns. Good editors will be happy to provide this; it is in their best interests to have things sorted out as early as possible. Good editors will also always provide reasons for their decisions and actions. Authors more readily accept negative decisions when they are backed up with solid reasoning. This also maintains good relations and helps prevent authors being reluctant to submit future manuscripts to the journal.

It is important that editors are given complete editorial independence in their decisions on what to accept and include in their journals. The owners and publishers of journals must not try to influence their decisions in any way; this would be unethical. Decisions should also not be dictated by commercial considerations or influenced by factors such as the nationality, ethnicity, political beliefs, race or religion of the authors. A number of organisations have codes of conduct on both these aspects, for example, the World Association of Medical Editors (WAME, 2011a,b) and COPE (2011b, sections 6 and 16). COPE has also published a Code of Conduct for Journal Publishers (COPE, 2011c) that emphasises the importance of editorial independence. The WAME guidelines (2011a) recognise that there are some limits to editorial freedom and that the owners of journals have the right to remove editors, 'but they should dismiss them only for substantial reasons such as a pattern of bad editorial decisions, disagreement with the long-term editorial direction of the journal, or personal behavior (such as criminal acts) that are incompatible with a position of trust'.

Reviewer acknowledgement and appreciation

Reviewers should, each time they review a manuscript, be thanked for their review, notified of the decision and sent all the reviewers' reports (anonymised unless open review with revealed reviewer identity is used). This is very easy to do with online systems so there is no excuse not to. Not only is it courteous, it helps reviewers see things they have missed and better understand the scope of a journal and the quality it is looking for. *The EMBO Journal* has started to send reviewers all the other reports before the decision is actually made (calling this 'cross-peer review'), actively encouraging them to comment on each other's reports. The feedback can then be used to inform the decision. Reviewers are not generally, except in a few journals or for specific tasks such as statistical appraisal, paid. This issue has often been debated, but payment is generally thought not to be an effective or appropriate method of compensation (see, for example, WAME, 2007). The opinions of reviewers on this have been found to be divided, but with a majority thinking it would make the cost of publishing too expensive (Ware and Monkman, 2008). Because most reviewers are also authors (Ware and Monkman, 2008), a give-and-take relationship exists, and they benefit from critical appraisal and feedback on their own manuscripts. This of course only works if individuals take on their fair share of the reviewing load, and (as mentioned above) doubts have been expressed about this and the 'tragedy of the reviewer commons', where there is every incentive to submit manuscripts but little incentive to review (Fox and Petchey, 2010). It is, to a certain extent, up to editors to make sure that at their journals there is some degree of equality in the submission–reviewing balance.

Journals have devised various non-cash ways to reward their reviewers, including such things as public acknowledgement in a list published, usually annually, in the journal, free journal subscriptions or discounts on books, waivers of publication charges, gifts of various sorts (e.g. CDs, calendars, offprints), invitations to special receptions, CME (Continuing Medical Education) credits, letters of endorsement and personalised certificates. And, of course, good reviewers are often invited to join the editorial boards of journals for which they review. These sorts of acknowledgement are, however, by no means universal, and greater recognition of the work carried out by reviewers, by both publishers and employers, has been called for (UK House of Commons Science and Technology Committee, 2011, paragraph 164). This brings with it the need for all publishers to have in place robust systems for recording the work carried out by reviewers, and is another area where schemes such as ORCID will make it easier to assign credit accurately.

Consistency in decision-making

Achieving consistency in decision-making across a journal that is selective in what it publishes (i.e. does not base acceptance on just soundness) is important, both for the quality of the journal and in fairness to all its authors. Each journal needs to work out how this will be achieved and whose responsibility it will be to monitor it. Critical is that all the individuals with editorial decision-making responsibilities are made aware of editorial policies and standards when they join the journal, and the whole editorial board is kept updated when change are made. Where there are restrictions on how many articles a journal can publish, these individuals also need to be kept informed on how many manuscripts are being accepted across the journal and advised whenever the threshold for acceptance is changed, so that a backlog isn't built up. They also need to be told when the remit on scope or type of submission changes, so that manuscripts that fall outside these aren't inappropriately accepted. Once authors have been told a manuscript has been accepted, that must be viewed as a commitment to publish. Decisions shouldn't be reversed unless serious problems are found with a paper, and new editors shouldn't overturn decisions made by the previous editor unless serious problems are identified (COPE, 2011b, sections 3.2 and 3.3, respectively).

Rejected manuscripts – review 'wastage'?

What of the reviews for the manuscripts that are rejected? In most journals these will just be left in the records and archived along with the submission and its associated correspondence. In an attempt to alleviate the burden on the reviewer pool, some publishers have introduced a system of 'cascading' submissions and reviews. When a manuscript is rejected, the authors are given the opportunity to have it passed on to another journal, along with the reviews. This system is used successfully by a number of publishers (e.g. Nature Publishing Group, BioMed Central, PLoS, the IOP Publishing, the Royal Society of Chemistry, and the European Molecular Biology Organization, EMBO), but it is always the author's choice whether to take up the transfer option or to submit afresh and get new reviews. Journals vary as to whether or not the reviewers' names are passed on with the reviews, and this probably affects what the new editor decides to do: they can elect to send manuscripts for additional review if they feel it is necessary, and are probably more likely to do this if they do not know the identities of the reviewers of the reports that have been passed to them from another journal. Cascading becomes more problematical between publishers, as exemplified by The Neuroscience Peer Review Consortium (http://nprc.incf.org/). This was set up in January 2008 as an alliance of neuroscience journals whose editors were concerned that they were seeing many solid manuscripts being rejected because of space limitations or because articles weren't suitable for their journals. Journals within the Consortium (at the end of 2011 there were about 40) agree to accept manuscript reviews from other members of the Consortium. There seems only to have been one public update report (Saper and Maunsell, 2009), but from that it appears that the percentage of manuscripts being received/forwarded to other members is low (1–2 per cent). Aside from concerns about lack of awareness amongst authors and because there are many more neuroscience journals outside of the Consortium than in it, there are issues of commercial advantage, as explained by Philip Campbell, the editor of *Nature*, who has said (Campbell, 2011, paragraph 58):

> 'This facility is controversial within NPG. We invest significant sums of money in our professional editors spending time both in the office and in visits cultivating contacts with referees, and fostering insightful refereeing as best we can. To then hand on the reports and names to another publisher is to some extent undermining our competitive edge. Indeed, the principle [sic] competitor of NN[*Nature Neuroscience*], *Neuron*, is not a part of the experiment, and we might well not have joined the experiment if it was.'

New models of peer review

The Internet and electronic publishing have presented opportunities to experiment with new approaches, and although traditional pre-publication peer review is highly valued it needs to be open to improvement and innovation. A number of models have been introduced, some are now quite established and others are being run experimentally for trial periods. A small selection is given below.

Combining traditional and open review

Attempts have been made to couple a period of public, open commenting with more conventional, confidential review. One of the best-known models is that in use at the journal *Atmospheric Chemistry and Physics*. Here, after pre-screening by the editorial board, submissions are posted on the journal's website as 'discussion papers'. A moderated, interactive public discussion period of 8 weeks follows during which reviewers chosen by the journal post their comments, remaining anonymous if they choose, along with anyone else who wants to, but whose identity must be disclosed. After this period, authors are expected, within 4 weeks, to publish a response to all the comments. It is only after this that the editorial decision and recommendations are made. All discussion papers and the associated comments remain permanently archived. The model seems to have been successful for this journal (see Pöschl, 2010, for a progress report), but even so, the level of commenting from the scientific community is relatively low (see below for further discussion of this issue), with only about one in four papers receiving comments in addition to those from the chosen reviewers (Pöschl, 2010). *The Journal of Interactive Media in Education* is another journal that combines private and public review.

Such approaches may not be suitable for all journals or for all disciplines. For example, when the journal *Nature* experimented with optional open review running in parallel with its conventional, confidential peer-review process, uptake by authors was low (5 per cent), particularly so for cellular and molecular fields, and only 54 per cent of the papers that were available received comments (*Nature*, 2006a). On analysis, the comments were of limited use to the editors in decision-making. 'Pre-print' or 'e-print' posting, as it is known, and open commenting may not work in fast-moving areas such as molecular biology where concerns about being scooped are common, or in disciplines such as chemistry where patents may be involved (Parker, 2011). In the physics community, however, pre-publication e-print posting with the opportunity for community commenting is the norm and has been very successful: arXiv (http://arxiv.org/), the e-print server in the fields of physics, mathematics, non-linear science, computer science, quantitative biology, quantitative finance and statistics, was established in 1991, and in 2011 contained nearly 700 000 e-prints and served about 1 million full-text downloads to around 400 000 distinct users every week (Ginsparg, 2011). Authors can go on to submit their work to journals for publication, and in the majority of the areas covered most do (although there is considerable variation amongst the sub-disciplines; Davis, 2009b).

One journal that has experimented successfully with open, public, peer review is the *Shakespeare Quarterly*, a well-established humanities journal. In 2010 it opened up the review of some articles submitted for a special issue on 'Shakespeare and New Media' to public commenting (*Shakespeare Quarterly*, 2010). To ensure there would be comments from experts, the guest editor invited around 90 scholars to comment. Some did, along with self-selected commentators, and high-quality feedback was received. Some junior scholars were, however, put off commenting in case they contradicted the more senior ones. One of the reasons the experiment was generally successful was probably due to the time and effort put into the project by the editor: 'it was as controlled a process as traditional peer review. It was just controlled in a different way' (Howard, 2010).

Selection of articles to review by reviewers rather than selection of reviewers by editors

Examples include 'open (participatory) peer-review' (an open-peer-review experiment at the *Journal of Medical Internet Research*), where reviewers can sign themselves up either as reviewers for specific articles (the abstracts of submitted articles which authors have agreed can be posted are listed on the site) or to be added to the reviewing database. This is similar to the model used for many years at the *British Journal of Educational Technology*, where members of the reviewer panel of over 250 are invited to 'bid' for newly submitted articles. Once or twice each month, the list of the titles of new articles is circulated to the panel, who choose those they think will be of interest to them and are in areas where they are familiar with the topic. In PeerChoice, being trialled by Elsevier, reviewers can use analytics software to select articles that match their interest and competency (Elsevier, 2011b).

Greater author control

At *BMC Biology*, authors are allowed to opt out of re-review by the reviewers after revision to meet the original criticisms. The editors must then decide whether the authors' responses are reasonable. At *Biology Direct*, authors have themselves to get three members of the editorial board to agree to be responsible for reviewing the manuscript.

Accompanying commentary on publication

The journal *Behavioral and Brain Science* has an 'open peer commentary' feature. Here, particularly significant and controversial work is accompanied by 10–25 invited commentaries from specialists, together with the authors' responses to them. *BMC Biology* also publishes an invited commentary from an expert for those cases in its author-opt-out scheme (see above) where revisions aren't as extensive as they should be or there are other limitations, so that readers are aware of these.

It is clear that experimentation is going on at a number of journals and that there is the potential to 'pick-and-mix' the various features being tried. It will therefore be invaluable to other journals for the results of such experiments to be reported, helping inform decisions on changes they may be thinking of making. There may be both discipline- and journal-related indicators to consider for successful adoption. *Nature* (2006b) has published a series of analyses and perspectives of peer review from a range of stakeholders that includes new models and approaches. The archive of the now closed *Peer-to-Peer* blog on nature.com also contains much useful and insightful information on various aspects and innovations of peer review (http://blogs.nature.com/peer-to-peer/).

Post-publication review and evaluation

Even though, traditionally, peer review of scholarly work has taken place before publication, there have been opportunities for further review and commenting after publication. These have, however, been limited. With the advent of new social media and networking channels not even dreamed of until relatively recently, the opportunity exists for peer review to continue to a much greater extent and much more easily after publication. And not just in the previous traditional context of, for example, 'letters to the editor', which represent a limited and mostly moderated and selective mechanism for views to be expressed, but along a spectrum that goes from that rather restricted case to the situation where anyone from anywhere in the world can take part: from a researcher in the same field to the amateur with an interest in the area, from the fanatic who enters online discussions to promote their pet theories or grievances to the Nobel laureate whose theories have been recognised by the highest award. This openness brings with it some issues: for example, who and what to trust? In open forums the responsibility rests with the reader. But they can be helped to judge the reliability and trustworthiness of contributions and points made by having transparency – who the comments are from, the contributor's background experience and, crucially, what their affiliations are (so that potential competing interests can be taken into account). Levels of moderation and the amount of information required from contributors vary from field to field and journal to journal. But in making the decision on where on this spectrum journal editors want feedback on their journal articles to fall, the potential importance of comments from outside the immediate community should not be underestimated.

Commentary, article-level metrics and e-letters

A number of publishers have opened up articles in their journals to post-publication commenting, most notably BioMed Central, PLoS and the BMJ Group. PLoS has also introduced 'article-level metrics', where all the articles published in its journals have details on usage, citations, social bookmarks and blog posts, as well as reader ('star') ratings and comments (PLoS, 2011). The aim is to help readers determine the value of the articles, both to them and to the wider community. *AIP Advances*, a new journal from the American Institute of Physics, is also offering article-level metrics, in an effort to allow articles to be judged on their own scientific merit. A common problem with post-publication commentary is getting people to take part. The level of engagement – with the exception of the *BMJ*, which seems to receive many 'rapid responses' to its articles – is generally low (Priem, 2011), which has been a disappointment to many. Schriger *et al.* (2011) analysed post-publication commenting in medical journals and found 82 per cent of the articles had no responses, prompting the authors to conclude (p. 153) that 'post-publication critique of articles ... does not seem to be taking hold.' There are probably a number of reasons for low participation: people are busy enough doing all the other things they need to, there's no incentive to engage because this activity attracts no 'credit', there may be reluctance to criticise openly the work of others (or indeed fear of being publicly criticised in return). There is also a problem with author engagement. Author participation is important, but a reluctance to respond has been found (Gøtzsche *et al.*, 2010). Online commenting and collaboration can work, for example as in the Polymath Project (Gowers, 2009), where over a thousand comments were received and a major mathematics problem solved after only 7 weeks – so maybe lessons can be learnt from the area of open science (Nielsen, 2011)?

New social media

New social media – such as blogs, Facebook, Twitter – present the opportunity for rapid feedback with extensive reach, bringing enormous potential benefits: alerting others to work they may not have otherwise seen, offering refinement and analysis, and bringing together people from different fields and geographical areas who then perhaps start to collaborate. Very important is the ability to alert people to published work that is problematical or suspect, either because of issues with the methodology or because of fabrication, falsification or other unethical behaviour. And because this can happen very quickly – sometimes within hours of publication – it can help minimise the damage that can occur when work that is suspect remains appearing sound in the scholarly literature. There have been some high-profile examples of work being criticised and found to be wrong very soon after publication as a result of vigorous activity in the blogosphere. For example, when in December 2010 a paper was published online in *Science* reporting a bacterium that can grow using arsenic instead of phosphorus and which incorporates arsenate into its nucleic acids (Wolfe-Simon *et al.*, 2011), postings critical of the methodology and interpretation appeared almost immediately (Redfield, 2010). The story continued over the following months, predominantly through the Twitter hashtag #arseniclife, which has come to symbolise successful post-publication review and members of the scientific community working together and openly, along the way also influencing the way the public thinks (Zimmer, 2011). Similar criticisms and blogosphere activity (Mandavilli, 2011) followed publication of a paper claiming to have identified genetic signatures allowing prediction of exceptional longevity in humans (Sebastiani *et al.*, 2010). The same media, however, also present the opportunity for concerted and rapid criticism of individuals, which may be unwarranted or false, even defamatory, and that is an issue that concerns many.

Post-publication evaluation

There is one well-established 'post-publication peer review' service, Faculty of 1000 (F1000, http://f1000.com/), which uses 'Faculties' of experts to provide named evaluations and ratings of published research across biology and medicine. The service started in 2002 (Wets *et al.*, 2003), with just over a thousand members (hence the name), and it prides itself that the majority of its evaluations are not from what are thought of as the top-tier journals. It now has over 10 000 members, who are asked to select the best articles they have read in their specialties, highlighting the key findings and putting the work into context. As more repository-type journals, where sound work is published without any selection for interest, potential impact or various other parameters, come into existence (see above), the need for, and expectation of, such post-publication services – across all disciplines – will undoubtedly increase. There is great scope for expansion of post-publication evaluation in a number of forms, involving individuals, journals and organisations.

With work being discussed potentially via various social media and by numerous people there is also great interest in finding ways to aggregate all this information and quantify it in some meaningful way to gauge the impact of research. The field is very new, and the challenges considerable, but initiatives such as 'altmetrics' (Priem *et al.*, 2010; Mandavilli, 2011) have already been set up and more are likely to follow.

Conclusion and outlook

So where does peer review currently stand? Despite some claims that it is 'broken' or 'in crisis', many feel that pre-publication peer review is not something that they want to see disappear. Mark Ware reviewed the state of journal peer review at the end of 2010, and concluded that 'far from being in crisis, peer review remains widely supported and diversely innovative' (Ware, 2011, p. 23). Fiona Godlee (2011), editor of the *BMJ*, has commented about peer review, that: 'At its best, I think we would all agree that it does improve the quality of scientific reporting and that it can improve, through the pressure of the journal, the quality of the science itself and how it is performed.' The UK House of Commons Science and Technology Committee inquiry into peer review concluded (2011) that, although pre-publication peer review is not perfect and there is much that can be done to improve and supplement it (paragraph 278), 'peer review in scholarly publishing, in one form or another, is crucial to the reputation and reliability of scientific research' (paragraph 277).

There are without doubt problems, variations in quality and considerable scope for improvement. Editors and publishers need to work together to ensure not only that their peer-review processes are of the highest quality, but that they also evolve and adapt to what is required by the communities they serve. There is no room for complacency. At this stage in the history of journal publishing, three and a half centuries on from the appearance of the first journals, there is greater opportunity for innovation and experimentation than ever before, and this should be embraced. For the first time the two traditional functions of pre-publication review have been separated: a pre-publication check for methodological and reporting soundness, and post-publication evaluation for interest, importance and potential impact. This model is attractive to many because it allows research to be published without delay, enabling researchers to move on without wasting time submitting work that is sound to journal after journal in the quest for publication, and others to benefit as soon as possible from their findings. The existence of a number of repository-type journals should help ensure healthy competition and the maintenance of high peer-review standards. Publication is closely linked to the assessment of researchers and their work by their institutions and the research funders. For as long as they require the 'badge' of a high-impact journal, the pressure on researchers to publish in those journals will remain. Post-publication evaluation services, however, offer the potential to assess and highlight work not just in the short term, but over the longer time period that it takes some work to be recognised. With the 'publish all, filter later' model (Smith, 2010b) it would be impossible to distinguish what is sound from what is not, or what is evidence-based rather than opinion, and so this is not in the view of many a realistic way forward. However, with the 'publish all that is sound, evaluate later' approach, researchers and the public can remain confident that what they are reading has been checked by experts.

Peer review is facing new challenges. Vast amounts of data are being generated in some disciplines. Some of this needs to be assessed by reviewers during peer review, or at least seen by them to enable them to assess what does need to be included or made available in appropriate repositories for others to access and use. This brings up issues of data availability, usability and storage, with all the technological and economic implications, areas which are under intense investigation and discussion (e.g. Royal Society, 2011b). Although reviewers have expressed willingness to review authors' data (Ware and Monkman, 2008), the potential burden should not be underestimated, as expressed by one researcher (Nicholson, 2006): 'The scientific community needs to reassess the way it addresses the peer-review problem, taking into account that referees are only human and are now being asked to do a superhuman task on a near-daily basis.'

Concerns about the increased burden on reviewers and the 'wastage' of reviews in the quest for publication have led to 'cascading' submission and review, and this may be something that more journals adopt, especially within individual publishers or between the sister journals of organisations.

The journal publishing landscape is a rapidly evolving one and it is likely that the diversity of peer-review models will increase. It is clear that different disciplines and communities, even different journals, have different requirements, and what works for one may not for another. Also, decisions will, to some extent, be dictated by authors and their research funders. But in this varied and rapidly evolving landscape there is little doubt that peer review – which is basically scrutiny and assessment by experts – will continue as an important component of the scholarly publishing process.

Sources of further information

Council of Science Editors (CSE, http://www.councilscienceeditors.org/). CSE's White Paper on Promoting Integrity in Scientific Journal Publications, 2009 Update. http://www.councilscienceeditors.org/i4a/pages/index.cfm?pageid=3331 (accessed 3 January 2012).

Elsevier Peer Review resources. http://www.elsevier.com/wps/find/reviewershome.reviewers (accessed 3 January 2012).

Godlee, F. and Jefferson, T. (eds) *Peer Review in Health Sciences*, 2nd edn. London: BMJ Books.

Hames, I. (2007) *Peer Review and Manuscript Management in Scientific Journals: guidelines for good practice*. Oxford: Blackwell Publishing and ALPSP. http://eu.wiley.com/WileyCDA/WileyTitle/productCd-1405131594.html

International Society of Managing and Technical Editors (ISMTE, http://www.ismte.org). Resource Central, a collection of resources, tools, instructions and articles to assist editorial offices in peer-review management processes. http://www.ismte.org/Resource_Central (accessed 3 January 2012).

Lock, S. (1985) *A Difficult Balance. Editorial Peer Review in Medicine*. Philadelphia: ISI Press.

Research Information Network (2010) Peer Review: a guide for researchers. http://www.rin.ac.uk/peer-review-guide (accessed 3 January 2012).

Wiley-Blackwell, Best Practice Guidelines on Publication Ethics: A Publisher's Perspective. Available at http://www.wiley.com/bw/publicationethics/ (accessed 3 January 2012).

References

Adams, J., King, C. and Ma, N. (2009a) Global Research Report: China. Thomson Reuters. November 2009. http://researchanalytics.thomsonreuters.com/m/pdfs/grr-china-nov09.pdf (accessed 4 January 2012).

Adams, J., King, C. and Singh, V. (2009b) Global Research Report: India. Thomson Reuters, October 2009. http://researchanalytics.thomsonreuters.com/m/pdfs/grr-India-oct09_ag0908174.pdf (accessed 4 January 2012).

Adams, J. and Pendlebury, D. (2011) Global Research Report: Materials Science and Technology. Thomson Reuters, June 2011. http://researchanalytics.thomsonreuters.com/m/pdfs/grr-materialscience.pdf (accessed 4 January 2012).

ALPSP/EASE (2000) Current practice in peer review: results of a survey conducted during Oct/Nov 2000. http://www.alpsp.org/Ebusiness/Libraries/Publication_Downloads/Current_Practice_in_Peer_Review.sflb.ashx?download=true (accessed 6 January 2012).

ALPSP and Kaufman-Wills Group (2005) The facts about open access. A study of the financial and non-financial effects of alternative business models for scholarly journals. http://www.alpsp.org/Ebusiness/ProductCatalog/Product.aspx?ID=47 (accessed 6 January 2012).

British Antarctic Survey (2011) Written evidence submitted to the UK House of Commons Science and Technology Committee Inquiry into Peer Review (8 March 2011, PR 40). http://www.publications.parliament.uk/pa/cm201012/cmselect/cmsctech/856/856vw_10.htm (accessed 4 January 2012).

Burnham, J.C. (1990) The evolution of editorial peer review. *JAMA*, **263**: 1323–9.

Campbell, P. (2011) Written evidence submitted to the UK House of Commons Science and Technology Committee Inquiry into Peer Review (10 March 2011, PR 60). http://www.publications.parliament.uk/pa/cm201012/cmselect/cmsctech/856/856we11.htm (accessed 4 January 2012).

COPE (2011a) How should editors respond to plagiarism? COPE discussion paper, April 2011. http://www.publicationethics.org/files/COPE_plagiarism_discussion_%20doc_26%20Apr%2011.pdf (accessed 6 January 2012).

COPE (2011b) Code of Conduct and Best Practice Guidelines for Journal Editors. March 2011. http://www.publicationethics.org/files/Code%20of%20conduct%20for%20journal%20editors4.pdf (accessed 6 January 2012).

COPE (2011c) Code of Conduct for Journal Publishers. March 2011. http://www.publicationethics.org/files/Code%20of%20conduct%20for%20publishers%20FINAL_1_0.pdf (accessed 6 January 2012).

Davis, P. (2009a) Open access publisher accepts nonsense manuscript for dollars. *The Scholarly Kitchen*, 10 June 2009. http://scholarlykitchen.sspnet.org/2009/06/10/nonsense-for-dollars/ (accessed 4 January 2012).

Davis, P. (2009b) Physics papers and the arXiv. *The Scholarly Kitchen*, 17 June 2009. http://scholarlykitchen.sspnet.org/2009/06/17/physics-papers-and-the-arxiv/ (accessed 4 January 2012).

Davis, P. (2010) Privatizing peer review – the PubCred proposal. *The Scholarly Kitchen*, 16 September 2010. http://scholarlykitchen.sspnet.org/2010/09/16/privatizing-peer-review/ (accessed 4 January 2012).

DeMaria, A.N. (2010) Peer review: the weakest link. *JACC (Journal of the American College of Cardiology)*, 55: 1161–2.

Elsevier (2011a) Evidence given by Mayur Amin to the UK House of Commons Science and Technology Committee Inquiry into Peer Review, 11 May 2001. Transcript of oral evidence, HC 856, Q127. http://www.publications.parliament.uk/pa/cm201012/cmselect/cmsctech/856/856.pdf

Elsevier (2011b) PeerChoice pilot general information. http://www.elsevier.com/wps/find/P04.cws_home/peerchoice (accessed 4 January 2012).

Fanelli, D. (2009) How many scientists fabricate and falsify research? A systematic review and meta-analysis of survey data. *PLoS ONE*, 4(5): e5738. doi:10.1371/journal.pone.0005738

Fox, J. and Petchey, O.L. (2010) Pubcreds: fixing the peer review process by 'privatizing' the reviewer commons. *Bulletin of the Ecological Society of America*, 91: 325–33.

Fuyuno, I. and Cyranoski, D. (2006) Cash for papers: putting a premium on publication. *Nature*, 441: 792.

Garfield, E. (2006) The history and meaning of the journal impact factor. *JAMA*, 295: 90–3.

Ginsparg, P. (2011) ArXiv at 20. *Nature*, 476: 145–7.

Godlee, F (2002) Making reviewers visible: openness, accountability, and credit. *JAMA*, 287: 2762–5.

Godlee, F. (2011) Evidence given to the UK House of Commons Science and Technology Committee Inquiry into Peer Review, 11 May 2001. Transcript of oral evidence, HC856, Q97. http://www.publications.parliament.uk/pa/cm201012/cmselect/cmsctech/856/856.pdf

Godlee, F. and Dickersin, K. (2003) 'Bias, subjectivity, chance, and conflict of interest in editorial decisions', in F. Godlee and T. Jefferson (eds). *Peer Review in Health Sciences*, 2nd edn., pp. 91–117. London: BMJ Books.

Gøtzsche, P.C., Delamothe, T., Godlee, F. and Lundh, A. (2010) Adequacy of authors' replies to criticism raised in electronic letters to the editor: cohort study. *BMJ*, 341: c3926.

Gowers, T. (2009) Is massively collaborative mathematics possible? *Gowers's Weblog*, 27 January 2009. http://gowers.wordpress.com/2009/01/27/is-massively-collaborative-mathematics-possible/ (accessed 4 January 2012).

Grant, R.P. (2010) On peer review. *Confessions of a (former) Lab Rat*, 15 April 2010. http://occamstypewriter.org/rpg/2010/04/15/on_peer_review/ (accessed 4 January 2012).

Hames, I. (2007) *Peer Review and Manuscript Management in Scientific Journals: guidelines for good practice.* Oxford: Blackwell Publishing and ALPSP.

Howard, J. (2010) Leading humanities journal debuts 'open' peer review, and likes it. *The Chronicle of Higher Education*, 26 July 2010. http://chronicle.com/article/Leading-Humanities-Journal-/123696/ (accessed 4 January 2012)

ICMJE (2011) Uniform requirements for manuscripts submitted to biomedical journals. Ethical considerations in the conduct and reporting of research: conflicts of interest. http://www.icmje.org/ethical_4conflicts.html (accessed 3 January 2012).

Jaschik, S. (2011) Rejecting double blind. *Inside Higher Ed: Times Higher Education,* 31 May 2011. http://www.timeshighereducation.co.uk/story.asp?storycode=416353 (accessed 4 January 2012).

Jefferson, T., Alderson, P., Wager, E. and Davidoff, F. (2002) Effects of editorial peer review: a systematic review. *JAMA*, 287: 2784–6.

Jefferson, T., Rudin, M., Brodney Folse, S. and Davidoff, F. (2007) Editorial peer review for improving the quality of reports of biomedical studies. *Cochrane Database of Systematic Reviews* 2007, Issue 2. Art. No.: MR000016. doi: 10.1002/14651858.MR000016.pub3.

Kronick, D.A. (1990) Peer review in 18th-century scientific journalism. *JAMA*, 263: 1321–2.

Laine, C. and Mulrow, C. (2003) Peer review: integral to science and indispensable to *Annals*. *Annals of Internal Medicine*, 139: 1038–40.

Lawrence, P.A. (2003) The politics of publication. *Nature*, 422: 259–61.

Lawrence, P.A. (2007) The mismeasurement of science. *Current Biology*, 17(15) R583–5.

Lock, S. (1991) *Introduction to the third impression. A Difficult Balance: Editorial Peer Review in Medicine.* London: BMJ. Originally published 1985. Philadelphia: ISI Press.

Mandavilli, M. (2011) Peer review: Trial by Twitter. *Nature* 469: 286–7.

Martinson, B.C., Anderson, M.S. and de Vries, R. (2005) Scientists behaving badly. *Nature*, 435: 737–8.

McCook, A. (2006) Is peer review broken? *The Scientist* 20(2): 26.

Nature (2006a) Overview: *Nature*'s peer review trial. http://www.nature.com/nature/peerreview/debate/nature05535.html (accessed 4 January 2012).

Nature (2006b) Nature's peer review debate. http://www.nature.com/nature/peerreview/debate/index.html (accessed 4 January 2012).

Nature (2011) Nature Publishing Index 2010 China. http://www.natureasia.com/en/publishing-index/china/2010/ (accessed 4 January 2012).

Neylon, C. (2010) Peer review: what is it good for? *Science in the Open*, 5 February 2010. http://cameronneylon.net/blog/peer-review-what-is-it-good-for/ (accessed 4 January 2012).

Nicholson, J.K. (2006) Reviewers peering from under a pile of 'omics' data. *Nature*, 440: 992.

Nielsen, M. (2011) Open science. *Michael Nielsen, author blog*, 7 April 2011. http://michaelnielsen.org/blog/open-science-2/ (accessed 4 January 2012).

Parker, R. (2011) Evidence given to the UK House of Commons Science and Technology Committee Inquiry into Peer Review, 4 May 2001. Transcript of oral evidence, HC856, Q8. http://www.publications.parliament.uk/pa/cm201012/cmselect/cmsctech/856/856.pdf

Petchey, O. and Fox, J. (2011) Progress on obtaining journal-level data on the peer review system. *PubCreds: Fixing the Peer Review Process by 'Privatising' the Reviewer Commons*. 18 February 2011. http://www.ipetitions.com/petition/fix-peer-review/blog/5040 (accessed 4 January 2012).

Ploegh, H. (2011) End the wasteful tyranny of reviewer experiments. *Nature*, 472: 391.

PLoS (2011) Article-level metrics http://article-level-metrics.plos.org/ and Article-level metrics information http://www.plosone.org/static/almInfo.action (accessed 4 January 2012).

Pöschl, U. (2010) Interactive open access publishing and public peer review: the effectiveness of transparency and self-regulation in scientific quality assurance. *IFLA Journal*, 36: 40–6.

Priem, J., Taraborelli, D., Groth, P. and Neylon, C. (2010) altmetrics: a manifesto. 26 October 2010 (modified September 2008, 2011). http://altmetrics.org/manifesto/ (accessed 4 January 2012).

Priem, J. (2011) Has Journal commenting failed? *Jason Priem, author blog*, 7 January 2011. http://jasonpriem.com/2011/01/has-journal-article-commenting-failed/ (accessed 4 January 2012).

Pulverer, B. (2010) A transparent black box *EMBO Journal*, 29: 3891–2.

Redfield, R. (2010) Arsenic-associated bacteria (NASA's claims). *RRResearch*, 4 December 2010. http://rrresearch.fieldofscience.com/2010/12/arsenic-associated-bacteria-nasas.html (accessed 4 January 2012).

Rohn, J. (2010) Peer review is no picnic. guardian.co.uk, 6 September 2010. http://www.guardian.co.uk/science/blog/2010/sep/06/peer-review (accessed 4 January 2012).

Rossner, M. and Yamada, K.M. (2004) What's in a picture? The temptation of image manipulation. *Journal of Cell Biology*, 166: 11–15.

Royal Society (2011a) Knowledge, networks and nations: global scientific collaboration in the 21st century. RS Policy document 03/11, March 2011.

Royal Society (2011b) Science as a public enterprise. http://royalsociety.org/policy/projects/science-public-enterprise/ (accessed 6 January 2012).

Saper, C.B. and Maunsell, J.H.R. (2009) Editorial. The Neuroscience Peer Review Consortium. *Neural Development*, 4: 10 (http://www.neuraldevelopment.com/content/4/1/10).

Schriger, D.L., Chehrazi, A.C., Merchant, R.M. and Altman, D.G. (2011) Use of the internet by print medical journals in 2003 to 2009: a longitudinal observational study. *Annals of Emergency Medicine*, 57: 153–60.

Sebastiani, P., Solovieff, N., Puca, A., *et al.* (2010) Genetic signatures of exceptional longevity in humans. *Science*. Published online 1 July 2010. doi:10.1126/science.1190532

Sense About Science (2009) Peer Review Survey 2009: Full Report. http://www.senseaboutscience.org/data/files/Peer_Review/Peer_Review_Survey_Final_3.pdf (accessed 6 January 2012).

Shakespeare Quarterly (2010) *Shakespeare Quarterly* Open Review: Shakespeare and New Media. http://mediacommons.futureofthebook.org/mcpress/ShakespeareQuarterly_NewMedia (accessed 4 January 2012).

Shao, J. and Shen, H. (2011) The outflow of academic papers from China: why is it happening and can it be stemmed? *Learned Publishing*, 24: 95–7.

Smith, R. (2006) Peer review: a flawed process at the heart of science and journals. *Journal of the Royal Society of Medicine*, 99: 178–82.

Smith, R. (2010a) Classical peer review: an empty gun. *Breast Cancer Research*, 12 (Suppl. 4): S13 doi:10.1186/bcr2742

Smith, R. (2010b) Scrap peer review and beware of 'top journals'. BMJ Group blogs. 22 March 2010. http://blogs.bmj.com/bmj/2010/03/22/richard-smith-scrap-peer-review-and-beware-of-%E2%80%9Ctop-journals%E2%80%9D/ (accessed 6 January 2012).

Spier, R. (2002) The history of the peer-review process. *Trends in Biotechnology*, 20: 357–8.

Tananbaum, G. and Holmes, L. (2008) The evolution of Web-based peer-review systems. *Learned Publishing*, 21: 300–6.

Tenopir, C., Allard, S., Bates, B., Levine, K.J., King, D.W., Birch, B., Mays, R. and Caldwell, C. (2010) Research publication characteristics and their relative values: a report for the Publishing Research Consortium, September 2010. http://www.publishingresearch.net/documents/PRCReportTenopiretal Jan2011.pdf

UK House of Commons Science and Technology Committee (2011) Peer review in scientific publications. Eighth Report of Session 2010–12, HC 856. London: The Stationary Office Limited. http://www.publications.parliament.uk/pa/cm201012/cmselect/cmsctech/856/856.pdf; http://www.publications.parliament.uk/pa/cm201012/cmselect/cmsctech/856/85602.htm (accessed 4 January 2012).

van Rooyen, S., Godlee, F., Evans, S., Smith, R. and Black, N. (1998). Effect of blinding and unmasking on the quality of peer review: a randomised trial. *JAMA*, 280: 234–7.

Velterop, J.J.M. (1995) 'Keeping the minutes of science', in M. Collier and K. Arnold (eds). *Proceedings of the Second Electronic and Visual Information Research (ELVIRA) Conference*, pp. 11–17. London: Aslib.

Vines, T., Rieseberg, L. and Smith, H. (2010) No crisis in supply of peer reviewers. *Nature*, 468: 1041.

Wager, E. and Jefferson, T. (2001) Shortcomings of peer review in biomedical journals. *Learned Publishing*, 14: 257–63.

WAME (2007) Rewarding Peer Reviewers: Payment vs Other Types of Recognition, WAME Listserve Discussion 12 February 2007 to 20 February 2007. http://www.wame.org/resources/wame-listserve-discussion/

WAME (2011a) The Relationship Between Journal Editors-in-Chief and Owners. Policy Statement posted 25 July 2009. http://www.wame.org/resources/policies#independence (accessed 3 January 2012).

WAME (2011b) Geopolitical intrusion on editorial decisions. Policy Statement posted 23 March 2004. http://www.wame.org/resources/policies#geopolitical (accessed 4 January 2012).

Ware, M. (2005) Online Submission and Peer Review Systems: A review of currently available systems and the experiences of authors, referees, editors and publishers. ALPSP Research Report. http://www.alpsp.org/Ebusiness/ProductCatalog/Product.aspx?ID=40 (accessed 6 January 2012).

Ware, M. (2011) Peer review: recent experience and future directions. *New Review of Information Networking*, 16(1): 23–53.

Ware, M. and Mabe, M. (2009) The STM Report. An overview of scientific and scholarly journal publishing. International Association of Scientific, Technical and Medical Publishers. September 2009.

Ware, M. and Monkman, M. (2008) Peer review in scholarly journals: perspective of the scholarly community – an international study. Publishing Research Consortium (PRC) Research Report. http://www.publishingresearch.net/documents/PeerReviewFullPRCReport-final.pdf

Weller, A.C. (2001) *Editorial Peer Review: Its Strengths and Weaknesses*. ASIST Monograph Series. Medford, NJ: Information Today, Inc.

Wets, K., Weedon, D. and Velterop, J. (2003) Post-publication filtering and evaluation: Faculty of 1000. *Learned Publishing*, 16: 249–58.

Wolfe-Simon, F., Blum, J.S., Kulp, T.R., *et al.* (2011) A bacterium that can grow by using arsenic instead of phosphorus. *Science*, 332: 1163–66.

Zimmer, C. (2011) The discovery of arsenic-based Twitter. How #arseniclife changed science. *Slate*, 27 May 2011. http://www.slate.com/id/2295724/ (accessed 4 January 2012).

3

The scholarly ecosystem

Michael Jubb

Abstract: This chapter examines some key trends in the funding of research, especially the funding of basic research by governments and other public bodies; and highlights the pressure to increase the contribution of research to innovation, economic performance and the fulfilment of social needs. It also examines where basic research is conducted in different countries, in universities and research institutes; how research careers are developed under the increasing pressure of competition; and how universities both support and manage researchers. Finally, it examines how research is conducted by both individuals and teams; how researchers both consume and create information in the course of their research; and how the research process is changing in different disciplines as a result of technological change.

Key words: Research, researchers, funding, competition, information, universities, technology.

Introduction

Researchers are driven by a desire to enhance our knowledge and understanding of the world we inhabit: the end product of their work, if successful, is new knowledge, typically based on a combination of newly discovered or developed data and information, set alongside data and information which has been taken from the work of previous researchers. The result is greater understanding and a newly enhanced knowledge base.

Scholarly publishing fulfils a relatively small but critical role in the wider landscape of research across the globe, enabling researchers to communicate their findings. Publishing depends on the activities of researchers, both as producers and as consumers of scholarly content. But researchers in turn depend on a publishing infrastructure to enable them to communicate their findings effectively both to their fellow researchers and to wider communities. This chapter presents a picture of the nature and scale of the research landscape, delineates some key features and trends over the past few years, and considers some key aspects of the research process and how it is changing.

Funding of research by governments, business and other organisations

Across the 34 members of the Organisation for Economic Co-operation and Development (OECD), gross expenditure on research and development (R&D) amounted in 2008 to $964 billion.[1] Roughly 35 per cent of investment in R&D takes place in North America, 31 per cent in Asia and 28 per cent in Europe; the rest of the world (Latin America and the Caribbean, Africa and the Middle East, and Oceania) together account for about 6 per cent. Expenditure has increased by over 60 per cent in real terms since the mid-1990s, and in major research countries has tended to exceed the rate of growth in gross domestic product (GDP). Thus in the US the average annual growth in R&D expenditure over the past 20 years has been 3.1 per cent in real terms, as compared with average growth in GDP of 2.8 per cent. The result is that across OECD countries as a group, R&D represents a growing proportion of the economy as a whole: R&D expenditure grew as a proportion of GDP from 1.9 per cent in 1981 to 2.3 per cent in 2008.

Of course, not all of this expenditure results in research findings and outputs of the kinds that are reported in scholarly books and journals. The business sector is the major source of funding for R&D among the members of the OECD, and the majority of those funds are devoted to 'experimental development': the development of products, processes or services. In the US, for example, development of this kind accounts for over 60 per cent of the total expenditure on R&D. The more fundamental 'basic' or 'applied' research that is reported in the scholarly literature thus represents just a part of the overall expenditure on R&D. Expenditure on basic research – that is, according to the definitions developed by the OECD, 'experimental or theoretical work undertaken primarily to acquire new knowledge of the underlying foundation of phenomena and observable facts, without any particular application or use in view' (OECD, 2002) – thus amounts in the US to 17 per cent and in France to 25 per cent of total expenditure on R&D (National Science Board, 2010).[2]

In China it accounts for about 5 per cent of activity (Ministry of Science and Technology of the People's Republic of China, 2007).

Governments fund a significant proportion of all recorded R&D expenditure; but they tend to be the major funders of basic and applied research. In the US, for example, the Federal Government accounted in 2008 for about a quarter of all R&D expenditure, but 57 per cent of the funding for basic research. And in the major research-producing countries, governments have tended over the past decade to increase their research budgets quite sharply. Thus in the UK the budgets for the Research Councils increased by 78 per cent in real terms between 1998 and 2008, while the block grant allocated to universities to support their research activities increased by 62 per cent.[3] In the US, the Federal budget for basic research rose by 20 per cent in real terms between 2000 and 2008, although the sharpest increases were in the early part of the decade (National Science Board, 2010, Appendix Table 4-18). Such sharp increases have become less common since 2008, but it is notable that the economic stimulus package enacted in early 2009 through the American Recovery and Reinvestment Act provided a considerable one-off increase in the Federal R&D budget of over $18 billion.

Governments have been prepared to increase expenditure in this way because they believed that it is necessary in order to achieve economic success. The UK was typical in adopting the kind of strategy announced in its *Science and Innovation Investment Framework*, published in 2004 (HM Treasury *et al.*, 2004).[4] This announced that: 'For the UK economy to succeed in generating growth through productivity and employment in the coming decade, it must invest more strongly than in the past in its knowledge base, and translate this knowledge more effectively into business and public service innovation.'

The new strategy promised to make good past under-investment in the science base, and to raise science spending faster than the trend rate of growth of the economy to achieve that end. But the investment was for a purpose, and brought with it a renewed emphasis on the linkages between research and innovation, and translating the results of research into tangible outcomes for the benefit of society and the economy. 'Knowledge transfer' and working collaboratively with business were key themes in this strategy, which was accompanied by the development of targets and performance indicators, along with periodic reviews to track performance and progress. Similar themes have been repeated in the funding and policy papers issued by the new Coalition Government elected in 2010 in the UK, which have used remarkably similar language (Department for Business Innovation and Skills, 2010).

> 'Our world-class science and research base is inherently valuable, as well as critical to promoting economic growth. Investment in science and research creates new businesses and improves existing ones; brings highly skilled people into the job market; attracts international investment and improves public policy and services. The UK's world-class research base will be a key driver in promoting economic growth.'

None of this is unique to the UK. The OECD's Ministerial Committee for Scientific and Technological Policy identified in 2004 the pressure for publicly funded research 'to increase its contribution to innovation, economic performance and the fulfilment of social needs' (OECD, 2004, 2009). In Japan, the Science and Technology Agency has made investment in research a foundation for its economic strategy,[5] and similar points were made in the review of Australia's innovation system (Cutler and Co., 2008).

The OECD Ministerial Committee also noted, however, that governments were wrestling with questions of 'how best to restructure and reform public research organisations to improve their contributions to social and economic problems without sacrificing the objectivity and independence of their advice and their ability to pursue curiosity-based research'. More recently, the European Union has noted the need to address: 'both a competitiveness challenge (closing Europe's gap in innovation) and a cultural challenge (integrating research and innovation to focus on societal challenges)' (European Union 2011, p. 1).

The struggle to balance these different kinds of goals continues and is reflected in the strategic aims and objectives of major funding bodies. The Higher Education Funding Council for England (HEFCE), which provides block grants to universities to support their research activities, for example, defines its aim in this area as: 'to develop and sustain a dynamic and internationally competitive research sector that makes a major contribution to economic prosperity and national wellbeing and to the expansion and dissemination of knowledge.'[6]

In China, the Law on Science and Technology Progress makes repeated mention of the role of science and technology in 'economic construction and social development'.[7] Funding bodies that provide project-based rather than block grants to support research typically make the link even more explicit. Thus, the US National Institutes of Health (NIH) defines its mission as: 'to seek fundamental knowledge about the nature and behavior of living systems and the application of that knowledge to enhance health, lengthen life, and reduce the burdens of illness and disability.'[8]

In similar vein, the Australian National Health and Medical Research Council, like similar funding bodies in other countries, has put an increasing emphasis on translational outcomes of medical and health research; while the more broadly based Australian Research Council talks of 'capturing and quantifying the outcomes of research and knowledge transfer and the contribution of research to the economic, social, cultural and environmental well-being of Australians.'[9]

This focus on research as a key underpinning of economic performance and social well-being means that Government funding of scientific research – in both research institutes and universities – has shown an increasing tendency to be based on performance criteria; and in countries such as the UK and Australia, this has been accompanied by large-scale research assessment exercises undertaken by national agencies. The impact on universities will be considered in the next section.

While science policy in many countries is based on the belief that investment in research is intimately tied to economic growth, evidence about the nature and scope of the linkages is far from conclusive. This is not surprising, as the relationship between science and innovation is non-linear, and complex outcomes may differ substantially between different countries and disciplines. We do not understand the mechanisms through which investments in R&D – still more the investments in basic research – and the immediate results in the form of new knowledge or technologies, interact with other features of societies and economies to produce innovation and growth. Impacts often come after considerable time-lags, and are complex to identify and analyse. Hence there is renewed interest in developing capacity and capability to assess the impact of research through programmes such as the National Science Foundation's (NSF) Science of Science and Innovation Policy (SciSIP) programme in the US.[10] The challenges faced by such programmes are, however, formidable.

Research and researchers

There were some 4.2 million researchers in the OECD countries in 2007, an increase of 48 per cent since 1995. The rate of increase has been even sharper, of course, in some emerging research countries, and on some measures China now has more researchers than the US.

Research and where it is conducted

In all the top ten research nations, the business sector is the largest performer of R&D, accounting for expenditure ranging from 78 per cent in Japan and 72 per cent in China and the US to 49 per cent in Italy. But most basic research – on average more than three-quarters in the OECD – is undertaken in universities and Government research institutes. There are significant differences between countries, however, in how the research base is organised, and where researchers are located; and the balance between universities and national research institutes varies hugely. Thus in the Russian Federation, around 90 per cent of basic research is conducted in research institutes; while in the Nordic countries around three-quarters and in the US nearly three-fifths is conducted in universities. Nevertheless, in the US, intramural R&D performed in agencies and laboratories of the federal Government, and in federally funded research and development centres accounts for over 10 per cent of all R&D, and a slightly higher proportion of basic research (National Science Board, 2010, Chapter 4).

In some European countries, recent developments may tend to shift more research activity towards the university sector. In Russia, for example, new federal universities have been established by merging existing universities and research institutions (Kuznetsov and Razumova, 2011). And in China there is a clear shift away from the previous dominance of the Chinese Academy of Sciences and its institutes towards the funding of researchers in universities.[11]

There are similar differences in the location of researchers. In the UK, there is a relatively small number of research institutes run centrally by the Research Councils, but 73 per cent of researchers are employed in universities, and only 3 per cent in Government departments or institutes. In Germany, on the other hand, with its well-developed infrastructure of institutes run under the auspices of the Fraunhofer Gesellschaft, the Helmholtz Association, the Leibnitz Association and the Max Planck Society,[12] 44 per cent of researchers are located in universities, and 12 per cent in the Government sector.

The proportions of university-based research that is funded by Government on the one hand, and business or other organisations on the other, also show significant differences across the OECD. In the major research nations, Government is the largest source of funding for university research, with proportions ranging from 52 per cent in Japan to 65 per cent in the US, and 80 per cent in Germany and Switzerland. Business support for university-based R&D, on the other hand, averages only around 6 per cent across the OECD; but that average conceals a range from 35 per cent in China, and 31 per cent in Russia, to between 1 and 3 per cent in Japan, France and Italy. In the US, it is about 6 per cent. The balance is made up from other sources, including non-profit organisations, funds from overseas and funds controlled by universities themselves. In the US, for example, over 20 per cent of the funds to support research in universities is provided by the universities themselves.

Research careers

Research careers typically begin in universities with study for a doctorate. In the major research nations, research funders and universities devote considerable resources to the support of doctoral students, although the mechanisms and forms of support differ significantly. Doctoral education is increasingly seen as a commodity with measurable economic value. Thus in the US, the NIH and the NSF support large numbers of doctoral students as research assistants funded through grants to universities for academic research. In the UK, the Research Councils earmark doctoral training grants to universities to enable students to carry out a doctoral-level research project together with taught coursework. Both countries seek to attract doctoral students from other countries, and in the US, for example, foreign students on temporary visas account for more than half the doctoral degrees awarded in several disciplines, including engineering, physics, mathematics, computer science and economics (National Science Board, 2010, Chapter 2). Such students are attractive to universities and funders not least because many of them choose to stay once they have gained their doctorate, and pursue their careers as highly qualified researchers in their new country: more than three-quarters of foreign recipients of US doctorates plan to stay in the US.

The US, Germany and the UK are the major producers of doctoral award-holders globally, accounting for nearly half the total among OECD countries.[13] A key concern in many countries is the success rate for those entering doctoral programmes, and the time taken to complete a doctoral degree. A recent study in the US indicated that the 10-year completion rate across 30 institutions averaged 56.6 per cent, with a range across disciplines from 41.5 per cent in computer and information sciences to 77.6 per cent in civil engineering. In the UK, the Research Councils as well as individual universities have made it a priority over the past decade to increase completion rates, which for Research Council-supported students are now typically over 80 per cent after four years (Council of Graduate Schools, 2008).[14]

The next career stage for many researchers is a postdoctoral appointment, the number of which has tended to increase in many countries. Although it is difficult to get precise numbers, this growth has become a major issue of concern in both the US and the UK. Increases in competition for permanent academic posts, and the growth of collaborative research in large teams, have led to large numbers of highly qualified researchers working on short-term contracts with relatively low pay and few benefits, thus delaying the start of their independent careers either within or outside the research community. In the US, about a quarter of those who gain doctorates get to a tenure track position within 4–6 years of gaining doctoral status. In the UK, it is estimated that 30 per cent of science PhDs go on to postdoctoral positions, but only about 12 per cent of those go on to secure a permanent academic position (Royal Society, 2010). The problem is that while the number of postdoc posts has increased at the base of the career pyramid, the number of permanent and more senior posts has not increased to anything like the same extent. In the US, for example, while the number of full-time tenured faculty increased by a third between 1979 and 2006, their proportion of the academic workforce fell from 69 to 62 per cent; over the same period, the proportion of postdocs rose from 4 to 9 per cent (National Science Board, 2010, Chapter 2). This position has been made worse by the economic recession, which has made many universities reluctant to appoint new permanent staff. Policy-makers in the US, the UK, Sweden and other countries are struggling to find solutions to the problem, which is an acute one for the university sector in many countries.

Funding; competition and assessment

Competition for posts and for funding is indeed an increasingly prominent feature of the research landscape, especially in universities. Success in winning research income is a key performance indicator for many universities. It features, alongside bibliometric measures such as numbers of papers published and citations to those papers, in the calculation of the various global league tables produced by the Shanghai Jiao Tong University, Times Higher Education, Quacquarelli Symonds and others, as well as in similar exercises in individual countries. Research income typically comes in two forms: project funding, which is awarded, on the basis of a project specification, to an individual or group to undertake a specific research project that is limited in scope, time and budget; and institutional funding, often in the form of an annual block grant, which is provided to an institution to support its general research activities, without identifying specific projects or activities to be undertaken.

In Germany, for instance, the Federal Government – through the Ministry of Education and Research – and the Länder (the 16 states which form the Federal Republic) provide institutional funding to some 750 research establishments, including universities. Both the Federal Government and the Länder also provide direct funding for specific projects within a framework of programmes in particular areas of research, as well as to basic research projects independent of any programme. They also provide the majority of funds for the German Research Foundation (DFG), whose chief task is to select the best research projects by scientists and academics at universities and research institutions on a competitive basis and to finance those projects.[15]

In the UK, universities receive block grant to support their research activities through the Higher Education Funding Councils for England, Scotland, Wales and Northern Ireland, respectively. The amount that each university receives is determined primarily by the results of the Research Assessment Exercise (RAE), which takes place every few years; the most recent was in 2008, and the next, under the new title of Research Excellence Framework (REF), will take place in 2013. The key outcome of the process is a rating of the quality of the work produced over the period intervening between successive exercises by the researchers entered into some 70 subject-based 'units of assessment'. These ratings, along with associated volume measures, constitute the basis of a formula which determines the amount of block grant that universities receive each year to support their research activities (not their teaching) until the next exercise is undertaken.

UK universities also bid for project-based grants and doctoral studentship awards from the Research Councils. Here one of the main concerns, for the Councils as well as universities, has been the low success rates for applicants, and what might be done to ameliorate the position when success rates fall to around 20 per cent[16] or lower. From the Councils' perspective, the problem is that they receive, and have to assess through a costly peer-review process, many more high-quality applications than they are able to support. From the universities' perspective, the problem is the time and effort involved in preparing and submitting many more applications than are likely to receive funding. Similar problems have arisen in Australia, where success rates for some Australian Research Council awards have fallen well below 20 per cent.[17]

In the US, the Federal Government does not provide support for research in universities in the form of a general block grant, although some state funding for universities probably does support some research activity at public universities. The Federal Government provides all its funding for university research in the form of support provided through agencies such as the NIH (by far the biggest provider), the NSF and the Department of Energy, for specific, individually costed, projects. This means that the Government and its agencies are more directly involved than in many other countries in determining which projects will be supported from public funds; but it avoids the need for large-scale assessment exercises such as in the UK. It is also noticeable that as in other countries, funding tends to concentrate on a relatively small number of universities: in 2008 the top 20 universities accounted for 30 per cent of all university expenditure on R&D, a proportion that has remained stable for the past two decades (National Science Board, 2010, Chapter 5).

Managing and supporting research

Universities thus face increasing pressure to manage as well as support the activities and performance of their researchers. At the highest level, this means that most universities have established mechanisms for developing a clearly articulated research strategy, typically with the active involvement of a Research Committee; and that a senior member of the university's management team (in the UK, a Pro Vice Chancellor or Deputy Principal) is responsible together with that committee for monitoring, reviewing and delivering that strategy and its key objectives.

But the increasingly complex and competitive research landscape requires structures of support and management below that strategic level. Institutional funding for research is accompanied by increasing demands from governments for scrutiny and the demonstration of quality, value-added outputs and impact in return for the supply of taxpayer money. And the ways in which research grants and contracts are bid for and won means that developing and sustaining a university's or a department's research portfolio is not straightforward. Moreover, success in securing research funding brings with it a range of obligations: grants and contracts are often tied to tightly specified milestones and outputs, rigorously monitored and heavily audited. Together these developments have created a need to support and manage research portfolios more closely. Activities that in earlier years were left to researchers themselves are now more closely linked to the university's strategic objectives; and dedicated support services have been established to operate on the interface between researchers and corporate management.

Such developments have led some to detect a strengthening of hierarchical management in universities, and a weakening of academic self-management. There is thus talk of a 'paradigm shift' in authority relationships, with university managers experiencing both pressure to improve research performance, and more opportunities to manage research activity. But the inherent uncertainty of scientific research, and the diversity of research cultures and peer-group judgements, imposes limits on managers' ability to control. Research teams retain considerable autonomy over how they conduct their research, and research strategies and priorities are informed by the judgements of key members of the research community. Moreover, there is considerable debate over the appropriate mechanisms for research management, and measures for assessing performance; the literature on performance indicators for research is extensive (Whitley *et al.*, 2010).

Research support units within universities vary hugely in size and shape, and in how they are organised: some are highly centralised, while others operate more as teams distributed across departments and faculties (Green and Langley, 2009). They undertake a wide range of functions including identifying and publicising research funding opportunities; supporting researchers in developing project proposals, especially on matters such as costing; negotiating contracts with external sponsors; project management and financial control; monitoring and reporting to funders; and knowledge transfer, commercialisation and dissemination. Some universities have set up internal research assessment processes and mechanisms for internal peer review of project proposals before they are submitted.

As part of these developments, many universities are developing and implementing current research information systems (CRISs) which bring together data and information about the research projects that have been and are being undertaken across the institution; funding agencies, programmes and funding schemes, and forthcoming calls; proposals being submitted to or under consideration by those funding agencies; research results in the form of publications, patents and other intellectual property; and about the performance of individuals, groups and departments. For universities, a CRIS provides a tool to assist in policy-making, evaluation of research based on outputs, documenting research activities and outputs, project planning, and providing a formal log of research in progress.

Not all researchers welcome these kinds of developments, or share the kind of view of the world they represent: many regard the requirement to submit information about their work as a burdensome chore, and resent the monitoring and management of their activities and performance as an unwelcome intrusion. Most researchers are focused on research, not the ancillary things that surround it. Many of them regard budgets, standards, regulatory requirements, financial and progress reporting and so on as at best necessary evils and at worst bureaucratic obstacles that get in the way of their work. Seen from this perspective, research support services can provide a very valuable service in helping to overcome such obstacles. Any requirements that add to the obstacles by introducing new tasks or burdens tend, on the other hand, to be resented.

The more effective and user-focused research support offices, and the more sophisticated CRISs, however, can provide useful support to researchers by alerting them to funding opportunities, locating new contacts and networks, supporting them in developing research proposals as well as reports to funders, providing links to scholarly publications and other outputs, and so on. The key point is to ensure that researchers perceive real benefits for a relatively small amount of input effort.

Researchers and the research process

To create the new knowledge which is the objective of research, researchers need to obtain data. Some of this comes from primary sources (experimentation, observation, archival documents, interviews and so on, depending on the subject matter and the nature of the research), but much is derived from the existing knowledge base. Thus during the course of their work, researchers are both producers and consumers of data and information resources.

Many different models of the research process have been devised, but there is common agreement on the key stages, which involve defining a research question and then:

- identifying existing knowledge which is relevant to the question;
- accessing, analysing and evaluating existing data and knowledge;
- designing a methodology and a process for generating new data and knowledge;
- writing a research proposal and submitting it to a funding body;
- collecting or creating new data and analysing it;
- combining old and new knowledge to answer the research question and to enhance understanding;
- reporting and disseminating the outcomes of the research in a form which is both sustainable and retrievable.

The process is not linear, of course; and it typically involves a number of loops backwards and forwards – as well as stops and starts – between the defining of a research question and the dissemination of the results of a project that seeks to answer it. Moreover, the activities and the detail of the processes involved in information discovery, data collection, processing, analysis, information management, access and dissemination vary hugely across different subjects, disciplines, and individual researchers and research groups. Similar kinds of activities are configured together in very different ways; and the practices of individual groups often involve multiple information cycles leading to intermediate outputs (tools, methodologies, half-processed data and so on) which then form the inputs for other cycles of activity.

Individuals and teams

In the sciences, most current research is conducted by groups or teams of researchers: there are relatively few researchers who undertake research projects as individuals without the support of a team. In the social sciences and the humanities, individual research is still common, but team-based research is becoming increasingly common too. There is no typical research group or team: they vary in size, structure and scope, as well as in the roles that individual members perform. But it is common to have a principal investigator (PI) working with a range of colleagues who may include junior and senior tenured staff alongside postdocs and doctoral students, as well as technicians. Larger groups may include lab or project managers.

Individual members of research groups typically have specific roles within the group – often according to their level of seniority – and their activities may vary sharply as a result.

PIs, for example, often combine research with a range of other teaching, management and administrative responsibilities; they may be involved in developing and running a wide variety of research and related activities, involving relationships with a diverse range of people and organisations, including local colleagues, national and international peers, and funding and regulatory bodies. They are often responsible for preparing new research proposals as well as reporting to funders on completed projects, knowledge transfer activities and so on.

Postdocs are often the key team members who devote their efforts mainly and directly to the research activity of their group. In some cases, where they have developed the necessary expertise, they may also provide specialist support in areas such as statistics and modelling.

Doctoral students' work tends to be even more tightly focused on a specific aspect of the group's research. They tend to have a relatively narrow set of relationships primarily but not exclusively with local collaborators, and their information-handling activities are often less complex than those of other members of the team. Similarly, technicians' activities tend to focus around the functioning of experimental equipment and protocols. Lab and/or project managers usually focus on managing meetings, meeting reports, staff project reports, visitors' agendas and so on, and sometimes maintaining the group's website.

Researchers as information consumers

Although roles and practices vary considerably within and between groups, and across subjects and disciplines, at key stages in the research lifecycle it is clear that all researchers are information consumers. They discover and gain access to the information they need nowadays predominantly through web-based resources, including generic search engines such as Google as well as specialist bibliographic search and retrieval tools such as PubMed; on-line publications; and dedicated websites that they trust as authoritative. Most scientists now use the physical library relatively little; and even in the humanities, researchers are increasingly finding the resources they need online.

Many studies have noted (see, for example, Research Information Network, 2009a) that researchers appear to have a limited awareness of the range of information services and resources available to them, and the number they use seems surprisingly small. They also show loyalty to particular resources or services that they like or trust and find easy to use. A fundamental reason for this narrow, often opportune, choice of information tools and resources is that researchers lack the time to review the whole information landscape, or to learn how to exploit a wider range of resources and services to best effect. They are more likely to supplement their search strategies by seeking advice from colleagues (scientists more than information professionals) as to the most appropriate and useful sources of information.

In the UK and the US at least, articles in scholarly journals are the single most important kind of information resource for researchers, alongside conference proceedings in some disciplines such as engineering. And usage is increasing: surveys in the US indicate that the number of articles they read increased from *c.*150 to *c.*280 between 1977 and 2005 (Tenopir *et al.*, 2009); and usage of e-journals in UK universities has been increasing at an annual rate of over 20 per cent (Research Information Network 2009b). But there is an increasing array of other kinds of information including protocols, techniques, standard operating procedures (SOPs), technical product information, reference works and databases which researchers need to access during the course of their research. Social media are also becoming increasingly important for some researchers, although evidence of take-up across the research community as a whole is as yet slight, probably because there is not yet the critical mass of individuals using such services to make it worthwhile for the purposes of enhancing research.

Generating and analysing data

Many areas of research are now characterised by the generation of volumes of data unthought of even a few years ago. Low-cost sensors mean that environmental scientists, engineers and other researchers can use a range of instruments long term to generate data relevant to their work on a 24/7 basis. Synchrotrons, telescopes, satellites, lasers and other instruments can generate terabytes (10^{12} bytes) of data every day; and in the life sciences, high-throughput gene sequencing platforms can produce similar volumes of data in a single experiment. Projects that generate tens of terabytes of data are now common; and at the largest end of the scale, the Large Hadron Collider will produce tens of petabytes (10^{15} bytes) of data a year. These developments have given rise to talk of a data deluge, and more recently of a new 'fourth paradigm' for research: following the moves from empirical to theoretical to computational science, it is suggested that we now need to think in terms of data-intensive science (Microsoft, 2009).

The data come in many different formats, shapes and sizes: observational, experimental, surveys, models and simulations; and from large international projects down to the work of small teams and individuals. Handling all the data requires new ways of working. E-science and cyberinfrastructure initiatives in the UK, the US and other countries have involved developing the capability and capacity to undertake computationally intensive science in distributed network environments, and projects using very large datasets that require grid computing. The complexity of the software and infrastructural requirements mean that many e-science projects involve large teams, and heavy investment in the processes for curating and analysing the data.

Even beyond the bounds of formally designated 'e-science', technological advance has brought fundamental change not only in the methods of scientific research but also in the infrastructure necessary to conduct it. Many researchers face increasing complexity in preparing, managing and analysing data; and as datasets grow larger, established data management techniques and off-the-shelf analysis tools are no longer adequate. In many areas of the life sciences, for example, researchers may need to draw on a wide range of genomics data, as well as data from other disciplines such as chemistry and clinical medicine, or from multi-scale mathematical models. The problem is that the datasets that researchers create and/or wish to use are often only partly connected, and incompatible in format, so that both discovery and integration are significant challenges.

There is thus increasing interest in the need for and development of schemas and ontologies to facilitate the indexing, cross-searching, aggregation and integration of data. There is also an increasing demand for workflows that provide systematic and automated means of undertaking analyses across a range of diverse datasets and applications; and also of capturing the process so that the method and the results can be reviewed, validated, repeated and adapted (see, for example, Taylor *et al.*, 2007). Workflows configured in this way can co-ordinate multiple tasks, such as running a program, submitting a query to a database, submitting a task to a cloud or grid, or summoning a service over the web to use a remote resource. Outputs from one task constitute inputs to subsequent tasks.

Finally, there is increasing interest in the sharing of data across organisations and disciplines, and in making it more generally available as a key output of the research process. Many funding bodies now require applicants to submit data management plans as an integral part of their project proposals, and include a requirement to make data available to others. They see this as part of their commitment to getting best value for the funds they invest, not least by reinforcing open scientific enquiry and stimulating new investigations and analyses. But they also recognise that different fields of study require different approaches, and that what is sensible in one scientific or technological area may not work in others; and that there is thus a need to determine standards and best practice, as well as encouraging the development of scientific cultures in which data sharing is embedded.[18]

There is also broad recognition of the need to develop an infrastructure (Research Councils UK, 2010) of facilities that link multiple laboratories and observatories, instruments, users and data; and especially large databases and services that allow researchers to 'bring their computations to the data, rather than the data to the computations'. And developing new capacities and skills in the research base is an essential part of building that infrastructure. New kinds of science require close collaboration between scientists from different domains, and working with computer scientists and technologists to provide new ways of conducting research through high-quality data acquisition, simplified large-scale data management, powerful data modelling and mining, and effective sharing and visualisation.

Communicating research

Researchers publish and disseminate their work in many different ways: through formal publication in books and in learned and professional society journals; through conferences and their proceedings; and through a variety of less formal means, now including social media. The choices researchers make are underpinned by a number of interrelated motives beyond the simple desire to pass on their findings to those who may be interested in them. These motivations include the desire not only to maximise dissemination to a target audience, but to register their claim to the work they have done, and to gain peer esteem and the rewards that may flow from that.

In deciding when, where and how to communicate their work, researchers may have to make choices between speedy dissemination to a desired audience, and less speedy publication in a high-status journal. Such choices are made more complex because researchers know that publications serve not only as means of communication (Research Information Network, 2009c). They can be monitored or measured as indicators of quality or impact (in the academic world and more widely). And articles in scholarly journals dominate all other forms of publication, partly because they are more easily ranked and measured using a series of readily available and increasingly sophisticated metrics. But many researchers feel uncomfortable with the dominance of the article – particularly the article published in a high-status journal. They are concerned that communications through other channels – including those that are better suited to applied or practice-based research, and to communicating with non-academic audiences – seem to have low status and prestige in the academic world. There are also concerns about the impact on researcher behaviour in areas such as policy development, which may have a significant social or political impact, but do not feature much in research performance metrics. The introduction of impact assessments in the forthcoming Research Excellence Framework in the UK has been designed in an attempt to address such concerns.

The only major exceptions to the dominance of the journal article is the continuing high status attached to monographs and edited volumes in the humanities, and to practice-based outputs in the arts. Yet even in the humanities journal articles are now by far the largest publication format by volume, and there are increasing concerns about the decline of the book, attributed variously to shrinking library purchase budgets, publishers' reluctance and the pressures of research assessment regimes.

Increasing numbers of researchers in all disciplines are also making at least occasional use of one or more social media for communicating their work; for developing and sustaining networks and collaborations; or for finding out about what others are doing. But frequent or intensive use is rare, and some researchers regard blogs, wikis and other novel forms of communication as a waste of time or even dangerous. Moreover, most who use social media do not see them as comparable to or substitutes for other channels and means of communication, but as having their own distinctive role for specific purposes and at particular stages of research. And frequent use of one kind of tool does not imply frequent use of others as well. Current levels of take-up are therefore relatively low, even though attitudes towards social media are broadly supportive (Research Information Network, 2010; CIBER, 2010).

Commonalities and differences

As noted at several points above, although it is possible to present a generic picture of the research process, practice varies across disciplines, but also between different groups operating in different institutional settings within similar research fields. Disciplinary cultures have a powerful influence on practice. But so also do other factors including: access to funding; the size of the group or project; the volumes of data being handled; the complexity or heterogeneity of that data; the complexity of the analysis or computation required; and the nature and scale of any collaboration across disciplinary, institutional or national boundaries.

In the life sciences, for example, large-scale proteomic or genomic research programmes are characterised by high-volume sharing of largely standardised (and thus homogeneous) data. Systems biology, which attempts to pull together diverse data (such as genomic, gene expression and metabolic data), is characterised by large-scale processing but of much more heterogeneous kinds of information, which may pose a challenge for researchers seeking to integrate the different taxonomic structures that have emerged in specialist domains.

Similarly, in the humanities, a single researcher in a discipline such as philosophy may operate in a complex set of informal relationships with other scholars, and use a wide range of tools and techniques to organise and analyse their data. Researchers in a field such as corpus linguistics, by contrast, use complex datasets and a range of methods to assemble a corpus which they may then need to clean and reformat before they can begin to annotate and analyse the data, using a range of bespoke software or off-the-shelf packages.

Understanding the practices and the needs of researchers in different subjects and disciplines, or operating in different contexts, is therefore a complex process: what works in one setting may well not work in another.

Competition and collaboration

Researchers have for long both competed and collaborated with each other. As funds are finite, individuals, teams, institutions and nations compete for resources, for doctoral students and for research posts in order to pursue their interests and sustain their work. They also compete for impact (in the form of citations, innovations and so on) and for prestige (in the form of prizes, of ratings in assessment exercises such as the UK's RAE, of rankings in league tables and so on). And competition is increasing as a result of increased pressure on funding resources; the changing expectations of funding bodies; and globalisation, with new competitors in emerging nations.

Much attention has been paid to the development of 'big science' of the kind exemplified by the Large Hadron Collider at CERN, or the Human Genome Project, and the teams of hundreds or thousands of researchers associated with them. But most researchers do not work in big teams with big budgets. Rather, they work in groups that operate in a relatively unstructured way and on a relatively small scale; and they typically have a series of informal as well as formal relationships with other individuals and groups both within the institution in which they work, as well as with others outside. Senior researchers, in particular, often operate as part of a number of more or less overlapping collaborations and relationships.

Even in the humanities the 'lone scholar' has for long been essentially a myth. Such scholars may work for the most part on their own on projects they themselves design and undertake; but they engage in a wide range of informal discussions and dialogue with colleagues working in cognate areas. And technological developments are both facilitating and driving collaboration between researchers. Internet connectivity means that it is easier than in the past to share ideas, data, tools and workflows. So the costs of collaboration are falling on the one hand, while the increasing complexity and cost of the infrastructure needed to support many kinds of research means that there is an increasing imperative to work across traditional boundaries to exploit that infrastructure to the full.

But it is not just technology that is driving growth in collaboration at local, regional, national and international levels. Governments and other funders are also promoting collaboration by their emphasis on multidisciplinary research that addresses large-scale issues and problems such as environmental change, sustainable energy, health and well-being.[19] There is also growing interest in seeking to develop a deeper understanding of the linkages between research and innovation, or healthcare outcomes; and of how to achieve successful interactions between the business and research sectors.

From a research perspective, collaboration with other universities, with industry and with public and voluntary sector bodies can help to drive success for individuals (in securing grants and contracts, and greater citation and other impacts for their work); for institutions (in helping to build critical mass, leverage of research opportunities and winning funding); and for nations (in supporting innovation and the development of knowledge-based economies). In Europe, the framework programmes for research of the European Commission have been a major driver for collaboration. The Seventh Framework Programme has provided 50 billion euros for research and development over the seven years from 2007 to 2013, the great majority of which has gone to projects requiring participation from several different countries.

One indicator of the extent of collaboration is co-authorship of the articles reporting the results of research. As is well known, the proportion of science and engineering articles that are co-authored has been growing, from 40 per cent of the global total in 1988 to 64 per cent in 2008; and the average number of authors per article has risen too, from 3.1 to 4.7. Of course, part of this simply reflects the growth of research teams, as distinct from collaboration across institutional or other boundaries. But more than half of articles published by authors from US academic institutions now include a co-author from another institution; and globally, the articles that list institutions from more than one country grew from 8 to 22 per cent between 1988 and 2008 (National Science Board 2010, Chapter 5). For major research nations in Europe – France, Germany, Netherlands, Switzerland, the UK – around half or more of science and engineering articles published include an author from another country. Such collaboration, particularly with long-term partners, tends to produce papers with higher citation impact.

Looking forward

This brief overview has highlighted some trends, some of them in tension with each other, in a complex landscape. There is no reason to believe that most of those trends, and the tensions, will not remain for the foreseeable future. Thus research will continue to be driven by the intellectual curiosity of researchers, but also by the imperatives and policies of the major funders of research, primarily Governments. It remains an article of faith for Governments – even those experiencing fiscal difficulties – that continued public investment in research is essential for the success of their economies and for the well-being of their societies; that a high-quality research base makes a country attractive for inward investment by international business; and that publicly funded research plays an important role in raising the productivity of R&D in the business sector and has a positive impact on innovation in the economy as a whole.

But in straitened economic circumstances especially, Governments and other funders seek a return on their investment in research. There are some suggestions that the greatest productivity increases in the long term come through breakthroughs in knowledge and understanding that derive from basic research. But the evidence of relationships between investment in basic research and economic growth is not strong; and Governments tend to wish to see returns in relatively short timescales. Hence the increasing stress on collaboration and knowledge exchange with the business sector and other organisations, and efforts to develop and tighten the linkages between research and innovation. Hence also the development of targeted technology-transfer and knowledge-exchange programmes; and the increasing emphasis on monitoring and assessing the performance of the publicly funded research base. Such monitoring and assessment often covers not only primary results and their quality, but success in patenting, licensing, transfer agreements and co-operative R&D relationships (see, for example, National Science Board 2010, Chapter 4). There is no sign that these trends will weaken.

Nor will the focus from Governments and other funders on addressing major global challenges such as public health or reducing poverty. Indeed, this has been part of a long-term trend to encourage researchers from different disciplines and organisations to come together to share ideas, skills and techniques to address complex problems; to provide access to new ideas and insights; to create critical mass in research skills and expertise; to share costs and risks, and to ensure efficient use of expensive facilities; to produce higher-quality results in shorter time frames; and to provide more pathways to achieve economic and social impact.

Multi-disciplinary and cross-disciplinary work co-exists, however, with strong, but changing, disciplinary cultures. Even as disciplines evolve, and new ones such as bioinformatics emerge, there is little sign that such cultures are breaking down, or that they will not remain a key feature of the landscape in the future. Indeed, for many researchers, their allegiance to their discipline is as strong as – or even stronger than – that to their institution. It is from their peers working in cognate areas, after all, that they seek the recognition and esteem they need to advance in their careers; and this becomes increasingly significant as competition for funds intensifies. The forces of globalisation could also help to reinforce disciplinary communities and cultures at the same time that they facilitate collaboration and cross-disciplinary working.

At a global level, as we have seen, China, India, Brazil, Iran and other Asian countries are already playing an increasingly important role in the research landscape; and that role will increase further as that of Western Europe and North America continues to decline proportionately. It is important to distinguish, however, between a proportionate and an absolute fall in contributions to the global research effort. What we are seeing as a result of the emergence of new countries is a significant increase in that effort and the resources – financial, human and infrastructural – devoted to it; and there is no sign of significant reductions in contributions from Western countries in absolute terms. Collaboration and movement of researchers between them and the newer countries are growing, and will become an increasingly important feature of the landscape. Perhaps more challenging will be the fostering of co-operation with researchers in countries of the developing South, where resources of expertise and facilities are more thinly spread. At present, such collaborations as exist tend to be dominated by researchers from established research nations. Developing more equal relationships and helping to build research capabilities and capacities in the countries of the South is a significant challenge for the future.

Notes

1. Figures in this section are taken from OECD Science and Technology Main Indicators unless otherwise referenced.
2. See also Chapter 4 of *Science and Engineering Indicators 2010*, National Science Foundation, available at http://www.nsf.gov/statistics/seind10/start.htm
3. Table 1.2, *SET Statistics*, Department of Business, Innovation and Skills, available at http://www.bis.gov.uk/policies/science/science-funding/set-stats. For an overview of the funding of research in the UK, see *Making Sense of Research Funding in UK Higher Education*, Research Information Network (RIN), 2010, available at http://www.rin.ac.uk/system/files/attachments/Making_sense_of_funding.pdf
4. See also the *Innovation Nation* White Paper, published by the Department for Innovation, Universities and Skills in 2008.
5. Japan Science and Technology Agency: www.jst.go.jp/EN
6. http://www.hefce.ac.uk/research/
7. http://www.most.gov.cn/eng/policies/regulations/200412/t20041228_18309.htm
8. http://www.nih.gov/about/mission.htm
9. *Strategic Plan 2010–11 to 2012–13*, Australian Research Council, 2010, p. 14.
10. http://www.nsf.gov/funding/pgm_summ.jsp?pims_id=501084 .
11. See the list of grants in Chapter 5 of the *Annual Report 2009* of the National Natural Science Foundation of China, available at http://www.nsfc.gov.cn/english/09ar/2009/pdf/005.pdf
12. For an overview of the research landscape in Germany, see http://www.research-in-germany.de/dachportal/en/research-landscape/2866/research-landscape.html.
13. It should be noted, however, that important countries such as India, China and Brazil supply no PhD data to the OECD.
14. See, for example, the *BBSRC Annual Report and Accounts, 2009–10,* Biotechnology and Biological Sciences Research Council, 2010; and the *ESRC Annual Report and Accounts, 2009–10*, Economic and Social Research Council, 2010.
15. Federal Report on Research and Innovation 2010, Bundesministerium für Bildung und Forschung (BMBF – German Federal Ministry of Education and Research) Referat Innovationspolitische Querschnittsfragen, Rahmenbedingungen (Innovation Policy Framework Department) 11055 Berlin, Germany.
16. That was the success rate for applicants to the UK Medical Research Council in 2009–10. See http://www.mrc.ac.uk/consumption/idcplg?IdcService=GET_FILE&dID=26844&dDocName=MRC006981&allowInterrupt=1
17. See the Australian Research Council *Annual Report 2009-10*, available at http://www.arc.gov.au/pdf/annual_report_09-10.pdf
18. For an example of a policy statement from a major UK research funder, see the Biotechnology and Biological Sciences Research Council's *BBSRC Data Sharing Policy* Version 1.1. 2010.

19. See, for example, the UK Research Councils' '*Cross-Council Research Themes*' at http://www.rcuk.ac.uk/research/xrcprogrammes/Pages/home.aspx

References

CIBER (2010) *Social Media and Research Workflow*. London: CIBER, University College London and Emerald Publishing.

Council of Graduate Schools (2008) *PhD Completion and Attrition: Analysis of Baseline Program Data for the PhD Completion Project*. Washington, DC: Council of Graduate Schools.

Cutler and Co Pty Ltd. (2008) *Venturous Australia*, available at http://www.innovation.gov.au/Innovation/Policy/Documents/NISReport.pdf

Department for Business Innovation and Skills (2010) *The Allocation of Science and Research Funding 2011/12 to 2014/15: Investing in World-Class Science and Research*.

European Union (2011) *Innovation Union Competitiveness Report 2011: Executive Summary*, available at http://ec.europa.eu/research/innovation-union/pdf/competitiveness-report/2011/executive_summary.pdf

Green, J. and Langley, D. (2009) *Professionalising Research Management*, available at researchsupport.leeds.ac.uk/images/uploads/docs/PRMReport.pdf

HM Treasury, Department of Trade and Industry, and Department of Education and Skills (2004) *Science and Innovation Investment Framework, 2004–2014*. London: Her Majesty's Stationery Office.

Kuznetsov, A. and Razumova, I. (2011) Selling to the BRIC – Russia: scholarly e-products and the Russian market. *Learned Publishing*, 24:2.

Microsoft (2009) *The Fourth Paradigm*.

Ministry of Science and Technology of the People's Republic of China (2007) *China Science & Technology Statistics Data Book 2007*.

National Science Board (2010) Science and Engineering Indicators 2010. Arlington, VA: National Science Foundation (NSB 10-01).

OECD (2002) *Frascati Manual: Proposed Standard Practice for Surveys on Research and Experimental Development*.

OECD (2004) *Science and Innovation Policy: Key Challenges and Opportunities*, available at http://www.oecd.org/dataoecd/24/11/25473397.pdf

OECD (2009) 2009 *Interim Report on the OECD Innovation Strategy*, available at http://www.oecd.org/dataoecd/1/42/43381127.pdf

Research Councils UK (2010) *Delivering the UK's e-infrastructure for research and innovation*.

Research Information Network (2009a) *Patterns of Information Use and Exchange: case studies of researchers in the life sciences*.

Research Information Network (2009b) *E-journals, their use value and impact*.

Research Information Network (2009c) *Communicating Knowledge: how and why researchers publish and disseminate their findings*.

Research Information Network (2010) *If You Build it, will They Come: researchers perceive and use Web 2.0*.

Royal Society (2010) *The Scientific Century: Securing our Future Prosperity.*

Taylor, I.J., Deelman, E., Gannon, D.B. and Shields, M. (2007) *Workflows for E-Science: Scientific Workflows for Grids.* London: Springer.

Tenopir *et al.* (2009) Electronic journals and changes in scholarly article seeking and reading patterns. *Aslib Proceedings*, 61, 1.

Whitley, R., Glaser, J. and Engwall, L. (eds) (2010) *Reconfiguring Knowledge Production: Changing Authority Relationships in the Sciences and their Consequences for Intellectual Innovation.* Oxford: Oxford University Press.

4

The digital revolution

Michael Clarke

Abstract: The digital revolution is without a doubt the most significant event in information dissemination since Gutenberg's printing press and arguably marks a much bigger shift in human communication. This chapter discusses the impact of the digital revolution on scholarly publishing and professional communication thus far and describes the key trends and technologies shaping the future of the industry. These include evolving online publishing platforms, Web 2.0 technologies that use audience participation and network intelligence, mobile technologies that enable information professionals to access information anywhere, semantic technologies that transform how we discover information, and workflow integrations that channel the right information to the right individual at the right time.

Key words: Digital publishing, electronic publishing, online publishing, mobile, mobile web, smartphones, e-readers, tablets, Web 2.0, semantic technology, semantic web, workflow integration, personalization.

Introduction

Printed matter following the invention of Gutenburg's printing press is termed '*incunabula*', which is Latin for swaddling clothes, and refers to the infancy of the form. Books from this period (c. 1439 to 1501) often featured embellishments, marginalia and other elements to give the appearance of being hand written. It wasn't until the 16th century that books started to evolve to a form very similar to those found on the shelves of bookstores and libraries today.

The digital revolution is without a doubt the most significant event in information dissemination since the Gutenberg revolution, but just like that revolution we began with an *incunabula* period. However, instead of mimicking manuscripts, the first phase of the digital revolution produced mere simulacra of printed publications: online journals and electronic books that looked and functioned as much like their print counterparts as possible. The typeset PDF was and remains the dominant mode of distribution for journals. For e-books, the PDF or EPUB edition similarly seeks to replicate the print edition as faithfully as possible. Indeed, even the dominant metaphor of the web, the web *page*, is a reference to our print heritage.

There are signs, however, that we are emerging from our *incunabula* period to new, digital native forms of publishing. Web 2.0 technologies are changing how professionals locate and share information. Semantic technologies are transforming how information products are developed and discovered. Mobile devices are changing the way scholarly information is distributed. And researchers and scholars have changing expectations for the way in which information and services from publishers will fit in to their workflows. This chapter discusses these developments and their impact on scientific, technical, medical (STM) and scholarly publishing.

Online publishing platforms

While electronic publications, in their various forms, date back to the 1960s, the era of electronic publication as the *primary* mode of dissemination began in the mid-1990s and coincided with the rise of the World Wide Web (Tenopir and King, 2000). As most academics and researchers were already connected to the Internet and accustomed to information retrieval systems and email, the move to online publications was relatively straightforward. Commercial publishers made investments in building large-scale publishing platforms such as ScienceDirect (Elsevier), InterScience (Wiley), Synergy (Blackwell), SpringerLink (Springer) and Nature.com (Nature Publishing Group). Many not-for-profit organizations – especially those in the biological sciences – moved their journals relatively quickly to platforms developed by HighWire Press, Ingenta, MetaPress, Ovid or Atypon Systems. A number of not-for-profit organizations focused on the physical sciences took more of a do-it-yourself approach. Organizations including the University of Chicago Press (which had an emphasis, during the 1990s, on astrophysics), the American Institute of Physics, the Institute of Physics, the Optical Society, the American Geophysical Union, the Institute of Electrical and

Electronics Engineers (IEEE) and the American Physical Society all developed their own in-house platforms.

The development of online publishing platforms coincided with an industry shift from subscription sales to site licensing and, ultimately, the Big Deal (Bergstrom and Bergstrom, 2004). Elsevier led the way, borrowing the site licensing concept from enterprise software, selling the entirety of the content on its ScienceDirect platform for one, deeply discounted (when considered on a per-title basis) price. This move to site licensing allowed scholarly publishers to fund the continued investment in digitization. As a consequence, the industry shifted quickly from a print-centric subscription model to an online-centric licensing model as compared with adjacent markets such as news, magazines or trade publishing.

The great limitation of these platforms, however, was books – or rather the lack thereof. Most of these platforms did not feature books, or if they did, they were hosted in a limited capacity (and often were treated, from a display perspective, as if they were journals). Generally speaking, the shift to online distribution of books has lagged journals by over a decade. This delay is due to a combination of technological factors, limitations in existing business models and market receptivity.

Institutional budgets for periodicals and books were often managed separately and periodicals budgets during this period had greater flexibility. Moreover, moving from a journal subscription model to a site license model was a relatively simple transition – they are both based on an annual payment for a content set that is regularly updated. Books have historically been sold on a one-time purchase basis with no updating (with a book, an update is considered a 'new edition' and normally requires a subsequent purchase). And finally the production of books is much harder to streamline in the way journal production can be streamlined. Elements valued in book publishing, such as bespoke design and typography, do not lend themselves to scale. Moreover, books are much more structurally complex than journals, with sections, chapters, subsections, callouts and other elements that are not standardized from book to book, even when published by the same publisher.

The principal challenge to wide-scale adoption of digital books, however, was (and remains) reader technology. Journals are consumed on an article-by-article basis. An eight-page article can be downloaded from the web and easily printed from an office printer. In fact, printing out a single article is more convenient than carrying around a printed journal issue. Moreover, a journal article is short enough that screen reading is comfortable for many users. Books, however, are often consumed in long-form and can run to hundreds of pages. That is too long for most people to consume on a laptop or desktop computer screen and not practical to print from an office printer. The wide-scale adoption of digital books has therefore been waiting patiently for the last decade and a half for reading technology to catch up with production and distribution technology. The introduction of electronic readers (e-readers) and tablet computers, as discussed below, marks the beginning of this transition and, not coincidentally, corresponds with steep increases in the sales of electronic books.

While there were (and remain) many challenges to the digital dissemination of books, there were notable early successes. McGraw-Hill's development of its Access Medicine portfolio, the American Psychiatric Association's development of the Psychiatry Online Library and the *Oxford English Dictionary* are just a few of the better known electronic book offerings. Moreover, book aggregation platforms by ebrary, Knovel, Rittenhouse, Safari Books Online and others helped realize both a viable business model and market receptivity. Today, nearly all the major online platforms include increasing amounts of book content. Libraries are purchasing digital books and readers are accessing them online, albeit with the limitations in reader technology described above.

A perhaps greater challenge than the integration of books and other content assets of STM and scholarly publishing platforms is the flexibility of the platforms to meet the evolving needs of the marketplace and to adapt quickly enough to a rapidly changing technological environment with expectations often set in the consumer marketplace or other adjacent information spaces. The macroscopic trends impacting STM and scholarly publishing – including Web 2.0 tools and technologies, semantic technologies, workflow integration and mobile devices – all present challenges for online platforms and are discussed in more detail below.

Web 2.0

Where scholarly publishing was an early adopter of the web and enabling technologies such as SGML (Standardized General Mark-up Language – the precursor of XML), the industry ceased to remain in the vanguard for the next technology wave: Web 2.0. The term 'Web 2.0' was popularized by Tim O'Reilly (O'Reilly, 2005) and refers to then-emerging online technologies that include social media, new media crowdsourcing, and other terms for aggregating participatory audiences or otherwise utilizing the intelligence of networks.

The participatory themes described by the Web 2.0 moniker are in some ways native to scholarly publishing and communications while in other ways they are exogenous. Scholarly publishing is inherently participatory. Scholarly articles and monographs are 'user-generated content'. Authors, reviewers and readers are often the same people. Journals publish a great many letters. And journals and scholarly monographs support a real, physical community of professionals who often congregate regularly at one or more specialist meetings to present their work. In short, many of the Web 2.0 tools and technologies were not embraced by scholars and scholarly publishers because their communities had long since developed institutions and practices for participatory exchange.

Equally problematic, the often unmediated participation found in many Web 2.0 applications was, and remains, contrary to many of the principles and purposes of scholarly publishing. While most professional scholars participate in the scholarly publishing process, they do so in carefully prescribed ways. Reviewers are invited by editors. Editors are appointed by committees. Authors are only published after review by selected peers. This system supports a strata of scholarly brands – including an author's institution, funding agency and the journal or press they are published by – which are perceived as signifiers of quality.

Beyond signifying quality to readers, publication is often a requirement for career advancement. In the sciences, publication in peer-reviewed journals remains standard practice and a researcher's work, including the rank of the journals in which he or she has published, is often a key consideration in grant reviews, tenure decisions and other career milestones. In the social sciences and humanities, publication of a monograph by a university press plays a similar role. The various forms of participation encompassed by Web 2.0 tools and applications – such as blogging, commenting, micro-blogging and shared bookmarking – are not typically considered in career advancement decisions and therefore are not considered as worthwhile. Surveys of commenting in online journals, for example, have shown little uptake and no significant increase over the years (Schriger *et al.*, 2011).

Despite these obstacles, there have been a number of notable attempts to bring Web 2.0 tools and applications to scholarly publishing – particularly in the sciences.

Professional networks

Professional networks are sites that provide a forum for individuals to interact, via discussion forums, peer-to-peer communications, comments, shared links or other functionality. Nature Network was the first network of this kind. The site was originally launched to provide a community forum for researchers in the Boston area. Nature Network London followed soon after. Eventually, the network became broader and the Boston and London sites (along with New York) were transitioned to subsidiary 'hubs'.

A number of networks for scientists followed in *Nature*'s path. 2Collab was developed by Elsevier but was discontinued in April 2011. UniPHY, from the American Institute of Physics, has taken a different approach by focusing on just the physical sciences and mapping author associations from published research papers in order to pre-populate an individual's networks with colleagues. Perhaps the most widely used networks today are ResearchGate and Mendeley, both start-ups funded by venture capital and both broad networks aimed at connecting nearly all fields of academia.

Sermo was the first online professional network for physicians. Participation is limited to those with a medical degree (as opposed to Nature Networks which anyone can join). Perhaps the most notable thing about Sermo is its business model. Sermo sells access to its forums and data to commercial organizations such as pharmaceutical companies, and physicians (while identified and validated upon enrolment in Sermo) participate anonymously. Sermo therefore functions as a kind of large-scale anonymous focus group, complete with paying clients behind the mirror.

While Sermo was the first to launch, several other networks for physicians have followed. Doc2Doc is a network developed by the BMJ Publishing Group but open to global participation. Asklepios, on the other hand, is sponsored by the Canadian Medical Association and limited to physicians from that country. Ozmosis is a physician network that supports itself by providing workflow integration tools to institutions.

Shared bookmarks

Shared bookmarking sites were popularized by Delicious, a start-up service that was acquired, and subsequently divested, by Yahoo! Such sites enable users to post and share the websites they find interesting or useful. The value of bookmarking sites is fourfold:

1. one's bookmarks are available from any computer;
2. one can share one's bookmarks with others;

3. one can discover related websites by seeing what others who bookmarked the same website as you also bookmarked; and
4. one can follow specific users, such as colleagues, to keep abreast of their readings.

Following Delicious, several social bookmarking resources were developed for the STM and scholarly market, including CiteULike and Connotea. Additionally, many professional networks, such as Mendeley, include a component of social bookmarking.

Virtual reality/gaming

The role of gaming and so-called virtual reality remains experimental within STM and scholarly publishing but is worth noting due to the traction it has gained in the consumer space. Several STM and scholarly publishers, including Nature Publishing Group and the IEEE, have experimented with interfaces in Second Life, a massive multi-player online game (Nature Publishing Group discontinued its Second Life interface, cleverly called 'Second Nature', in 2010). Second Life players can interact with publisher artifacts (including applications such as molecular models) and participate in job fairs, lectures, symposia and other events. While initiatives such as these are nascent, they are worth following as new communication, presentation and business models may emerge.

Blogging networks

With numerous independent blogs by scientists on platforms such as WordPress or Typepad, there have been a number of efforts at aggregating the audience by developing science-focused blogging networks. The most notable such networks are ScienceBlogs, Nature Blogs and PLoS Blogs. Additionally, many publishers have begun their own 'official' blogs associated with specific publications. These include the *New England Journal of Medicine*, *Journal of the American Medical Association*, *Pediatrics* and *Health Affairs* among many others.

While blogs by and for scientists proliferate, the genre has yet to find a comfortable home in the scientific communication ecosystem. Research is not published in blogs, but rather in journals. Less formal communications continue via email and at conferences. What then is the function of science blogs? Are they for scientists or for the general public? Are they a place for scientists to have more speculative discussions that are not appropriate for peer-reviewed venues? Such questions become even more difficult to answer when a journal starts a blog under the journal brand. How is a blog post different from an editorial or commentary? These questions remain as blogging continues its emergence and evolution in scientific communication.

Workflow integration

'Workflow integration' is a term that is currently in vogue in scholarly publishing. While users of the term may have field-specific meanings in mind, I will use the term here in its widest possible sense to include whatever point at which one seeks information in the context of one's professional life.

- A student's workflow could include using a textbook in a course, studying for an exam or accessing reference materials.
- A clinician's workflow could include providing information to a patient, look-up of diagnostic criteria or drug interactions, consultation of treatment guidelines or review of material for maintenance of certification.
- A researcher's workflow might include review of laboratory protocols, assessment of primary literature, analysis of datasets or the composition of journal papers.

These are all professional workflows and all provide numerous points at which information or services are needed. The goal of 'workflow integration' is to make the relevant information or service available at the right point in the workflow and with a minimum of friction, thus saving the professional time and thereby providing a more valuable product or service. A small sample of workflow integration product and service categories is given below.

Document distribution

Document distribution services have long prospered as a means of connecting busy professionals with articles and other content. Such services are proliferating in a wide range of offerings and business models. Some, like Reprints Desk and Infotrieve, continue to provide document delivery in much the same way it was practiced a few decades ago, albeit with online ordering systems and digital delivery. ArXiv, the venerable physics pre-print server, is arguably a kind of document delivery system. Physicists have long passed pre-prints to colleagues for feedback prior to publication, a practice made more efficient by ArXiv, which centralizes the activity. PubGet focuses on connecting researchers to article PDFs as efficiently as possible by streamlining the search and retrieval process. And DeepDyve provides article rental via a subscription plan targeted to individuals and professionals in small- to mid-sized companies.

Mendeley provides perhaps the most innovative example of document distribution. They have taken the approach of developing a professional network that is based on document sharing. Users are encouraged to upload their own papers to their profiles to share with colleagues. They then can bookmark the work others have loaded and share individually or in groups. They are therefore part professional network, part document distributer, part social booking site and part document management system.

Point of care decision support

Clinicians working at the point of care seek very different types of information, for very different purposes, than medical researchers working in the lab or field. A clinician needs succinct information that helps him or her diagnose a patient, prescribe the appropriate treatment or review how to perform a procedure. In the past, locating the relevant medical reference text off the bookshelf was the most efficient means of finding this information. In today's fast-paced clinical settings, that is often not feasible. Publishers have responded by developing decision support resources that often combine digitized reference material, integration with drug databases, and purpose-developed content and tools. The most prominent examples include MD Consult and Clinical Key from Elsevier, the Access Medicine portfolio of speciality products from McGraw-Hill, Medscape from WebMD and Up-to-Date from Wolters Kluwer.

Continuing education/maintenance of certification

Physicians, lawyers, nurses and other professionals are required in many countries to pass licensing and recertification exams and receive ongoing training to maintain good standing in their profession. While study guides for such exams have long been common, they have largely moved online and have become increasing interactive, accounting for differences in individual knowledge progress. Examples include McGraw-Hill's

UMLEasy, which prepares students for the United States Medical Licensing Examination; the American Academy of Pediatrics' PREP the Curriculum, which prepares physicians for the pediatric speciality board exam; and ACCP Seek by the American College of Chest Physicans, a mobile application that helps physicians prepare for certification or recertification in pulmonary, critical care and sleep specialities.

Laboratory workflow support

While scientists working in laboratories need to keep up with research in their field and so are avid consumers of journal articles, they also have a need for information that helps them conduct the experiments that they are paid to perform. A number of publishers, including Nature Publishing Group and Cold Spring Harbor Laboratory Press, have developed online protocols to provide precisely this type of support. Protocols are like recipes for performing aspects of experiments and include information on equipment, sequence and technique. The most novel entrant in this category is the *Journal of Visualized Experiment*, which provides peer-reviewed and professional recorded videos of laboratory experiments. McMillan has developed a new division, called Digital Science, to develop an array of products that assist researchers with day-to-day work, including tools for equipment sourcing, chemical compound searching and research tracking management.

Manuscript submission and review

Perhaps the earliest example of a successful, widespread, online workflow tool in scholarly publishing is that of manuscript submission and review systems. Such systems allow authors to submit manuscripts online and enable publishers to process manuscripts through an editorial process that often includes peer review by outside experts. Prior to the adoption of such systems, manuscripts were submitted and subsequently circulated via post, adding days if not weeks to each step of the editorial process.

STM and scholarly publishers moved to online manuscript systems en masse in the mid-1990s in concert with the industry move to online publishing platforms. While a number of publishers developed their own systems in-house, most used third-party systems provided under a software as a service architecture. Leading pioneers include Aries Systems, ScholarOne (now a division of Thomson Reuters), HighWire Press and E-Journal Press.

Content integration

While it might seem obvious that there is no such thing as 'journal readers' or 'book readers' as professionals distinct from each other, publishers have long operated their businesses as if this were true. Book and journal divisions are more often than not operating in silos with separate management, separate marketing and even separate online platforms. Researchers and other readers, however, do not limit their reading to particular formats but rather read multiple formats within a topical area. An engineer who specializes in microfluidic devices in nanotechnology will be interested in relevant technical reports, conference proceedings, journal articles and monographs on that topic.

A few publishers are delivering this kind of integrated content portfolio. Most of the large commercial publishers – including Wiley, Elsevier and Springer – include both books and journals on their online platforms. In physics and engineering, where technical reports and conference proceedings have long held more importance than in other fields, integrated portfolios are far more common. Publishers such as SPIE (the international society for optics and photonics) and IEEE have long combined their digital assets in 'digital libraries' that better reflect user information seeking behaviour. In the medical sciences, the American Psychiatric Association (APA) was a pioneer with the creation of PsychiatryOnline, which brings together the APA's guidelines, continuing medical education, journals, textbooks, news, and reference works in one online portfolio.

Mobile devices

One of the primary reasons for the continued use of paper copies is their convenience and portability. A printed book, journal or a printed copy of an article PDF is far more convenient for long-form reading than reading on a computer screen for many individuals. In addition to being available off-line, the printed object can also be read more easily in a variety of situations and locations from planes and trains to sofas and beds. Any move to complete digital consumption of scholarly material requires a digital reading device (or devices) that provides all of the advantages of paper – portability, ease of annotation, lack of eyestrain – along with the advantages of digital delivery (the ability to access vast amounts of reading material in a slim device, backlighting, etc.).

Such devices are now being developed. Smartphones, e-readers and tablet computers (to say nothing of laptop computers) have made great strides in the last 5 years, with Apple and Amazon as the key innovators around device manufacture. These devices have been adopted quickly by academics and other information professionals. A recent Outsell report indicates that 70 per cent of US faculty and 83 per cent of college students in the US use a mobile device of some kind (Worlock, 2011). While there is not one device that 'does it all,' these three categories of devices target different use cases and market segments.

Smartphones

Recent advances in mobile computing and mobile device manufacture are transforming the way people interact with information the world over. Smartphones have existed for nearly a decade in the form of Palm Treos, Blackberrys and various phones for the mobile version of the Windows system. While a number of early innovators emerged in the STM publishing space with workflow decision support tools for clinicians (most notably Epocrates), these devices appealed to a small niche of professionals and were used primarily for email and administrative functions such as electronic calendars and notation.

The launch of the iPhone, followed by the subsequent development of Google's Android operating system and more recently a refreshed Windows system, have moved the adoption of smartphones from a niche, business communication tool to a powerful delivery platform for STM and scholarly information. In the US, for example, 81 per cent of physicians are using smartphones, and 75 per cent own an Apple mobile device (iPhone, iPod or iPad) (Manhattan Research, 2011). Statistics were not available as of this writing for overall scholarly adoption of smartphones, but their adoption among all consumers in the US is approximately 40 per cent and climbing (Kellogg, 2011). Using this figure as a floor and physician adoption as a ceiling, we can postulate that the overall adoption of scholarly professionals is between 40 and 81 per cent. The actual number as of this writing is almost irrelevant due to the steepness of the adoption curve. With prices falling dramatically, it is a safe operating assumption that smartphone adoption will reach near ubiquity in STM and scholarly markets in developed countries in the next 5 years. In less developed economic regions, especially Asia (Qing, 2011) and South America (Gomez, 2011), smartphone adoption, while lagging Europe and North America, is growing rapidly.

While smartphones are excellent delivery systems for a wide variety of content, they are not ideal for journal articles, textbooks, scholarly monographs and other long-form reading or multi-media formats requiring larger display (procedural videos, for example). This has not prevented STM and scholarly publishers from developing an array of device-native applications and websites optimized for the smartphone. These include applications for single journals, such as *Nature* as well as applications for content portfolios such as the journals of the American Chemical Society. It also includes purpose-built applications such as ACCP Seek, developed by the American College of Chest Physicians for maintenance of certification.

E-readers and tablets

There have been numerous attempts to popularize e-readers and tablet computers over the last decade and a half, with little result until quite recently. The market was not ready and the technology was not sufficiently advanced. Moreover, no one had seamlessly linked the devices to content sources, until Amazon introduced the Kindle. The Kindle was revolutionary as it enabled one-click wireless download of any digital book available via Amazon. Tens of thousands of books were just a click away. Part of the reason for the Kindle's success is that it is a purpose-built device: it is for book reading. It does not do much else and the display and size makes it less than ideal for other content formats such as magazines, textbooks or journals.

The iPad, by contrast, with its larger dimensions, color screen and touch pad, is a multi-purpose device, designed for reading, watching videos, surfing the web, reading email and running any number of thousands of applications (including the Kindle application). Unlike the Kindle, the iPad is great for reading journal articles, textbooks, magazines, and other content formats. The downside of the iPad is that it is much more expensive than the purpose-built Kindle.

The introduction of viable reader technology may very well signal the beginning of the end of printed books as a dominant information dissemination vehicle in STM and scholarly publishing. Print distribution ceased to be relevant over a decade ago in journal publishing but has remained the primary dissemination mechanism for long-form reading, including monographs, textbooks and reference works. This is because long-form reading was not practical on a computer screen – even that of a laptop. Modern e-readers and tablets designed with long-form reading in mind, and able to accommodate high-resolution color imagery and user annotation, are now available. And they will get dramatically better and dramatically cheaper over the next 3–5 years. Amazon released its next-generation color Kindle (Fire) in late 2011 at a price point that is scarcely more than the price of some textbooks. While sales of e-books represent only 6.4 percent of total book sales (US) at this point, publishers must, given the steepness of the adoption curve, assume that the rapidly advancing e-reader technology will be more than adequate for the needs of most professional users and that dramatically falling prices will render the devices ubiquitous (Association of American Publishers, 2010). Indeed, some universities and medical schools have already starting requiring them (Conaboy, 2011).

In addition to the improvements in e-reader and tablet hardware, great strides have been made in software standards. EPUB 3 and Kindle Format 8, both recently released, have significantly improved support for document formatting, allowing many of the complex structures found in STM and scholarly books, such as tables and mathematics, to be rendered as precisely in electronic format as they are in print. Additionally, these new formats provide much greater control for rendering document fonts and layout, which is essential for publishing text that contains non-Latin alphabets.

There are significant implications for STM and scholarly publishers, many of which have built content development workflows and business models around the print format. Such workflows will need to be re-engineered as will the business models and distribution partnerships that support their products. This is already beginning to happen as textbook publishers are now partnering with start-up ventures such as Inkling, which has developed a platform for digital textbooks on tablets (Reid, 2011). Some publishers, including PLoS, Elsevier and the ACCP, are developing tablet applications directly. Others are disseminating books via Kindle and other digital distribution streams. And others still are optimizing online book content for tablet reading. Indeed, to this last point, the line between application and online website is blurring with the emergence of HTML5, which is capable of supporting increasingly sophisticated online applications that can store content offline on users' devices as needed. While still an emerging technology, HTML5 has the potential to further transform how users interact with information, standardizing a viewing experience across many devices.

Semantic technology

The *meaning* of content is currently written so that humans, not computers, can understand it. Semantic technologies provide a layer of metadata to content that allows computers to understand and make connections to it. For example, XML provides information about document structure. HTML provides information about a website's structure. But neither, by itself, can tell a computer what the content in a document or web page is *about*. Semantic technologies provide this machine-oriented content information via an overlay of metadata. These metadata can come in the form of taxonomy, ontology, entity extraction or a combination of all three.

Taxonomy

A taxonomy is a hierarchical framework, or schema, for the organization of organisms, inanimate objects, events and/or concepts. From a computing standpoint, however, there are some important differences between a classic Linnaean taxonomy and a taxonomy that is useful in application logic. Taxonomies used for computing may assign multiple parents to a given taxon or root term. Taxons need not live in only one branch of a taxonomic tree but may be related to several. Taxonomies used in application logic also place a great deal of emphasis on lexical equivalents or synonyms. This is because computers do not know about synonyms unless they are explicitly told about them. Any first-year medical student can tell you that 'heart attack', 'ST-Elevated Myocardial Infarction' and 'STEMI' all refer to the same disease event, however even the most advanced computers require a thesaurus to make such connections.

Ontology

An ontology is a structural framework for organizing information about relationships between concepts, objects or events. An ontology explains how elements of a taxonomy are related to each other. Drug X, for example, may treat condition Y, but with adverse effect Z. While the relationship between drug X, condition Y and adverse effect Z are easy for humans to comprehend (because our languages evolved with our brain functions in mind – literally), computers need these relationships mapped in different ways.

Entity extraction

Entity extraction is the process of locating specific types of digital objects. These might include people, places, academic institutions, chemical compounds, genetic sequences, laboratory equipment, diagnostic devices, surgical equipment, clinical trials or any number of other nouns. The purpose of locating such objects is often to provide the reader with more context about the object. For example, a paper containing a particular chemical compound might link to a database with more information about that compound. Likewise for gene sequences or clinical trials. The identification of laboratory or surgical equipment might be used to provide links to purchase the equipment. Individuals might be identified to provide a list of all work authored by that individual. Entity extraction can be used in concert with taxonomies and ontologies to provide a more precise layer of semantic metadata.

Publisher interests in semantic technology

It is important here to disambiguate between the 'Semantic Web' and 'semantic technologies.' The term 'Semantic Web' is used, often synonymously with 'Web 3.0', to refer to the notion of interoperable datasets – or linked data. Many prominent individuals in computing science, government and beyond – including Tim Berners-Lee, the architect of the Web – are actively promoting the need for more interoperability of scientific and government data, not least of all due to the sheer volume of data being produced (Berners-Lee, 2009). *The Fourth Paradigm* (Hey *et al.*, 2009) has generated a great deal of discussion around the increasing role of computing in making sense of the vast datasets being produced by today's scientific research.

While interoperable data are of doubtless importance to scientists and technologists, it is not the area where semantic technology is most of value to *publishers*. Publishers are primarily concerned with semantic technology that enriches content for specific use cases: product development, search engine optimization and user personalization. These use cases are being served now by utilizing semantic technologies without depending on the larger development of the Semantic Web.

Product development

Wide-scale data interoperability requires many organizations both to agree upon standards and to invest in the necessary infrastructure [e.g. RDF (Resource Description Framework) triple stores, domain taxonomies, universal identifiers]. While such efforts are worth pursuing, it is not necessary to wait until they are in place for publishers to use semantic metadata for their own product development.

Product development at the publisher level need only depend on the efforts of that organization. Examples of STM and scholarly information products that have used semantic metadata include Wolfram Alpha, the Royal Society of Chemistry's ChemSpider, the Journal of Bone and Joint Surgery's *JBJS Case Connector*, and Elsevier's *Clinical Key*. In the consumer space, Netflix, Amazon, Pandora and Zappos, among others, use semantic technology to significantly enhance their services. STM and scholarly publishers in many ways have less friction to overcome than their consumer counterparts as there has already been a great deal of work done in creating scientific and medical taxonomies and much of it is publically available. Such public domain schemas ensure future interoperability as new resources that appear in the marketplace will want to map to any domain standards.

Publishers and other information professionals are also beginning to use advances in natural language processing (NLP) to drive product development. NLP is used in speech recognition workflow tools such as the Dragon Diction application. NLP can, however, be used as an aide to the development of controlled vocabularies, especially enterprise schema that represent classification of a proprietary content set. It can additionally be used in concert with text mining to provide researchers with new filtering systems and more comprehensive analysis tools (Williams, 2011).

Search engine optimization

Semantic metadata can be used to increase traffic from search engines as such metadata can provide search engines with more information about the content being searched. While the leading search engines maintain their own sets of synonyms, they may not be as complete as those that can be provided by a specialized publisher.

If a unit of content is published, for example, that refers to the acronym 'ALS', how is a search engine to know whether the content is about 'advanced life support', 'antilymphocyte globulin' or 'amyotrophic lateral sclerosis'? If the last, will that unit of content appear in search queries for 'Lou Gehrig's Disease'? Will it know that amyotrophic lateral sclerosis is a kind of bulbar motor neuron disease and would be relevant to searches on that topic? What about searches for spinal cord diseases? The kind of connections and topical hierarchy that might be obvious to anyone familiar with a topic often elude search engines on all but the more popular searches.

Recently, several of the leading search engines have begun working together, via Schema.org, on the development of standards that will facilitate a greater level of metadata exposure (Guha, 2011).

User personalization

While usually thought of in terms of *content* enrichment, semantic technologies can additionally be brought to bear to enable computer applications to better understand the *people* who are using them. People can inherit the semantic traits applied to content they interact with. Based on reading, searching or browsing interests – or the alerts the person has set up for him- or herself – an application can make personalized recommendations for additional reading. In other words, applications can increasingly utlize semantic technologies to anticipate the needs and interest of users to save them time.

In the consumer space, this type of personalization is increasingly common. Dynamic personalization and adaptive information environments driven by semantic technologies are used by Amazon to recommend products, by Pandora to recommend music, by Netflix to recommend movies and by Facebook to filter news feeds. In the STM and scholarly space, this type of personalization has not yet been deployed although less dynamic personalized services have existed for some time. *Journal Watch*, by the Massachusetts Medical Society, for example, provides a topical alerting service across a range of specialties.

The challenge with regard to STM and scholarly applications is in making the filters transparent to users. While it may not be terribly important to Pandora users why one song is recommended over another, for STM and scholarly users the stakes are higher. A researcher needs to be able to see all the available research on a topic before selecting various filters – and he or she needs to be cognizant of what is being filtered out. Recommendation services will be less problematic in this regard as compared with search filters.

Conclusion and outlook

One of the most heated discussion topics over the last decade and a half in scholarly publishing is whether and/or when print publication will cease. Over the same period of time, however, technology has rendered the question irrelevant. The Web has already become the primary mode of dissemination of scholarly information and print is now an ancillary distribution channel. With digital printers now capable of producing high-quality print copies of books and journals with very low print run (including single copies) the question of how long print copies of books and journals continue to be distributed is simply a function of how long there are individuals and institutions willing to pay for such copies. Much as there remains a niche market for vinyl records, there is likely to remain a niche market for printed artifacts.

On the one hand, the digital revolution is over. The wheel has spun and we are in a profoundly different era than we were a few decades ago. On the other hand, we are just now emerging from the *incunabula* period of digital publishing. Up until this point, digital products have largely been simulacra of print artifacts. We now see the first stirrings of entirely new types of information products, delivered across a dizzying array of devices, through an ever-expanding universe of business models, and via formats that are evolving before our eyes. In this sense, the digital revolution is just beginning as we are in the process of shifting to digital native products and services that are conceived, developed and delivered via digital means. These products and services will less and less resemble the print artifacts they are replacing, just as printed books bear only superficial resemblance to the codices that came before.

References

Association of American Publishers (2010) *Book Stats 2010*. Washington, DC: Association of American Publishers.

Bergstrom, C.T. and Bergstrom, T.C. (2004) The costs and benefits of library site licenses to academic journals. *Proceedings of the National Academy of Sciences USA* 101: 897–902.

Berners-Lee, T. (2009) 'Linked Data', Talk at TED (February 2009). Retrieved from: http://www.ted.com/talks/tim_berners_lee_on_the_next_web.html

Conaboy, C. (2011) Medical student essentials: Stethoscope, iPad. *The Boston Globe*, 29 August.

Gomez, J. (2011) Latin America Telecom Insider. *Pyramid Research*, 3(6): November.

Guha, R. (2011) Introducing schema.org: Search engines come together for a richer web. *The Official Google Blog*, 2 June. Retrieved 2011 from: http://googleblog.blogspot.com/2011/06/introducing-schemaorg-search-engines.html

Hey, T., Tansley, S. and Tolle, K. (eds) (2009) *The Fourth Paradigm*. Redmond, WA: Microsoft Research.

Kellogg, D. (2011) 40 Percent of U.S. Mobile Users Own Smartphones; 40 Percent are Android. *Neilsenwire*, 1 September 1. Retrieved 2011 from: http://blog.nielsen.com/nielsenwire/?p=28790

Manhattan Research (2011) *Taking the Pulse U.S.* v11.0.

Reid C. (2011) McGraw-Hill, Pearson invest big in Inkling digital textbook platform. *Publishers Weekly*, 25 March.

O'Reilly, T. (2011) What is Web 2.0: Design Patterns and Business Models for the Next Generation of Software. O'Reilly Media (2005). Retrieved from: http://oreilly.com/web2/archive/what-is-web-20.html

Qing, L.Y. (2011) Android sees 1,000 percent growth in SEA. ZDNet Asia, 10 November. Retrieved 2011 from: http://www.zdnetasia.com/android-sees-1000-percent-growth-in-sea-62302815.htm

Schriger, D.L., Chehrazi, A.C., Merchant, R.M. and Altman, D.G. (2011) Use of the internet by print medical journals in 2003 to 2009: a longitudinal observational study. *Annals of Emergency Medicine* 57: 153–60.

Tenopir, C. and King, D. (2000) *Towards Electronic Journals*. Alexandria, VA: Special Libraries Association.

Worlock, K. (2011) The Use of Mobile Devices and Content in US K-12 and Higher Education Markets. Outsell, 31 March.

Williams, C. (2011) Computer that can read promises cancer breakthroughs. *The Telegraph*, 21 November.

5

Publishing and communication strategies

David Green and Rod Cookson

Abstract: This chapter details publishing and communication strategies within the context of the digital technology revolution. The major focus is on scientific and academic journals publishing but the chapter also discusses the little-detailed tradecraft involved in the historical strategic development of particular product types against a backdrop of wider market evolution. Illustrative case-study exhibits are presented detailing the strategic development of selected products and markets, as well as to explain the powerful Network Effects that underline the success of journals that work to more closely match their communities.

Key words: Publishing strategy, communications strategy, product development, market development, market penetration, diversification, Ansoff matrix, Network Effects, economies of scale.

πάντα χωρεῖ καὶ οὐδὲν μένει
'Nothing Endures but Change'
Heraclitus, *c.* 535–475 BCE

Introduction

Heraclitus of Ephesus can truly be considered the Publisher's philosopher. He elaborated the doctrine of change being central to the universe, and he established the term 'Logos'[1] in Western philosophy, meaning both the source and the fundamental order of the universe.

Change does indeed seem to have been endemic in the publishing and communication worlds since the beginning of the technological and industrial wave based on the invention of the microprocessor in 1971 (Figure 5.1). For the last 20 years or more, every time publishers have gathered together, the talk has been of nothing but change – changes in technology, economic and political context, library finances and sociocultural change. Although there is a real tradition and continuity in our industry, we can take another image from Heraclitus, that even though a person steps in the same river, those who step into it are always washed by different waters: 'each individual atom of water, does not constantly change; the totality of things constantly changes' (Shiner, 1974).

This period since 1971 has also witnessed the current wave based on information and communication technologies (ICT), initially leading to process revolutions in our industry, and increasingly now, as we truly enter the deployment phase in the 2010s (Figure 5.2), to new products emerging. This digital revolution has driven a paradigm shift in our industry from print-based manufacturing to online service provision, causing major disruptions for both markets and products. As with any technological revolution, there are both threats and opportunities which arise from these 'waves of creative destruction' (Schumpeter, 1975).

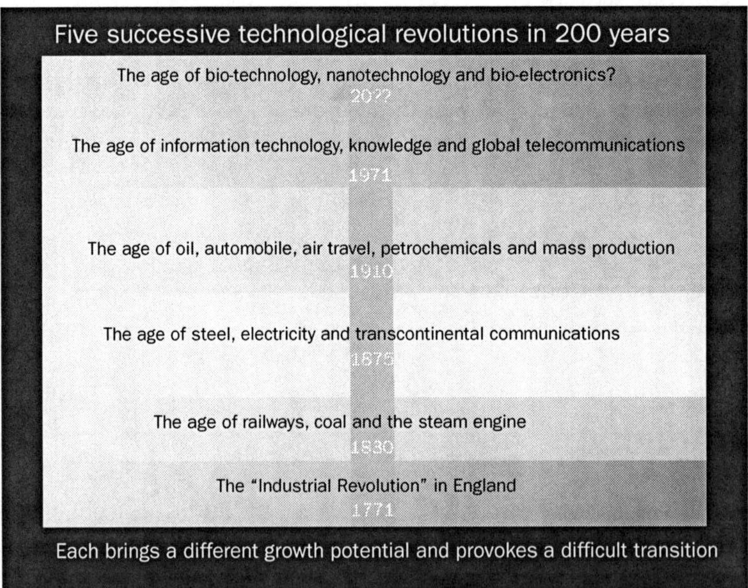

Figure 5.1 Kondratiev waves in history

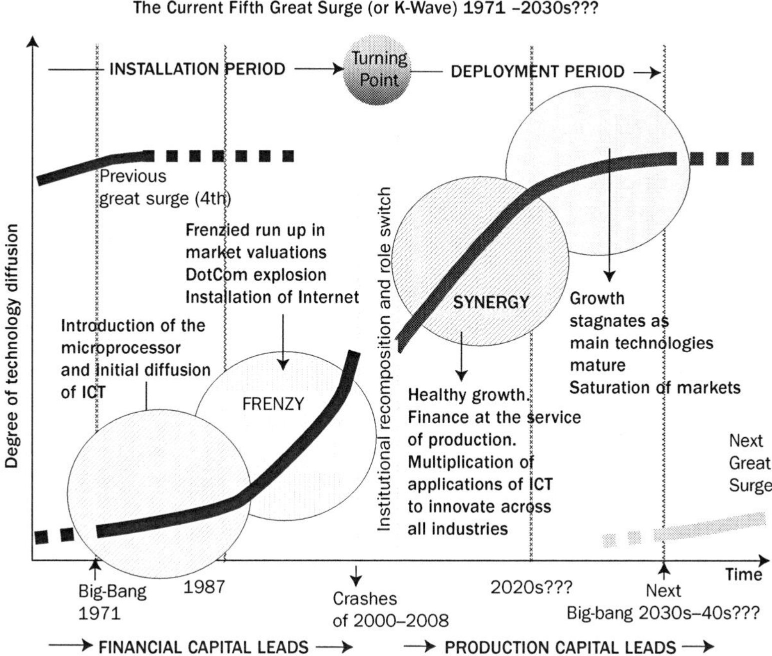

Figure 5.2 5th Great Surge based on ICT

Source: Based on the work of Carlota Perez, in particular *Technological Revolutions and Financial Capital*, figure 7.1, p. 74. Edward Elgar Publishing, 2002. Reproduced with permission. The authors are indebted to Professor Perez for elaborating this version especially for this chapter.

Further, the economic analysis conducted by Carlota Perez indicates the role played by financial capital in the global publishing industry from the 1980s up to the early years of the 21st century. Her analysis also clearly indicates the turning point that the industry has now reached, a theme that we develop later in this chapter.

These concerns that disruption was beginning to occur in our industry were most graphically raised by the physicist Michael Nielsen at a workshop for editors at the American Institute of Physics in 2009, to be found on his blog – 'Is scientific publishing about to be disrupted'.[2] Nielsen's views and recent championing of Open Science[3] have raised many issues. The key points of his hypothesis are:

- Scientific publishers should be terrified that some of the world's best scientists, people at or near their research peak, people whose time is at a premium, are spending hundreds of hours each year creating original research content for their blogs.

- In comparison, scientific journals are standing still.
- Scientific publishing is moving from being a production industry to a technology industry.
- The cost of distributing information has now dropped almost to zero, and production and content costs have also dropped radically.
- The world's information is now rapidly being put into a single, active network, where it can wake up and come alive.
- The result is that the people who add the most value to information are no longer the people who produce and distribute it, but rather the technologists, the programmers.

Contrary to the Nielsen hypothesis, if one area of publishing has responded to the challenges of digital technology, and embraced many opportunities offered, it has been journals publishing. The essential lacuna in Nielsen's hypothesis is his confusion of science and research with their mediation into peer-reviewed content, and the incredibly complex set of services, activities and products that publishers bring to the material output of the academic and research worlds.

This chapter will focus on both products and markets, referring along the way to the key media, but always within the context of the digital technology revolution. For this reason – and also because it represents the specialism of the authors – we will focus on scientific and academic journals publishing. The chapter features exhibits predominantly taken from Taylor & Francis's publishing programme as illustrative case studies on the strategic development of products and markets.

Strategic developments in the scientific and academic publishing industry

Since the year 2000, it is estimated that the journals industry has invested over £2 billion in technological systems, as well as innovated in areas such as electronic editorial systems, author tools, production workflow, plagiarism checking, content management, online content platforms, global sales management and many more elements that are outlined in Figure 5.3. We hope to show that in the Web 3.0 world and beyond,

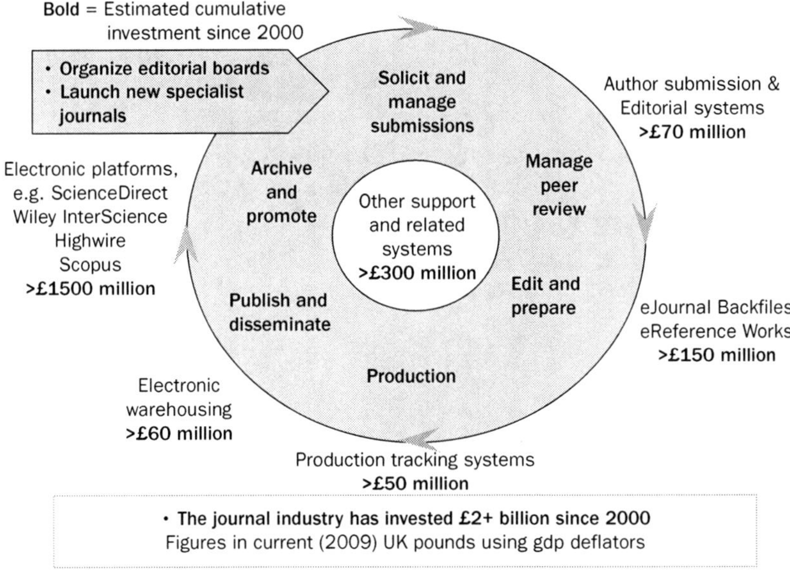

Figure 5.3 The scale of journal publishers' technological and content investment since 2000

Source: 'Access to Research Outputs: A UK Success Story', PA, STM, ALPSP London 2010.

which values expert material and the transmission of peer-reviewed knowledge, journals and the publishing industry are rising to the challenge – with other media still highly valued despite the changed technological and economic contexts.

From its initial origins as recording the minutes of science, in the 20th century journals were often viewed as a slightly 'eccentric offshoot' of monograph publishing that publishers had to be involved in to cover fully their fields of publishing. Both Elsevier and Robert Maxwell began the industrialisation of journal publishing in the late 1940s and 1950s, not the least of the innovations being the pre-paid subscription, aggressive launching of international titles (such as Elsevier's *Biochimica et Biophysica Acta* in 1946) and titles in applied science, and computer-based subscription management and fulfilment (Cox, 2002).

Yet journal publishing at that time and up until the mid to late 1980s was very much based on a 'black box' business model, with the content put together by author, editor and peer reviewer, and consumed by researcher/reader (and the same academic or scientist may play each of these roles at different times), with the 'industry' operating on the outside of the academic world dealing with production, printing, marketing and sales, subscription management and distribution – a relationship between publisher, library agent and librarian. But it was always the case, as with book commissioning, that good relationship management was a key skill for the publisher – getting the best editors, linking with eminent learned societies, and selecting a good, balanced editorial board who would not only add lustre to the title but help promote and sell subscriptions to their and their colleagues' institutions.

Abstracting and indexing – secondary publishing

Technology began to drive e-publishing in the 1960s and 1970s. This involved delivery of secondary publishing abstracting and indexing products (A&I) initially with the Dialog system, which was one of the predecessors of the Internet, as a provider of bibliographic information. Initially databases such as ERIC (education), INSPEC (electrical engineering) and MathSciNet (mathematical sciences) were delivered as magnetic tapes, but by the 1980s a low-priced dial-up version of a subset of Dialog was marketed to individual users as *Knowledge Index*. This included INSPEC, MathSciNet and more than 200 other bibliographic and reference databases. Even at this early stage, subscribers to the A&I databases were linked to document retrieval services such as CARL/ Uncover, who would go to physical libraries to copy materials for a fee and send it to the service subscriber.

The origins of A&I products can be traced back to *An Index to Periodical Literature*, first published in 1802 by William Frederick Poole, who had recognised that periodical articles were often being overlooked due to a lack of an effective indexing service. Originally, abstracting services developed to aid research scientists in keeping abreast of an exponential growth in scientific journal publications, focusing on comparatively narrow subject areas.

From their origin as a service to the scientific community, the number of abstracting services has grown to an estimated 1500 today, many of which were founded in print but are now to be found online. The conversion of print to online format allowed libraries to build in links to their own online public access catalogues (OPACs) as well as to electronic and print document delivery services. More recently, Jasco (2007) has argued that traditional abstracting services may eventually be outmoded because more efficient searches can be made using powerful search engines. However, quantum improvements in search and retrieval software have not necessarily meant that the task of identifying relevant material has been made any easier for the researcher. There is still enormous value in A&I services being structured on the basis of application of a bespoke taxonomy developed by subject specialists, which can provide much more granular and targeted search results than Google or even specialist search software (see Exhibit 1).

Such challenges to commercial producers of A&I services have been met by producers of bibliometric databases (e.g. SCOPUS™) where the value of cross-referencing, citation and other metadata have been recognised as quality indicators and thus drivers of publication metrics, which allow users to identify quantifiably authoritative pieces of research from within an access-controlled online environment. The original purpose of A&I services to help researchers overcome the difficulties of tracing potentially useful articles scattered over not only the extant print periodical and other literature, but now predominantly the Internet, remains valid. More than ever, discoverability and search and navigation are central to research providers and users. The challenge for A&I service producers today is to retain integrity, identity, validity and authority in an age of seemingly ubiquitous sources of one-off and serial research and scholarly literature. Additionally, from these searches, rapid delivery of the primary material needs to be designed in, as well as linking to datasets, chemical reference works, handbooks, patent databases, etc., meeting the challenges of linking on the semantic web.

Within the physical sciences A&I databases have for long been a key tool for the research community, and in the online age have rapidly developed to incorporate many features making the access and usage of the data faster, more intuitive and enriched. An indexing service gives a full bibliographical reference whilst an abstracting service in addition provides a brief summary of the article or reports content. All forms of A&I can be searched by subject topic, author(s) name or subject keywords such as the chemical, plant or process name. A&I providers now need to develop and make available searchable related datasets, reference links, related patents and as the provisions develop further structural tagging and bespoke identifiers such as the International Chemical Identifier – InChI (see Exhibit 2).

Exhibit 1: Scientific A&I database case-study – Chemical Abstracts Service

A major example of an abstracting and indexing database that has developed in tandem with the web is the **Chemical Abstracts Service**, which is a division of the American Chemical Society. In this example proprietary databases have been developed and expanded over numerous years and have thus become recognised by chemical and pharmaceutical companies, universities, government organisations and patent offices globally as an important source of chemical information. Chemical Abstracts Service has become vitally important to the physical sciences community by combining their databases with advanced search and analysis technologies, delivering current, complete and cross-linked digital information allowing scientific discovery. This information contains full linking of metadata and data sources.

What makes Chemical Abstracts important to researchers is that at its core is a periodical index providing summaries and indexes of disclosures in recently published scientific documents across all major publishing houses. The index incorporates 8000 journals, technical reports, conference proceedings, theses and dissertations as well as numerous new books in any of 50 major languages. In addition, the index incorporates patent specifications from 27 countries and two international organisations, giving the full database enriched content for the researcher to draw upon.

As well as the published articles and reviews, patents are also covered in detail by Chemical Abstracts and they account for over 15 per cent of the documents available for search and retrieval. The majority of patents that are of interest to chemists cover compositions of substance (i.e. new chemical compounds, mixtures, pharmaceuticals) or processes (i.e. synthesis). Patents are also beginning to include three-dimensional atomic structures, structural databases and their uses, as access to information becomes easier. As hundreds of thousands of patents are issued annually by countries, a great deal of scientific and editorial effort has gone into organising these patent documents for effective retrieval via A&I services such as Chemical Abstracts.

Exhibit 2: InChI – web-based storage and retrieval of chemical information

An example of how the provision of information digitally is developing is the InChI (International Chemical Identifier). InChIs are constructed of text strings comprising different layers and sublayers of information defining a compound or substance. The different layers of defining the chemical are separated by slashes (/). To ensure users easily understand how to find a particular chemical each InChI string starts with the InChI version number followed by the main layer.

So as to determine a particular chemical the main layer contains sublayers for the particular chemical formula, atom connections and hydrogen atoms which uniquely identifies the chemical. Depending on the structure of the molecule the main layer may be followed by additional layers, for example for charge, stereochemical and/or isotope information. This information can then be overlaid by scientists, publishers and database providers to enable web-based linking between sources of chemical content whether web-page, journal or magazine, or database, leading to article text identifying the compound or structure being discussed (the InChIKey and InChI is exact to each chemical).

By searching on the identifier via a resolver (such as the ChemSpider Inchl Resolver) a lookup is performed between a shorter InChIKey and the full InChI, returning digitally all relevant compound or publication information. The software to enable these searches is freely downloadable online, highlighting how information can easily be sourced and returned in the digital age.

http://www.inchi-trust.org/index.php?q=node/6

Abstracting and indexing are becoming ever more interactive for the researcher or academic by developing newer and faster ways of getting to the relevant information from the literature (see Exhibit 3). This now includes such techniques as content and data mining, which is defined as the automated processing of considerable amounts of digital content for

Exhibit 3: Social Science database case-study – *Educational Research Abstracts Online/ERA*

The Social Science database *Educational Research Abstracts Online/ERA*, in the mid to late 1990s, was a 'flat text' (print) abstracting journals programme. This comprised ten segmented A&I print publications in the field of education which served a useful current awareness purpose to the individual user. The challenge was to convert this into a unitary, searchable and structured online database, which could represent the 'front-end' of global educational research, and offer the user a route into the full-text documents that lay 'behind' the abstract.

This has been achieved to a large extent via reference linking which either allows access to subscribed-to primary material, or a click-through to a document delivery/pay-per-view (PPV) service via the British Library Document Supply Centre (BLDSC). The next phase of development for *ERA* is to capitalise on the semantic search capabilities of the worldwide web, in order to weave its content into the wider research literature now available online.

the purposes of information retrieval (be it structural data, tabulated results or data analysis), information extraction and meta-analysis. As the services available continue to develop, semantic annotation giving a meaningful context for information content could develop into a new standard for STM content, and facilitate improved and deeper search and browse facilities into articles and research. Enhancements in the capability for A&I to perform in-depth searches have meant that recently there has been consistent development of automated extraction tools which then present the important elements contained within documents and articles, including not only the expected scientific elements (genes, proteins, chemical compounds, diseases) but also now business-relevant elements such as company names, people/academics, products and places. The continuing development of these techniques aids in identifying the relationships between the elements the reader is interested in within significant numbers of documents.

Journals – primary research publishing

At the beginning of the 1990s there were very few full-text primary journals distributed via the Dialog system mentioned above, and fewer than a dozen titles had been launched for online delivery as ascii text via email. In 1991 Paul Ginsparg began the LANL preprint server for physics at Los Alamos (now known as arXiv), which at the time was seen as a major threat to the existence of traditional physics journals (although it has transpired that this system itself has required significant funding, and the preprint server has come to play a different role from the journal publication of versions of scientific record). At the same time, the results of the ADONIS project, digital scans of biomedical journals on CD, led to the launch of a (not very long-lived) commercial product. There then began a period of intense experimentation, often involving libraries and technology providers in addition to both commercial and learned society publishers. In 1992 the American Association for the Advancement of Science launched the *Online Journal of Current Clinical Trials*; Elsevier started Project Tulip with the University of California system, delivering scanned images of materials science journals to UC libraries; and the Red Sage project (named after a congenial restaurant favoured by publishers in Washington, DC), a collaboration between ATT Labs, UC San Francisco and a group of learned society and commercial publishers and university presses, sought to develop an experimental digital journal library for the Health Sciences. These projects all provided valuable data, insights and experiences, but at this time the online product essentially represented a 'dumb' digital replication of the print version.[4]

By 1995–96 most major publishers were announcing their intentions to produce online versions of their print editions, and experiments such as the UK SuperJournal project began to look at how e-journals were actually used, and the features that users wanted (see Exhibit 4). What is remarkable is both how much attachment there still was to the print paradigm in the 1996–98 period, and how, in little over a decade, all of the requested core user requirements are now taken for granted by users of online journals.

At the turn of the millennium, most major publishers had full e-versions available of their journals, and some e-journals were already starting to contain features that were not available in the print version. In addition, publishers' versions were also starting to compete with aggregators' licensed versions of full-text databases – such as BIS, EBSCO Publishing, Ovid and BIDS. These aggregated databases typically provided unlinked 'dumb' online versions which simply replicated the print edition. Publishers responded both by seeking embargoes on their content

Exhibit 4: The SuperJournal project

The SuperJournal research project was funded by UK JISC in the eLib Programme, to study the factors that would make electronic journals successful. The objective was to identify the features that deliver real value, and to explore the implications with stakeholders in the publishing process: readers, authors, libraries and publishers. The research was conducted over three years (1996–98) and the project ended in December 1998. The project developed an easy-to-use electronic journal application and made clusters of journals in Communication and Cultural Studies, Molecular Genetics and Proteins, Political Science and Materials Chemistry available to UK university test sites via the World Wide Web. At the start of the project readers were asked about their expectations for electronic journals. For two years their usage was recorded and analysed. At the end of the project, they were asked to comment on what they did and didn't like about SuperJournal, and the features they wanted in future electronic journals and services. Key findings were that users wanted:

- a critical mass of journals in each field,
- certain key functionality – browse, search and print,
- a deep and permanent backfile,
- seamless discovery and access, but with a choice of services for finding what is needed in their subjects, and
- the time-saving convenience of desktop access, as well as the broadest possible choice of content

http://www.superjournal.ac.uk/sj/index.htm

appearing in the aggregators' databases, and by starting to build additional features into their own e-versions. At a fairly rapid pace, the process change that had begun in the journals business in the 1990s started to drive the potential for new types of product based on digital content.

Further, journals and the activities surrounding research activities and the publishing workflow began to change. This can be seen reflected in what has been termed the 'new research and learning landscape', shown in Figure 5.4. This landscape integrates the publishing process much

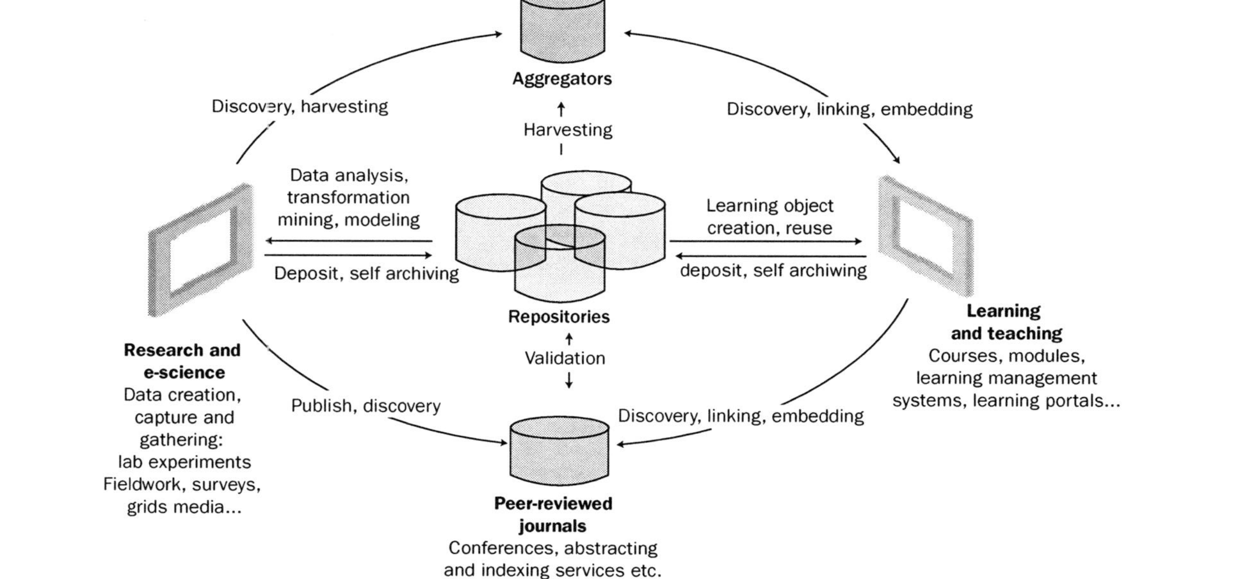

Figure 5.4 Journals in the new research and learning landscape

Source: L. Dempsey, 'The (Digital) Library Environment: Ten Years After', *Ariadne*, Issue 46, 2006, UKOLN, University of Bath http://www.ariadne.ac.uk/issue46/dempsey/, figure 2, which is adapted from the OCLC *Environmental Scan* (see http://www.oclc.org/reports/escan/research/newflows.htm), which is in turn adapted from Liz Lyon, 'eBank UK: Building the links between research data, scholarly communication and learning', *Ariadne*, July 2003, Issue 36: http://www.ariadne.ac.uk/issue36/lyon/

more into the academic and research process. Publishers can no longer sit as part of a 'black box' process outside the academic and research worlds, but must be integrated into it as a full partner. There has always been a teaching role for many journal articles, and this has been embraced much more in recent years with the decline of a lot of research and monograph publishing, and often due to the long gestation period of book publishing as opposed to article publication.

In addition, the shift from print to online has led to a significant change in workflow whereby the print version (perhaps a single archival volume or an amalgam of issues printed together) becomes an 'offcut' of a fully digital flow process from author to reader (Figure 5.5). The attention of publishers has also moved much further from production of publishing products to provision of publishing services within research networks, as shown in Figure 5.6. This in turn can be seen both as the fundamental shift from journal to network and as a precursor to potential new products, especially driving innovations in 'multi-layered' network products of varieties of book, journal and reference content, including multimedia, datasets, etc.

Alongside these changes in both processes and the publishing landscape, journal publishers have been required to demonstrate the value of the services that they are providing – much of which is of course driven by investment in technological systems as well as through changing the 'terms of trade' of the business. So we can list the following:

- online submission and peer review systems,
- smarter search and navigation in 'discoverability' technologies,
- author templates and authoring tools,
- originality checking with the Cross-Check system,
- getting author and researcher rights in balance through new copyright and licensing initiatives,
- developing new business models,
- providing legal advice to editors and learned societies,
- driving reputational factors such as branding and trust factors through publishing integrity programmes and third-party metrics,
- and not least serving editors and authors through providing clearly targeted channels of research dissemination in marketing, sales and promotional activities.

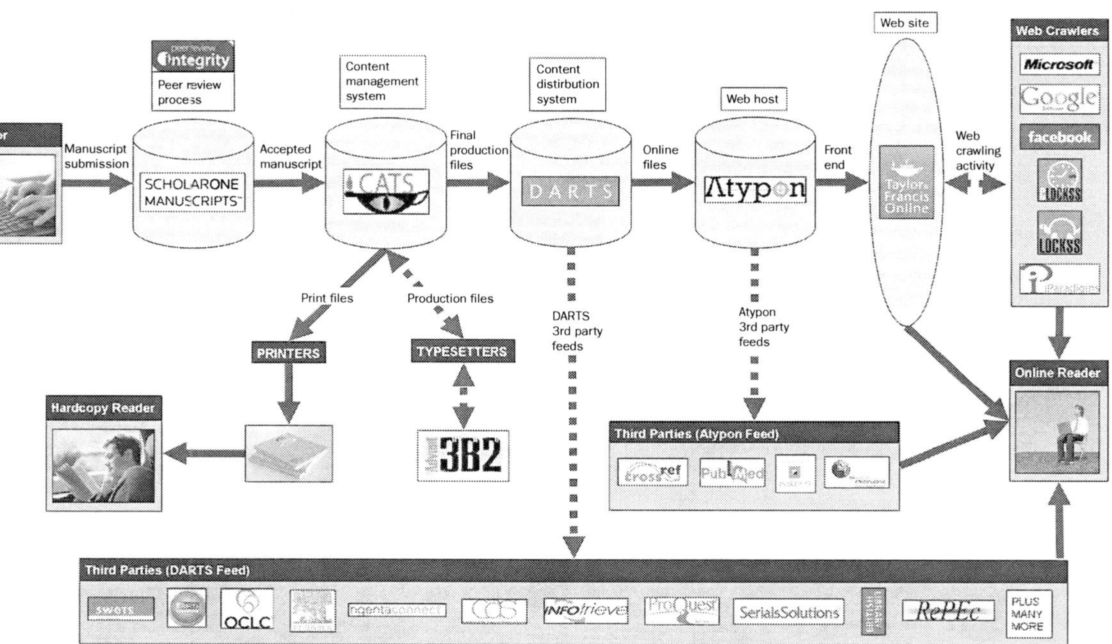

Figure 5.5 The online journal article workflow in the 21st century (Taylor & Francis example)

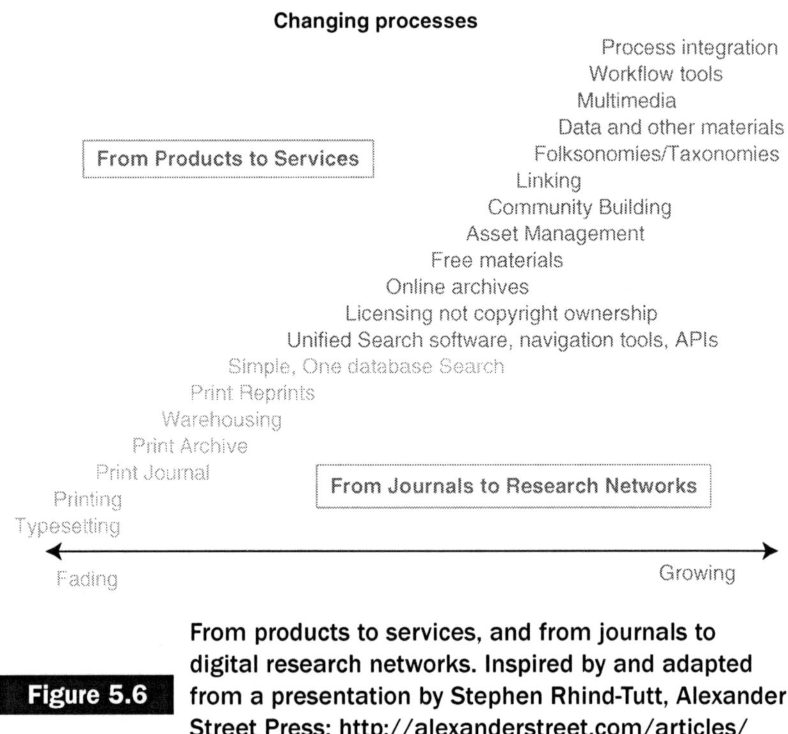

Figure 5.6 From products to services, and from journals to digital research networks. Inspired by and adapted from a presentation by Stephen Rhind-Tutt, Alexander Street Press: http://alexanderstreet.com/articles/index.htm

Although the decline of the journal has been much heralded, with the development of large databases of journal content on the one hand, and the individual article pay-per-view (PPV) market developing on the other, the fact is that it is the journal, its brand and the reputational factors associated with it that still provides the key trust factor to the content. This will continue to be the case in the future online 'multi-product content' or 'multi-layered content', supplying journal and book content along with associated data and supplementary materials.

Monographs

By 1997, a conference sponsored by the Association of Research Libraries in the USA was contemplating the decline of the scholarly monograph, with some referring to 'its comatose body'.[5] Indeed, one reason given for the continuing popularity of the research article, and its growing role in coursepacks and as teaching tools, is that monographs are seen as declining in relevance and timeliness by the reader, and in viability by the commercial publisher, and even in sustainability by the university presses. Every publisher uses the term in a slightly different way, but in general 'monograph' has become a catch-all term for a book that is not of a reference type, that is of primary material, and which may be multi-authored, single-authored, or an edited collection.

It is worth drawing a distinction between humanities titles, the viability of which are fundamentally dependent on the credibility of the scholar(s) as author(s); social science monographs, which are today dependent on the globalisation of markets and new markets as library budgets shrink in established markets in the US and Europe; and STM titles, which face the same phenomenon as social science, but with the added twist of a degree of dependence on the market vicissitudes of practitioner, professional and industrial audiences. But in the second decade of the 21st century, the essential commercial equation that a commercial scholarly monograph publisher makes as the publishing decision is:

$$\text{Quality of work} \times \text{Number of people interested in topic/subject} = \text{Go/No-go}$$

In general, however, university presses cannot take this approach and make as narrowly commercial a publishing decision, as they are much more producer-led rather than reader-led, and highly dependent on their host institutions or supporting foundations for sustaining their quality and prestige publishing. For the most part, on the basis of this model, commercial book publishers find it hard to compete with the prestige of university presses when it comes to the commissioning of the highest prestige material.

But there is no doubt that there is a funding crisis for the traditional university press model, as they try to come to grips with the new digital culture and the challenges of the Open Access lobby in both journal and book publishing.[6] The free online and digital print-on-demand (POD), a model that has also been recently espoused by Bloomsbury Academic among other commercial publishers, is unproven and potentially hastens income decline as more people become comfortable reading online (driven not least by new-generation e-reader platforms and mobile technology). There is a real need to retain strong revenue streams as new layered content with multimedia features becomes available, such as the recent launch of *The Waste Land* app.[7]

Successful commercial monograph publishing is in fact in rude health in the 2010s. Although unit sales have shrunk by around 75 per cent since the early 1990s, a multifold increase in publishing output has balanced this decline, and, with changes in digital process and the marketplace, the economics of monographs have perhaps never been healthier. This derives from a number of factors, based partly on the pricing up of hardback library editions, and the adoption of a POD paperback edition if there is sufficient perceived demand in addition to library sales. Other factors include:

- lower costs through digital processing;
- add-on revenues and enhanced editions through e-books;
- new sales channels such as Amazon and e-book stores;
- new rights deals and licensing deals with e-book aggregators;
- new value being driven from the back list and sales revivals of out-of-print through digitisation.

There are also significant developments through application of new digital possibilities by offering enhanced collections, particularly in STM subjects, in the form of enhanced databases (see Exhibit 5).

Exhibit 5: Enhanced database case-study: CRCnetBASEs

The CRCnetBASEs were launched in 1999 as one of the first online e-book providers in academic publishing. Since then they have grown to include more than 7000 online references in more than 40 subject disciplines. CRCnetBASEs offer instant access to one of the world's premier scientific and technical references with added support for libraries. The largest repository of scientific and technical information is the SCI-TECHnetBASE, which holds all online CRC Press content. It includes the entire line of science and technical books published through the CRC imprint. The database contains more than 6000 online volumes and is continually growing. Users can conduct sophisticated searches across the entire site or by sub-discipline and create an online resource centre tailored to the needs of the library or organisation.

As the CRCnetBASEs have developed they have incorporated the facility to allow converting raw materials or chemicals into more useful forms for spearheading the hunt for valuable new materials or techniques by providing the references and resources to generate this work. They also offer insights from experts on how to ensure processes are operated safely, sustainably and economically. In particular they can be used as a collection of interactive databases and dictionaries, allowing researchers to perform exhaustive searches using a variety of criteria, including structure searching and, in the CHEMnetBASE, incorporating up-to-date chemical tagging via the InChI project. It also provides ways to create customised tables and export the data in a choice of formats, allowing the researcher the ability to maximise the scope of the information available to them.

Furthermore, it is possible to access a Combined Chemical Dictionary (CCD), a chemical database containing entries on over 570 000 substances including:

- Dictionary of Natural Products
- Dictionary of Organic Compounds
- Dictionary of Drugs
- Dictionary of Inorganic and Organometallic Compounds
- Dictionary of Commonly Cited Compounds
- Dictionary of Marine Natural Products
- Dictionary of Food Compounds
- Dictionary of Carbohydrate.

This allows users to search content using the intuitive and powerful MarvinSketch Java Applet and JChem search engine from ChemAxon™ and allows users to draw their own structure queries. A polymers property database also offers a source of scientific and commercial information on over 1000 polymers where each entry includes trade names, properties, constituent monomers, commercial applications, manufacturing processes and references, enhancing the user's experience and offering much greater usability.

Products such as the CRCNetBASE, whilst fundamentally a database of online book products, therefore keep fully abreast of technological developments in digital content provision and linking, thus continually enhancing the value proposition as key digital STM resources.

Textbooks

As monographs appeared to decline in the mid-1990s, so there was a shift among publishers as they piled into textbooks, seeking to replicate the ones that were commercially successful propositions. A new generation of student customers to repeat sales year on year is superficially very attractive. The textbook is also a high-cost, labour-intensive product. It needs to be kept up to date as a full subject review; it requires top authors who need to be kept happy and they will require a significant financial interest in the work; there need to be good in-house development editors who are able to monitor and interpret intelligence on courses in the main markets that the book will serve; and the digital opportunities for 'add-ons' such as CD-ROMs, companion websites, multimedia supplementary material, etc., all come at a cost.

Thus the market has been starting to resist what are becoming very expensive items, and the textbook business is somewhat idiosyncratic in that the people who are recommending the books through adoption for their courses are not the ones who have to pay. Various phenomena are causing problems for the current textbook market:

- the burgeoning second-hand market
- 'student sharing'
- the increased risk of piracy
- competition from new digital media, such as companion websites, bespoke coursepacks (based on current book and journal content) and virtual learning environments.

Nevertheless, a successful textbook in a key subject which keeps up to date and makes the most of digital possibilities remains highly viable for the astute and experienced publisher (see Exhibit 6).

Reference works (including encyclopaedias)

The large reference work and encyclopaedia continue to go through hard times under the challenge of digital. Witness the demise of *Encyclopaedia Britannica* under the challenge of Encarta in the 1990s, and now, as a top reference publisher said to us recently, 'We are getting murdered by Wikipedia and other free reference content'. A good reference work or encyclopaedia has great potential as an online digital product, especially when linked as a multi-layer with a publisher's other digital content, but

Exhibit 6: Textbook case study – *Molecular Biology of the Cell* (Garland Science)

'This is a large book, and it has been a long time in gestation—three times longer than an elephant, five times longer than a whale.' From the Preface of the first edition of *Molecular Biology of the Cell.*

The first edition's author team comprised James D. Watson, Bruce Alberts, Dennis Bray, Julian Lewis, Martin Raff and Keith Roberts who started writing the book in 1978. It was published in 1983 to considerable acclaim (Friedberg, 2005). It is often referred to as 'the Bible' of cell biology due to its role in establishing the parameters of cell biology literacy.

Throughout its five editions the standards set in the first edition have been adhered to, as follows:

Authorship: Alberts, Lewis, Raff and Roberts have been joined by Alexander Johnson and Peter Walter. Each of the authors is responsible for a cluster of chapters while Roberts conceptualises and sketches the illustrations. The chapters are extensively reviewed by scientific experts in the numerous sub-fields covered in each chapter. For each edition, there may be as many as 250 expert reviewers. Each chapter undergoes extensive developmental editing to ensure that the level, voice and style are consistent throughout.

Illustrations: More than half of the illustrations are original to the book. The authors take great care to explain the concepts as carefully in the pictures as in the legends and text. The rest of the illustrations are from scientific literature to ensure scientific accuracy and authority.

Pedagogy: The structure of *Molecular Biology of the Cell* is based upon a formula invented by James Watson for the first edition of *Molecular Biology of the Gene*. Each chapter is divided into short sections under declarative headings known as concept headings.

A brief version of *Molecular Biology of the Cell, Essential Cell Biology*, was published in 1997 and quickly established itself as the leading undergraduate cell biology textbook.

Both books are accompanied by a library of cell biology videos and animations which both reinforce the text's concepts and expand on the content and scope of the book. Other supplements include PowerPoint slides of all figures, extensive problems, quizzes and test questions.

Both books are now available in downloadable e-book format for purchase in their entirety, as individual chapters and for limited-term rentals. In the first six months sales of the e-books are still a small proportion of print sales, although demand is growing and it is expected that e-books will comprise a sizeable proportion of sales within the next 12 months as more cheap e-readers are sold. *Essential Cell Biology* is soon to be available in media-integrated format for use on the iPad, and eventually, for Android devices.

Twenty-five years after the publication of the first edition of *Molecular Biology of the Cell*, it remains the leading book in sales and in intellectual achievement. The global course market is approximately 250 000 students and has been stable for the last 10 years.

the investment required is not insignificant. And the integration of different products is not necessarily straightforward, especially when that content has been digitised to different standards, in different formats or is sitting on different platforms. Despite this, successful products still remain (see Exhibit 7).

There has, however, been growth in recent years of shorter reference works – handbooks – collections of survey articles/entries of around 5000–7000 words (such as the current volume). These are especially popular in STM subjects, and are typically cheaper than monographs in hardback, as most will have the potential for industrial or professional sales. A good, definitive reference handbook can gain real prestige by putting a real stamp on a particular field – as traditional print or replica e-book.

Technical proceedings

Technical proceedings as a product have not changed dramatically in recent years, reflecting their primary purpose as an archival record. They

Exhibit 7: Encyclopaedia case study – The *Routledge Encyclopedia of Philosophy*

The original product

The *Routledge Encyclopedia of Philosophy*, or *REP*, was published as a ten-volume set in 1998. A CD-ROM was also offered as part of the package. The culmination of seven years of intense work by the General Editor Edward Craig and a team of over 20 subject editors, *REP* numbered over 1300 contributors and 2000 entries. Shortly after release of the print version work began on a fully searchable and extensively cross-referenced dynamic Web version, the *Routledge Encyclopedia of Philosophy Online*. Launched in 2001, *REP Online* expands this acclaimed *Encyclopedia* well beyond print reference boundaries. The full content of the classic ten-volume set remains at its core, but *REP Online* is a living, growing resource growing along with the discipline itself. Each year the *REP* releases a diverse range of new material, including newly commissioned entries by leading scholars and revised versions of existing entries. By 2010 *REP Online* contained over 100 new and revised entries.

The marketplace

The market for large-scale online academic reference products such as *REP Online* is driven mainly by academic libraries, which form the core customer base for *REP Online*. Whilst the market for multi-volume print-based reference works has diminished significantly, demand for quality, peer-reviewed academic reference works available online remains strong. The North American market is particularly important. In 2011 individual subscriptions became available for the first time. The marketplace for such digital products faces competition from a variety of sources, some in the form of similar subscription-based products from other publishers and some from free resources such as *The Stanford Encyclopaedia of Philosophy*.

Challenges

As with journals, delivering a steady stream of new quality content remains a key challenge for any online digital reference product such as *REP*. Other challenges come in the form of working with external platform providers and keeping essential parts of the site, such as the home page, up to date; the archiving of entries when revisions or replacements are commissioned; and maintaining the *REP* profile through reputational and trust factors in a marketplace increasingly populated by unreviewed content which can be freely accessed.

remain popular in applied scientific and technical disciplines, such as computer science, where a greater tradition exists for publishing conference papers alongside books and journal articles. Technical proceedings are indeed moving increasingly online, sold as e-books, although often as a supplement to the print edition rather than a substitute.

The digital age brings a number of new challenges and opportunities for publishers of technical proceedings. Dual pressure comes from conference organisers demanding a lower upfront financial commitment towards publication alongside greater project management support from the publisher to bring the publication together, including electronic submission and review software, author templates and instructions, handling of author queries, and managing copyright transfers. Customers are also demanding more sophisticated online products, which may further put pressure on publishers' margins through the need to intervene more on manuscripts to improve consistency of style, introduce XML tagging to aid search and discovery, and host authors' supplementary material.

Delivered effectively, these new requirements can enhance the product, maximise visibility and reinforce good working relationships between the conference and publisher, but the specialisation and investment now involved in securing technical proceedings contracts and selling them in sufficient quantities have narrowed the range of publishers involved in this sphere. Further, Open Access advocates within fields such as computer science have been urging simple author posting of conference proceedings in repositories, as an example of DIY publishing.

Exhibit 8: A technical proceedings case study

Since the 1970s, a prestigious professional membership society based in the UK has published the proceedings of its annual conference on state-of-the-art technical developments in the fields of infrastructure and engineering. The *c*. 70 papers appearing in the final publication total up to 700 pages, and are thoroughly reviewed and selected by a panel of experts drawn from academia and industry.

The organizers pass accepted and edited papers to a commercial publisher as camera ready copy, with a preface prepared by the editorial panel. The publisher adds a contents page, paginates and adds heads and footers to the manuscripts, designs the cover, and then prints, binds and delivers copies in bulk to the conference for distribution to delegates.

The publisher offers the proceedings for general sale after the conference through all usual channels, priced at approximately £150/US$220, with strong appeal to academic and professional libraries as an archive volume. Sales in the low hundreds are typically forecast and prove profitable, with the conference receiving a royalty.

Product development vs. market development

So far, we have looked at the many and varied outputs of scholarly communication as, effectively, standalone products. A single book or database appeals to a set of researchers active in a specific field. Commercial success is a function of the inherent quality of the book or database, how effectively it is promoted to potential customers and how able (and, more importantly, willing) they are to pay.

Does this mean that the performance of a scholarly publishing house is simply the sum of the sales of its products? On a crude level, the answer is of course 'yes'. What it overlooks, though, is a key element in determining underlying and future performance – the competitive environment in which a firm operates.

Take a simple example. Publisher X may have the best book on Genetic Regulation this year and achieve excellent sales. Next year, Publisher Y may put out a superior book in the same field which has far greater appeal for customers. Sales of Publisher X's book are extremely disappointing in the second year. The book is unchanged, but its performance is now lacklustre. It has suffered because its 'market penetration' – the book's share of total sales of Genetic Regulation texts – has declined due to the competing book. Publisher X can respond with a vigorous marketing campaign. Given that there is now a superior product on the market, the results of this are likely to be modest. The book's sales have peaked and will soon decline toward zero (or to the online 'Long Tail', which is much the same thing).

The typical scholarly monograph has a sales life cycle lasting several years. A very few exceptional titles continue selling for a decade or more (Nitterhouse, 2005). To manage this inevitable life cycle pattern of peak and trough, publishers build portfolios of products in their chosen subject areas, with new content added each year. As the sales of individual products move into decline, new products pick up the slack, ideally creating a stable financial performance for the publisher.

Exploring scholarly communication with Ansoff's Product/Market matrix

This portfolio strategy is an example of 'Product Development', one of four core strategies for competitive markets outlined by Igor Ansoff in his Product/Market matrix (Figure 5.7) (Ansoff, 1987).

Fighting for share of an existing market – the 'Market Penetration' strategy – is what Publisher X does when promoting its Genetic Regulation book aggressively to counteract the competitor title. It is a way of extending a book's sales life. Decline will still come, but hopefully later, and with the additional revenues earned outstripping marketing spend.

Product Development – building a portfolio of Genetic Regulation texts – will enable Publisher X to generate a healthy, stable business. This business, however, will only ever be a portion of total sales of books in the field. In other words, it is limited by the size of the publishing market in Genetic Regulation. Publisher X can focus on high-margin products within existing markets, constraining monograph output and emphasising textbooks, and perhaps deploying telesales teams to maximise sales. This is in effect a coping strategy. Sooner or later, the market's limits will be

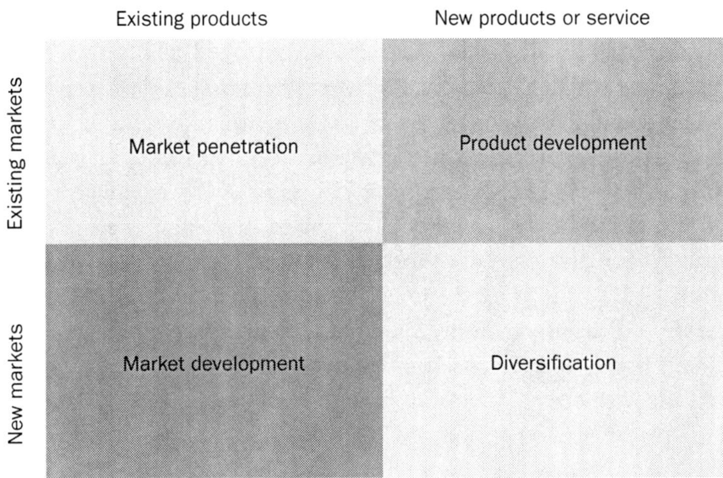

Figure 5.7 **Igor Ansoff's Product/Market matrix**

Source: Igor Ansoff (1987) *New Corporate Strategy*. New York: Wiley. Reproduced by permission.

reached. Further progress depends on Ansoff's other two strategies – 'Market Development' or 'Diversification'.

Market Development involves finding new customers for existing products. This can either mean selling to non-purchasing customers in current markets or seeking new customers in different segments. Publisher X's Genetic Regulation book may have sold well in North America, but have scope to improve in Europe with effective marketing. Alternatively, having sated demand with Genetics researchers, Publisher X might develop a secondary market with Botanists interested in gene regulation. These new markets may be relatively small but, as costs are limited to sales, marketing and distribution, margins can be high.

Publishers are not always the driver of Market Development strategies. Amazon now accounts for 25 per cent of university press book sales (Esposito, 2009) and has expanded the customer base for scholarly books beyond publishers' traditional markets. This is a significant departure from historical practice, where publishers would select and negotiate the market and segments in which a book is sold.

Diversification is the biggest leap of all – creating new products in new markets, preferably building on strength in related areas. It targets the most vibrant, dynamic segments of a market, but is high risk – in terms of both the chance of failure in an unknown market and forgone opportunities in familiar segments. For this reason, Diversification has been called the 'suicide cell' of Ansoff's matrix. And scholarly publishing is an industry which has historically been averse to speculative endeavour, let alone suicidal behaviour. There are consequently few examples of successful product diversification in scholarly and professional publishing. Most impressive is LexisNexis, now a division of Elsevier, with turnover of £2.6bn in 2010.[8] This mighty oak grew from a full-text search facility indexing legal cases in New York and Ohio, launched by Mead Data Central as LEXIS in 1973. By 1980, Mead had hand-keyed all US federal and state legislation, creating a unique, comprehensive resource for the US legal profession. That same year, NEXIS was added, providing journalists with a searchable database of legal news articles (Harrington, 1984). Another illustration, also from Elsevier, is Scopus, which expanded a family of abstracting and indexing products into a comprehensive bibliometric resource capable of competing with Web of Science. A third example is Wiley Job Network, a paid-for recruitment site built on the back of Wiley's publishing business (see http://www.wileyjobnetwork.com).

We mention Diversification in passing. Many of the products created – being in new market segments – cease being scholarly publishing as we recognise it. The rewards can be large, but the risks involved should not be underestimated.

Why Ansoff's model works differently for journals

Translated from books to journals, Ansoff's four strategies take rather different form. Why? Books and journals both experience economies of scale, meaning that unit costs typically decline as portfolios or print runs grow. Journals additionally have 'Network Effects'. This means that their value increases *exponentially* as their community grows (see Exhibit 9). Books conversely have intrinsic value, purchased simply for what is inside their covers.

While a book business benefits from scale, a journal business requires both scale *and* widespread accessibility and visibility within its research communities. This fundamental difference between books and journals was for a long time concealed beneath the superficial similarity of the two printed products, leading some people to assume that the same publishing strategies work for both. This is not the case, as we shall explore.

Exhibit 9: Network Products – and the power of Network Effects

Products which become more valuable the more they are used (and the more users they have) are said to have 'Network Effects'. These are also called 'positive externalities'. Classic examples include telephone networks (of curiosity value if one person owns a phone, hugely powerful once millions connect) and Facebook (of increasing value to users as more of their friends join). Products and markets with Network Effects increase in value *exponentially* the more they are used (Katz, 1994) Metcalfe's Law formalises this for telephone networks, stating that the value of a telecommunications network is proportional to the *square* of the number of users the network has (Gilder, 2003).

Journals exhibit strong Network Effects. If 10 000 scholars read a journal online, it is heavily cited, has a high Impact Factor and is influential in its discipline. A journal with 50 readers is an obscure title in a research niche. All other things being equal, usage determines the relative value of these two journals, even though the cost base of the two is identical. Phil Davis and Leah Solla have generalized this relationship for Chemistry journals, tentatively showing that journal usage has a Power Law relationship with the size of the user base, rising exponentially as users increase (Davis and Solla, 2003).

Books, on the other hand, have no Network Effects. Their value is intrinsic. The hundredth person to read a book has the same reading experience as the first, and value is not changed through use. Whilst uninterested in Network Effects, a book publisher will be highly conscious of economies of scale. A print run of 10 000 books has far lower unit costs than one of 50 copies, creating a far higher margin on each book sold.

Network Effects matter because they amplify differences between journals, and do so disproportionately. The reasons for this are self-evident. A journal in a global 'Big Deal' has higher readership than a self-published title with a handful of subscribers. Likewise, a journal at a subject-specialist publisher like the American Medical

Association is more visible and more highly read than one at a publisher with no other Medical titles. Sales reach, learned society memberships, prominence within a research community, promotion, online platform and researcher habit all generate positive externalities. Some people argue that Open Access, semantic enrichment, data integration and other techniques for embedding content more deeply in the research community have similar effects. The jury is still out, but we should expect that some of these initiatives will prove useful. Journals with strong Network Effects see readership and Impact Factor rise consistently, drawing in a better and better selection of the available papers. Ultimately, these journals rise to the top of their fields, with a hierarchy of journals arrayed below them in accordance with their externalities.

So far, so conventional. Do we really need Network Effects to explain how the journal market operates? We do, and Metcalfe's Law sheds light on why. There are a finite number of researchers in any field. Tenopir and King (2008) have found that the average US scientist reads more than 280 articles annually (obviously this varies between disciplines), a number which is increasing but again is finite. As journals with greater Network Effects gain quality papers, other journals must lose out, concentrating good research increasingly in small clusters of titles. And indeed this is what we see. In Environmental Science, for instance, more than 77 per cent of all JCR-ranked research was published in journals of 100+ papers in 2010, up from 69 per cent in 2006. Over the same period, the median size of journals in the area rose from 68 to 80 articles.[9]

In the wider world, markets governed by Network Effects are extremely hierarchical. The 90 per cent+ market share that Microsoft enjoyed in computer operating systems for some years is the extreme, monopolistic end of the spectrum. Ted Lewis, however, has demonstrated that an equilibrium state for a network market with four significant players is 63 per cent share for the market leader, 26 per cent for the 'fast follower', and just 8 per cent and 2 per cent for the two 'laggards' (Lewis, 2009). The proportions vary between markets and depending on how many participants a market has, but the principle is clear – a single dominant player tends to gain a significant structural advantage in network markets.

What is the optimal strategy for a journal publisher in the age of Network Effects? It is likely to be a hybrid. Journal publishing still contains large fixed costs – for example, in building and developing online platforms, editorial and production processes, and in operating global marketing and sales forces. Economies of scale make many of these costs relatively low as journal portfolios grow. Network Effects meanwhile rise as accessibility and visibility increase, making journals more valuable as their circulation and embeddedness in the research community rise. Publishers who can achieve universal access and high visibility in their research communities, whilst being large enough to achieve economies of scale – and generate positive cashflow – will dominate the next decade of journal publishing.

Intriguingly, this future is business-model neutral. Everything is in play.

Journals succeed when an active, well-networked Editor serves a viable research community to a high standard. Put another way, a network product (the journal) converts the expertise of a network (the research community) into tangible, digestible outputs (articles, issues). Henry Oldenburg achieved this with the launch of *Philosophical Transactions of the Royal Society* in 1665. He could do so because a core 'invisible college' (the membership of the Royal Society) had been deliberately constructed (de Solla Price and Beaver, 1966). Its output was a network product which happened to be a printed journal, the best dissemination technology of the time.

Three significant changes have occurred since the time of Oldenburg, however:

1. *Enhanced communication* – digital technology and the development of social media have transformed researchers' modes of communication, allowing a journal's editorial team to be much closer to its research community and facilitating much faster communication.
2. *Bibliometric analysis* – enabling the editorial team to see clearly the research publication trends in their field of interest, and the position their journal occupies within it.

3 *Authors have a voice* – and are systematically contributing to the journal publishing process for the first time.

Why do these developments matter? They are important because it is now both feasible and realistic for journals and other academic and scientific publications to be finely attuned to their audience and author base, and to evolve in step with their research community. What was previously a staccato back-and-forth exchange characterised by long silences is becoming a continuous process of co-creation, with scholarly communication leading and catalysing cutting-edge research. The more closely a journal matches its community, the more powerful the Network Effects the journal creates.

Let us return to Ansoff's Product/Market matrix and examine why the underlying differences between books and journals might favour divergent publishing strategies. We will not dwell on Diversification strategies, which so often create products other than journals.

Like their book counterparts, journals publishers naturally pursue a Market Penetration strategy for some titles – trying to increase market share for existing journals in existing markets. This involves familiar spadework – setting up electronic submission systems, operating production management systems, producing high-quality print and online issues with increasing rapidity, promotion, conference representation, indexing in a disturbingly wide variety of sources, managing Editorial Boards so that they benefit a journal, improving the author experience, and so on. A competent publisher will undertake these activities as a matter of course.

The journals strategy conundrum – product or market development?

The core decision a publisher must make is whether to concentrate on Product Development (launching new journals or acquiring titles) or Market Development (selling current journals to new audiences) – or try both. Which approach is best varies with each different journal list.

Product development in journals publishing

Product Development in a journals business focuses on building networks of researchers around a title. In practice, this depends upon both the Editor's and the publisher's ability to refine and improve the journal in light of that community's evolving needs, so generating the strongest Network Effects. We consider this in the context of new launch journals first.

Achieving best fit with the community takes many forms. For instance, new technologies can help researchers work more effectively. In 2008, Taylor & Francis' journal *Food Additives and Contaminants* spun off a Part B publishing surveillance papers. Food scientists need to keep track of problems highlighted in these surveillance papers, often wanting to engage the detail of the data rather than the accompanying research article. We thus built a dedicated database containing the datasets of all papers published in *FAC* Part B, allowing researchers to search systematically for data on additives and contaminants pertinent to their research.

New journals can also provide higher levels of service than incumbents. *Remote Sensing Letters* launched in 2010 to provide rapid communication in the remote sensing field. The Editors aim to make decisions on papers within 50 days of submission, and after acceptance edited articles are published online on average in 30 days. The response has been emphatic. The journal received 174 submissions in its first year, whilst usage in the first half of 2011 is 67 per cent up on the same period in 2010. *RSL* will receive it first Impact Factor in 2012.

Effective launches can help new research communities consolidate. The award-winning Routledge journal *Jazz Perspectives* has provided a rallying post for researchers in its field, whilst *Celebrity Studies* is currently raising the prestige of an intriguing interdisciplinary research area. Taylor & Francis' journal *Environmental Communication*, driven forward by Editor Professor Steve Depoe, helped the International Environmental Communication Association (IECA) form in 2011. The IECA already has 214 members,[10] still part way through its inaugural year.

What is true of new journals often applies to existing journals. Professor Len Evans, Editor-in-Chief of *Biofouling*, identified that authors increasingly expected very quick turnaround times. In 2007, Taylor & Francis established a 3-week Accept-to-Online-Publication time for the journal, backing the new service level with vigorous promotion. Between 2007 and 2010, full rate library subscriptions increased by 14 per cent (they had previously been in decline), revenue rose 134 per cent and gross margin improved significantly. Submissions over the same period grew by 148 per cent, full text downloads by 222 per cent and citations by 60 per cent. The journal has never been in better shape.

Such initiatives enable a journal to mesh efficiently with its community, extending its network of researchers. Their benefit is multiplied many times when sales reach makes the journal available widely across the globe. It makes no difference how this sales reach is achieved – consortial deals and Open Access can both deliver very wide readership.

Quite how much expanded sales reach can enhance a journal is demonstrated by a natural experiment. *Environmental Technology* joined Taylor & Francis in 2008, just short of the journal's 30th anniversary. Between 2007 (the last year with the previous publisher, where it was published online but had no consortial sales deals) and 2010 usage increased by a breathtaking 2726 per cent. The Impact Factor is on a strong upward path, rising in 2009 and 2010, and the journal will publish 67 per cent more pages in 2012 than it did in 2007.

Sales models can create substantial challenges for publishers pursuing a Product Development strategy through new journal launches, however. Should new journals be included in sales deals to drive usage and gain an Impact Factor in the shortest time, or excluded to allow full rate subscriptions to grow? Some publishers have concluded that there is no answer to this riddle, and now only launch new titles on Open Access models. This throws up questions itself. Why should an author pay to publish in an unproven title? There is a genuine concern that Open Access publishing may not serve poorly funded, niche research areas effectively, especially those in Humanities and Social Science, and that it will become increasingly difficult to find appropriate outlets in these fields.

What is undeniable is that journals need to maximise access to their research networks, and so generate strong enough Network Effects to compete with established journals. Which economically sustainable business model is best able to deliver this access will be the subject of heated discussion for many years to come.

Market development in journals publishing

A journals Market Development strategy utilises many of the same approaches, but has the differential goal of establishing a title within an unfamiliar research network. Verspagen and Werker (2003) conducted an interesting study of how a mix of existing and new journals moved into the field of Evolutionary Economics after its rebirth in the early 1980s. Most successful of all was *Research Policy*, a wide-ranging journal which researchers identified as the most important journal in this field both pre-1985 and in 2003. The journal was established at the start of the period, but diversified to capture this emergent area and remain a key outlet within it.

As well as expand across disciplinary boundaries, a journal can spread its geographical footprint. *Regional Studies* introduced German and French abstracts in 2002 to build readership in those countries and raise the Regional Studies Association's profile there. Spanish abstracts followed in 2004, and Mandarin in 2008. Between 2002 and 2010, published papers from German and French researchers grew by 50 per cent and citations to the journal by 170 per cent,[11] testament to the success of this targeted internationalisation strategy.

But how do Editorial initiatives of this sort help develop a business? Journal publishing is what is sometimes called a 'dog food business'. Purchasers are not reached directly, but rather by influencing users. Market share is built first in the form of quality articles, which drive readership and so citations, generating high Impact Factor. This in turn draws in better submissions, raising the standard of articles published. It is often described as a 'virtuous circle', and is a demonstration of Network Effects in practice. Increasingly, librarians refer to usage data when deciding whether to renew a subscription or to purchase a large sales collection. It follows that Market Development strategies which successfully increase a journal's quality and worldwide appeal will tend to generate revenue for the publisher, even if this takes the negative form of protecting revenue which would otherwise have been lost.

Market development strategies can also directly earn revenue. Paid supplements are a very profitable addition to the journal mix, bringing high-margin income for relatively little work. It is still possible, if rare, for journals in the Medical and Pharmacological sectors to earn six-figure sums from supplements each year. Similarly, article reprints have underlain the profitability of Pharma journals for decades. What has become apparent in recent years, however, is that these non-recurrent sales can disappear rapidly in the face of recession, government regulation and low-cost online alternatives. They are unlikely to regain their former importance.

As with books, not all Market Development is publisher-driven. Google is now a powerful source of journal readership and draws in pay-per-view sales from a much broader-based audience. DeepDyve (www.deepdyve.com) wants to make a business from selling journal content outside traditional markets, using an 'iTunes' business model for short-term rental of articles at low prices. Meanwhile peer-to-peer networks like Mendeley (www.mendeley.com) have the potential to open up new markets whilst simultaneously demonetising them, a sort of 'peer-to-peer' model of article posting. The Chinese curse exhorts: 'May you live in interesting times'. These are interesting times indeed.

Choosing between product and market development

Our original question asked whether a journal publisher should emphasise Product or Market Development, or indeed both. There is no simple answer to this – it depends on the circumstances of an individual journal list and the environment it operates in. What we can say is that the research community continually grows and evolves. Much of this change can be accommodated by existing journals (Ansoff's Market Penetration strategy). But emerging research areas may require different kinds of journals (think of the innovative *Journal of Visualized Experiments* or *Journal of Maps*, for instance). Publishers must continue to expand their portfolio to meet these changing requirements, through launches or acquisition. If they don't, other publishers will almost certainly occupy the vacant ground. Most likely, several publishers will have journals in a field, competing for primacy. The winner, as we have noted before, will be the one whose journals are best able to generate Network Effects and draw the community together around them.

If Product Development is an essential strategy for keeping a publisher's portfolio aligned with research output, there is also a place for Market Development. This may best be thought of as a higher level activity – a means of extracting greater revenue from maturing journals.

When a journal is young, Product Development is the optimal strategy. As it grows and establishes itself, the focus shifts to Market Penetration. And finally, as the journal matures, it should seek out opportunities for revenue from non-traditional markets – stressing Market Development. Ansoff's matrix gives us a key to managing the life cycle of a journal.

Programme management and portfolio development

We now turn to how, and why, publishers build portfolios of journals. Historically, the barriers to entering scholarly publishing have been high. Typesetting and printing were highly skilled tasks before Desktop Publishing, and were costly. Conversely, incentives were limited, with most scholarly publishing performed by university presses and learned societies as a labour of love. These society journals – located at the centre of perhaps thousands of researchers in a given subject – had excellent, unparalleled connectedness to their research community, providing a large competitive advantage.

As we have seen, the world began changing with Robert Maxwell's commercialisation of scholarly publishing in the 1950s, and was then transformed by the affordable, powerful computer technology from the 1980s. Now, one person can launch and run a journal. They may not do it well, but if they can generate sufficient submissions, they will be able to publish articles and issues, and perhaps to generate revenue.

Does that mean that everyone will develop portfolios of successful journals? A glance around the scholarly publishing world suggests not. Elsevier, Springer and Wiley published 46.9 per cent of all articles indexed in Thomson Reuters' *Journal Citation Reports* in 2009.[12] Independent presses publish individual titles for sure, and small clusters possibly, but to develop a quality programme requires scale and many, many skills. Indeed, managing a large journal portfolio is significantly more complicated than was ever the case in the past. Aside from academic Editors, it requires the collaboration of experts in copy-editing, typesetting, proof reading, printing, warehousing, online publication, digital conversion and content management, website design and hosting, submissions and review software, sales systems, customer services, marketing, library relations, editorial management, bibliometrics, finance, strategy and human resources, *inter alia* – and probably needs to be able to deploy these skills in many countries globally.

Why do publishers go to the trouble of building large journal programmes? The short answer is that only on very large lists can both economies of scale and Network Effects be fully realised. The coexistence of these two forces has long been recognised as a characteristic feature of the software industry (Schmalensee, 2000). Journals, unlike books, are beginning to behave like an online business.

Network Effects and economies of scale

Economies of scale are generated in familiar ways: printers make special rates for a publisher who brings 1000 journals; it is more affordable to attend a conference relevant for 50 journals than to display a single title, and likewise to spread the investment required for an online platform across a large portfolio; global sales teams generate more revenue per transaction on larger lists. These economies of scale provide a business with the cashflow needed to fund future investment and development. Network Effects enable the publisher's journals to compete effectively in the market. They are maximised by worldwide sales reach, excellent peer review systems, production which is in step with the research community, a richly interlinked online platform, researcher loyalty and effective marketing strategies.

A journal publisher that currently achieves economies of scale but not Network Effects may well be profitable and successful today – but won't be in a decade's time. Both are now essential for success, and both are optimised on very large portfolios.

Publishers have attained large scale through four basic strategies:

- *Society Friend* – providing flexible, tailored services which make learned societies want to publish with you. At a certain point, positive feedback loops kick in, as societies trust publishers associated with high-quality society journals and who have the infrastructure (both in systems and attitude) required for effective society publishing. *Blackwell, the so-called 'honorary not-for-profit' prior to their acquisition by Wiley, built a comprehensive journal business with this strategy through the 1990s. Sage is now seemingly trying to replicate that strategy.*
- *Factory Ships* – build presence by creating fleets of very large, well-managed journals and actively seeking out quality papers. This is analogous to the Factory Ships which dominate modern fisheries, locating fish with advanced sonar and harvesting them on an industrial scale. The strategy particularly suits owned journals, where a publisher has a free hand to amend the journal to best suit the Factory Ship role. As large journals tend to be cost-efficient, this can be a highly profitable publishing model. *Elsevier has been extremely effective at acquiring and developing Factory Ship journals, particularly in STM disciplines.*
- *Platform Publishing* – this is a software industry concept, which involves taking a successful product and cloning it for a new field. Wiley's phenomenally successful For Dummies series is a classic example of platform publishing, taking a clearly defined formula and adapting it for a wide range of topics. A different take on platform publishing is given by Cell Press, where Elsevier have created a family of five quality journals around the single title *Cell* since its purchase in 1999. Even more prolific has been *Nature*, which has now sired 37 daughter journals, all bearing the name '*Nature...*'.
- *New Kid in Town* – when one has little or no presence in a discipline, an option is to launch titles in emerging and evolving research fields.

The risks of launching in an unknown field are, of course, high, and librarians are additionally reluctant to subscribe to new titles. For these reasons, many established publishers have turned away from new journal launches. It is perhaps not a coincidence that smaller, 'upstart' publishers have launched titles in the niches left unoccupied, with mixed success. Well-thought through, intelligently conceived launches – like those of Public Library of Science – have flourished. Many others have not. *Routledge has attained a leading position in Social Science fields such as Education, Politics and International Relations, and Area Studies, driven mainly from a strategy of launches by the then Carfax imprint in the 1985–95 period.*

Starting with a core of quality titles makes all of these strategies easier. Having business intelligence gleaned from strategic priorities of government and funders' research priorities, as well as links with key up-and-coming scientists and academic research 'stars' can help sharpen the portfolio focus. Throughout, the goal should be to produce good journals publishing high-quality papers. It is not necessary for a title to be the best in its field, but it must serve its research community supremely well, continuously evolving in the light of feedback from scholars. If any of these strategies are done well, they can then be monetised through employing an appropriate business model.

Delivering on publishing strategies

In reality, most publishers blend these approaches depending on the opportunities of their particular market segments. For example, a significant portion of Elsevier's Factory Ship journals arrived in acquisitions such as North Holland (1971), Pergamon (1991) and Academic Press (2001), while Elsevier's market-leading presence in Food Science and Geography arose from the New Kid in Town strategy of systematically launching journals in emerging disciplines. Meanwhile, Elsevier publishes many high-quality society journals in the Health Sciences, and pursues Platform Publishing with the highly successful Trends journals and Advances annuals. There is no one right way, but rather a suite of strategies to be employed according to the specific external conditions of any journal market, and internal corporate environment.

The desired end point is a comprehensive, quality journal portfolio in the publisher's chosen subject area(s). This allows economies of scale to be realised, and significant Network Effects to be generated. For some publishers, one subject or a cluster of related subjects is enough. The American Institute of Physics has recently refocused on its core journal programme, for instance (Bousfield, 2011). Others aspire to complete spectrum coverage. An intriguing area for future investigation will be how journals with different roles in the research community – review journals, mainstream Factory Ships, niche sub-field outlets, letters journals, thought leaders, and so on – combine to form journal ecosystems within (or without) a publisher's portfolio.

A key task becomes the development of metrics to understand journal health and ensure that each title in a portfolio makes a genuine contribution to the portfolio. If not, disposal or closure may be required. Writing almost 15 years ago, Gillian Page, Bob Campbell and Jack Meadows provided checklists for assessing the health of a journal and determining remedial action if it is ailing (Page *et al.*, 1997). These contain sensible advice and proven formulae for managing complex situations. Today's reality is perhaps more pragmatic. Faced with engrained difficulties, the simplest option is to consult the journal's authors through a longitudinal or web survey, examine the journal's key bibliometrics against its close competitors and discuss the results with the Editor-in-Chief. If a clear action plan is not produced, the journal may well have reached its final destination. There is so much information available today that the challenge is not so much defining malady, but rather creating a consensual, robust plan for resolution.

As we earlier observed, the changing dynamics of journal publishing have favoured certain publishers over others. Where once large society journals were dominant, they have increasingly ceded primacy to Factory Ship journals (currently, the state-of-the-art repository for Network Effects) and the nascent 'mega-journals' like *Zootaxa* and *PLoS ONE*. A key question now for journal publishers is whether self-organising groups of researchers, drawn together around issues of Open Access and data transparency through social media, will take the mantle from Factory Ships. This question won't be answered for many years to come.

Arguments around the 'Serials Crisis' are much wider than differing business models – they hinge on who has the power (and moral authority?) to control the research communication process, and what level of services and quality standards (and their inherent costs) are required by those producing and consuming (and assessing?) the material output of research communities worldwide. Will semantic tagging marginalise established journal publishers? Will automated parsing systems render traditional copy-editing and typesetting irrelevant? Will Open Data – i.e. the notion that some data should be freely available to everyone to use, data-mine, mash up and republish as they wish, without restriction by copyright, patents or other 'ownership' mechanisms – redefine the relationships between researcher, government, research funder and publisher? We can but guess at the answers to these questions, but the journey is likely to be eventful!

What publishers can do now is continue to manage their journal portfolios intelligently with the long term in mind, manage each journal individually, invest in technology which improves researchers' publishing experience and experiment in search of newer, more powerful modes of communication. Positioned thus, they will be able to incorporate and benefit from breakthrough technologies when they arrive.

The Tao of Academic Publishing

The world has changed, but the fundamentals haven't. The other major philosopher who employs a river-image is Wittgenstein. He distinguishes between the movement of the waters on the riverbed and the shift of the bed itself; and states that the bank of the river consists partly of hard rock subject to no alteration or to only an imperceptible one, and partly of sand, which may get washed away, or perhaps more sand will be deposited (Wittgenstein, 1979). For our purposes, the moving waters could be seen here as representing the changing journal content and its surrounding context and technologies, and the riverbed as the basic structure of scholarly communication with the solid rock and the more mutable sand. Will the rocky riverbed itself change, with some of the river banks getting swept away – a true paradigm shift heralding a new age of scholarly communication – or is it all just the sand and shingle moving around with the flow of the waters?[13]

Scholarly publishing involves groups of researchers judging what is worthwhile work through conference presentations, sharing drafts and research outputs, informal discussion and ultimately peer review; publishers then convert this material into readable and/or functional form and distribute it to small groups of researchers active in that field through journals; researchers read and cite the work, citing papers of most relevance, and so create a hierarchy of importance for papers, journals and authors; in turn, this influences future submission behaviour, creating a strong positive feedback loop.

Put another way, there are huge volumes of communication between researchers about their work. Publishers convert this into formal, version-of-record papers – which are the building blocks of future science. Modern publishers have taken on the mantle of latter-day alchemists, turning the lead of grey literature into the gold of highly cited papers.

As Michael Mabe notes elsewhere in this volume, the journal age was launched by Henry Oldenburg in 1665, establishing the four principles of registration, dissemination, peer review and archive. These have been the constants, the unchanging, immutable bedrock of scholarly communications – yet are there signs, for example in the rise of the scientist's blog, that they represent a riverbed which is eroding? To these principles we may now add further key publishing requirements which the journals industry is best placed to provide, namely discoverability and access – and which can be characterised as representing a new, more permanent deposit on the riverbed and river banks.

Vannevar Bush announced the beginning of the end of this first journal age with his 1945 essay, 'As we may think' (Bush, 1945). Bush dreamt of a time when a globally networked community of scientists collaborated together for the common good. There are many indications that that time has come.

Potentially, we now stand at the beginning of the second journal age.

Familiar attributes guide good publishers – service for authors, relationship management, the centrality of peer review, dissemination and high-quality publications, *inter alia*. On these solid foundations, network science is rising, shaped by powerful Network Effects and lubricated by incredibly rapid, seamless communication between scholars. It will be a fluid, continuously evolving form of science, closer to the evolution of synapses in a brain than the clattering iron frame of a printing press. Above all else, it will be a competitive world, in which progressive, valuable initiatives are rewarded and useless, irrelevant activities are not. We can be certain that community relevance, brand, quality, reputation and the trust factor – all deriving from 'root journals' – will continue to play a strong role in research network communication processes and products.

Book publishing is experiencing transformation on a similar scale. Whether this signals the end of the modern book age – as ushered in by Johannes Gutenberg with movable type printing in 1439 – or simply the latest reinvention of an endlessly reinvented industry remains to be seen.

What bedrock strategies should guide the publisher in times of such profound change? Happily, the core values of effective publishing remain unchanged:

1. Treating each publication as its own 'small business' is a real differentiator even within the business template – the aim should be for each publication to serve its own particular niche and network to the highest standard possible.
2. Is each title positioned to deal with our changing world? Every publication needs to re-examine its aims and scope and its editorial policies as new technology opens up new content and market opportunities.
3. The external environment is harsh and will show up the badly equipped – so publishers need to deal with pressures from researchers, authors, editors, societies, research funders, libraries and governments, and be efficient in dealing with them.
4. We should be as concerned with the intellectual health of our publications as we are with their commercial health – as a quality driver.
5. Quality and excellence will be rewarded, in better publications, better usage, better sales, better revenues and better returns.

It is up to us who work in the industry to follow the Zen of Publishing, and balance the Yin of Change with the Yang of Continuity.

> 'Returning to the source is stillness, which is the way of nature. The way of nature is unchanging. Knowing constancy is insight.'
> Lau Tzu, *Tao Te Ching* (*c.* 604–531 BCE)

Acknowledgments and sources of further information

We would like to thank the following colleagues at Taylor & Francis Group for their contributions to and assistance in developing this chapter: Alan Jarvis, Denise Schank, Ian White, Daniel Keirs, Colin Bulpitt, Tony Bruce, Jo Cross, James Hardcastle, Oliver Walton and Lyndsey Dixon. The responsibility for the use of their helpful information and contributions remains, of course, the authors'.

Thanks to Bob Campbell and Ian Borthwick for their editorial guidance, and especially to Bob Campbell for helping develop the philosophical aspects of this chapter.

We are also grateful for industry material available through the trade bodies', researcher and industry groups' websites, where there is a motherlode of further information and references:

Publishing Research Consortium (PRC): http://www.publishingresearch.net/

International Association of Scientific, Technical and Medical Publishers (STM): http://www.stm-assoc.org/

Association of Learned, Professional and Society Publishers (ALPSP): http://www.alpsp.org.uk/

UK Serials Group (UKSG): http://www.uksg.org/

Publishers Association (PA): http://www.publishers.org.uk/

The Association of American Publishers (AAP): http://www.publishers.org/

Society for Scholarly Publishing (SSP): http://www.sspnet.org/

Research Information Network: http://www.rin.ac.uk/

Centre for Information Behaviour and the Evaluation of Research, University College London: http://www.ucl.ac.uk/infostudies/research/ciber/downloads/

Notes

1. Word, reason, plan, or account, the fundamental order in a changing world. There is a publishing journal, founded by Gordon Graham, formerly Chairman of Butterworths: *LOGOS: The Journal of the World Book Community* http://www.brill.nl/logos
2. http://michaelnielsen.org/blog/is-scientific-publishing-about-to-be-disrupted
3. http://www.openscience.org/blog/?p=269
4. A good source tracking the development of e-journals in the 1990s is Okerson (2000).
5. http://www.arl.org/resources/pubs/specscholmono/renfro~print.shtml
6. http://www.aaupnet.org/images/stories/documents/aaupbusinessmodels2011.pdf
7. http://touchpress.com/titles/thewasteland
8. *Reed Elsevier Annual Report 2010* (2011), accessed online 26 September 2011: http://reports.reedelsevier.com/ar10/business_review/lexisnexis/2010_financial_performance
9. Data collated from Thomson Reuters' 2009 Journal Citation Reports, with thanks to James Hardcastle in Taylor & Francis' Research & Business Information team.

10. Data retrieved from http://environmentalcomm.org/founding-members on 27 September 2011
11. Data retrieved from Thomson Reuters' Web of Knowledge on 27 September 2011.
12. Data collated from Thomson Reuters' 2009 Journal Citation Reports, with thanks to James Hardcastle and Jo Cross in Taylor & Francis' Research & Business Information team.
13. We are grateful to our Editor, Bob Campbell, for bringing the philosophers' river-images to our attention and starting to elaborate this idea in the context of a possible journals industry paradigm shift.

References

Ansoff, I. (1987) *New Corporate Strategy*. New York: Wiley.

Bousfield, D. (2011) AIP chooses to focus on core business. *Outsell Insights* 28 June 2011.

Bush, V. (1945) As we may think. *The Atlantic* 176(1): 101–8.

Cox, B. (2002) The Pergamon phenomenon 1951–1991: Robert Maxwell and scientific publishing. *Learned Publishing*, 15: 273–8.

Davis, P.M. and Solla, L. (2003) An IP-level analysis of usage statistics for electronic journals in chemistry: making inferences about user behavior. *Journal of the American Society for Information Science and Technology* 54(11): 1062–8.

Esposito, J. (2009) Creating a consolidated online catalogue for the University Press community. *LOGOS: The Journal of the World Book Community* 20(1–4): 42–63.

Friedberg E.C. (2005) *The Writing Life of James D. Watson*. Woodbury, NY: Cold Spring Harbor Laboratory Press.

Gilder, G. (1993) Metcalfe's law and legacy. *Forbes ASAP.*

Harrington, W.G. (1984) A brief history of computer-assisted legal research. *Law Library Journal* 77(3): 543–56.

Jasco, P. (2000) A look at the endangered species of the database world. *Information World Review* 164: 72–3.

Katz, M. (1994) Systems competition and network effects. *Journal of Economic Perspectives* 8(2): 93–115.

Lewis, T.G. (2009) *Network Science: Theory and Practice*. Hoboken, NJ: Wiley.

Nitterhouse, D. (2005) *Digital Production Strategies for Scholarly Publishers*. Chicago: University of Chicago Press.

Okerson, A. (2000) Presentation to an EBSCO Seminar, 'A History of E-journals in 10 Years: and What it Teaches Us', Jerusalem, 13 August.

Page, G., Campbell, R. and Meadows, J. (1997) 'Managing a list of journals', *Journal Publishing*. Cambridge, UK: Cambridge University Press, pp. 321–45.

Schmalensee, R. (2000) Antitrust issues in Schumpeterian industries. *The American Economic Review* 90(2): 192–6.

Schumpeter, J.A. (1975, orig. pub. 1942) 'Creative destruction', *Capitalism, Socialism and Democracy.* New York: Harper, pp 82–5.

Shiner, R.A. (1974) Wittgenstein and Heraclitus: Two River-Images. *Philosophy*, 49: 191–7.
de Solla Price, D. and Beaver, D. (1966) Collaboration in an Invisible College. *American Psychologist* 21(11), 1011–18.
Tenopir, C. and King, D.W. (2008) Electronic journals and changes in scholarly article seeking and reading patterns. *D-Lib Magazine* 14(11/12).
Verspagen, B. and Werker, C. (2003) The invisible college of the economics of innovation and technological change. *Estudios de economía aplicada* 21(3): 393–419.
Wittgenstein, L. (1979) *On Certainty*. Oxford: Basil Blackwell.

Development of journal publishing business models and finances

John S. Haynes

Abstract: This chapter provides an overview of journal publishing business models highlighting revenue generation, cost management and aspects of financial performance including the profit and loss statement. It also provides an overview of financial management for a portfolio of journals.

Key words: Journal publishing business models, revenue generation, cost management, profitability.

Introduction

The opportunities and challenges facing today's journal publishers are both exciting and daunting. A financial perspective is essential not only for large commercial publishers managing many titles but also for learned societies publishing a single journal that helps support other society programs. A successful scholarly journal program requires the creation and development of a high-level business strategy as well as the ability to implement cost-effective programs for authors, readers, editors, referees, librarians and other customers. The essential component of a successful business strategy involves a sustainable business model in which revenues are in balance with costs and overheads so as to meet financial objectives in an ongoing way.

This chapter sets out to review journal business models and finances and outline how new developments have impacted on the business of running a successful journal program. This is relevant today, as journal publishing is undergoing a significant transformation that may be as disruptive as the changes taking place in other content industries such as newspapers, magazines and music.

The first journal devoted wholly to science was *Philosophical Transactions*, created by Henry Oldenburg in 1665. Oldenburg published the journal at his own expense under an arrangement with The Royal Society that would have allowed him to retain any profits. It seems that the journal was not a financial success during Oldenburg's lifetime. Fast forward 350 years to the present day and if Oldenburg were still around he would have been surprised to see the business models playing out in the world of scholarly publishing.

In the last decades of the 20th century journal publishing tended to be an industry of slow change. In terms of business model there was little innovation with the traditional subscription model in ascendance. In contrast, the last 10–15 years have seen publishers enter a more active period of new business model development, with new players, innovation and entrepreneurship. A number of factors are driving these changes, such as:

- Economic disruption in mature markets (e.g. Western Europe, North America and Japan)
- Continued growth in the number of researchers worldwide and the associated growth in the research literature
- The continued popularity and success of the journal as a means to communicate and disseminate scholarly research and serve as a means of 'scholarly reputation management'
- New technology
- Regulation and legislation from governments and their agencies
- The emergence of a small number of large publishers
- Funding agencies, such as NIH, Wellcome Trust and Max Planck Society, taking a more active role in scholarly communication

The framework for this chapter revolves around a number of themes. The first relates to business models and revenue generation. The second theme covers cost management, for example how outsourcing and technology play a role. The next provides an overview of financial strategy, profitability and pricing, highlighting the importance of the three financial statements, particularly the profit and loss statement. The final theme before the conclusion is about journals as a portfolio.

Business models for scholarly journals

The term business model simply relates to how revenue is generated. Scholarly journal publishing is similar to other content industries in respect of the business models available. Whether it be newspapers (advertisers and readers), music (CD sales, iTunes downloads), television/radio (subscriptions, personal pledges, advertisers), there are essentially four revenue-generating business models:

- The reader/user or their proxy pays for content (the traditional subscription model)
- The author or their proxy pays for publication services (author pays)
- Financial support or subsidy from a sponsor
- Aggregating and packaging audiences to sell advertising

This section reviews each of these four business models. In terms of revenue generation, publishers can apply a single business model or models in combination. As for any business, the challenge is to have a sustainable model that meets customer needs in a competitive market, where revenue growth is likely to be a relevant financial objective.

Reader pays model

The reader pays model involves a subscriber paying a fee for an agreed period of time, usually one calendar year, to access content. In the past, the fee was usually paid in advance with the publisher delivering the printed issue at a determined frequency throughout the year. Nowadays, content is typically delivered incrementally online as each article is published with print as an optional extra, sometimes for an additional fee. The subscriber may be an individual but is typically an institutional library. In terms of cash flow, this model is beneficial to the publisher because subscription fees are paid in advance of the subscription period before many costs are incurred by the publisher.

Before the internet era, institutional libraries (for example, academic, government, corporate libraries) would typically subscribe to individual titles selected by an acquisitions or collection development librarian in consultation with a library committee composed of faculty. The primary mode of delivery was print. Since the development of online journals and with the emergence of a small number of very large publishers, content has been bundled into so-called 'Big Deals'. The Big Deal was created partly in response to the so-called 'serials crisis'. This can be described as a ratchet effect in the following way: there is a growing number of researchers in the world. These researchers conduct more research and publish more research articles. This has resulted in journals getting larger and more new journals being launched. Consequently, journal subscription rates rose faster than the cost of living and faster than library budgets. Consequently, libraries cancelled subscriptions to journals, limiting access to content. Annual subscription prices were ratcheted up another notch to take account of subscription attrition.

For some journals as well as there being an institutional subscription market, there is also a market for personal subscriptions to individuals. The best examples are *Science* and *Nature* which include magazine-style content blended with broad scientific coverage. Other examples are titles for a professional audience such as engineering and medicine. Learned societies often make their journals available to members as part of the membership package or at a low personal rate.

The individual market can be an important segment for some journals to widen readership, increase visibility and generate revenue. The dynamics between these two segments of the market needs to be fully understood to make effective pricing decisions. Publishers are tending to see individual subscriptions decline. This is partly as journals get larger and require more shelf space in the office, and also because institutional libraries and publishers have been successful in licensing content and making it easily and conveniently available online, removing the need for researchers to wait for the printed issue to arrive.

The dynamics between print and online editions, and institutional and individual sales, can be further complicated where journals have a significant revenue from classified or display advertising in the print edition. Media rates for selling online ads are much lower than selling ads in a printed issue and publishers are finding 'yields' from online advertising are much lower than for print. This situation is not likely to change in the near future, making publishers with significant print advertising revenue reluctant to cease the hard copy, with its associated costs.

In the print world, an institution often subscribed to multiple copies of the same journal (main library, department reading rooms, etc.). In the online world, these multiple subscriptions are being replaced gradually by a single campus-wide licence providing access to the online version, sometimes as part of multi-year deals. Part of this trend has also seen libraries discontinuing print subscriptions all together. The transition from print to online has been continuing since the mid 1990s and for some publishers the proportion of subscribers taking online only can be as high as 70 per cent. For the publisher, this requires decisions and policies on how to price legacy print subscriptions, terms and conditions for site-wide licenses and when to stop producing print issues all together.

As in any market, supply and demand are important economic factors. In scholarly journals, the demand curve continues to climb as more researchers fuel the growth of existing journals and spawn the development of new titles, for example in new or interdisciplinary research fields. Mabe (2003) has estimated that the number of journals has grown steadily over the last 200 years at around 3.5 per cent per year. On the supply side, the academic library (the primary paying customer for academic journals) is under continued financial pressure as a result of library budgets not keeping pace with inflation or even declining in absolute terms. The long recession starting in 2008 has seen renewed economic pressure in the three large mature markets of the USA, Western Europe and Japan. It seems likely that these financial constraints will continue and have a serious impact on all stakeholders in the journals enterprise. Consequently, publishers are eagerly establishing new markets, for example, in the so-called BRIC (Brazil, Russia, India and China) countries, and looking for innovative ways to add value, for example the use of semantic technology to enrich and tag content.

Publishers and librarians have also responded to the supply and demand pressures, publishers by bundling content and librarians by forming purchasing consortia or collectives.

Bundling and multi-journal packages

The last 20 years has seen the emergence of a small number of very large STM publishers. Currently, the four largest STM publishers (Elsevier, Wiley-Blackwell, Taylor & Francis and Springer) account for a combined total of approximately 6000–7000 journals. Each of these large publishers has created multi-journal packages bundling journals into online collections. These bundles are offered to librarians at a price that reflects a discount from the 'catalogue' price. Discounts vary but are typically in the 15–20 per cent range. This approach has become known as the 'Big Deal' and is sometimes referred to as the 'all you can eat' model.

Smaller and medium-sized publishers and society publishers have also followed suit. The Royal Society of Chemistry offers RSC Gold and American Institute of Physics has AIP Complete. For society publishers with only a single title or small list, then the option to bundle is restricted unless they co-operate with other organisations. The ALPSP Learned Journals Collection (in partnership with Swets) is an initiative whereby smaller ALPSP member publishers work together, through Swets (a subscription agent), to sell a combined package of their journals to consortia and other large customers. This cross-publisher package is an effective way for librarians to acquire content from multiple smaller publishers (http://aljc.swets.com/).

Consortia

In response to the increasing pressure on library budgets and the challenge librarians face to stretch acquisition funds ever further, libraries have grouped together into cooperatives or purchasing consortia. The development of consortia started in the late 1980s, OhioLINK being one of the first examples. This has grown to be a consortium of 88 Ohio college and university libraries, and the State Library of Ohio, that work together to provide Ohio students, faculty and researchers with the information they need for teaching and research (http://www.ohiolink.edu/).

Consortia operate along the following broad lines:

- Content is licensed from the publisher for a multi-year term (often 3 years)
- The 'base' price paid by the consortia to the publisher is typically the total amount of the subscription value of previously subscribed content from each of the consortia members
- There is a premium or access fee that is negotiated between the publisher and consortium that enables members of the consortium to access previously unsubscribed journal content
- Annual price increases are usually subject to a price cap
- There is a method to add new content to the collection at an agreed price

Consortia have provided a mutual benefit for both publisher and librarian. Consortia members have access to more content for a relatively low additional cost, whilst the publisher benefits from additional revenue and increasing the visibility of their content at a larger number of institutions. The International Coalition of Library Consortia has over 200 active members around the world and their website provides useful background (http://www.library.yale.edu/consortia/). The Consortium Directory Online (www.consortiumdirectory.com) is a comprehensive directory of the library consortium market and a useful resource for publishers. With the impact of the long recession of 2008 still being felt in academic libraries, the need for publishers and library customers to have flexible solutions in place in these uncertain times will be a key component in the continued development of consortia.

For useful background on licensing models and public domain templates for standard license agreements, a useful site can be found at http://www.licensingmodels.org/.

Pay-per-view purchase and rental

Pay-per-view (PPV) is another form of 'reader pays' model. Most PPV schemes operate on the basis of charging a fee (ranging from a few dollars up to the $20–30) to a reader who would not normally have access to a title because they are not based at a subscribing institution. PPV revenues generally make up a small percentage of total revenue for any journal, in comparison with subscription revenue and license fees. For new journals, where the library has not yet decided to subscribe, then PPV converting into a subscription once a pre-set threshold of PPV purchases has been recorded is one method that some publishers are adopting to launch new titles.

The concept of article rental is also under development, with a growing number of publishers experimenting with this model. One example is a service from DeepDyve (http://deepdyve.com). The service allows readers to rent an article for an agreed period of time (24 h, 7 days, etc.) for a small fee (typically 99 cents *a la* iTunes) and providing a full-text version of the article with limited functionality compared with online HTML or PDF versions. For example, the renter often cannot save, store or print the article. It is early days yet to say how or whether this model will be popular with users and whether publishers can make sense of it financially – for example without cannibalising other sales. This low price model does have a lot going for it in terms of providing a meaningful response to 'disenfranchised' individuals who are not at well-resourced institutions, and possibly provides a low-price way forward in relation to public access.

Digital archives and back files

In recent years publishers have created online archives containing digital files that go back to the first issue of the journal. For publishers with long histories these projects can require significant upfront investment in digitisation costs.

Publishers are making this archival content available in two main ways. The first method involves a lease or rental scheme. Here, the subscriber maintains access to the archive by paying the publisher an annual license fee. The fee may be part of the annual subscription or an additional payment may be required. The second way is via a one-off outright purchase. In this case, the back file can be regarded as a separate product. Access to the back file product continues regardless of whether the subscriber maintains the current subscription.

For back files, the publisher needs to decide when the current 'content wall' starts and back file content wall ends and what fee to charge for the additional back file content as a rental and as a one-off purchase.

Back file projects continue to prove popular with libraries who can now provide researchers with seamless online access to current volumes and the complete back file. This also means they can convert precious physical space in the library to serve other purposes. For publishers, back file projects have added to the journal's asset value and up-front costs are recouped in a relatively short period of time – typically 12–18 months.

For smaller and medium-sized publishers, there are cooperative efforts providing effective solutions; for example, JSTOR (http://www.jstor.org/) collaborates with hundreds of publishers and content providers to preserve and broaden access to their scholarly content.

In the case of online-only products such as a digital archive, the question arises of what access is provided to the customer at the end of the license period. In the print world it is clear that the subscriber retains the print copy for future use. In the online world the publisher has several options and can decide to provide ongoing access after cancellation of a license, and this may include the need for the customer to pay an annual maintenance fee to the publisher to maintain the customer's access to previously licensed content.

In summary, the reader pays model, typically via a subscription or license, retains a strong position as a sustainable business model for journals. However, it also faces perhaps the biggest challenge and potential for disruption. Partly as a result of this, the author pays model has attracted growing interest in recent years.

Author pays model

Partly in response to the growing pressures on academic library budgets, there are an increasing number of publishers and journals that are adopting an 'author pays' model. This is known as Open Access (OA) publishing where authors publishing in the journal are required to pay a fee (often termed an 'Article Processing Charge', APC) and in return, articles are made freely available online to all at no charge. APCs range from a few hundred dollars to several thousand dollars with the average somewhere in the range $1500–2500 per article. The author pays model has also been termed the 'gold route' to OA. As far as cash flow is concerned, this model is less advantageous to the publisher than the subscription model as revenue flows (author payments) are more in phase with outgoing expenses.

It is relevant to note that charging authors is not new and goes back to publishers levying 'page charges' on authors. These charges were based on the understanding that authors benefit from publishing in a journal and should be asked to support part of the costs. Typically, such charges would cover so-called 'pre-press' or 'first copy' costs, i.e. the costs of preparing an article for publication which would typically include:

- peer review and other editorial costs
- typesetting and copy editing

So called 'run-on' costs would be covered by the reader through subscription charges. Run-on costs would include manufacturing costs (printing, paper) and distribution. This page charge/subscription fee model is an example of a hybrid business model.

Some journals employ a tiered page charge scheme where charges are triggered once a page limit is exceeded. Page charges are sometimes voluntary and waiver schemes are also available for authors who are not in a position to pay. These variations are also used by some OA publishers.

In the late 20th century pages charges declined or charges were made voluntary rather than mandatory. This trend was driven largely by commercial publishers who in the 1960s and 1970s developed journals that were free to the author and relied exclusively on subscription charges.

Where society journals still have page charges then a possible way forward to a full OA model would be to increase author fees and reduce subscription prices, eventually removing subscription charges altogether.

Another option for author side payments is to charge authors a 'submission fee', whereby the author is charged a fee whether or not the article is published. This spreads the financial costs beyond solely published authors. Thus far, it appears that few journals are willing to adopt this variant as possibly they fear it might deter submissions.

The number of OA journals continues to grow and the take-up of OA can also be measured in terms of the growing number of OA publishers, ranging from not-for-profits – like the Public Library of Science – to commercial OA publishers – such as BioMedCentral (acquired by Springer in 2008), Hindawi (based in Egypt) and InTech (based in Croatia). The OA model clearly works for some publishers in some subject areas and it is now more of a question of how quickly the model will develop and move into other disciplines. Authors in some fields (predominantly biomedical) have been early adopters, chemistry has been less embracing, and it is likely that in other fields (e.g. mathematics) researchers with limited or no access to funds will be less attracted to the author pays model. The same applies to authors in developing countries where funds to pay OA fees would represent a significant cost, putting these researchers at a disadvantage (unless they were subsidised in some other way).

The trend to launch new journals under an OA model is partly driven by financial considerations. Starting up new subscription-based journals takes more upfront investment of money (with payback over 5–7 years), whereas OA journals are more 'pay-as-you-go'. The new OA publishers have been able to ramp up a lot of journals very quickly.

How the OA business model impacts financially on institutions depends on a number of factors such as: total expenditure on OA articles against expenditure on subscription products and the rate of transition from one model to the other. A Research Information Network (http://www.rin.ac.uk/) study ('Heading for the open road: costs and benefits of transitions in scholarly communications') identifies five different routes for achieving a sustainable transition, and compares and evaluates the benefits as well as the costs and risks for the UK.

For any scheme requiring author payment, it is important that publishers adopt clear policies to ensure that an author's ability to pay is separate from editorial acceptance, creating a 'firewall' between the editorial office and finances.

Hybrid open access

So-called hybrid OA is where a journal offers authors an option to pay to make their article OA. Articles from authors who don't pay such a fee are only available to subscribers. An example of this hybrid model is '*Oxford Open*' (http://www.oxfordjournals.org/oxfordopen/) offered by Oxford University Press. Many publishers now have a hybrid scheme in place although there is varied take-up from authors. Fees are similar to those for gold OA titles. Publishers offering hybrid OA are adopting a policy to reduce subscription prices in proportion to the revenue generated by author fees so as to avoid any claim of 'double dipping' from author fees and subscription charges.

Author self-archiving and institutional/subject repositories

In relation to OA, there is also the so-called 'green' route. The green route requires the author to deposit a version of their article in a subject-based or institutional repository. The version may be a pre-print or post-print version of the article and may not be the same as the final 'Version-of-Record' article published in the journal depending on copyright policies of the publisher.[1]

In contrast to gold OA, where there is a business model for revenue generation, with green OA there is no clear business model and this concerns those wanting a sustainable system.

The best examples of subject-based repositories are those in physics, maths and computer science (arXiv) and Research Papers in Economics (RePEc). For most of its almost 20 years of existence, arXiv has relied on funding agency support alongside support from its host institution (currently Cornell University). More recently it has launched a 'Sustainability Initiative' which is a collaborative business model. Rather than being supported by a single organization, arXiv is now supported by more than 100 other institutions who have a collective interest in the longer term sustainable development of the system.

This brings us on to the next business model, subsidy and how this applies in scholarly publishing.

Subsidy

Subsidies can take different forms from real financial resource through to resource in kind, donations of time and non-financial resource such as space, computer equipment and expertise. Many small publishing ventures and start-ups are funded in this way until they develop a sustainable financial model for the longer term. It can be a somewhat precarious existence to be a beneficiary of someone's largesse.

Perhaps the best recent example of subsidy funding a start-up is that of the Public Library of Science (PLoS). PLoS was founded in 2000, and received a grant of $9 million from the Gordon and Betty Moore Foundation to help support the creation and launch of a high-profile OA journal – *PLoS Biology*. Since then, PLoS has gone on to launch other high-profile journals, community-style journals and *PLoSOne*, all of them based on the OA model. PLoS is now financially self-sustaining and the rapid growth and success of *PLoSOne* has been one of the contributing factors.

As an aside, the *PLoSOne* model is different from most journals in a number of ways. As mentioned above it depends on a gold OA business model and employs a Creative Commons licensing scheme where authors retain copyright. The journal adopts the principle of peer review, but has implemented peer review in a different way from most journals. Rather than being asked to judge scientific quality or significance of an article – the scheme used by most traditional journals – referees are asked to judge on technical correctness, validity of the experimental method, whether conclusions flow from results, etc. Scientific quality and significance are then judged post-publication by readers using article-based metrics such as downloads and post-publication commentary.

The dramatic success of *PLoSOne* (it rapidly became the world's largest scientific journal in terms of articles published) has led to the model being copied by a number of other publishers who have created their own versions of *PLoSOne*. These now have their own term: 'mega-journals'.

Other countries also support scholarly journals through subsidy. For example, in Japan, many learned society journals are partially supported by a subsidy system called 'kakenhi'. This is a system of grants-in-aid that provide financial support or subsidy for many Japanese learned society journals. The dependence on government agencies to support a national scholarly publishing system may remove some market pressures, until of course government decides that there are other national priorities and journals have to fund their own way.

Another example of subsidy is SciELO – Scientific Electronic Library Online. This is a model for cooperative electronic publishing of scientific journals on the Internet designed to meet the scientific communication needs of developing countries, particularly Latin American and Caribbean countries. SciELO is product of a partnership among regional, national and international institutions. In a similar way, BioOne is a collaborative venture of learned societies in the biological sciences where each founding organisation continues to make financial and/or in-kind contributions to BioOne's development. BioOne provides a means for smaller societies to gain market impact and presence online and a means to provide libraries with a high-quality collection. ProjectMuse has similar objectives for learned society journals in the humanities and social sciences.

Advertising and sponsorship

There are a very small number of high-profile journals that generate significant revenue from advertising, both classified – i.e. principally career sections and advertisements for jobs – and display ads – i.e. for products and services. These are publications such as *Nature* and *Science* which are as much magazines as they are journals and have a much broader reach in terms of subject coverage. They also have very large readerships and circulations – institutional and individuals – which mean that advertisers can reach a large audience for their products and services. Advertising in most scholarly journals has generally a much more limited potential because of the smaller readership. There are exceptions of course, and these are typically in fields where the readership has a professional base such as medicine or engineering. The transition from print to online for these journals has been another challenge as advertising rates for online publications are typically a fraction of advertising rates in printed journals.

Sponsored sales of single issues

Sponsored sales of single issues can be a significant income stream for some journals. This involves a sponsor (often a corporate organisation) purchasing a particular journal issue in bulk because the contents of the issue are relevant to their business. Journals in the medical field (e.g. *New England Journal of Medicine*, *The Lancet*) can generate significant revenue from sponsorship of this kind where a pharmaceutical company might purchase 100 000 copies of a report on a successful clinical trial. For smaller clinical journals such sales can represent an important secondary income.

Sponsored sales whilst being a positive boost for sales and providing additional visibility for the journal brand, can be unpredictable from year to year. There are also possible ethical issues to steer clear of when selling content in this way and making sure there is a clear 'firewall' between editorial control and the sponsors' interests. In the last couple of years such revenues have been declining, partly because of the current economic situation and perhaps partly because the pharmaceutical companies are looking at other ways of promoting their products.

Other revenue

Publishers can also earn additional revenue from their digital content, often in the form of royalties or license fees, by making their content available through other channels such as third-party aggregators. These aggregator databases are intended to access segments of the market that are difficult or costly for the publisher to access. To avoid the possibility of cannibalising revenue from current subscriptions, publishers have the option to embargo content in these databases so that access is only to prior years and not to current content.

Cost management

As well as revenue generation and growth, publishing is also focused on cost management. Today's digital publishing landscape is very different from the world of printed journals, yet most journals still have printed editions that are manufactured and distributed. The end result is that there are more cost categories to plan, budget and control.

Editorial office support

There are a number of activities that incur costs surrounding the editorial process. The journal needs an effective system to support the process of managing submission of articles, peer review and manuscript tracking. Almost all journals now use a software system to manage these processes either developed in house or leased under a license from a specialist service provider. Consequently, the publisher is faced with a 'make or buy' decision, where factors to take into account include:

- The degree of control required over the development path. For example, does your particular journal or community need a customised interface or specific features and functionality? Or will a more generic solution meet your needs?
- What is the cost of ownership – how does the cost and benefit of developing and operating your own system compare with accessing a system built, maintained and developed by a third party?
- Is developing software core to your mission and does it allow you to achieve your business goals?

Licensing software from a supplier of course means there are external costs and license fees rather than internal salaries and consultants fees involved. Peer review software companies charge on the basis of a fee for each manuscript submission that goes through the system.

In addition to software, managing a journal office includes costs for peer review management, manuscript checking, author support and administration. These costs can be as salaries for in-house staff or payments and stipends to support external editorial offices housed at the editor's research institution. All of these costs usually scale as the size of the journal grows. A useful business ratio to keep track of here is cost per submitted manuscript and how this scales with volume of articles. Another useful metric is revenue per article – particularly if your journal is considering moving from a subscription to an author pays model.

Production costs

Production is another set of publishing activities that has changed significantly in recent years with associated cost implications.

Production includes typesetting (usually in the form of XML composition), copy editing and page make up – the so-called 'pre-press' activities. Many of these activities, particularly pre-press, were done in local markets by small to medium-size vendors close to home. Nowadays, much of this production activity is outsourced to large companies based off shore in places like India. Cost-effective management of production vendors has become an essential skill as well as the ability to negotiate service levels and prices and manage expectations. Travel budgets for production staff have risen accordingly. With this off-shoring and outsourcing has also come economies of scale that have driven down prices significantly. In such an environment it is unlikely that production departments will find it beneficial to enter multi-year agreements with vendors – better to have the ability to renegotiate with existing suppliers and/or negotiate with potential new suppliers as competition, technology changes and economies of scale drive prices down further. Finance Directors will be looking to see price per page metrics trending downwards.

As the transition continues away from print then other potential costs savings are available; for example, print-on-demand technology provides publishers with a cost-efficient method to manage print runs and warehousing costs. In an innovative move, some publishers have adopted a 'rotate and condense' print format that accommodates two pages on a single page with significant cost reductions.

Online delivery

While production costs have come down, the new activities associated with online production and delivery have added new costs. A publisher now needs to build an online delivery platform or rent space with a journal hosting provider (another 'make or buy' decision). Technology costs scale in a marked contrast with how editorial or production costs scale. Technology costs typically have a large fixed cost component and small variable costs (as content is added to the platform) whereas production costs tend to scale proportionately according to the size of the journal. One can list many different requirements needed for successful online journal platforms, such as:

- Search engine optimisation
- Semantic technology for content enrichment
- Delivery of metadata to secondary services
- CrossRef – membership fees and fees associated with deposit of content; plus CrossCheck and CrossMark – also from CrossRef
- Maintaining and preserving the digital archive (formerly the preserve of the librarian)
- Collaboration with other archival solutions, e.g. LOCKSS, CLOCKSS, Portico
- Usage statistics and COUNTER compliance
- Delivery to mobile devices
- Creation of apps

This list will only continue to evolve and grow with new developments in the market and emerging opportunities for the management of scientific data. The challenge is to assess how each of these activities and processes adds value compared with its impact on your cost base and ability to generate a return on investment.

Marketing and sales costs

As for many other parts of the journal publishing value chain, marketing and sales have not been spared from significant strategic and operational change.

With the move away from annual journal subscriptions based on simple price lists published in a catalog, to online information products bundled via a license negotiated with the customer, there are a great many new costs associated with these different practices: for example, legal costs of creating and managing licenses, and sales staff costs associated with face-to-face discussions with library customers to negotiate mutually beneficial deals, new requirements to mine customer data and drive sales success. There is also a need for software and systems to manage these data and the associated business transactions, such as:

- Customer Relationship Management (CRM) software
- Marketing campaign software for email communications
- Tools for social media marketing
- Access control and e-commerce systems
- Web analytics

With more and more marketing being managed via sophisticated software, the world of marketing (whether it is author marketing, usage marketing or content marketing) is becoming evidence based and analytically driven. Many of these systems are web based and provide valuable tools to staff in the office and on the road. New systems mean additional costs and the challenge is to show a positive return on investment. In addition to these new activities, there remain costs of other activities, such as exhibiting at conferences. Editors and societies demand it, but it is hard to determine whether it is cost effective.

Financial management and performance

Understanding financial performance is critical to success in any business and this applies equally to journal publishing. Unfortunately, some publishing managers and staff acquire financial understanding in rather a 'hit and miss' fashion; others are fortunate enough to benefit from rounded management training and a close relationship with their finance department and management accountant.

Financial strategy and pricing

An important first step in any assessment of publishing finances is clarity on the organisation's financial strategy and how this fits within its overall mission. A profit motive is clear in any commercial organisation whilst for a not-for-profit then financial aspects are just as important even if the goal is to break even financially as well as serve the mission.

Pricing of journals and information services is more an art than a science. Pricing partly depends on the objectives of the owner and the strategic and business goals the organisation sets out to achieve. Pricing is also about value and understanding the value your customers place on your product in a competitive market. An effective pricing strategy should also be part of the marketing mix and although costs are important to keep in mind when making pricing decisions, cost-based pricing is more likely to be appropriate for commodity-style products rather than a journal publishing a unique collection of content.

Value, of course, tends to be in the eye of the beholder and understanding the value proposition of your journal means having a deep understanding of your customers and the competitive market. A highly cited quarterly review journal is likely to represent a different value proposition from a large rapid communication journal, for example. Being closer to the customer is much easier in the online world particularly as usage defines a value metric and usage is now well calibrated through the COUNTER system (http://www.projectcounter.org). Ratios such as 'cost per download' (CPD) are now terms commonly in the vocabulary of publishers and librarians where librarians set CPD thresholds and if a journal exceeds a particular CPD value then this triggers a closer review or even cancellation of the title in question. For OA journals, setting appropriate article processing charges for authors requires a similar philosophy concerning value, the competitive market and financial objectives.

Revenue comes in many flavours, as indicated in the business models section above. For each business model, there needs to be an appropriate pricing scheme. As well as multiple journal bundles, pricing discounts and consortia licenses, some publishers have been successful with tiered pricing schemes. This is where each customer is assigned to a tier according to a metric or set of metrics that relate to the value a customer places on having access to the content. For example, a small two-year college might place a lower value on having access to research content than a large research intensive university and prices should vary accordingly. Other pricing schemes use full-time equivalent number of faculty or researchers as a measure, and the Carnegie Classification (http://classifications.carnegiefoundation.org/) has been used by publishers as a means to set prices according to the value a customer is likely to place on having access to content. Product tiering is another common pricing strategy, where the customer pays a premium for value-added features; this strategy is less common in journals publishing.

Given that most publishers are in business to maximise access and distribute their content widely, pricing models that are more restrictive and meter usage are less likely to support objectives and goals for the publisher and tend to be unpopular with librarians as well. A key message is to keep pricing schemes transparent and simple to communicate to all concerned.

The financial statements

Three financial statements are required to manage any business: the profit and loss statement, balance sheet and cash flow statement. There are many useful books available on finance for non-financial managers; for example, *Financial Intelligence: A manager's guide to knowing what the numbers really mean* is a practical guide with informative sections on each of the three financial statements (Berman and Knight, 2006).

Profit and loss (P&L) statement

The P&L statement is usually the one that most managers and publishing staff will to be familiar with. The purpose of the P&L statement (sometimes called the 'income statement' or 'statement of earnings') is to attempt to measure whether the products or services that a company provides are profitable when everything is added up. The P&L statement represents the best attempt to show the sales a company generated in a given period of time (e.g. a month, a quarter, 12 months), the costs incurred in making those sales over the same period and the profit or surplus, if any, that remains.

The P&L statement may be for the entire company, a division, or a single product or service. Publishing staff as they reach higher into the organisation will take on what is termed 'P&L responsibility' for their journal or portfolio. Each journal should have its own P&L statement and often for publishers with larger journal portfolios, each publishing manager will have an aggregate P&L statement for the journals they have P&L responsibility for.

The P&L statement is presented in a common structure with three main categories of headings. Sales or revenue is at the top and this is what people commonly mean when they refer to 'top-line growth'. Costs and expenses are the middle section of the P&L statement, and profit or surplus is at the bottom, hence – the 'bottom line'.

A brief, simplified example of what a Journal P&L looks like is given in Table 6.1.

The P&L statement is an important document for managers in order for them to run the business and to understand how decisions (e.g. on pricing and discounts) have an impact on revenue, and how other

Table 6.1 **Illustrative profit & loss (P&L) sheet ($, thousands) for a hybrid journal's position at the end of July**

	Previous year actual	Current year budget	Year-to-date (YTD) actual – July	Forecast	Variance: Forecast vs. budget
Subscription revenue					
Institutional subscription	505	520	391	528	8
Individual subscription	10	8	3	7	–1
Society member subscribers	20	17	7	17	0
Consortia access fees	54	65	42	59	–6
Other revenue					
Reprints	10	9	4	9	0
Offprints (authors)	5	5	2	5	0
Advertising (display and classified)	45	54	38	65	11
Pay per view	5	5	1	4	–1
Open access fees	25	38	26	46	8
Back file sales	180	250	138	250	0
Total revenue	859	971	652	990	19
Costs					
Editorial office support	105	106	69	109	3
Editor-in-chief stipend	50	50	25	50	0
Manuscript submission, review, tracking software system	26	26	17	27	1
Copy editing	53	53	32	53	0
Typesetting	35	35	21	34	–1
Platform costs	53	56	34	56	0
Paper, print, binding	130	119	71	117	–2
Distribution	15	13	8	13	0
Postage	18	16	10	16	0
Marketing and sales costs	81	88	40	103	15
Total costs	566	562	327	578	16
Gross margin	293	409	325	412	3
Gross margin as a percentage of revenue	34%	42%	50%	42%	
Overheads	98	98	47	98	0
Net margin	195	311	278	314	3
Net margin as a percentage of revenue	23%	32%	43%	32%	

Note: Gross margin is equal to total revenue less total costs. Net margin is equal to gross margin less overheads.

decisions on costs (e.g. hiring new staff, purchasing new equipment or paying vendors) impact the bottom line. The format of most budgets will usually follow the same format as the P&L statement.

The big proviso in how to interpret a P&L statement, inherent in any P&L, is that they reflect estimates and assumptions made by the finance department. For example, when should a publisher recognise revenue from a subscriber if the subscriber pays a full year in advance of the subscription period? Should it recognise revenue on the P&L when the invoice is sent to the customer, when the customer sends payment or when the publisher starts dispatching issues of the journal? In fact it is typical for publishers to use the so-called 'matching principle' to match revenues against costs. For example, this would mean that for a monthly journal one-twelfth of the revenue received would be apportioned to the P&L each month. Similarly, consortia access fees might be added on a pro-rata basis according to online usage metrics.

Another proviso is that the P&L tells us about what has happened, rather than providing information we need to predict or forecast what will happen in the future. So as well as using the P&L statement as a management tool, it us important to develop other metrics that are more forward looking, for example the number of new customers added, market spend per new customer or sales from new products against sales from old products.

As we have seen above, there are different methods available for a journal to generate the funds it needs to be a viable and sustainable operation. The other side of the financial equation for any successful business involves balancing revenues against expenses, costs and overheads in order to break even or generate a profit or surplus.

There is no typical journal, each one being different in terms of its size, scale and market. Larger journals may benefit from economies of scale; high circulation titles have potential for advertising, whereas journals in the social sciences and humanities are typically much smaller and therefore cost less to produce; STM journals in particular can become large operations in their own right.

Other important financial statements

Financially intelligent managers should not only understand the P&L statement but also be aware of and get acquainted with two other important financial statements. These are briefly defined here and for further background the reader is referred to one of the many books on financial management for non-financial managers.

Balance sheet

Companies prepare a balance sheet to provide a summary of their financial position at a given point in time (so balance sheets always have a date, typically at the end of an accounting period such as a month, quarter, financial year). The balance sheet is simply a statement of what a company owns (its assets), what it owes (its liabilities) and its book value, or net worth (also called owners' equity or shareholder's equity).

The balance sheet is used as an important indicator of a company's financial health. It is useful to a banker, an investor or owner of a business for assessing risk as well as inventory management. It helps answer questions such as: Is the business in a position to expand? Can the business easily handle the normal financial ebbs and flows of revenues and expenses? Should the business take immediate steps to bolster cash reserves?

Analysis of the balance sheet can identify important trends, particularly in the area of accounts receivable and payable. Is the receivables cycle lengthening? Can receivables be collected more aggressively? Is some debt uncollectable? Has the business been slowing down payables to forestall an inevitable cash shortage?

The balance sheet is also used as part of the due diligence process by external investors and/or for mergers and acquisitions.

Cash flow

The cash flow statement shows how a company acquired and spent its cash during a given period of time. If you're a publisher in a large organisation, changes in your company's cash flow will not typically have an impact on your day-to-day job. But in fact it is the most important statement. If your organisation runs out of cash you simply don't have a business. So senior management certainly needs to understand cash flow management.

Journals as a portfolio

Large publishers usually divide their programs up along subject lines with portfolios managed by a group of staff charged with growing the program and building the business. Good financial management (revenues and costs) is part of this. For smaller society publishers, a key question is whether to 'self publish' and carry out the main publishing activities independently or to contract out the publishing function in whole or in part to a commercial publisher. For learned societies with a single journal or small group of titles it is becoming increasingly complex to go it alone and so partnerships between societies and commercial publishers continue to grow.

For commercial publishers seeking to grow the portfolio, adding society journals can be an effective method to achieve this goal. As society journals are added to the portfolio, some costs will scale with activity (e.g. production costs) but other costs, for example sales costs, will largely remain fixed. In this way, the publisher grows revenue by adding new titles, whilst spreading fixed costs over a larger number of journals. This can be part of an effective financial strategy.

The society also benefits by gaining access to economies of scale (e.g. production) and efficient access to a market via the publisher's sales force. For small and medium-sized societies, this approach can be an effective way to manage their journal assets and manage investment and risk.

When a society publisher contracts out its publishing to a commercial publisher, the most common arrangement is one based on a royalty payment. In this case, the publisher will manage the costs of publishing the journal, collect the revenue and provide the society owner with a royalty. The royalty may be a percentage of revenue or percentage of gross or net profit.

Larger societies, more aware of journal assets, are pushing for guaranteed levels of income when negotiating new agreements and often using consultants/agents to help them in such negotiations.

Launching new journals

Research continues to grow and publishers have responded to market needs by launching new journals in emerging fields and interdisciplinary topics. Launching new journals compared with managing an existing journal program requires a different mind-set, for example the approach to risk and investment. Launching new journals can be an effective way to grow the business and a number of factors need to be taken into account, such as:

- What business model to choose and how long will it take to make a return?
- How big is the available market?
- What will it cost to reach key segments of that market effectively?

- How will growth scale and impact upon editorial and production costs?
- How to deliver the journal – print as well as online?
- What other resources are required?
- What marketing budget is needed for launch and how will this be focused on attracting authors and readers?

A successful journal launch is always a team effort and it is strongly recommended that one of the team has a strong financial background if you don't have a management accountant on hand. This will help create and develop the business plan before launch and help monitor risks and provide forecasts as the journal develops.

Conclusion and outlook

As long as the journal continues to serve valuable functions in the scholarly community then publishers will continue to have an opportunity to develop and tailor appropriate business models to suit market needs.

A successful journal has many key characteristics and this chapter has attempted to show that one of these characteristics is the need to have sustainable business models in place. This requires a good understanding of revenue generation, pricing strategy and cost management. As you move higher up any organisation, the focus changes from individual title performance to portfolio management and creating successful growth strategies.

Knowledgeable financial staff are located close by in most organisations and it is strongly recommended that you get to know the way around your journal finances by getting closely acquainted with the chief financial officer or management accountant for your journal. Working collaboratively you will be able to deliver top line growth and a stronger bottom line.

Note

1. An NISO/ALPSP Journal Article Version Technical Working Group has made recommendations describing the versions of scholarly journal articles that typically appear online before, during and after formal journal publication.

Sources of further information

Cox, J. and Cox, L. (2008) *Scholarly Publishing Practice: Academic journal publishers' policies and practices in online publishing*. ALPSP Research Report, Third Survey.

Heading for the open road: costs and benefits of transitions in scholarly communications – a study commissioned by Research Information Network (RIN), JISC, Research libraries UK (RLUK), the Publishing Research Consortium (PRC) and the Wellcome Trust. April 2011.

King, D.W. and Alvarado-Albertorio, F.M. (2008) Pricing and other means of charging for scholarly journals: a literature review and commentary. *Learned Publishing*, 21: 248–72.

Nagle, T., Hogan, J. and Zale, J. (2010) *The Strategy and Tactics of Pricing*, 5th edn. New York: Prentice Hall.

References

Berman, K. and Knight, J. (2006) *Financial Intelligence: A manager's guide to knowing what the numbers really mean*. Cambridge, MA: Harvard Business School Press.

Mabe, M. (2003) The growth and number of journals. *Serials* 16(2): 191–7.

Development of book publishing business models and finances

Frances Pinter, with the assistance of Laura White

Abstract: This chapter covers the various forms and financial profiles of academic and professional book publishing. It looks back at the history of how this genre developed and how it is now adapting to the opportunities and challenges of the digital age. Ranging widely it covers hotly debated issues such as copyright, licensing terms, open access, digital production workflows and what steps need to be taken to make the most of digital while still preserving the values and skills of professional publishing.

Key words: Academic book publishing, scholarly book publishing, professional book publishing, open access and books.

Introduction

In this chapter we shall be looking at the development of book publishing business models, the finances that underlie them, market drivers and what we might expect during the second decade of the 21st century. It is being written from the vantage point of the end of 2011 – probably about half way through a 20-year transition that is in equal amounts painful and exhilarating. The promises of the new technology seem limitless. Change is happening at a breathless pace in some areas, while certain aspects of publishing remain constant, some would say even backward. Publishing executives today are taking decisions that will shape the landscape of academic communications and the role the industry plays in it, while at the same time the room for manoeuvre is constrained by factors well outside their control.

The history and landscape of academic book publishing

Scholarly book publishing as a part of the publishing industry rose rapidly with the expansion of higher education after the end of the Second World War first in the USA. By the 1970s many areas of scholarly publishing were prospering. In America the dramatic growth of university presses contributed to a wider dissemination of scholarship than ever before. By the end of the 20th century there were nearly 90 university presses, many that also published materials of local interest and books of wider general appeal, gravitating primarily to the fields of humanities and social sciences. Indeed in America many serious presses found ways of broadening the appeal of scholarly research by grooming academic authors to write significant popular books that became bestsellers and were highly influential in shaping public thinking on any particular issue. For these select few authors the earnings could be significant, even reach seven figure royalty earnings (Greco *et al.*, 2008).

In the UK the expansion of higher education came later, although publishers began to see the potential from the late 1960s and early 1970s. The university press landscape was dominated by the two large publishers, Oxford University Press and Cambridge University Press.

For most academics in the social sciences and humanities, the publication of their original research in the form of monographs was enough to meet their needs for tenure and promotion, and for the publisher print runs of 2000–3000 copies was the norm by the early 1970s.

The publishing of monographs in the English language was predominantly an activity of American and British publishers (with some in Canada and Australia and a few such as Elsevier in Europe), although as English became the dominant language in business and scientific communications, other academic presses in Europe and increasingly further afield chose to publish in English.

As university presses grew stronger a tension arose between them and commercial academic presses. The hidden subsidies that university presses receive from their parent institutions coupled with their tax-exempt status created an unfair playing field according to commercial publishers. This has not, however, deterred a healthy commercial sector from evolving in both English and other world languages.

Textbook publishing, on the other hand, tends to be local at primary and secondary education levels. At university level the US and UK publishers competed for market share on an increasingly global scale. Publishers exported (and often localised) tertiary-level content in many parts of the world, finding lucrative markets in smaller and/or poorer countries that could not sustain the width and breadth afforded by the UK and US companies.

In the US textbooks are used much more widely in the teaching process with students often able to pass satisfactorily through a course with only one core textbook recommended by the instructor. In the UK tertiary education is moving in that direction, although it has a tradition of encouraging wider reading from a variety of sources. With over 3000 universities and 2000 community colleges the US market dwarfs the UK with its 180 institutions of higher education. Therefore, US publishers were and continue to be better placed to make large investments in textbooks that sold in tens and hundreds of thousands of copies each year. UK publishers, by contrast, relied much more on the export market, especially to Commonwealth countries.

Today the market for English language academic books is global and the publishing industry that produces them is global too. The main publishers, OUP, CUP, Palgrave, Taylor and Francis, Pearson, Springer, Wiley-Blackwell and Elsevier, all have offices around the world. Their main markets are North America, Europe and Asia Pacific, but their reach is into every country that has a university and now Internet access.

Professional publishing

Professional publishing for the professional market is increasingly dominated by large conglomerates based in North America. In the legal and tax sectors technology suppliers are growing more quickly than both traditional and online publishers, and it is fair to say that a number of the larger players are now less interested in the single book written on a specialist topic by a practitioner or academic. Instead they now tend to focus on the deep content sets they own and aggregate (much of which are primary sources and legislation) and build online databases where they can then slice and dice content for different segments of the market. The ability to hold and manipulate huge volumes of data is crucial, with military-grade technology and back-up systems to mitigate risk.

However, several UK-based independents are growing their businesses successfully through a largely hard-copy offering. What the future will look like is hard to gauge but a combination of large online databases, books and e-books seems likely with the demise of loose leafs and CD-ROMs a medium-term certainty.

Content is king in the professional space, but the delivery mechanisms and value proposition need to be right. As the market becomes more commodity-based, it is likely that the margins will deteriorate in the long term from the very high margins that have been achieved historically.

In the UK the big publishers have seen erosion in growth rates in the last 5 years or so. This is due to customers cancelling hard copy subscriptions, take up for online services being slower than anticipated, smaller players offering cheaper alternatives and the buying/negotiating skills of customers improving. That said, margins in the larger companies are still comfortably over 20 per cent and likely to remain there for a period of time as cost cutting mitigates lower growth rates.

Actual numbers of lawyers and accountants continue to grow so the markets served are growing and are likely to continue. The concept of the professional body has become increasingly popular and many new 'professions' have come to have their own professional bodies. The challenge for the professional publisher is that the actual overall revenues on offer are declining due to the market trends above. In the longer term one could imagine margins steadying at a lower rate once the customer and supplier arrive at a position that is sustainable for both.

Some of the larger publishers serving the professional market also publish business books for the consumer market (such as Wiley Blackwell) and have authors that serve both sectors.

The impact of digitisation and digital publishing

Today, with the impact of digitisation we are seeing a blurring of the boundaries between different types of publications (including both journals and books). Learning materials are becoming referred to as 'learning objects', with the distinct objective of taking content out of pigeon holes and allowing for their deconstruction – to be reassembled by teachers and learners themselves rather than be packaged and presented as a static object by intermediaries such as publishers.

Research findings are now circulated freely on the Web prior to or even instead of formal publication. In many areas multimedia is making inroads as ways of enhancing the flat text. The pressures for free access to end-users through the open access (OA) movement (discussed below) is threatening the business model that initially tried to replicate the print world online. New distribution channels are proliferating for every kind of publication. Authors are demanding higher royalties and publishers are investing heavily in new processes, staff training and new business models.

'Pre-press' production process

In production the defining moment came when publishers were able to apply XML (Extensible Markup Language), which is an accepted set of rules for encoding documents in machine-readable form. XML allows publishers to repurpose and reflow their content in as many formats as required, whether to facilitate custom publishing or simply allow a single e-book to be read on a multiplicity of devices. It is hard to overestimate both the challenges and the opportunities this has created for the industry.

Metadata

Metadata describe data around content. In the old-fashioned print world this has usually meant the bibliographical information found in publisher promotion materials and library card catalogues. In the digital world there has been an explosion in how metadata have come to be used to tag every piece of information not just about the book, but in the book. This allows publishers and users to manipulate content in interconnected ways undreamt of just a few decades ago. The significance of this, again, cannot be overestimated.

Printing

The printing industry has also seen the sweep of digital impact on how it carries out its business. While litho printing is still the preferred method for print runs of over 400–500 copies, there are now two additional possibilities that provide cost-effective ways of producing books.

Print on demand (POD) designed to print single copies reached the market some 15 years ago. However, the initial machinery was expensive and therefore required centralisation of a large amount of printing. This has now improved considerably and we are moving towards small efficient machines that allow for dispersed printing around the globe.

The more recent arrival of the short-run digital printing option is the preferred method for runs from around 25 to 400 copies. This suits monographs publishing very well.

Apart from allowing publishers to print only the quantity they require for whatever period they wish, this flexibility also allows publishers to decide whether they will print to hold stock or only print when stock is required (as Springer does with its e-copy/my copy programme) – delivering directly from the printer. The new textbook publisher Flat World Knowledge chooses to circumvent warehousing in this way, although for how long this will be possible is hard to tell. More traditional publishers start with litho, print short digital runs if necessary as sales slow down and then progress to POD with the digital file held by the printer to be used after orders come in. Amazon and other large retailers also offer this POD service to publishers.

Reading devices

The hardware industry is producing more and more user-friendly devices on which content can be published. Whether mobile devices, tablets such as the iPad or bespoke reading devices such as the Kindle, we have them, people want to use them and applications for them are inevitably mushrooming all around us. No one knows for sure which will be profitable, and are able to deliver content in pedagogically sound ways, best loved by students and researchers. A few early studies such as the one carried out by Princeton University suggest that students are not entirely convinced of their utility. However, it is likely that e-readers will find their place amongst a variety of tools in the student's rucksack.

Publishers have tended to be fearful of digital piracy cannibalising sales and have been relying on Digital Rights Management (DRM) technologies that have costs attached to them. However, DRM is contentious and most technologies are hacked sooner rather than later. Soft DRM is therefore becoming the preferred approach, with such practices such as watermarking or disclosing the purchaser's identity when sharing illegally.

New business models

New business models are primarily in the digital (i.e. electronic) realm and fall into two categories, toll-based and OA. These changes impact on the traditional print model, where print is either abandoned or becomes just one of many delivery options.

The distinction between toll-based and OA refers to who pays for the publishing process and when in the publishing process these costs of publishing are paid.

Toll-based sales of subscriptions to e-journals came about fairly easily and is now virtually complete [with 96 per cent STM (Science, Technical, Medical) and 87 per cent HSS (Humanities and Social Sciences) of all English language scholarly journals available digitally (Ware and Mabe, 2009, p. 19)]. These subscription-based products tend to be sold primarily to institutional libraries and professional practices. However, books are migrating more slowly. 'E-book' is a generic term that covers anything that resembles a book in digital format and is used for both academic and trade titles – both of which have very different market and sales profiles. It can therefore be confusing when looking at trends, even though both are going up.

Some types of trade books have tripled their market share in the past 3 years from the base of 3 per cent in 2009. However, there is no way of knowing whether this steep rise has occurred because of the hype around the new readers and will therefore plateau out at a relatively modest level. In academic and professional publishing, by contrast, the e-book has distinct benefits to scholarly communications, in terms of discoverability, citations, concurrent usage in libraries, etc. E-book sales are rising exponentially. Bets are on as to when e-sales will exceed 50 per cent, expected within 2–5 years. There will still be a large market for print books. Apart from the big textbooks (for the time being) printed books will increasingly be produced on demand or virtually on demand in very short digital print runs.

How readers consume content will, in the end, determine the formats in which they are delivered. While there is a demand for printed editions, publishers and printers will be more than happy to supply them.

However, there are numerous variables that will determine how this shapes up:

- Library offerings via e-book aggregators
- The variety, quality and price of reading devices
- The take up of reading on digital devices
- Flexibility afforded by publishers in their business models regulating and charging for access to content
- How attractive publishers can make their content
- The extent to which readers are able to customise their books through a mix and match of the materials and compose their own custom built book

The stakeholders and market drivers of digital book publishing

Publishers are reacting to the abundance of content online (especially free content) by refocusing their role in the value chain. No longer considering themselves as gatekeepers, which their access to capital for investment effectively defined them as such in the last century, they are searching for ways of adding value.

Scholars

As a first step to understanding the value chain in book publishing, we need to consider the requirements of scholars themselves. They grasp the potential of digital access and distribution to information and scholarship and are asking publishers to accommodate or get out of the way. The framework is set for building a technical environment to 'support information, data-intensive, distributed, multidisciplinary research and learning' (Borgman, 2007, p. 262). This direction is being endorsed by research funding bodies. E-research and e-infrastructure required to deliver and communicate the findings is another pressure to change the existing business models. However, the rate of change differs from one discipline to another and within disciplines – and not always along obvious generational divides.

In his book *The Digital Scholar*, Weller (2011) discusses the convergence of digital, networked and open technologies and the way it is transforming the way scholarship is conducted, with huge implications for collaboration, dissemination, methodology and pedagogy. The question that remains to be answered is whether publishers as we know them today will adapt as successfully to this changing landscape as they did to the rapid growth of the scholarly and higher education communities themselves.

Nevertheless, the reliance on publishing in its traditional form for career progression remains strong. While this continues to be the case academics will look to publish their works in whatever format is required of their disciplines and look to publishers for selection, adding value by editing, formatting, producing, promoting and branding – giving it that all important seal of approval. In economic terms this alliance between author and publisher has been referred to as 'co-creators of value' (a concept often attributed to John Banks, University of Queensland).

Libraries and library suppliers

We do know that librarians are especially keen on reducing their intake of printed matter and move to digital content. This will greatly reduce their need for additional shelf space. It also allows them to ingest digital content into their catalogues in ways that allow for the monitoring of usage. This has in turn led to Patron-Driven Acquisition (PDA) models (discussed below) that in due course may lead to more selective purchasing taking the 'just in time' as opposed to 'just in case' philosophy to a much higher level of precision than ever imaginable with printed books.

Librarians are redefining their own professions. They are becoming increasingly important in helping their patrons navigate around not only their own collections but around the whole of the Web, including the massive amount of free content. Libraries, too, are pushing for access to e-books for their patrons on a multiplicity of devices.

The large e-content library suppliers are aggregating content into databases, but this tends to include monographs and reference works only, as publishers are wary of including e-textbooks for fear of losing control of their content. These aggregators began offering content in much the same way as traditional book library suppliers. Their offerings are effectively from a catalogue of e-books aggregated from a number of individual publishers. Libraries can either buy subset packages or pick and choose individual titles, depending on which plan they subscribe to.

Just as with the traditional supply of print books these aggregators are enhancing their offerings by additional services that allow for extra efficiencies and cost savings to the libraries (e.g. the supply of metadata in bespoke forms).

PDA is a method by which the content of an e-book can rest inside a library catalogue and purchases are triggered based on usage by end-users. Once titles are triggered, the library generally owns it on a perpetual basis. However, there are a number of variants on this model, including the ability to 'borrow' an e-book on a short-term loan basis.

Ebary have been the latest to adopt this model, running a pilot programme which they afterwards extended due to its success. NetLibrary have a PDA programme – e-books are purchased at the first use, and once the purchase is made the academic library then owns that e-book. Ingram's MyiLibrary runs its Patron Select programme. First access to an e-book comes at no cost. On the second time access is made, the library is charged and the e-book is licensed to that library for a specific duration of time.

The politics of access

Access to knowledge has become a hotly contested issue of fundamental human rights, especially in developing countries (see Krikorian and Kapczynski, 2010). Several declarations such as the Budapest and Berlin Declarations have called for content to be free at point of use. This kind of position would have been intellectually untenable in the past when the container (the printed books) and vehicles (physical shipment) that transported knowledge needed to be paid for. However, in the digital age, content, it was said, wanted to be free. Of course, this was an exaggeration and after a decade of wrangling over business models it is now increasingly accepted that scholarly monographs and textbooks need to undergo professional handling and that it is primarily publishers that have the skills of selecting, organising independent peer review, editing, formatting, branding, marketing and making the content available in multiple formats on multiple platforms.

It was never the case that all content was closed. Programmes to make printed books available in developing countries have been funded by western governments and philanthropic organisations for some time. As soon as digital communications made instant access possible, bodies such as EIFL and Research4Life (including HINARI, OARE and AGORA) were created to make journal content either very inexpensive or entirely free to developing and transition countries.

However, publishers have often been their own worst enemies in the public relations war. When the OA movement began at the turn of the century with the creation of journals that were free to the end user and the publishing process was paid for from research funds some mainstream publishers reacted with outrage. Now Springer owns BioMed Central, one of the pioneering open access initiatives, and properly funded open access is seen as a viable option to the subscription-based model.

Although there is no consensus on whether OA will become the dominant model in journal publishing, it is easier to see how it can operate in the STM journal space where publication fees amount to only a tiny amount of any research budget. It is harder to envisage across HSS where research budgets are much smaller or even non-existent.

In the case of books there have been only a few experiments with OA which will be described below. Of course, the input costs of a 300-page book are clearly much greater than those of a 20-page journal article. These sums would be much harder to extract from research budgets, although funders are being encouraged to consider their role in the dissemination process.

For example, Amsterdam University Press was charged with the administration of OAPEN, a European Union-funded project that is a collaborative initiative to develop and implement a sustainable OA publication model for academic books in the Humanities and Social Sciences. The OAPEN Library aims to improve the visibility and usability of high-quality academic research by aggregating peer-reviewed OA publications from across Europe. It serves as a test-bed to see if an OA model can be sustainable. OAPEN has its roots in the continental tradition of publishing, where there is much more funding available for the publishing of scholarly monographs whether in print or electronic versions. OAPEN is advocating for a greater institutionalisation of such funding.

In addition to the gold standard of OA (where the author or research funder pays a fee for publication) there is also the green route whereby content is held in institutional repositories on an OA basis. While some funders and universities have mandated OA, and some countries are thinking of doing so on a national basis, this movement towards institutional repositories has not been entirely successful. This has been due to a number of factors, including a reluctance of many academics themselves, as well as insufficient funding for management and promotion of content.

Professional publishing remains relatively immune from the OA pressures as the content is generally aimed at improving the professional's ability to increase their earning power. Unlike educational and research materials it is usually not the case that the creation of the content is paid for out of the public purse.

The shape and development of new book publishing business models

To understand the seismic shifts taking place now we need to map out how things were, how things are today, how things will be and how we are going to get there – perhaps.

We are going to look at four types of publications – monographs, edited volumes, textbooks and reference works – and three types of subject areas – HSS, STM and Professional (usually includes Law, Business, Accounting) (Table 7.1).

Until recently only a few commercial and university presses were prepared to experiment with open content licensing. Now many have done so, although only a few have dedicated programmes that are committed to the model, which works as follows.

Table 7.1 **Recommended retail price scale for books (based on a sample from half a dozen large publishers), largely hardbacks (except textbooks) of around 300 pages**

	Monograph	Edited volume	Textbook	Reference work
Humanities and Social Sciences (HSS)	£40–90	£40–120	£15–30	£50+
Science, Technical, Medical (STM)	£50–120	£75–150	£25–50	£100+
Professional	£60–150	£80–200	£25–75	£100+

The basic premise of OA is that the work should be free online on a licence that restricts the user to non-commercial uses only. That leaves the publisher with all the commercial rights, including print and digital, for commercial exploitation. The publisher can then make the book available in a number of different formats: print, stand alone e-book available on a multiplicity of devices in different formats, and as an enhanced e-book giving extra value to a library edition for example or providing additional materials which are paid for either by subscription or as one-off purchases.

Attempts to make this model work began with publishers simply selling print books while posting their content online for free. Sometimes they placed a specific customised licence on the digital version that restricted further commercial exploitation. More recently, however, there has been a general acceptance of the Creative Commons Non-Commercial licence (and sometimes using the CC+ designation that adds information about further reuse beyond the scope of the licence).

Taking our initial typology of books, we'll also look at some of the experiments going on now and see what the business models are and how they are faring across the range of book publications (as illustrated in Table 7.2).

Costs – print versus digital

For any book publishing programme (be it traditional or experimental) to be successful and sustainable, the publisher's foundation is stable funding and strong financial control, so it is important to understand how the costs are managed.

Table 7.2 **Experiments in open content book programmes**

Book type	Open content example
Monographs	Bloomsbury Academic; HSRC Press; Michigan University Press; OAPEN
Edited collection	Bloomsbury Academic
Textbooks	Flat World Knowledge; OER efforts
Reference works	Wikipedia

In the traditional model publishers followed a fairly standard way of costing their books. It all began with the individual title. There was a straightforward distinction between fixed costs (copy editing, typesetting, formatting, proofreading, design) of the book amortised over a print run – usually representing around 18 months of sales – and variable costs that represented costs such as first print runs, royalties and distribution charges. Other costs were treated as fixed or variable depending on how the company conducted its business. Large companies have their own warehouses and sales teams and assign a cost to each copy of the printed book. This is a backward way of treating a fixed cost as a variable as the actual costs of bringing a title to the market have to be successfully amortised over each copy. Small publishers tend to outsource sales, marketing, warehousing, etc., and they know from the contract with their service providers just how much they will be charged – usually expressed as a percentage of sales.

For this reason publishing is often referred to as a 'mark-up' business. All companies know the multiple of their fixed costs (however calculated) required to arrive at a minimum net receipt per book, then multiplied by the print run to provide a figure – which is then expressed as a gross margin. Tucked into the equation is a percentage of sales required to cover overheads, which again varies from company to company.

While overheads are expressed as a percentage of each copy sold, everyone is aware of just how many copies need to be sold to cover the actual overheads associated with the project and then how many projects need to be put through each year to cover the costs.

Below we shall discuss monographs in more detail but here we see how the costs of traditional monographs break down on a book-by-book basis. A publisher can calculate in his or her head how many copies they need to sell in order to cover fixed costs and make enough of a contribution to overheads to cover the cost of handling a project. An example of the breakdown of costs and income on a book is presented in Table 7.3, working to a rough total of 400 unit sales. In digital publishing we simply have no idea yet how much our costs *per 'unit' sold* or even cost *per project* will actually be when taking into account the unknown amounts of time we are all spending trying to develop new business models.

The problem with digital publishing is that there is no comparable concept as 'the copy'. There is, in effect, only one copy of the text, the master digital file, and what the publisher is selling is access. Whether this is on subscription expressed as payments per page, per chapter or per book, for a limited period of time, or on a perpetual access licence, for single or multiple devices and single or multiple readers for a tiered set of charges, depending on the size or wealth of an institution or country is causing problems with the basic expenditure and revenue models. Although there may be no warehousing costs, there are higher marketing

Table 7.3 Cost sheet for a monograph retailing at £50 (per unit, assuming 400 copies sold, and digital printing)

Sample cost sheet for a print monograph	
Typical retail price	50
Net receipt	
(*assuming 35 per cent trade discount*)	32.5
Origination costs (*includes design, copy editing, typesetting, print*)	6
Royalty (*assuming 5 per cent of net receipt*)	1.63
Gross profit	
(= *Net receipt minus origination cost and royalty*)	24.87
Gross profit (of net receipt)	77%
Other costs	
Distribution	3.25
Marketing	1.95
Overheads (*includes rent, utilities, staff, finance costs, etc.*)	17.7
Net profit	
(= *Gross profit minus other costs*)	4.87
Net Profit (of Net Receipt)	15%

costs and there is pressure to raise author royalties. We really have little idea what the ratios will look like once the digital models settle down and publishers are able to again calculate in their heads what the price of a 'book' of a certain number of words should be.

Looking at the drivers of digital publishing we see several operating across types of publications and many more that are specific to each type. Cost savings across all types is a short-term myth even if in the long run there will be savings on paper and physical distribution.

For publishers there is a real problem in devising new ways of managing their digital investment. Should this include re-skilling existing staff or the upheaval of hiring new staff with the appropriate skills? What will it take to alter traditional patterns of workflow? Does one write off these investments as they are incurred or handle them more like software – to be written off the balance sheet over a period of years?

For the time being publishers have to invest massively in the transition and returns are likely to go down before they start to climb again (and not forgetting that we are still in the midst of the most serious recession since the depression of the 1930s).

Monographs

'A work of scholarship on a particular topic or theme which is written by a scholar (or scholars) and intended for use primarily by other scholars. The scholarly monograph is a focused work of scholarship pitched at a relatively high level of intellectual sophistication.' (Thompson, 2005, p. 84).

Monographs are generally considered to be the lowest risk and carry the lowest investment. They are the product of original research and are generally sold to academic libraries. While historically they may have sold up to 3000 copies, today they sell between 200 and 600 depending on the subject and price. In general, HSS titles sell for anything from £40 to £80, STM at slightly higher prices and Professional books starting at £70 and selling well into the hundreds of pounds, as illustrated in Table 7.1. Academics in HSS subjects need and want to publish book-length material while for STM academics there is greater prestige (and therefore of more importance for promotion) to publish in journals. Professional books tend to be produced by professionals who want a foot in the academic door, or academics who use the publication as a way of promoting consultancy and other services. Some of the larger publishers have moved out of monographs publishing altogether because the size of each project does not warrant the overheads.

Monograph publishing has been one of the first areas in scholarly publishing to experiment in Open Content Book Programmes. Bloomsbury Academic's experimental business model is often described using an ice cream analogy. The core monograph (or research-led publication, as they call it) is published on their website in HTML on a Creative Commons Non-Commercial (CC NC) licence. They also sell the print version (either in hardback, paperback or both), stand alone e-books for reading devices such as Kindle and Sony, e-books through aggregators such as MyLibrary and Ebrary, and a library PDF. Some e-books have additional resources bundled in. To date, print books are selling in the quantities anticipated, although the size of the sample and length of time that this imprint has been publishing (since 2010) is too small and short to evaluate its success.

Other publishers are now allowing authors to publish their monographs on a CC NC licence upon request, although generally they don't like it and are fearful of the possible impact on sales. Nevertheless there is interest in making this model work. It is unfortunate that the technology made it possible at about the time that libraries faced real spending cuts and so it is impossible to determine whether any drop in sales might be due to OA or just a drop in budgets and hard choices needing to be made.

A study at Amsterdam University Press (Snijder, 2010) of 400 primarily backlist titles concluded that while there was an increase in discoverability and accessibility, the test ran for too short a period to tell whether OA would result in greater sales.

Edited volumes

Edited volumes are generally spoken about in the same breath as monographs and they have a similar financial profile. Because they involve multiple authors, publishers prefer to rely on the volume's editor (usually an academic in the field and often a combination of a senior academic who lends their name and a junior who does all the work). Nevertheless, there are hidden costs to edited volumes such as the issuing of multiple chapter contracts (such as with this book) and discussions amongst contributors.

Edited volumes tend to include reports on original research or they are commissioned instead of a single-author work because there is no one who knows enough in both breadth and depth to cover all the topics pulled together in the volume (such as this book).

Edited volumes may cross over into the textbook and or the handbook arena, again because it is deemed to be the best way of covering a range of issues that have a natural link (again such as this book). The history of edited volumes is chequered. Academics believe that these contributions are less highly regarded than journal articles, and librarians are believed to prefer single-author monographs to edited volumes, although the evidence on this is scanty.

Edited volumes are a curious hybrid. They are neither journal articles (although some may have chapters that have been recycled as journal articles), nor exclusively conference proceedings (although some may be), nor always representing original works. Long the stepsister of monographs, conventional wisdom had it that the printed edited volume sold less well than single-authored monographs.

Today the edited volume often tackles interdisciplinary themes that are beyond the ability of a single individual to handle. As studies become more interdisciplinary more edited volumes are produced with the express purpose of acting as textbooks.

Within the digital realm edited volumes have an insecure future as OA e-books. They are not funded by outside sources such as open journal articles. They run the risk of the most interesting chapters being cherry picked online by readers, making the decision to buy a whole book (whether print or digital) a much less purposeful acquisition. And yet it is the edited volume that most easily lends itself to customised publishing – which, should there be sufficient demand, could yield profitable income.

Textbooks

'In the broadest sense, a textbook could be defined as a book which is written for and used by teachers and students for the purposes of teaching and learning.' (Thompson, 2005, p. 196).

As already indicated there are significant differences between US and UK textbooks, with the UK producing more upper-level supplementary texts and the US specialising in large textbooks for the core curriculum of lower-level undergraduate courses. Because of the high investment required there are only a few very large players at the lower levels of the curriculum. In the UK there are more openings for niche textbooks, even at the lower levels for smaller publishers.

All of the three subject areas (HSS, STM and Professional) require textbooks and these are mainly conceived by editors in publishing houses who keep an eye on what is needed for courses. Authors are paid either by fees or by royalties. The competition amongst publishers is in getting the best authors and understanding the requirements of lecturers so as to be able to guide the authors to produce the most successful textbook in the field. There has been an increasing migration into higher education publishing by those who began originally as academic publishers concentrating on monographs.

The largest textbook experiment is Flat World Knowledge, a new company founded in 2006 with the vision of using the free-to-promote purchases of the same content in a number of different formats, along with supplementary materials in teachers and student aids. It publishes the core textbook online in HTML and all books are on a CC NC licence. Students can buy the printed version for around $30 in black and white and $60 in colour. These are supplied on a POD basis as Flat World has shunned the logistics of operating a more traditional fulfilment service through holding stock in a warehouse. They therefore have no inventory costs. Because of its promise to produce the print books less expensively than competitors it has attracted many excellent authors and generated a lot of publicity around its new business model.

Textbooks and custom publishing

Another approach affording lecturers greater flexibility over content is the trend towards offering the opportunity to customise textbooks through the mixing and matching of chapters from a number of sources. In some cases this is restricted to material from a single publisher, whereas in others lecturers can upload their own content or materials from other sources.

DynamicBooks, a new software initiative from Macmillan, is just one of many now allowing university instructors to edit digital editions of textbooks and customise them for their individual classes. Professors are able to reorganise or delete chapters; upload course syllabuses, notes, videos, pictures and graphs; and rewrite or delete individual paragraphs, equations or illustrations.

DynamicBooks gives instructors the power to alter individual sentences and paragraphs without consulting the original authors or publisher – no doubt causing questions to be raised concerning copyright.

Another example of a company offering similar services are http://academicpub.com who provide textbooks from a variety of publishers.

Reference works

'Reference works are an accumulation of discrete pieces of knowledge.' (Thompson, 2005, p. 323).

Reference works are produced in all subject areas and are generally commissioned and developed by the publishing house. They are priced anywhere from monograph level to hundreds or thousands of pounds depending on the level of investment and the size of the relevant market. These works are increasingly international and a number of European publishing companies such as Brill have carved out niches for themselves.

The digital era has transformed the business of reference publishing by allowing easy and inexpensive update of material. And as a result, this has changed the workflow structure and delivery, effectively spelling the end for printed reference works. Some reference works made a successful transition to digital, such as the *Oxford English Dictionary* which is about to cease print publishing altogether. Others have had greater difficulty, such as the world famous *Encyclopaedia Britannica* which contracted to less than 10 per cent of its historical high to now a profitable £50 million business.

The largest reference work publisher is Wikipedia. Its runaway success was initially seen as a threat to all encyclopaedias. However, due to questions over provenance and reliability, the value of quality-controlled content is increasingly becoming acknowledged. The question remains though: How much is the market willing to pay for high-quality content when there is so much available for free?

The new aggregated packages of content transcend the above distinctions. Digitisation has made this possible and a reality. Today, the large publishers are offering packages such as Palgrave Connect and Oxford Scholarship Online and other publishers are rapidly packaging up and digitising their complete lists.

Blended e-products

Scholarly communications are increasingly relying on multimedia. These were at first additional resources bundled in with the e-book package and sold as enhanced e-books. Today a more sophisticated form of blended media is emerging – multidimensional and open to all sorts of experimentation. Too much of such material, at too high a price is ignored by the community. Too little and too simple is quickly discarded as the next exciting product comes along. Publishers are, of necessity, making investment decisions without a clear idea of what the expected returns might be from this area.

Reference and textbooks have the greatest potential, while monographs are too specialised and each title creates too little revenue to find room to invest in enhancements. Most scholarly publishers rely on authors and their institutions to come up with additional content and resources. Edited volumes do have the potential for benefiting from enhancements as each chapter can only report on research in a manner that is as succinct as a journal article, so finding ways of providing the background data and additional information can at times serve the reader very well.

New companies are springing up everywhere to host e-book content and sell either the digital or print products as a result of showing as much as possible free without hurting sales. Indeed, models such as PaperC, which hosts textbooks and allows publishers to set the length of time readers may view the content (30/60/90 minutes) before closing access, hope to make their money by splitting the revenue with their publisher clients. All of these models are in some ways beholden to the 'freemium' model. They have all been influenced by Amazon's 'Look Inside' feature, which demonstrated that exposure can increase sales. Google Books followed the same principle.

Conclusion – the future of 'stuff'

It is a truism to say that we have moved from a world of information scarcity to information abundance. But this short phrase encapsulates why everyone in the academic communications chain is being forced to change their business model if they wish to stay in business. To find a way around all the 'stuff' that is expanding at a frightening rate on the Web, publishers, booksellers, printers, distributors, libraries and their suppliers are all changing to accommodate the changing usage patterns of academics and students. And the next decade will see a substantial increase in tools designed to help navigate around and make best use of the 'stuff'. In some cases we are pushing the change, but in most we are all responding to what is possible and what is desirable.

It is impossible to write a handbook on the subject that describes the status quo – because there is no status quo. The tectonic plates are on the move. There is no way of knowing yet whether it will create a tsunami of devastating proportions or whether the publishing industry as we know it will adapt and even with its new ways of operating and new business models, shake off the shackles of the past and find a healthy way forward in the digital realm.

The publishing industry is working hard to deal with the pressures on the industry – OA, open educational resources, institutional repositories, politics of access and licensing issues in the digital realm.

What the value chain will look like after an almost complete migration to digital in academic publishing is still unclear, although pieces are becoming clearer. Issues around the level and direction of investment during the transition are the questions that will preoccupy the industry for another 10 years.

Acknowledgement

We thank Martin Casimir of Bloomsbury Professional for input on professional publishing.

Further reading

Adema, J. (2010) *Overview of Open Access Models for E-books in the Sciences and the Humanities*. Accessed from http://www.aupress.ca/documents/OpenAccessModels_OAPEN.pdf

Cox, L. (2010) Scholarly book publishing practice. *Learned Publishing Journal* 23(4,347–56,doi:10.1087/20100412,http://www.ingentaconnect.com/content/alpsp/lp/2010/00000023/00000004/art00012

Ferwerda, E. (2010) *Open Access Monographic Publishing in the Humanities*. Accessed from http://iospress.metapress.com/content/l6wg61l0mg6426w8/fulltext.html

Griffiths, R.J. and Rascoff, M. (2005) *The Evolving Environment for Scholarly Electronic Monographs*. Accessed from http://www.ithaka.org/ithaka-s-r/strategyold/Environment per cent20for per cent20digital per cent20monograph per cent20publishing per cent20and per cent20distribution.pdf

Heath, M., Jubb, M. and Robey, D. (2008) *E-Publication and Open Access in the Arts and Humanities in the UK*. Accessed from http://www.ariadne.ac.uk/issue54/heath-et-al/

Hickey, H. (2011) College Students' use of Kindle DX to e-reader's role in Academia. Accessed from http://www.washington.edu/news/articles/college-students2019-use-of-kindle-dx-points-to-e-reader2019s-role-in-academia

JISC E-book Report. Accessed from http://www.jiscebooksproject.org/reports/finalreport

Macicak, S. (2009) *Patron-driven, Librarian approved: a pay-per-view model for e-books.* Accessed from http://uksg.metapress.com/media/cmwkwptvyh29e2jhpq0x/ contributions/h/8/5/7/h857558qvq02445k.pdf

Pearson Custom; http://www.pearsoncustom.com/

Pochoda, P. (2009) UP 2.0 'Some theses on the future of academic publishing'. *The Journal of Electronic Publishing* 13(1), Accessed from http://quod.lib.umich.edu/cgi/t/text/text-idx?c=jep;view=text;rgn=main;idno=3336451.0013.102

Podcast with Suzanne BeDell, STM book director at Elsevier. Accessed from http://www.sla-europe.org/2011/02/09/podcast-suzanne-bedell-stm-book-director-at-elsevier/

Presentation from ALPSP Seminar, (March 2010) The Future of Academic Book Publishing, Accessed from http://www.alpsp.org/ngen_public/article.asp?aid=111846

Publishers Association Annual Report (2011) Accessed from http://www.publishers.org.uk/index.php?option=com_content&view=article&id=1755:the-publishers-association-reveals-accelerated-growth-in-2010-digital-book-market&catid=503:pa-press-releases-and-comments&Itemid=1618

Scott, B. (2011) *Professional Publishing Revenues Rebound with Help from E-books and Online Strategies.* Accessed from http://bookpublishingnews.blogspot.com/2011/02/professional-publishing-revenues.html

Steele, C. (2008) *Scholarly Monograph Publishing in the 21st Century: The Future more than ever should be an Open Book.* Accessed from http://vnweb.hwwilsonweb.com.libproxy.ucl.ac.uk/hww/results/getResults.jhtml?_DARGS=/hww/results/results_common.jhtml.35

The Association of American University Presses (2011) *Sustaining Scholarly Publishing: New Business Models for University Presses.* Accessed from http://aaupnet.org/resources/reports/business_models/aaupbusinessmodels2011.pdf

University of Michigan Espresso Book Machine Experiment Study. Accessed from http://www.emeraldinsight.com/journals.htm?issn=0737-8831&volume=29&issue=1&articleid=1912300&show=html&view=printarticle&nolog=310677

Willinsky, J. (2009) Towards the design of an open access monograph press. *The Journal of Electronic Publishing* 12(1) http://quod.lib.umich.edu/cgi/t/text/text-idx?c=jep;view=text;rgn=main;idno=3336451.0012.103

References

Borgman, C. (2007) *Scholarship in the Digital Age: Information, Infrastructure and the Internet.* Cambridge, MA: MIT Press.

Greco, A.N. and Wharton, R.M. (2008) Should university presses adopt an open access business model for all their scholarly books? *Proceedings ELPUB 2008 Conference on Electronic Publishing.* Accessed from http://elpub.scix.net/data/works/att/149_elpub2008.content.pdf

Krikorian, G. and Kapczynski, A. (eds) (2010) *Access to Knowledge in the Age of Intellectual Property.* New York: Zone Books.

Snijder, R. (2010) The profits of free books: an experiment to measure the impact of open access publishing. *Learned Publishing*, 23(4). Accessed from http://www.ingentaconnect.com/content/alpsp/lp/2010/00000023/00000004/art00003

Thompson, J. (2005) *Books in the Digital Age*. Cambridge: Polity Press Ltd.

Ware, M. and Mabe, M. (2009) *STM Report: An overview of Scientific and Scholarly Journal Publishing*. Oxford: International Association of Scientific, Technical and Medical Publishers.

Weller, M. (2011) *The Digital Scholar: How Technology is changing Academic Practice*. London: Bloomsbury Dynamic Books; http://dynamicbooks.com/instructor-advantage/

8

Editorial and production workflows

Volker Böing

Abstract: This chapter deals with the growing complexity of today's scientific publishing business and describes possible solutions to tackle the challenges presented by the continuing growth of publication output, as well as the increasing variety of print and electronic formats required for book and journal content. The chapter describes the development of editorial and production workflows based on XML, as well as the integration and automation of systems through business analysis and the realisation of Business Process Management approaches.

Key words: Editorial workflows, production workflows, metadata, XML, validation, business process management, automation, quality assurance.

Introduction

For centuries, printed products such as books and journals were the only content media a publisher had to control and take care of, with clear supply chain responsibilities and roles. In parallel with the wider technological developments over the past 15 years (such as growth of the Internet), the academic and professional publishing industry has seen a rapid evolution of new digital publication channels and content formats that have become valuable parts of a publishing house's product portfolio. Furthermore, the scholarly publishing industry is confronted by the immense international growth in the number of researchers with a concomitant increase in publication output, especially from China and Asian countries which are investing more heavily in research and development (Blaschke, 2003; UNESCO, 2009). This immense increase in information (Marx and Gramm, 2002) and the associated management challenges are of critical importance to scholars, the publishing community and customers alike.

Electronic publishing (ePublishing) promises to cope with this growth in a timely and cost-effective manner, allowing publishing businesses to focus on content for online-first publication as well as reducing print and distribution supply chain demands through the adoption of new, digital printing processes.

Advances in formats and in editorial and production workflows

ePublishing has moved the focus away from print-only distribution channels to electronic-only (e-only) and multi-channel publication approaches (Research Information Network, 2010). Advances in digital printing technologies (BISG, 2010), such as short-run printing and print on demand (POD), have made it possible for publishers to move away from a strategy of printing huge initial quantities of stock which might later need to be pulped, depending on the reality of whether a product meets with market expectations.

The quality of digitally printed products has much improved over the last few years and customers rarely notice a difference between a digitally printed book and a book printed via offset. In offset printing, an image is transferred (offset) from the printing plate to a rubber blanket, and then again to the printing surface, whereas digital printing techniques start from a digital printing image in a computer which is then either produced via laser or inkjet printers. The initial effort required to set up an offset printing job is higher than that needed for digital printing but it is more cost-effective for larger print runs. For example, for a new edition with high potential sales, or for the reprint of a bestseller, a decision must be taken as to how big the offset print run will be. For a low print-run publication, printing to order or even taking an e-only approach would be a good solution to reduce warehouse costs and to allow publication of titles which would never have been published under the old cost- and budget-driven circumstances of a print-only world.

In the past, printing was the main purpose of a production workflow. Today, however, production workflows are themselves developing into content preparation process support systems which create the various formats needed to supply the different distribution channels. Printing uses just one of the many formats created. Today, some publishers approach publications primarily as e-only products, whilst creating print-relevant formats anyway and storing them in a central data repository. Whether these 'print-ready' versions are used at a future date is dependent on the publisher's product placement strategy and on the demands of the market.

As in other media-oriented industries, it should be up to the customer to decide how to consume content, and thus format (including print) becomes a matter of choice to be supported. One sample strategy for dealing with the new expectations for both online and print content is Springer's MyCopy, where low-cost print products are available on demand to customers who have access to related eBook packages. Other sample strategies are the 'Espresso' POD machine, or service providers such as BOD (Books on Demand), which allow individual copies of books to be loaded onto their system to be printed on-site and on demand at a host institution. Increasingly, academic and professional publisher outputs are heading online first, with print levels dropping, replaced and enhanced through new technologies, access models and discoverability tools. To manage these developments and avoid duplication of production efforts downstream, new editorial and production workflows need to be defined and established. But applying digital processes is a highly complex challenge, particularly given the growing amount of data, formats and electronic features compared with the print-oriented publishing process. As well as providing softcover and hardcover print versions, today's publishing business processes and IT systems have to handle various electronic formats such as PDF, HTML and ePub, which are required by different reading devices (from desktop computers to handheld readers and, increasingly, even smart phones).

Preparing content in each format from scratch can have major cost implications but is a necessary action when historical content also has to be accessed for today's business models. For frontlist title production, a complete set of formats is desirable and is only a minor effort when they are the result of the initial typesetting, editing and artwork processes for a publication. XML (Extensible Markup Language) derivatives such as ePub can be created from full-text XML, and a onetime investment in a style sheet often does the job without any extra costs.

However, a move from print-oriented to digital print-and-online publishing is not simply a question of production processes, as workflows are very much intertwined with other departments in a publishing company. This is particularly clear when one considers the need for appropriate upstream formatting of electronic files and the addition of adequate and correct metadata to allow for user discoverability in the new electronic architectures that lie downstream.

Metadata and XML-based processing

The previous section explained the demands and requirements of various content formats. One way to achieve these demands automatically is via a layout-independent XML file which can be used to render various content formats. But XML is not only beneficial for content processing, as it can also create data which hold the bibliographic metadata of a publication. Content may still be king but metadata are clearly master. Without a correct and reliable metadata description of content, the content itself is useless in an ePublishing environment where visibility and availability are so important. Every wholesaler needs to put content in the right corner of an online shop, every POD printer needs to print it according to the correct specifications and every librarian needs to place it on the correct shelf of a digital library; metadata are essential for all these purposes. XML coding of text and metadata provides machine-readable data for these various purposes, as well as for production tracking systems, and it has thus become a fundamental tool in electronic content management and production processes. XML is the basis for:

- metadata importing and exporting
- layout-independent content representation
- delivery consistency checking
- semantic enrichment
- cross-reference and forward-linking processes
- workflow job descriptions (technical production parameters and deliverables)
- derived product support

XML data are defined by a so called Document Type Definition (DTD), a set of rules, similar to the grammar of a language, controlling how certain data elements can be grouped and nested. Furthermore, the data elements themselves are defined in the DTD. Using the language metaphor, a DTD is the grammar and the vocabulary for XML files and it is possible to validate and to proof the correctness of sentences in this language against the rules defined. An XML element itself consists of a descriptive opening and close tag and the text content in between. A computer program (applications in this context are called parsers) reads through the 'sentences' in an XML file and can semantically interpret what certain text portions mean.

In the XML fragment represented in Figure 8.1, the parser can identify that after the element opening tag <JournalTitle> the title of the journal

```
<JournalInfo JournalProductType='ArchiveJournal'>
  <JournalID>412</JournalID>
  <JournalPrintISSN>0009-5915</JournalPrintISSN>
  <JournalElectronicISSN>1432-0886</JournalElectronicISSN>
  <JournalTitle>Chromosoma</JournalTitle>
  <JournalSubTitle>Biology of the Nucleus</JournalSubTitle>
  <JournalAbbreviatedTitle>Chromosoma</JournalAbbreviatedTitle>
</JournalInfo>
```

Figure 8.1 **Example of XML-encoded journal metadata**

follows until the closing tag </JournalTitle> is reached. The text content 'Chromosoma' thus is given a meaning and can be processed based on that meaning. XML Schema DTDs (Duckett *et al.*, 2001) also define rules about the content within the elements and it is possible to specify date ranges or character settings (for example) which are valid or not valid as content in the appropriate elements. A further step in validation efforts for XML data is Schematron (http://www.schematron.com/), which goes beyond format and content validity checks that can be achieved by DTDs and Schema DTDs by allowing an additional validation of XML content against certain business rules. The right elements may be used and the correct content type tagged with them but the overall XML file might still not be correct if the values of the various elements do not fit together and make sense according to business rules, which are clearly of great importance. For example, an XML feed from a peer-review system to a production environment which holds a <\SubmitOnline> date which is after the <\Accepted> date is correct with regard to the DTD and the structuring of the data but simply wrong according to the business rule that an article has first to be submitted before it can be reviewed and accepted for publication. This is a very easy example but to identify such rules can be a very labour-intensive and painful exercise when finding new items that have not been thought of from the beginning and when addressing processing errors featuring incorrect data.

The combination of metadata and content structures in one DTD is advisable and hugely beneficial as it brings metadata and content together in one complete electronic package. Such an approach provides elements and attributes for bibliographic data of a publication as well as for the body, front and back matter parts, which can all be described with the elements of one DTD. An XML file based on such a universal publication DTD holds everything which belongs to an article or chapter. Whether such an instance is stored on a file store or as entries in an object-oriented XML database is secondary from a production point of view but can make a difference in the way the XML can be used further down the line for the support of online platform functionalities or for the re-use of already published content.

Header information for journal and book content can contain basic descriptive information such as publisher location, journal title and ISSN. A subset of metadata information for journal content can be seen in Figure 8.1.

Complete and consistent metadata preparation allows for content packages to be clearly identified at any stage of production. This can also be applied to tables, figures and possibly other media objects within XML files, allowing automatic processing to be applied in a straightforward way. The deliverables can then be automatically placed in the correct folders in a file store, with metadata uploading to and updating the product database on import. Metadata updates from a product database to individual publications are possible, and metadata updates are also possible when the XML files are exported from a central production data repository, i.e. user changes are reflected 'on the fly' when working with XML and automated systems.

Full-text XML allows for layout-independent content representation (Figure 8.2), including the creation of ePub and HTML files, as well as

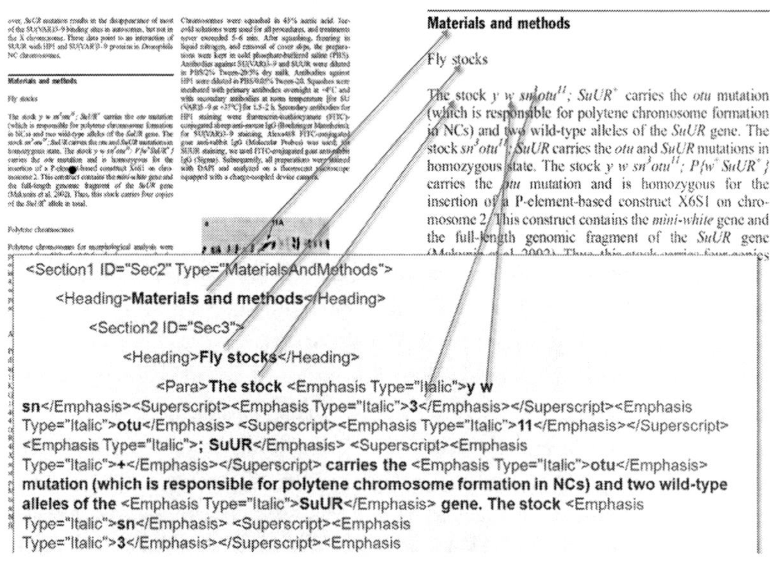

Figure 8.2 Layout-independent XML data and its use

serving as input for PDF-rendering engines to use in creating print and online files.

Full-text XML content also supports other products and services which are either not directly related to a publication itself or enrich the existing content. Examples include reference linking from article citations to related book and journal content available online, and cited by linking where articles maintain a record of citation by external publications.

Semantic enrichment (i.e. the identification and tagging of key terms and definitions for use in building linked relationships between contextually relevant material) makes chapter and article content more valuable for the end-user and increases the overall reading and usage experience (Figure 8.3). Full-text XML files can be used to create and feed into additional meta-products such as image databases by using semantically tagged image data created during the production process to retrieve and to re-use images from existing published content.

Ideally, the use of XML will already have started in the manuscript tracking/peer review system, providing the initial author and article metadata that can be used to create a technical representation of the future publication within a production IT system. On the content creation side, an author can already be provided with TeX or Word layout templates to ensure that the author uses only those structural elements that are supported by the publisher's XML DTD. The use of

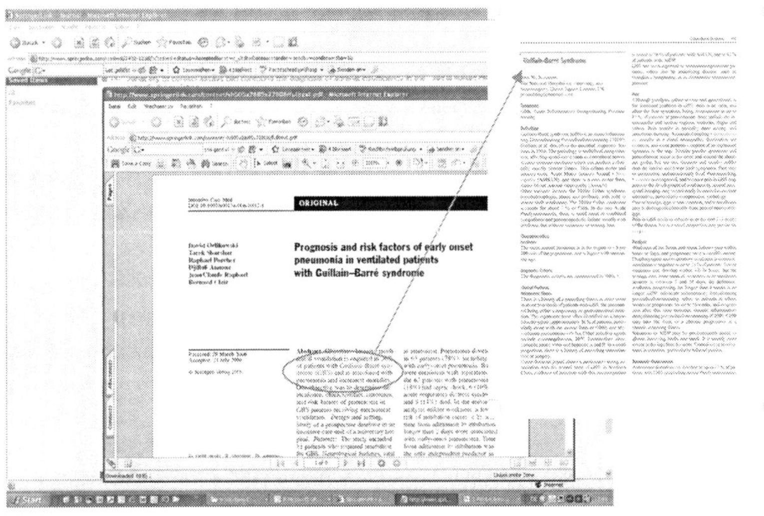

Figure 8.3 Example of semantic linking of terms and definitions

XML to transfer data via web services from one application to another is much more efficient and controllable than the 'watch-dog' application/script-based approaches of the past, where folders on a server were monitored for incoming data that were processed on arrival.

As well as the mere transfer of XML-encoded content and publication data, workflow requirements such as typesetting, artwork and language editing can also be described via XML and validated against expected results on receipt. Delivery consistency checking using XML parsing (checking the delivered content structure against the expected content structure) is relatively straightforward and avoids the kinds of inconsistent and incomplete data that later require painful correction.

Any new requirements arising for DTD and XML encoding of content and metadata can be made through backward-compatible upgrades. Occasionally, of course, major changes to a DTD will be unavoidable and so migration of existing XML markup may be required (which can be problematic for XML files in production, for example with vendors or at application servers awaiting automatic processing). While this can be quite a complicated operation, the benefits of integrated application systems and databases through XML and a DTD definitely outweigh such drawbacks.

Electronic production workflows

Standardisation and global approaches are key to achieving automation in the cooperation between external vendors and internationally operating publishers. Electronic production workflows transfer content items at various production stages between vendor (e.g. those responsible for typesetting, artwork or printing) and publisher IT systems.

Initiating a standardised electronic production workflow requires analysis and specification of the deliverables and processing requirements for the various steps within a journal and book production chain. Developing a common workflow and establishing technical language that both vendors and internal production staff alike can share and communicate with is the backbone of an electronic production workflow. To form a basis for cooperation and standardisation, the following mandatory fields are recommended for inclusion in such a workflow:

- Production Workflow Components (Chapters, Covers, Adverts, etc.)
- XML Creation
- PDF Requirements (Print & Online)

- Artwork Specifications
- Layout
- Trim sizes/Formats
- Author Instructions
- Quality Check Routines
- Copy Editing
- Proof Procedures
- Responsibilities

In the workflow diagram in Figure 8.4, an example of a possible journal production workflow is shown. The definition of stage numbers, which can be referenced in technical instructions and user handbooks, is very useful, while the use of discrete (article or chapters) and compound (issues and books) workflows will form part of a publisher's own specifications.

The discrete workflow shown starts with the initiation of an article object. This can be triggered by direct upload of manuscript data to a production workflow server by a user or through automatic transfer of author source data from a peer review system upon article acceptance. The responsible production personnel can, at this stage, finalise the initial metadata before the content preparation and author query phases of the workflow start in parallel. It is advisable to make use of the time required by the author to go through appropriate questionnaires and the

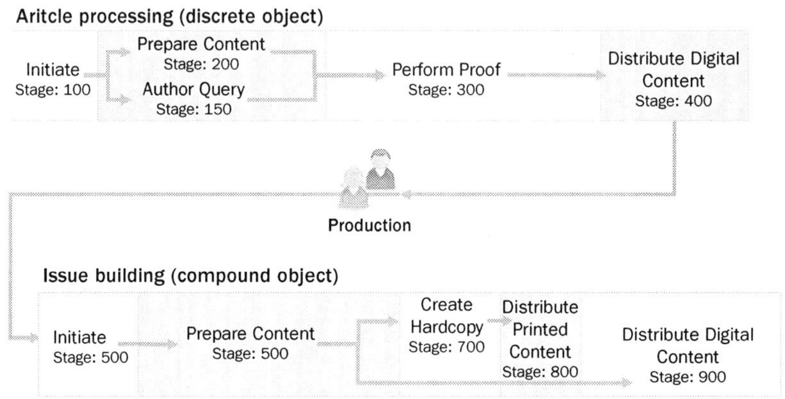

Figure 8.4 Example of a journal article production workflow representation

transfer of copyright to proceed with the first typesetting and language editing round. This keeps the overall publication time down and gives the author a timely publishing experience.

After finalisation of the proof stage an article can already be published online, at which point the article will be citable via its Digital Object Identifier (DOI). A DOI is a string of characters which is a unique identifier for content as well as being a permanent link to the content. Scholarly publishers assign DOIs through the CrossRef System. CrossRef issues the publisher with a prefix (e.g. 10.1007 for the scientific publisher Springer) and the publishers assign a unique suffix string identifying the publication itself. 10.1007/s00412-011-0329-6 identifies an article in the journal 'Chromosoma' and is resolved when used with the DOI Proxy server – http://dx.doi.org/10.1007/s00412-011-0329-6 – to the publisher's online platform by using the Uniform Resource Locator (URL) registered with the DOI (Figure 8.5). Such 'key/value' pairs allow publishers to update or change the physical location of content without altering the DOIs themselves: a DOI stays valid although the physical location of the content is changed; it is a permanent way to cite electronic versions of scholarly content. CrossRef provides services such as the reference linking process mentioned above.

Once all articles comprising a journal issue are published online, a compound workflow can begin to build the issue, assigning articles under the familiar volume, issue and year structure of a journal. Different approaches to issue building are practised by different publishers

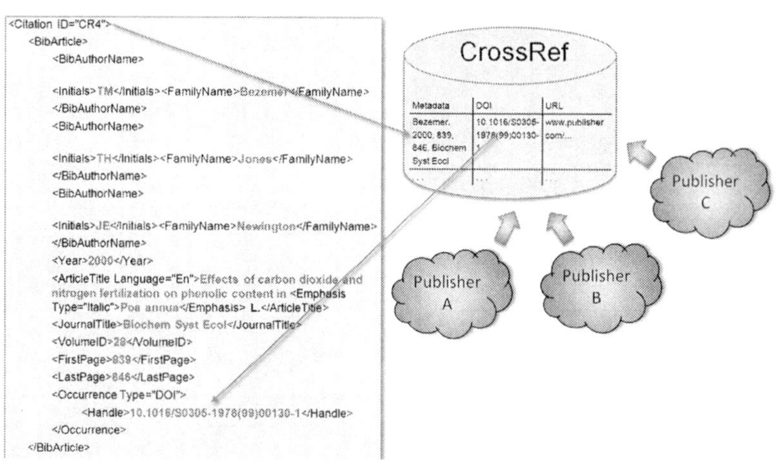

Figure 8.5 Reference linking and DOI metadata storage

depending on the needs and wishes of their customers, with some opting for a more or less automatic assignment of articles to an issue (first in, first out), and others deciding which articles should end up in a certain issue and, within that, in what sequence (here the editor-in-chief or members of the editorial board are likely to be most active in deciding the issue structure). When the issue structure has been built, the files can be sent for final typesetting and pagination, including updating bibliographic metadata at the article level. For those publishers adopting automatic issue building and assigning articles consecutively during the publication year, the final bibliographic metadata can be made available at the time of article acceptance and handover to production.

An electronic production workflow should streamline the production process and provide the ability to create all necessary output formats in one go, especially as customers are increasingly interested in XML, HTML, PDF and ePub outputs as replacements for, or additions to, a printed product. The number of formats which are actually stored in a publisher's content repository can be reduced to a layout-independent XML file of the content together with related media objects, in principle allowing for all other formats to be created on the fly. Data feeds in the form of ONIX or proprietary formats can be rendered alongside these content formats, depending upon customer requirements.

When implementing an electronic production workflow like the one described above, it is important to aim for a technical system design which is as configurable and modular as possible to enable sufficient flexibility for future development. This is particularly relevant to examples of workflow change and where new responsibilities crop up, as well as to supporting the potential for new product development. Such modularity means it should not be necessary to re-build major parts of a system or to interfere with existing, reliable and accepted functionalities. It should only be necessary to enhance the relevant content model or technical modules to provide additional functionalities or processes for new format outputs.

Business process management and IT systems development

Any definition of the term Business Process Management is heavily influenced by IT but an understanding of it in a broader sense, with an integrated view of management, organisation and control, allows a beneficial, goal-oriented approach to design and implement business processes successfully. IT is an important part of this and a supporting component (Schmelzer and Sesselmann, 2010).

Business process management analysis and specification approaches are critical to integrating global ePublishing systems composed of electronic manuscript submission, electronic and traditional print production processes, and associated business and market information subsystems.

Establishing 'who does what, when, and how?' across the publishing business process chain of editorial, production, sales, marketing and fulfilment for book and/or journal content is a challenge for any publisher to consider, and even more so to apply. Ideally, ePublishing systems should be put in place with the functionality to support the various departments and task-responsible people within the overall process chain. Although not everything that can be supported by IT system functionality has to be supported, everything that is required for consistent journal or book products should be mandatory in the content and workflow management systems. A global system should support mandatory steps from initial metadata gathering, through content creation and production, and on to transfer of data (content and metadata) between internal users, external vendors, customers, content aggregators and distributors.

An analysis of the business is the initial step to setting up any such system, as seemingly simple questions with regard to relevant technical parameters can result in a wide variety of answers. Such a variety of existing instructions can lead to a huge number of different production processes on the vendor's side, even if from a bird's eye view there is a one-to-one relationship between publisher and vendor; rationalising these approaches is important for establishing a robust and efficient system.

Business analysis can also have a value in itself, quite apart from helping to develop an appropriate technical workflow. In clearly answering the questions of 'who does what, when and how?', an analyst needs to review the roles, responsibilities and dependencies of particular business process steps in terms of both short-term needs but also looking to the longer term, i.e. investigating the potential for future improvements and optimisation of systems and procedures.

Given the impossibility of talking to all staff in medium to large companies, particularly those with multiple business locations across the globe, the introduction of a key-user concept is advisable, as this allows for representatives to be invited to explain the business process and discuss the specific requirements of their peer group. Extracting all the detail of common processes and potential future developments from the received insights and discussions will be a challenge. Many departments may have good reasons for their specific ways of approaching processes, including the simple fact that things are done in a certain way because that's how they have always been done!

In smaller companies, analysing 'who does what, when and how?' may be easier to accomplish but, simultaneously, resources to implement overall change may be more restricted. An alternative solution is to 'buy-in' pre-packaged systems from vendors who can effectively perform a 'business analysis' as part of their tendering and business development processes. Fast start-up and quick wins can be achieved by introducing such an environment based on a vendor's system but any further advantages can sometimes prove hard to achieve after the introduction of such a system. Suppliers of such systems sell a product for a number of publishers and the provided functionality is often the result of what is common amongst the existing customers, and so might not cater fully for an individual publisher's specific workflow. Nevertheless, especially for smaller publishers, this can be a very good solution if the appropriate competence team and IT organisation doesn't exist in-house.

As in every other business field, change can be perceived as a threat to existing procedures, and resistance is therefore to be expected if change is implemented the wrong way. But when change is approached in an open, flexible and cooperative manner, it can also be a great opportunity for fruitful discussions and a motivating experience for every participant. This is especially true where the potential for systems optimisation, and the great opportunity this presents for quality and efficiency, is recognised.

Bringing people on board during an analysis and design phase is crucial for the overall success of a business process management project. Getting a clear and logical conceptual framework that is easily understood in the first place improves user buy-in before the actual technical implementation starts. Indeed, even if the first version of an IT system does not match expectations, the trust gained during an initialisation, analysis and design phase can carry the project through.

Once agreement is reached on a conceptual framework for future internal and external business process steps and activities, the functional requirements can be developed through a technical design phase with developers and system architects. These developers and architects would ideally have already participated in the initial user/peer group discussions, in order to better understand where the system needs to be heading. They can also feed into these earlier discussions with appropriate interventions when visions of future system functionality lead proceedings in directions which cannot be realised without higher costs and more effort than is reasonable.

Continuous progress updating is advisable during the implementation phase to keep users informed about the realisation of concepts they took part in defining during the decision-making process. Agile programming methodologies, such as SCRUM,[1] can be very useful here, with small and fast development cycles providing reassurance that developments are heading in the right direction. Mock-ups and story boards can also provide useful means of ensuring transparent development.

To facilitate the technical implementation of the proposed IT system, a clear representation of the products and processes covered – including books and journals and the range of publication types in between – is required. This object model has to be well defined with a well-designed data structure that is flexible enough to fulfil all needs but without becoming too complex, or precluding future maintenance and further changes that may arise during the lifetime of the system (Figure 8.6).

The system should be able to support content management processes and workflows, contracts, content files and supplementary electronic materials, marketing texts, author biography and other publication-relevant material. At the end of a publishing process, a final record within the system should contain everything of relevance to print and online publication as well as long-term archiving and preservation, ideally reflected in an XML DTD for import and export of content and metadata.

Another important field where business process management approaches can be beneficial is in communication and data transfer with external vendors during the workflow stages of relevance to production. A clear specification of vendor tasks and expected deliverables can introduce a location-independent route to efficient product creation. The benefits of such a standardised way of publishing book and journal content are huge, although limitations here include a loss of flexibility in realising special requirements or ideas, given the complex nature of globally used systems with a limited potential for localised variations.

An Enterprise Content Management system (Figure 8.7) with the aim and scope described above is a 'living thing'. Permanent monitoring and an open ear to users and management is necessary for the continuity and value of this kind of asset.

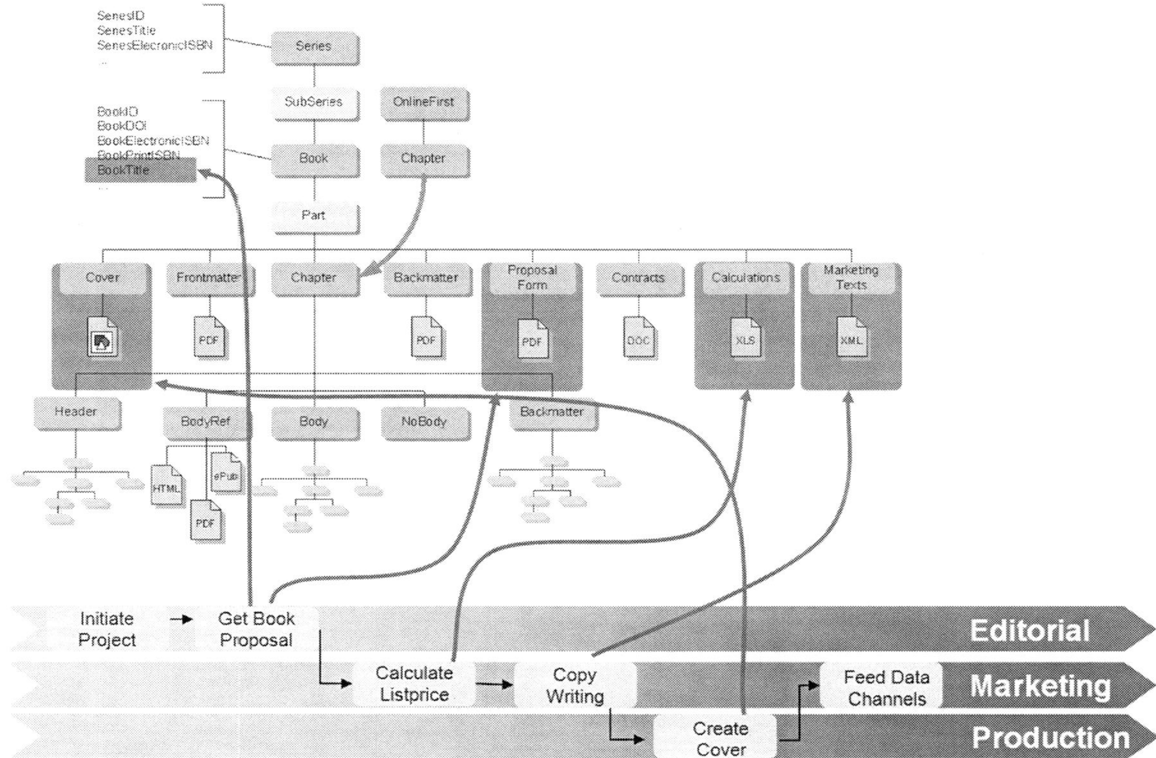

Figure 8.6 Example of a book object model and associated business processes

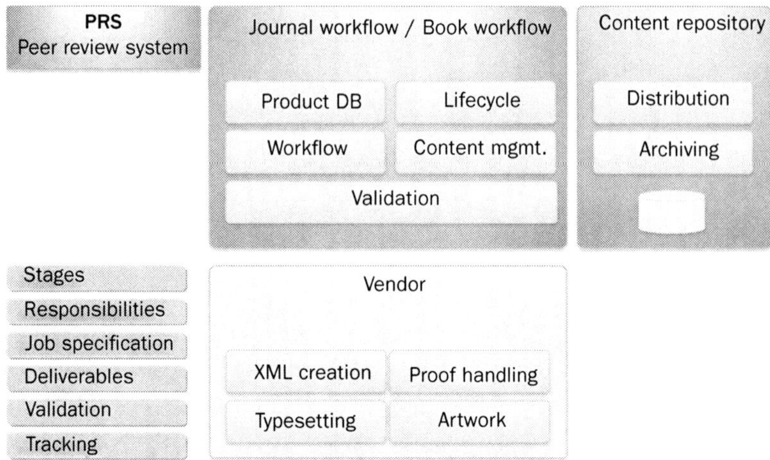

Figure 8.7 Example of an Enterprise Content Management model

The conceptual overview of a Process and Content Management system shown in Figure 8.6 names the main components of a possible publisher's IT infrastructure. Starting with a Peer Review System, where the decision-making process ('Should the title be published?') is supported and the collaboration of editorial and in-house or external reviewers takes place, such a system provides external as well as internal editorial board members with the appropriate means to cope with the publication queue of a journal. After a publication is accepted, an automatic transfer of initial metadata such as peer review dates, author contact information and the author's source data (manuscripts including the raw data for images, tables, text and possible electronic supplementary material) can greatly improve the overall turnaround time of a publication. Once accepted, product data and production systems take over, steering the production chain and providing life cycle, content management, validation and workflow functionality.

Such a product and production system provides an overview of frontlist title production as well as of the historical pool of publications. Product data and production systems can be integrated or separate, with a hand over to production step from a pure product database to a more content management-oriented production system. In the case of outsourced typesetting, artwork, XML creation and proof handling, vendors have to provide the appropriate IT infrastructure to do this work, as shown in Figure 8.7. In the case of in-house creation of content files, the production system on the publisher's side has to have the appropriate tools available to complete tasks. Finally, accepted and published versions of publications have to be archived and distributed, and such system functionality can be integrated in a single production IT system or be part of a separate one. In Figure 8.7, only the final version is sent to the archiving and distribution system, and the various previous versions created during the initial stages are deleted and vanish from the production system, where only the current frontlist title version remains. Throughout all of these system components, it is necessary to define tasks (up to job descriptions), stages, responsibilities, deliverables, validation rules and consistency constraints and to provide sufficient tracking and monitoring functionalities.

Quality assurance

Key performance indicators can show whether something is running well but they are of limited use in explaining the root cause of a problem within the publishing/production chain; they would not, for example, detect high attrition rates on the vendor's side as a reason for a sudden peak in disapproval rates in proof stages. Such staff turnover issues are of particular concern when outsourcing work to vendors (e.g. in Asia), making it necessary to continuously ensure a common technical basis of understanding amongst internal users as well as between internal staff and external vendors.

It is necessary to establish appropriate quality assurance measures to maintain and develop an integrated publishing approach. Continuous monitoring of usage (how working procedures are applied) and results allows a publisher to ensure that systems keep pace with the requirements of the business.

The following areas can be the subject of quality assurance measures:

- enforcement of standardised processes and production methods
- error reduction
- turnaround times
- disapproval rates
- training of users
- vendor and internal department audits
- author satisfaction surveys

Any updates or changes to the system arising out of quality assurance feedback or for other business reasons also need to be clearly communicated and incorporated into existing specifications if standardised approaches are to be maintained. In this respect, it is also important that vendor IT systems are able to communicate with a publisher's technical infrastructure.

Conclusion and outlook

Whilst in the past it was most important for a printed product to be in good shape with bibliographic metadata correct on the cover and on title pages, in today's digital arena this is not sufficient. Changes in distribution and fulfilment processes have seen a fall in book and journal print levels. Traditional production workflows are migrating to pure content preparation electronic workflows, handling new and more complex kinds of author source data in the same way, and using XML-based workflows to achieve layout-independent content that can be output to multiple print and electronic formats. These changes have led to publisher product databases playing a central role in any company's operations. To correctly maintain the effectiveness of this central resource, complete and consistent metadata are required.

Business process management can bring value to publishers in terms of the efficiency, sustainability, agility and quality benefits that analysis and specification can help to realise. Integrated content management systems are becoming a must-have item, especially for publishers with increasing book and journal throughput.

Looking forward, the technical potential of rendering engines and database publishing will allow publishers to manage and build their businesses, and it seems very likely that continuing advances in ePublishing will lead to even greater levels of automation, especially in the context of content production workflows.

Note

1. A methodology of agile software engineering with iterative, incremental software deployment cycles.

References

BISG (Book Industry Study Group) (2010) *Digital Book Printing For Dummies®*, BISG/Wiley; http://www.bisg.org/publications/product.php?p=20

Blaschke, S. (2003) Die Informationsexplosion und ihre Bewältigung: Gedanken zur Suche nach einem besseren System der Fachkommunikation. *Information – Wissenschaft und Praxis* 54(6); http://www.archive.org/details/DieInformations explosionUndIhreBewltigung

Ducket, J., Griffin, O. and Mohr, S. (2001) *Professional XML Schemas (Programmer to Programmer)*, illustrated edition. Wrox Press.

Marx, W. and Gramm, G. (2002) *Literaturflut – Informationslawine – Wissensexplosion. Wächst der Wissenschaft das Wissen über den Kopf?*; http://www.mpi-stuttgart.mpg.de/ivs/literaturflut.html

Research Information Network (2010) *E-only scholarly journals: overcoming the barriers*; http://www.rin.ac.uk/our-work/communicating-and-disseminating-research/e-only-scholarly-journals-overcoming-barriers

Schmelzer, 20J. and Sesselmann, W. (2010) Geschäftsprozessmanagement in der Praxis: Kunden zufrieden stellen – Produktivität steigern – Wert erhöhen, 7., überarb. Aufl. – Hanser Verlag

UNESCO Institute for Statistics (2009) *A Global Perspective on Research and Development*, http://www.kooperation-international.de/detail/info/unesco-institute-for-statistics-a-global-perspective-on-research-and-development.html

9

Electronic publishing standards

Todd Carpenter

Abstract: One key aspect of our new era of digital publishing is the standards upon which the publication process rests, from creation through distribution to preservation. The network of organizations developing standards in our community is varied and overlapping. So too are the standards. This chapter covers some background on standards and standards development, highlights some key existing standards in electronic publishing, and discusses some issues needing future standardization and some of the initiatives underway to address these issues.

Key words: Standards, NISO, ERM, digital, publishing, ISO, SUSHI, DAISY, XML, ISBN, ISSN, DOI, ISTC, ISNI, ORCID.

Introduction

Publishing is not a closed ecosystem involving only the publisher and the author. *Interoperability* is the key to cost-effective digital publishing such that it produces content that is discoverable, accessible and preservable, whether you are looking at the supply chain, libraries and other intermediaries, or end users. *Standards* are what ensure production efficiency and interoperability in every industry, and the use of standards has a long history in publishing. Along with the rapidly increasing growth of electronic content has come a new wave of standards for e-publishing. The complexity of the digital publishing supply chain requires significant consensus on distribution structures, authentication systems, identifiers and metadata to ensure overall interoperability and discoverability. This chapter discusses some background on standards and standards development, highlights some key existing standards in electronic publishing, and discusses some issues needing future standardization and some of the initiatives underway to address these issues.

Standards development

The advancements of the distribution of knowledge have often been traced to advances in the technology of distributing that content. From the creation of *incunabula*[1] (early printed books) in the 15th century, and from the development of the steam-powered printing press (Meggs, 1998) in the 19th century to the rapid movement of distributing content digitally toward the end of the 20th century, technological changes have radically altered how content is produced and distributed. When a new technology is first introduced, a variety of implementation methods are tested and implemented, but over time a few methods evolve into best practices. In our modern environment, one or more methods are eventually adopted as formal standards.

The International Organization for Standardization (ISO) defines a standard as a:

> 'Document, established by consensus and approved by a recognized body, that provides, for common and repeated use, rules, guidelines or characteristics for activities or their results, aimed at the achievement of the optimum degree of order in a given context.'[2]

While formal standards play an important role, equally important are the best practices and de facto standards that exist in our marketplace and which moderate much of what is accomplished in a variety of industries, particularly one as old and established as publishing.

Publishing standards

We don't often give much thought to the design and production elements of a book or journal, except possibly in noticing their absence. Things like page numbers, binding, title pages, indices, paper, font styles and basic page design structures are taken for granted, but all are examples of different types of standards that most publishers adhere to voluntarily. Although these practices are not frequently enshrined in formal documents, in a way that matches the ISO's definition, they are an ever-present element of publishing production, library management or the reading experience.

Many standards that have played a critical role for centuries in printed book and journal production and content distribution need to be reconsidered and adapted to the digital content environment. One good example of this is page numbering, which began as a production system for keeping plates and the subsequently produced sheets of paper in the correct order for binding the book. Today in an era of digital content with reflowable text – where the end-user can adjust the typeface, font or other traditionally fixed elements – the concept of a page number is nearly meaningless. And yet readers still rely on page numbering because it has become a useful system beyond its original production purpose. In part, pages are important because reading is often a social activity; while the act of reading may not itself be social, readers frequently want to share what they have read and discuss it with others.

Page numbers are a way of referencing something within a book or journal within that social context. This is especially true in the scholarly world, where citations and referencing content are critical elements in the process of research and publication. So even though the electronic format of content does away with the structural need for physical page numbers, a need still exists for some citation point that can be used for referencing.

This is an example of why standards development is so critical in the ongoing transition to digital content. In the coming years, standards development organizations (SDOs) will need to work through many similar issues to ensure new technologies are functional, appropriately usable and fully capable of supplementing or replacing their print counterparts. Much work has already been done to develop needed standards for electronic content, as this chapter will illustrate; but much more remains to be done.

Types of standards

There are a variety of ways in which people and organizations develop consensus around standards or best practices. These can range from completely independent, driven by the 'free hand of the market' to the extremely formal, driven by organizations focused specifically on the creation of standards. Both the method of development and the formality of the process used to develop the resulting standard determine its type. The two main recognized types of standards are *de facto* and *de jure*.

A de facto standard is one that has become accepted in practice but has not undergone any formal process to obtain consensus and may not even have publicly available documentation. Typically, de facto standards result from marketplace domination or practice. In the publishing world, page numbering, as discussed above, is an example of a de facto standard. A de jure standard is one that is developed through a formal process, usually managed by an official SDO. These standards typically require that the following principles be met (adapted from American National Standards Institute's Essential Requirements):[3]

- *Openness*: any affected and interested party has the ability to participate in the process prior to the standard's acceptance.
- *Balance*: participants in the standard's development should represent diverse interests and no single group should dominate a standard's development.
- *Due process*: development and approval of the standard follow a documented procedure for engaging and critiquing the project. Typically, there is also a right to appeal decisions.
- *Consensus*: a standard is approved only when agreement is reached by a specified number of voters, generally more than a majority, but not necessarily all voters.

Compliance with both de facto and de jure standards is voluntary. However, in some cases, de jure standards can be cited by legal code or regulation, which could make it mandatory to follow in the affected legal jurisdiction.

In some cases, a de facto standard is taken through a formal standards process and thereby becomes a de jure standard. One recent example is Adobe's Portable Document Format (PDF), which after many years as a de facto standard in the marketplace became an international standard (ISO 32000-1[4]) in 2008.

Standards development organizations

The community of organizations that create standards is a complex one, operating at industry, national and international levels. Most countries have a national standards-setting body, sometimes independent or non-governmental and sometimes formed and/or authorized by the government. Examples of such national bodies are the American National Standards Institute[5] (ANSI) in the US, the British Standards Institution[6] (BSI) in the UK, the Deutsches Institut für Normung[7] (DIN) in Germany, the Association Française de Normalisation[8] (AFNOR) in France and the Standardization Administration of China[9] (SAC).

The primary international standards body for publishing-related standards is the ISO.[10] ISO's voting members are the national standards bodies 'most representative of standardization in [their] country'.[11] ISO divides their standards work into Technical Committee (TCs), each of which has responsibility for a particular subject area and are identified by an ascending number scheme. A number of the standards related to electronic content, such as the International Standard Book Number (ISBN),[12] the International

Standard Serial Number (ISSN)[13] and the Digital Object Identifier (DOI),[14] are developed by TC 46 – Information and documentation.[15] A joint committee – JTC1, Information Technology[16] – of ISO and the International Electrotechnical Commission (IEC) is responsible for many of the standards related to format specifications and computer interactions, such as the JPEG 2000 image coding system.[17] National participation in this process is organized differently in each participating country, but most countries use some form of 'mirroring committee' of national experts to provide input into the relevant ISO work.

Currently within the US, there are over 200 ANSI-accredited SDOs[18] developing American National Standards in everything from manufacturing and safety to libraries and publishing. For electronic content, some of the key developers are: the Association for Information and Image Management[19] (AIIM), the National Information Standards Organization[20] (NISO), ARMA International[21] and the InterNational Committee for Information Technology Standards[22] (INCITS).

A number of other SDOs exist outside of the formal international and national bodies discussed above. Two international standards organizations, created specifically for internet- and web-related standards, are the Internet Society[23] [responsible for the Internet Engineering Task Force[24] (IETF)] and the World Wide Web Consortium[25] (W3C).

Many trade or professional organizations have one or more committees developing standards and guidelines in areas of interest to their members. Within the e-publishing world, examples of such organizations include: the American Library Association[26] (ALA), the Book Industry Study Group[27] (BISG), EDItEUR,[28] the International Digital Enterprise Alliance[29] (IDEAlliance), the International Digital Publishing Forum[30] (IDPF), the International Federation of Library Associations and Institutions[31] (IFLA), the National Federation of Advanced Information Services[32] (NFAIS) and United Kingdom Serials Group (UKSG).[33]

Some organizations form consortiums for the purpose of collaborating on the development of standards, such as the DAISY Consortium,[34] the Entertainment Identifier Registry (EIDR),[35] the Open Researcher and Contributor ID (ORCID)[36] and the Organization for the Advancement of Structured Information Standards[37] (OASIS).

Government agencies may also develop standards as part of their mission. In the US the National Institute of Standards and Technology[38] (NIST) develops standards in a wide variety of areas to further US innovation and industrial competitiveness. The Library of Congress[39] has developed numerous standards related to libraries, metadata and preservation.

What should be apparent from this SDO discussion is that there is no lack of organizations developing standards. Because the lines are not always clear where one organization's mission ends and another begins, there is often overlap and conflicts in the resulting standards. Most SDOs, though, are good at working together on areas of common interest and will try to stay abreast of each others' activities and collaborate whenever possible. However, it is not unusual to encounter situations where two organizations develop competing or incongruent standards due to either a lack of awareness of the other's work, 'forum shopping' (when developers try to find a receptive community), or to suit the specific needs of a particular community that could be somewhat different from those of another community.

Key standards in electronic publishing

A discussion of all relevant standards for electronic content could fill an entire book. As this discussion is limited, a representative sample of critical standards will be discussed in the areas of: (1) structure and markup, (2) identification, (3) description, (4) distribution and delivery, (5) authentication for discovery, (6) reference and linking and (7) preservation. A few standards discussed in this section have not yet been published, but they are included if the initiative is well on its way and/or a draft is available.

Structure and markup standards

One basis for understanding the need for structuring and marking up content is the simple fact that machines do not have the same level of understanding of nuances and inferences that human beings do. A person glancing at the title page of a book can easily tell which text is the title, which is the author and which is the publisher. A computer must have explicit markings to understand which text is which.

There are several benefits to producing content in structured content formats. The first of these is that it is easy to change the presentation of structured documents through the use of style sheets. In this way, the same content can be transformed from one page layout to another, for example, or from one screen size or rendering to another. This allows a publisher to produce a single source file for multiple final formats and reduces overall production costs. This capability is increasingly important as new rendering technologies and new mobile devices are constantly coming onto the market. Platform-agnostic file structures also aid in long-term preservation as they can be more easily migrated to new formats to prevent future obsolescence. Finally, structured content provides opportunities for both enriching or re-using content for a different publication or purpose, for example a teacher and student version of a textbook, a book compilation of journal articles, a web 'mash-up' of content or a multimedia version of a textual book. Increasingly, publishers are also exploring ways to semantically enrich content by linking words, phrases or references to other additional materials outside of the text. It is far easier to add links to references and terms or to add other tags and annotations using structured content than it is through more fixed formats, such as a PDF.

Extensible Markup Language (XML)

Markup languages, such as TeX,[40] LaTeX[41] (pronounced 'tech' and 'la-tech' as in 'technical', respectively) and Standard Generalized Markup Language (SGML),[42] were originally developed for production and typesetting of content for print production. SGML, published as the international standard ISO 8879 in 1986, defined how to create Document Type Definitions (DTDs), which are specific markup language applications. Most markup languages have developed from this initial SGML standard, including TEI,[43] DocBook[44] and the Hypertext Markup Language[45] (HTML) for presenting webpages.

A need developed for a slightly lighter-weight and more flexible structure than SGML that could also be used to transport and store data. The resulting language, developed by the W3C was introduced in 1998 as the Extensible Markup Language[46] or XML. At its heart, XML is a set of rules for how content should be structured and marked up using tags and a customized set of elements and attributes. The specific elements and attributes used and their relationship to one another are typically declared in a schema. By referencing this schema, a computer program can understand how to interpret the markup to act on it intelligently.

Journal Article Tag Suite (JATS)

In 1996, the US National Library of Medicine (NLM) launched an online reference system called PubMed, which pushed onto the world wide web the MEDLINE database of references and abstracts in the life sciences and biomedical sciences. In the development of this system, the National Center for Biotechnology Information (NCBI) of the NLM created a Journal Article and Interchange Tag Suite with the intent of providing a common format in which publishers and archives can exchange journal content. Since its enhancement and expansion in the early 2000s, the suite has become a de facto exchange format for journal content. In 2009, the NLM put forward the JATS for national standardization within NISO and it is currently being reviewed publicly and is due for publication in 2012.

Digital Accessible Information System (DAISY)

Another important benefit of structured content is the ability to improve accessibility of content to people with disabilities, particular for the visually impaired. One important standard in this space is the Digital Accessible Information System, or DAISY, standard.[47] This standard provides a means of creating books that include text-to-speech functionality for people who wish to hear – and navigate – written material presented in an audible format. The standard has recently been revised[48] to make it more modular and to expand its scope beyond the 'talking book' to cover a broad range of digital content types in a variety of formats. The revision specifies a framework that will 'provide the increased flexibility that producers were requesting to allow markup to be tailored to their unique needs' (Garrish and Gylling, 2011).

Identification standards

We use identifiers to distinguish things from one another (disambiguation) and to serve as a shorthand way of referring to the item. Ideally, every content item would have at least one unique identifier that applies to it and only to it. Because identifiers are used for different purposes, many items may have multiple identifiers. A book, for example, could be assigned an ISBN by the publisher and also receive a call number by a library that adds the book to its collection.

International Standard Book Number

The ISBN was designed as a product identifier for use in the supply chain. Separate ISBNs are assigned to a hardback, trade paperback and mass-market paperback version of the same book so that every trading partner would know exactly which of these products was involved in the transaction. The latest version of the ISBN standard (ISO 2108:2005) extends this concept to e-books, stating: 'Each different format of an electronic publication (e.g. ".lit", ".pdf", ".html", ".pdb") that is published and made separately available shall be given a separate ISBN.'[49]

Due to confusion in the industry, the International ISBN Agency issued *Guidelines for the Assignment of ISBNs to E-Books*[50] in 2009. Controversy over these guidelines remains due to many unique situations when dealing with electronic content. The number of ways that digital versions of the same content can differ from one file to another is exponentially higher than it is for the print world. This could result in an extremely large number of ISBNs being assigned to all the different variations of the same digital text.

For example, a digital file produced by a publisher could be wrapped in different digital rights management (DRM) by multiple suppliers further down the chain. Because the experience provided (or limited) by DRM impacts the user experience, it might be valuable to identify those digital objects separately. However, does each supplier need to obtain a new ISBN? A PDF file might have specific page layout formatting, while a reflowable version of the text for a mobile device might lack this presentation information. Some versions might have active links and searchable text, while others might simply be static page images.

An even more complex situation might be when the underlying file that is distributed is exactly the same, but a reader's ability to access certain features or functions is associated with the rights or access keys that the reader purchases. It is an open debate as to whether it makes sense to assign unique ISBNs to each of these manifestations of the underlying work.

A variety of organizations are currently exploring the ISBN for e-books issue and working to obtain some consensus in the community.

International Standard Text Code

The International Standard Text Code (ISTC) (ISO 21047[51]) is a relatively new identifier that was designed to uniquely identify the content of a textual work, regardless of its format or product packaging. The intended users of the ISTC are 'publishers, bibliographic services, retailers, libraries, and rights management agencies to collocate different manifestations of the same title within a work-level record' (Weissberg, 2009). There are a variety of use cases of work-level identification provided by the ISTC. From a library perspective, it would be valuable to know that you have the same text of a particular work in a variety of different forms.

Another use for the ISTC is in the compiling of sales data for best-seller lists across all the different formats of a work. When there were generally two manifestations (a paperback and a hardcover version) of a book, compiling sales data was comparatively simple. In a digital environment, when there could be dozens of manifestations, the value of having an ISTC as a work-level identifier could be quite significant.

The International ISTC Agency[52] reported in April 2011 that some 7000 ISTCs had been assigned and at least 70 000 more were pending. At this writing it is still too early to predict the uptake on using the ISTC and the different ways it might be applied.

International Standard Name Identifier

The e-resource isn't the only thing that could be identified in the publication process. There are a variety of people associated with content, including authors, editors, compilers, translators, performers, songwriters, producers and directors. While libraries have created and maintained name authority files for their collections for decades, other organizations, such as society publishers, abstracting and indexing services and rights organizations to name just a few, have managed their own repositories of name-related information. As a result, a given individual or entity has no unique naming convention or identifier that crosses over organizations and systems and might link together the various information about that person or entity.

Among the many serious challenges of maintaining information related to people is the rapidity with which information changes. People are constantly changing roles and positions, creating ever more content in a variety of forms and – with less frequency – changing names, retiring or dying.

In addition to the logistic challenges of continually updating this information, there are legal and policy issues surrounding privacy of personal data. Many countries have passed laws[53] regarding the handling of personally identifiable information and more legislation is pending.[54] As the number and scope of online name identifier registries increase, it is likely that the concerns regarding privacy and therefore the potential regulation of this information will increase in the future.

A soon to be published international standard for the International Standard Name Identifier (ISNI)[55] (ISO 27729) specifies an identifier for the public identity and disambiguation of parties associated with digital content creation, distribution and management. The party being identified could be a real person, a pseudonym, a fictional character, a group, an abstract concept or even a corporate entity. The administration system described in the standard provides for a minimum set of core metadata about the party to be provided at the time of registration and stored in a central repository. These metadata are used to determine if a party already has an ISNI when one is requested or if a new identifier is needed.

The VIAF (The Virtual International Authority File) project[56] – a name authority system developed as a partnership between the Library of Congress (US), the Deutsche Nationalbibliothek and the Bibliothèque Nationale de France, in cooperation with a number of other national libraries and bibliographic agencies – has provided its database of over 14 million authority files to the ISNI International Agency,[57] who will be managing registration. The ISNI Agency is matching the data files provided by its founding members to the VIAF files to make initial ISNI assignments where there are more than three VIAF sources or two independent sources confirming the data (Gatenby and MacEwan, 2011).

Open Researcher Contributor ID

The Open Researcher Contributor ID (ORCID)[58] initiative was the outcome of a meeting co-organized by the Nature Publishing Group and Thomson-Reuters in November 2009. The ORCID consortium was chartered with a mission to create 'a central registry of unique identifiers for individual researchers and an open and transparent linking mechanism between ORCID and other current author ID schemes.'[59] Potential uses of the system are envisioned as: linking together a researcher and his or her publication output, aiding institutions and professional societies in compiling their researchers' publication output, improving efficiency of project funding and aiding researchers to find potential collaborators.

Although the system is not yet publicly available, it has been described in its principles as a mix of computed information about researchers and user-provided information. Researchers will be able to create and maintain their own profile and set their own privacy setting; data will be released under the Creative Commons CC0 waiver. Public launch of the service is projected for autumn 2012.

There is potentially synergy between the ISNI and ORCID systems. Although no agreement yet exists, there is a possibility that the ORCID system could use the ISNI identifier scheme for the assignment of ORCID

IDs, which would mean both systems would be using the same number format and could interoperate. There could also be greater collaboration where, for example, the ORCID project could participate directly in the ISNI system as one of the Registration Agencies representing the researcher community.

The key difference between these two seemingly overlapping standards is that the ORCID is a sector-specific project for the researcher community, while ISNI is a generalized bridge identification structure bringing people-related data together from many diverse communities for disambiguation and linking. The metadata that would be relevant to describe the work of a researcher, such as their institutions, funding sources, research focus, papers and research affiliations, are quite specific and different from the data that would be necessary to describe the work of a guitarist in a band.

Institutional Identifier

Works, books and authors are not the only entities that need identification in a well-functioning content supply chain. It is also extremely useful to identify the organizational entities trading information. This is critical not only for the sales process from publisher to library, but also among libraries for resource sharing. There are a number of existing organization identification systems, although they are limited in scope and none takes into account the linkages and relationships between organizations in the scholarly community. To address this gap, NISO launched the Institutional Identifier (I^2) initiative to build on work from the Journal Supply Chain Efficiency Improvement Pilot,[60] which demonstrated the improved efficiencies of using an institutional identifier in the journal supply chain.

The I^2 working group has developed a metadata schema to map unambiguous identification of institutions and their related entitles. For example, the Welch Medical Library at Johns Hopkins University (JHU) Medical School is related to the Eisenhower Library at the Homewood campus of JHU, but in many instances, the two entities operate independently. There are also departments on campus that have similar ties and relationships with other entities within JHU and outside of it. In addition, the library and institution are members of a variety of consortia and regional entities. Mapping these relationships is critical for effective management of subscriptions, access control systems and other institutional cooperation.

I^2 is currently exploring collaboration with the ISNI International Agency to extend the use of the ISNI infrastructure and business model to institutions and to harmonize their metadata profiles. A likely requirement will be one or more ISNI Registration Agencies that specifically assigns and registers institution ID with the ISNI system (DeRidder and Agnew, 2011). It is anticipated that this system will be operational some time in 2012.

Description standards

Metadata, often called data about data or information, are used to describe, explain, locate or otherwise make it easier to retrieve, use or manage an information resource.[61] The metadata we choose to describe a thing are often for a specific purpose. When one is buying a journal, for example, the title, price, frequency of publication, and the address of the publisher where the payment should be sent are each relevant and critical data elements for that transaction. This can be contrasted with the back-end production metadata required for long-term electronic archiving of the journal, such as file format, creation application, encoding system, embedded fonts and color space.[62]

These collective distinctions about metadata, describing a thing and the classes of things, are based on a concept called functional granularity, which refers to the need to provide as much information as is needed to conduct a specific task. To conduct a purchase transaction, one must know the price. However, in the context of preservation, price is an irrelevant data element. Alternatively, knowing the title and author of a book might be sufficient in a rights transaction, but the size, shape and weight of a particular copy would be important to a shipping fee calculation. Curating metadata is a time-consuming and expensive investment, which often requires a business rationale to justify this investment. If there is no need to create or maintain metadata for a particular purpose, then it doesn't make sense to invest the significant costs required to maintain it. The challenge, however, is that one may not know all of the future needs related to the content item. For this reason there is no simple rule for what is the appropriate metadata quality or detail level.

Machine-Readable Cataloging

One of the more widely adopted standards for describing published works in the library community is the MAchine-Readable Cataloging (MARC) standard.[63] The current version, MARC 21, is a harmonization of the US and Canadian MARC standards and is jointly maintained by the Library of Congress and the Library and Archives Canada. This system for conveying the bibliographic information about a work consists of three core elements: the record structure, the content designation and the data content of the record. The record structure is described in two standards, *Information Interchange Format*[64] (ANSI/NISO Z39.2) and *Format for Information Exchange*[65] (ISO 2709).

The content designation is 'the codes and conventions established to identify explicitly and characterize ... data elements within a record'[66] and supports their manipulation. The content of data elements in MARC records is defined by standards outside of the MARC formats, such as AACR2,[67] Library of Congress Subject Headings[68] and Medical Subject Headings[69] (MeSH). MARC records form the basis for most collaborative cataloging initiatives and most library systems are built around the basis of MARC record data structures. The MARC record format is maintained by the Library of Congress, with input from the American Library Association's ALCTS/LITA/RUSA Machine-Readable Bibliographic Information Committee (MARBI).

There has been considerable movement toward adapting the MARC record structure as systems have improved and changed over the decades since it was introduced. This has included MARCXML,[70] a framework for working with MARC data in an XML environment, and MARCXchange,[71] a standard (ISO 25577) for representing a complete MARC record or a set of MARC records in XML.

The modern cataloging rules, the IFLA Anglo-American Cataloging Rules, version 2 (AACR2), that help to define what a cataloging record should include (i.e. the information contained within a MARC record) are also being changed to adapt to our new web-based, linked data environment. The AACR2 cataloging rules were revised into a linking data type of format called Resource Description and Access[72] (RDA) in 2010. These changes will significantly impact the systems that include or exchange bibliographic information. As use of RDA requires significant changes in cataloging practices and supporting systems, a full transition to the new format will take some time.

Online Information Exchange for Books

ONIX is an acronym for ONline Information Exchange and is used to designate a family of standards 'to support computer-to-computer communication between parties involved in creating, distributing, licensing or otherwise making available intellectual property in published form, whether physical or digital.'[73] ONIX for Books[74] is an XML structure for the communication of book product metadata in supply chain transactions. Originally developed by the Association of American Publishers and a variety of trade entities in the late 1990s, ONIX for Books is now published and maintained by EDItEUR in association with the Book Industry Study Group (BISG) and Book Industry Communications (BIC).

A typical ONIX record would include basic bibliographic metadata about the title, including author, subject classification, description and ISBN, as well as sales information such as price, availability, territorial rights and reviews. The ONIX for Books standard has been widely adopted by major publishers, trade organizations, major retailers and distributors as the primary way in which product information is distributed in retail trade. There have been a few initiatives to create mappings between the ONIX for Books system and the MARC record system to help improve interoperability[75] of metadata between the publishing and library communities.

Distribution and delivery standards

Once content is created it needs to find its way out of the publisher's production department and through a supply chain of distributors, possibly libraries, and finally into the hands of a reader. In a print environment, this process included printing the content, as well as warehousing and then shipping physical copies of the book to a retailer or end-user. In a digital environment, content is similarly produced, but packaging and distribution takes place in quite different ways and different and additional distributors are involved in the process.

The format of these digital files has been shifting quickly since electronic content distribution first became available. In the early days of electronic distribution, content was distributed as simple text files. These eventually were transformed into more complex structured documents, to digitally recreate the 'page' format and Adobe's PDF became a de facto standard for delivering a facsimile of the page as it had appeared in print. PDF eventually became an international standard as noted above.[4] Many publishers are now providing content directly via the World Wide Web in HTML format via their website and in various e-reader formats through third-party providers.

As content distribution has grown in complexity and the variety of devices on which content needs to be rendered has increased, there has developed a need for a common distribution format. The EPUB specification is the leading contender to resolve this challenge.

Electronic Publication (EPUB) format

EPUB® is a set of standards for creating and distributing reflowable digital content. Developed by the International Digital Publishers Forum (IDPF), the latest version, EPUB 3,[76] has a function called 'media queries' that allows the use of style sheets to control the content layout while still allowing for reflowable text, and to 'produce, for example, a two-page spread on a tablet held in landscape mode, a one-page two-column layout when that tablet is turned to portrait mode, and a single column format on a mobile phone, all from the same XHTML5 file.' (Kasdorf, 2011). XHTML5 is the latest version of the HTML specification from the W3C in XML format (as opposed to straight text). This markup form will closely match what is renderable by a modern web browser.

EPUB consists of three main elements: the content itself, some descriptive information about the content and its components, and a packaging structure to combine all of the content and metadata elements. The need for a standard in this space is significant because of the complexity of interoperation needed not only between the publishers and the supply chain, but also with the reading-device manufacturers. In addition, as publications become more interactive – including things like audio, video and other multi-media features – the need to rely on a common structure for distributing electronic content is increasingly critical.

Authentication standards

Publishers who license or sell subscriptions to their electronic content are interested in managing access to that content. There are a variety of systems for limiting access based on some form of end-user credentials, authentication of IP addresses or through use of proxy servers. All of these methods have drawbacks particularly with the increasing desire of users to access resources remotely and from mobile devices. As organizations, such as libraries, that license the content add more and more content from multiple providers, the maintenance of authentication credentials becomes more onerous. End-users may be faced with the situation of having to re-authenticate every time they change from one content collection to another. Balancing ease of use and security is the biggest challenge in selecting an authentication method.

Security Assertion Markup Language

A newer type of authentication system is gaining traction as a single sign-on solution, based on Security Assertion Markup Language

(SAML),[77] a standard for exchanging authentication and authorization data between an identity provider and a service provider. The most widely known implementation of SAML in the publishing community is Shibboleth.[78] With this system, the service provider's system requests a user's credentials from the organization's identity management system, which 'asserts' to the provider's system the relevant access rights. A user has only to log on to the home system once per session and all assertions passed between the home system and different providers' systems occur in the background without the user's involvement.

Reference and linking standards

For many decades, the only content available online were abstract and indexing databases and full text still had to be delivered on paper, usually at an additional cost to the end-user, and always with a delay. As more content, especially journals, became available online, the issue became how to redirect the end-user from their search result to the full-text content, especially when there were many databases and collections involved from different content providers. Reference and linking standards were the solution, allowing interoperability between disparate systems.

Digital Object Identifier

The Digital Object Identifier (DOI®)[79] is a system for providing persistent and actionable identification and resolution to resource objects in a digital environment. A continuing criticism of the Web is the problem of broken links. The DOI addresses this by assigning an identifier that is separate from the location of the item. A registry system[80] of DOIs contains metadata and a resolution link to the actual content. If the content's location changes, the resolution link can be easily updated in one place and all existing links to it will still work.

The strength of the DOI system relies not on disambiguity, as in identifiers like the ISBN, but on the use of the DOI name as a Uniform Resource Identifier (URI) and the application of the Handle system,[81] a global name service enabling secure name resolution over the Internet. The DOI offers the capability of embedding another identifier, such as a journal's ISSN or an e-book's ISBN, to allow even more interoperability. The syntax for a DOI is described in the ANSI/NISO Z39.84 standard,[82] but the entire DOI system has been approved as an international standard (ISO 26324[14]) that was published in early 2012.

The DOI system is in wide application and it forms the basis for the CrossRef system, initially designed for scholarly publishing reference linking. As of August 2010, CrossRef managed a database of more than 43 million items associated with a DOI. In 2010, the DataCite group formed to provide data linking and metadata for scholarly research data using the DOI system.

OpenURL framework

Due to the very nature of the Internet, there are often multiple copies of the same content available on the network. These may exist in mirrored sites, in institutional repositories, or in licensed content databases managed by the publisher and/or by third-party aggregation services. For libraries that provide access to many of these content resources to their patrons, how do you point the end-user from a search result to the most appropriate copy of a resource, for example one that the library has already paid for? The solution was OpenURL (Van de Sompel and Beit-Arie, 2001), which provides a context-sensitive link through the use of a resolver system called a knowledge base. The knowledge base matches the institution's specific resource availability, e.g. licensed journal databases, to the requested item and presents the user with one or more available options for linking directly to the resource, or even ordering it if no electronic version is available.

In 2004, a NISO working group took the de facto OpenURL specification and created a de jure standard (ANSI/NISO Z39.88-2004[83]) that expanded the capability of the OpenURL to be used in applications beyond the original 'available copy' solution. One example of such a new application is COinS (Hellman, 2009) (ContextObjects in Spans) that allows OpenURLs to be used in HTML. The OpenURL system has seen wide adoption in library systems and content distributors. The successful implementation of OpenURL is dependent on the accuracy of the information found in knowledge bases, which was becoming a growing problem. In 2008, NISO and the UKSG jointly launched the Knowledge Bases and Related Tools (KBART) project[84] to raise awareness of the importance of data quality in OpenURL knowledge bases and to improve the overall efficiency of the resolution system. The group issued a recommended practice (NISO RP-9-2010[85]) with data formatting and exchange guidelines for publishers, aggregators, agents, technology vendors and librarians to adhere to when exchanging information about their respective content holdings. As of mid summer 2011, there were

24 organizations (representing 55 publishers) that had endorsed[86] the KBART recommendations and were adhering to the best practices to improve their resolution services.

Preservation standards

Preservation is an activity that 'future proofs' content. While preserving physical items entails a lot of environmental attributes, such as acid levels, humidity and temperature, the range of possibilities with digital preservation fall broadly into four levels of very different preservation activities.

The first level of preservation of digital content relies on the physical preservation of the bits that comprise the document. This could be done using a variety of media, from hard disks, to flash drives, to computer hard drives or even network drives. You then need a technological layer of preservation, which means that you need to preserve not only the physical media, but also some method of reading or extracting the content from the storage device. The next layer of preservation is a formatting layer, where software must be available that can render the extracted files. Finally, there is a semantic layer of preservation, which ensures the rendered content has not been altered through the transformation process.

The process of preservation relies heavily on standards adherence to allow for content preservation. The creation of metadata describing the technical and format structures is crucial to understanding the form, structure and rights related to a content object. The *PREMIS Data Dictionary for Preservation Metadata*[87] defines preservation metadata as 'the information a repository uses to support the digital preservation process'.

The common file structures for creating and distributing content, described previously, will also help to ensure preservation of content and simplify the software needs to re-create content in its original form. There are models for how content should be replicated and stored and many projects, such as LOCKSS[88] and CLOCKSS,[89] build on network replication to ensure long-term availability of content. Finally, there are social and organizational structures related to long-term preservation, such as the creation of organizations like Portico,[90] whose mission is to actively pursue the preservation of content in partnership with publishers and libraries.

Non-traditional media content in digital form

Most journals today are distributed in electronic form and take advantage of the possibilities provided by digital distribution by adding citation linking (see DOI and OpenURL above), animated images, video, audio, extended tables, data sets or other related content, which does not fit within the construct of a print journal. Authors began to see the value in these new forms and began submitting this supplemental material along with their articles. Some publishers welcomed these submittals to enhance their electronic journal offerings[91] while others were at a loss as to what to do with this content.

The rapid increase in this non-traditional content is straining even the electronic distribution publication model because of the time, effort and skills necessary to vet these additional materials, the specialized software and practices needed to distribute and store them, and questions about the responsibility for long-term preservation. Some publishers have declared they would no longer accept supplemental materials (e.g. Maunsell, 2010) with journal articles or are limiting what can be submitted (e.g. Borowski, 2011). Still other journals are mandating the availability of supplemental materials, such as data sets, be open and publically available. Several grant-funding agencies are also requiring that data generated as a result of funded research be made accessible. Whether these materials will find their ways into the publication process remains an open question, but certainly linking at a minimum and more likely interoperation at some level will be required.

To help address these issues, a joint NISO and NFAIS working group[92] is exploring the business practices and technological infrastructure needs for Supplemental Journal Article Materials. The question of what constitutes supplemental materials is one factor that is critical to understanding any standard practices and was the first step in the group's project. This working group is expected to issue their recommended practices for publishers to handle these supplemental materials by the end of 2011.

Traditional journal articles with supplemental information are only one part of a much larger challenge related to the increasing reliance on data in the scientific process. New forms of publications are developing, such as 'data papers', which are simply available data sets with some associated metadata. The entire realm of data management, data citation and data reuse is fraught with complicated questions, which will require significant study and standards development. For example, traditional provenance questions need to be addressed, such as: Who created this data set? How can we be assured that the data set hasn't been altered or manipulated since its release or publication? If the data are a sub-set of a larger data collection, how was that subset created, and can it be recreated? If a data set is constantly being updated with new data, how can we return to the state of the database at the time the initial query was run, as new data may influence the results of an analytical tool?

There are a variety of communities looking at these questions. A W3C Provenance Incubator Group published a state-of-the art paper with a roadmap for possible standardization efforts.[93] Another group organized by the CODATA organization in partnership with the International Council on Scientific & Technical Information (ICSTI) is exploring the issue of data citation practices.[94] Other groups have conducted surveys of researchers (Tenopir *et al.*, 2011) and of institutional repository practice (Soehner *et al.*, 2010). The Data Cite[95] organization is working with some of the largest repository providers to develop standards for the application of DOIs to data sets and developing institutional best practices regarding data preservation and sharing. Finally, the semantic web community is working to provide linking opportunities[96] to connect disparate data sets and expand the ability to reuse and mash up heterogeneous data sets.

Conclusion

As the creation and distribution of content moves increasingly toward digital forms, the publishing community must address the many challenges confronting an industry being turned on its head because of new technology and user expectations. Systems for describing, communicating and preserving content that have served us well for decades, if not centuries, need to be re-evaluated and often revamped. The standards process provides an opportunity to conduct this evaluation in a thoughtful way that engages all of the relevant stakeholders in the process. Although there are many organizations engaged in developing standards in the electronic publishing space, stakeholders must work together to achieve an interoperable environment where content is created efficiently, is discoverable and retrievable in a digital environment, and will also be accessible not only for all users today but into the future as well. A lot of progress has been made over the past few decades, but even more work remains, especially given the near certainty that new technologies will continue to develop, expanding the need for new standards. As an industry, we certainly have our work cut out for us.

Notes

1. Incunabula – Dawn of Western Printing [website]. Based on Orita, Hiroharu. *Inkyunabura no Sekai (The World of Incunabula)*. Compiled by the Library Research Institute of the National Diet Library. Tokyo: Japan Library Association, July 2000. http://www.ndl.go.jp/incunabula/e/
2. ISO/IEC Guide 2:2004, *Standardization and related activities – General vocabulary*. Geneva: International Organization for Standardization, 2004.
3. *ANSI Essential Requirements: Due process requirements for American National Standards*. New York: American National Standards Institute (ANSI), January 2010 edition. http://publicaa.ansi.org/sites/apdl/Documents/Standards%20Activities/American%20National%20Standards/Procedures,%20Guides,%20and%20Forms/2010%20ANSI%20Essential%20Requirements%20and%20Related/2010%20ANSI%20Essential%20Requirements.pdf
4. ISO 32000-1:2008, *Document management – Portable document format – Part 1: PDF 1.7*. Geneva: International Organization for Standardization, 2008.
5. American National Standards Institute (ANSI) [website]. http://www.ansi.org/
6. British Standards Institution [website]. http://www.bsigroup.com/
7. Deutsches Institut für Normung (DIN) [website]. http://www.din.de/
8. Association Française de Normalisation (AFNOR) [website]. http://www.afnor.org/
9. Standardization Administration of the People's Republic of China (SAC) [website]. http://www.sac.gov.cn/
10. International Organization for Standardization (ISO) [website]. http://www.iso.org/
11. *Member bodies*. International Organization for Standardization website. http://www.iso.org/iso/about/iso_members/member_bodies.htm
12. ISO 2108:2005, *Information and documentation – International Standard Book Number (ISBN)*. Geneva: International Organization for Standardization, 2005.
13. ISO 3297:2007, *Information and documentation – International Standard Serial Number (ISSN)*. Geneva: International Organization for Standardization, 2007.
14. ISO 26324, *Information and documentation – Digital object identifier system*. Geneva: International Organization for Standardization, publication forthcoming (expected in 2011).
15. *TC46, Information and documentation*. International Organization for Standardization website. http://www.iso.org/iso/standards_development/technical_committees/list_of_iso_technical_committees/iso_technical_committee.htm?commid=48750
16. *JTC1, Information Technology*. International Organization for Standardization website. http://www.iso.org/iso/standards_development/technical_committees/list_of_iso_technical_committees/iso_technical_committee.htm?commid=45020
17. ISO/IEC 15444-1:2004, *Information technology – JPEG 2000 image coding system: Core coding system*. Geneva: International Organization for Standardization, 2004.

18. *ANSI Accredited Standards Developers* [Listing with Complete Scope Info]. New York: American National Standards Institute, 12 July 2011. http://publicaa.ansi.org/sites/apdl/Documents/Standards%20Activities/American%20National%20Standards/ANSI%20Accredited%20Standards%20Developers/JULY11ASD-2.pdf
19. Association for Information and Image Management (AIIM) [website]. http://www.aiim.org/
20. National Information Standards Organization (NISO) [website]. http://www.niso.org/
21. ARMA International [website]. http://www.arma.org/
22. InterNational Committee for Information Technology Standards (INCITS) [website]. http://www.incits.org/
23. Internet Society (ISOC) [website]. http://www.isoc.org/
24. The Internet Engineering Task Force (IETF) [website]. http://www.ietf.org/
25. World Wide Web Consortium (W3C) [website]. http://www.w3.org/
26. American Library Association (ALA) Standards and Guidelines [webpage]. http://www.ala.org/ala/professionalresources/guidelines/standards guidelines/index.cfm
27. Book Industry Study Group (BISG) [website]. http://www.bisg.org/
28. EDItEUR [website]. http://www.editeur.org/
29. International Digital Enterprise Alliance (IDEAlliance) [website]. http://www.idealliance.org/
30. International Digital Publishing Forum (IDPF) [website]. http://idpf.org/
31. International Federation of Library Associations and Institutions (IFLA) [website]. http://www.ifla.org/
32. National Federation of Advanced Information Services (NFAIS) [website]. http://www.nfais.org/
33. UKSG [website]. http://www.uksg.org/
34. DAISY Consortium [website]. http://www.daisy.org
35. Entertainment Identifier Registry (EIDR) [website]. http://eidr.org/
36. Open Researcher and Contributor ID (ORCID) [website]. http://orcid.org/
37. Organization for the Advancement of Structured Information Standards (OASIS) [website]. http://www.oasis-open.org/
38. National Institute of Standards and Technology (NIST) [website]. http://www.nist.gov/
39. Standards at the Library of Congress [webpage]. http://www.loc.gov/standards/
40. *TeX Frequently Asked Questions on the Web*, version 3.22. UK TeX Users' Group (UK TUG), last modified 27 April 2011. http://www.tex.ac.uk/cgi-bin/texfaq2html?introduction=yes
41. LaTeX – A document preparation system [website]. http://www.latex-project.org/
42. ISO 8879:1986, *Information processing – Text and office systems – Standard Generalized Markup Language (SGML)*. Geneva: International Organization for Standardization, 1986.
43. Text Encoding Initiative (TEI) [website]. http://www.tei-c.org/
44. DocBook.org [website]. http://www.docbook.org/
45. W3C Recommendation. HTML 4.01 Specification. World Wide Web Consortium, 24 December 1999. http://www.w3.org/TR/html401

46. W3C Recommendation. *Extensible Markup Language (XML) 1.0 (Fifth Edition)*. World Wide Web Consortium, 26 November 2008. http://www.w3.org/TR/2008/REC-xml-20081126/
47. ANSI/NISO Z39.86-2005, *Specifications for the Digital Talking Book*. Bethesda, MD: National Information Standards Organization, 2005. http://www.niso.org/standards/z39-86-2005/
48. NISO Z39.86-201x, Authoring and Interchange Framework (draft for trial use). Baltimore, MD: National Information Standards Organization, 28 March 2011. http://www.niso.org/workrooms/daisy
49. See clause 5.5 in ISO 2108:2005, *Information and documentation – International Standard Book Number (ISBN)*. Geneva: International Organization for Standardization, 2005.
50. *Guidelines for the Assignment of ISBNs to E-books*. London: International ISBN Agency, 2009. http://www.isbn-international.org/faqs/view/17
51. ISO 21047:2009, *Information and documentation – International Standard Text Code (ISTC)*. Geneva: International Organization for Standardization, 2009.
52. International ISTC Agency [website]. http://www.istc-international.org/
53. See for example the *European Union Data Protection Directive* (Directive 95/46/EC). http://en.wikipedia.org/wiki/Directive_95/46/EC_on_the_protection_of_personal_data
54. In the United States, the *Personal Data Privacy and Security Act* has been introduced in three of the last four congressional sessions but has yet to be approved.
55. ISO 27729, Information and documentation – International Standard Name Identifier (ISNI). Geneva: International Organization for Standardization, publication forthcoming (expected in 2011).
56. VIAF (The Virtual International Authority File) project [website]. http://www.oclc.org/research/activities/viaf/
57. ISNI International Agency [website]. http://www.isni.org/
58. Open Researcher Contributor ID (ORCID) webpage http://www.orcid.org/
59. *Mission Statement*. ORCID [website]. http://www.orcid.org/mission-statement
60. Journal Supply Chain Efficiency Improvement Pilot http://www.journalsupplychain.com/
61. *Understanding Metadata*. Bethesda, MD: NISO Press, 2004. http://www.niso.org/publications/press/UnderstandingMetadata.pdf
62. For more on metadata for preservation, see *PREMIS Data Dictionary for Preservation Metadata*, version 2.1, January 2011. http://www.loc.gov/standards/premis/
63. Library of Congress Network Development and MARC Standards Office and the Library and Archives Canada Standards and Support Office. MARC 21 [documentation website]. Washington, DC: Library of Congress, date varies depending on section. http://www.loc.gov/marc/
64. ANSI/NISO Z39.2- 1994 (R2009), *Information Interchange Format*. Bethesda, MD: National Information Standards Organization, 1994. http://www.niso.org/standards/z39-2-1994
65. ISO 2709:2008, *Information and documentation – Format for information exchange*. Geneva: International Organization for Standardization, 2008.

66. American Library Association's ALCTS/LITA/RUSA Machine-Readable Bibliographic Information Committee (MARBI). *The MARC 21 Formats: Background and Principles*. Washington, DC: Library of Congress, November 1996. http://www.loc.gov/marc/96principl.html
67. *Anglo-American Cataloguing Rules*, 2nd edn, 2002 revision. Chicago: American Library Association, 2002. http://www.aacr2.org/
68. *Library of Congress Subject Headings*. Washington, DC: Library of Congress, Annual. Five volumes. http://id.loc.gov/authorities#conceptscheme
69. Medical Subject Headings (MeSH®). Bethesda, MD: National Library of Medicine, continuously updated. http://www.nlm.nih.gov/mesh/
70. MARCXML [webpage]. http://www.loc.gov/standards/marcxml/
71. ISO 25577:2008, *Information and documentation – MarcXchange*. Geneva: International Organization for Standardization, 2008.
72. RDA: Resource Description & Access [website]. http://www.rdatoolkit.org/
73. ONIX [website]. http://www.editeur.org/8/ONIX/
74. *ONIX for Books*, version 3.0. EDItEUR, April 2009. http://www.editeur.org/93/Release-3.0-Downloads/
75. For more on ONIX and MARC interoperability, see Luther (2009).
76. *EPUB 3, Proposed Specification*. International Digital Publishing Forum, 23 May 2011. [This draft is expected to be finalized and published in autumn 2011.] http://idpf.org/epub/30/spec/epub30-overview.html
77. *Security Assertion Markup Language (SAML)*, version 2.0. OASIS, March 2005. http://saml.xml.org/saml-specifications
78. Shibboleth® [website]. http://shibboleth.internet2.edu/
79. The DOI® System [website]. http://www.doi.org
80. For an example of a DOI Registration Agency that provides a DOI lookup service, see: CrossRef [website]. http://www.crossref.org/
81. *Factsheet DOI® System and the Handle System® version 4.1*. The International DOI Foundation (IDF), 21 September 2006. http://www.doi.org/factsheets/DOIHandle.html
82. ANSI/NISO Z39.84 – 2005 (R2010), *Syntax for the Digital Object Identifier*. Bethesda, MD: NISO, 2005. http://www.niso.org/standards/z39-84-2005/
83. ANSI/NISO Z39.88 – 2004 (R2010), *The OpenURL Framework for Context-Sensitive Services*. Bethesda, MD: National Information Standards Organization, 2004. http://www.niso.org/standards/z39-88-2004/
84. Knowledge Base And Related Tools (KBART) project [webpage]. http://www.niso.org/workrooms/kbart
85. NISO RP-9-2010, *KBART: Knowledge Bases and Related Tools*. Baltimore, MD: National Information Standards Organization, January 2010. http://www.niso.org/publications/rp/RP-2010-09.pdf
86. KBART Endorsement [webpage]. http://www.niso.org/workrooms/kbart/endorsement/
87. *Introduction and Supporting Materials from PREMIS Data Dictionary for Preservation Metadata*, version 2.1. PREMIS Editorial Committee, January 2011. http://www.loc.gov/standards/premis/v2/premis-report-2-1.pdf
88. LOCKSS (Lots of Copies Keep Stuff Safe) [website]. http://www.lockss.org/
89. CLOCKSS (Controlled LOCKSS) [website]. http://www.clockss.org/

90. Portico [website]. http://www.portico.org/
91. *Elsevier's 'Article of the Future' is now available for all Cell Press Journals.* Elsevier Press Release, 7 January 2010. http://www.elsevier.com/wps/find/authored_newsitem.cws_home/companynews05_01403
92. NISO/NFAIS Supplemental Journal Article Materials Working Group [webpage]. http://www.niso.org/workrooms/supplemental
93. W3C Incubator Group. *Provenance XG Final Report.* World Wide Web Consortium, 8 December 2010. http://www.w3.org/2005/Incubator/prov/XGR-prov-20101214/
94. CODATA Data Citation Standards and Practices [webpage]. http://www.codata.org/taskgroups/TGdatacitation/
95. DataCite [website] http://www.datacite.org/
96. Linked Data [webpage]. World Wide Web Consortium. http://www.w3.org/standards/semanticweb/data

References

Borowski, C. (2011) Enough is enough [editorial]. *The Journal of Experimental Medicine*, 208(7): 1337. http://jem.rupress.org/content/208/7/1337.full.pdf

DeRidder, J. and Agnew, G. (2011) I^2 and ISNI: improving the information supply chain with standard institutional identifiers. *Information Standards Quarterly*, 23(3). doi: 10.3789/isqv23n3.2011.09

Garrish, M. and Gylling, M. (2011) The evolution of accessible publishing: revising the Z39.86 DAISY standard. *Information Standards Quarterly*, 23(2): 35–9. doi: 10.3789/isqv23n2.2011.08 http://www.niso.org/publications/isq/2011/v23no2/garrish

Gatenby, J. and MacEwan, A. (2011) ISNI: a new system for name identification. *Information Standards Quarterly*, 23(3). doi: 10.3789/isqv23n3.2011.02

Hellman, E. (2009) *OpenURL COinS: A Convention to Embed Bibliographic Metadata in HTML*, stable version 1.0. 16 June 16. http://ocoins.info/

Kasdorf, B. (2011) EPUB 3 (Not your father's EPUB). *Information Standards Quarterly*, 23(2): 4–11. doi: 10.3789/isqv23n2.2011.02 http://www.niso.org/publications/isq/2011/v23no2/kasdorf

Luther, J. (2009) *Streamlining Book Metadata Workflow.* NISO and OCLC, 30 June. http://www.niso.org/publications/white_papers/StreamlineBookMetadataWorkflowWhitePaper.pdf

Maunsell, J. (2010) Announcement regarding supplemental material. *The Journal of Neuroscience*, 30(32): 10599–600. http://www.jneurosci.org/content/30/32/10599.full.pdf

Meggs, P.B. (1998) *A History of Graphic Design*, 3rd edn. New York: John Wiley & Sons, Inc., pp. 130–133. ISBN 0-471-291-98-6.

Soehner, C., Catherine, S. and Jennifer, W. (2010) e-Science and data support services: a survey of ARL members. Presented at: *International Association of Scientific and Technological University Libraries, 31st Annual Conference*, 23 June. http://docs.lib.purdue.edu/iatul2010/conf/day3/1

Tenopir, C., Allard, S., Douglass, K., *et al.* (2011) Data sharing by scientists: practices and perceptions. *PLoS ONE* 6(6): e21101, doi:10.1371/journal.pone.0021101 http://www.plosone.org/article/info%3Adoi%2F10.1371%2Fjournal.pone.0021101

Van de Sompel, H. and Beit-Arie, O. (2001) Open linking in the scholarly information environment using the OpenURL Framework. *D-Lib Magazine*, 7(3). http://www.dlib.org/dlib/march01/vandesompel/03vandesompel.html

Weissberg, A. (2009) The International Standard Text Code (ISTC): an overview and status report. *Information Standards Quarterly*, 21(3): 20–4. doi:10.3789/isqv21n3.200904

10

Citation, bibliometrics and quality: assessing impact and usage

Adam Finch

Abstract: This chapter details the various methods of evaluating the impact of published research, with a particular focus on citations. The chapter gives an overview of the difficulties of measuring research impact and the solutions and controversies of citation analysis, then goes on to look at the indices that record citations between articles and the metrics that these data feed into. Also discussed are publishers' approaches to improving journal impact, various recent developments in citation analysis, such as the influences of early view and open access, and author metrics.

Key words: Research performance, Web of Science, Scopus, Google Scholar, Impact Factor, EigenFactor, SJR, SNIP, Open Access, early view, h-index, strategic journal development.

Introduction

One of the challenges facing organisations manufacturing or using a product is measuring its quality and comparing it with that of competitors in a standardised way; although it is different from normal commercial products in many respects, the same is true of research. In most cases, the primary initial output of research takes the form of journal articles, conference proceedings and books; these publications then become the focus of evaluation. Authors may need to prove the importance of their work when applying for a new post; institutions might wish to demonstrate and publicise their strengths; funding agencies seek to support the strongest research and evaluate the impact of the funding;

and Editors can build reputations by improving their journal. Indeed, for research, the importance of indicators of quality is twofold; not only are authors producing research, they are incorporating the research of others into their work and so need a way to identify crucial islands of work in the sea of information. As it is a priority for their key customers and clients, publishers too are increasingly focused on the best way to demonstrate the usefulness, and therefore the value, of the research they publish.

Fortunately, there are measurable elements associated with publications that have been used to analyse their quality. The best and longest established example is counting citations (Gross and Gross, 1927). When one publication includes another in its reference list, this is a citation. As research tends to build incrementally, each new conclusion based on and extending the established body of knowledge, these citations are taken as recognition of value in the cited work. The more a work is cited by other publications, the more valuable it is.

With the online revolution, usage too became a viable option. When the online version of a work is accessed, this can be counted like the hits measured for any page on the web. Less significant research may attract chance usage based on the relevance of the title or an author involved, but more significant work is likely to be more popular and accessed a great many times. It has been argued that usage data are in some ways more useful than citation data as they provide a more current picture of research importance (Bollen *et al.*, 2009).

Analysis of the content of a book or journal can also be a useful third approach. If articles or chapters dealing with a specific topic or from a certain author or institution are becoming more common, that may indicate a rise in the importance or acceptance of an idea or researcher. The study of the measurable elements of publications – citations, usage and content – is referred to as bibliometrics, although the term is most commonly used in publishing to refer to citation analysis.

There have been moves to use other data to evaluate research but these are not yet as widely accepted. Counting patents, for example, has been proposed, but as different countries and regions have different patent laws and databases, establishing counts and coverage is difficult. Features tracking references to research in social media and blogs have been introduced by some publishers (*PLoS One*, 2009) but this approach is too recent to have become mainstream and remains more open to manipulation than other methods. This said, citations and usage are not without their problems either.

Quality, impact and popularity

It is tempting to use terms such as quality, impact and popularity more or less interchangeably; however, there are subtle but important differences. Citations, for example, can only demonstrate the impact of a work on a subject area, not the rather more subjective property of quality; a citation can be made to a work that is poorly written or presented, or recognising value in only part of the research presented. Moreover, citations may be made in contention with the cited work. Usually, it could be argued, this ultimately helps to establish consensus on a certain topic and so is still a valuable contribution to knowledge. In all cases, however, impact rather than quality is being measured.

Likewise, usage shows popularity rather than quality. A certain proportion of all usage will be based on the title, author name or the source in which the work appears, and just because a reader looked at an article does not mean they found it useful or important. Thus one might take impact and popularity as measuring elements of quality but not the whole.

Both citations and usage also have limitations and drawbacks as the foundations of metrics. Citations are inherently retrospective; it may take an author several years to read a work, incorporate it into their research, write an article addressing the topic and have this article published. Furthermore, the databases that index these citations tend to cover more journals in the US and Europe than elsewhere (Harzing and van der Wal, 2008), and coverage of the literature across subject areas varies wildly. The average number of citations in each subject area also differs, being more numerous in medicine, for example, than in mathematics. Self-citation, where authors or journals preferentially cite their own work to inflate their performance, may also be an issue (Van Raan, 2008). Many citations contain bibliographic errors and some are made without the cited work being read (Simkin and Roychowdhury, 2003). Some authors even question the underlying assumption that citations can be used to fairly measure impact (Todd and Ladle, 2008).

Usage data are more problematic still. Unlike citations, no central or neutral organisation counts usage for articles that are published. Although the COUNTER project has provided an immensely useful standard for what is counted when a user accesses an article (Shepherd, 2002), different publishers vary in their treatment of usage aggregated through third-party hosts such as Ovid. Usage counts can also be affected by changes in the indexing policies of Google and other search engines, making fair comparison over time impossible. Usage looks only at the electronic version of an article, ignoring print usage. It is also easier to manipulate than citations because all that is required is a click of a button rather than the publication of a citing article. Last but not least, publishers are also reluctant to yield their usage data, as they could provide business intelligence to competitors. Although work on a Usage Factor is underway (Usage Factors, 2010), no journal usage metrics have yet been produced for a significant proportion of titles across publishers.

In any case, neither usage nor citations provide us with a complete picture of research impact. The former is an indicator of where useful research was sought, while the latter only shows the subset of instances where a researcher's use of the research was finally published. The situation was perhaps best elucidated by Carl Bergstrom: 'Usage data tell us where the net was cast; citation data tell us where the fish were caught' (Butler, 2009). Both approaches are utilised far more frequently with journal articles than with books. At the time of writing, only selected book series and collections of conference proceedings are included in either of the main citation indices and usage counts are most commonly provided by publishers for their journal products.

It is quite possible to undertake useful citation and usage analysis of book titles where the data exists, but for the aforementioned reasons, the commonly used metrics in publishing apply to journals and count citations rather than usage. It is these metrics on which this chapter will focus; but before metrics can be calculated, publications and citations must be recorded in a citation index.

Citation indices

There are currently three major, international citation indices available, each with different coverage of published research.

Web of Science

The longest-running citation index is the Web of Science (WoS), now owned by Thomson Reuters. WoS, which has existed since 1960 and indexes around 12 000 journals (Thomson Reuters, 2011c), is a part of the larger database, Web of Knowledge, which indexes some 23 000 titles with backfiles going back more than a century (Thomson Reuters, 2011b).

However, full bibliographic information and a breakdown of the citations received each year since publication are available for approximately 8300 Science titles, 2900 Social Science titles and 1600 Arts and Humanities titles (with some overlap) along with a selection of conference proceedings in the Sciences and Social Sciences. Journals apply for coverage and are admitted to the index if they can demonstrate that their articles are scholarly, peer reviewed, attract a basic level of citation activity and are international in authorship or editorial coverage. Foreign language titles can be indexed as long as the abstract is available in English.

The data available include author names and addresses, keywords, volume, issue and page numbers, date of publication and article DOI (Digital Object Identifier – a unique code for each article, book chapter or book). Standard web access to WoS limits the downloading of records to batches of 500, which can make data acquisition for large analyses time consuming. The main bibliographic information for each article and the breakdown of citations per year are acquired on two different screens with different outputs, which do not share a common identifier; this means that some initial work is often required pairing the metadata for an article with its citations.

It is possible to search the index by author, article or journal title, address, country, year and document type, as well as less frequently used fields such as grant number and funding agency; however, it is not possible to search by subject area or publisher, so publishers must take alternative routes to gathering these useful data.

In the latest version of WoS, version 5, institutional addresses are aggregated from the form in which they appeared on the original work. 'Lemmatisation' has also been introduced, meaning that, for example, US and UK variant spellings of the same word need no longer be searched separately (Thomson Reuters, 2011a). It has historically been tricky searching for authors, many of whom often share the same surname and initials (Deis and Goodman, 2007), but WoS has been enhanced to construct unique author sets to help disambiguate researchers and to include a separate author search page. It is also now possible to search by Researcher ID with links for each ID back to the full author profile on the Researcher ID site (Thomson Reuters, 2011a). Additionally, Thomson Reuters plans to deliver a solution to this as part of their Research in View product, by incorporating the ORCID (Open Researcher & Contributor ID) author unique identifier system (Haak, 2011).

A significant development in the WoS product is the Book Citation Index (BCI), scheduled for release in late 2011. Planned to initially contain approximately 25 000 volumes, the BCI will include much of the data currently available for journals and will be accessible through the same web interface. This is crucial for social sciences, arts and humanities titles, where a far higher proportion of the key literature appears in book form. It may also inaugurate a new era of citation analysis for books.

Scopus

Scopus is Elsevier's competitor to WoS, launched in 2004. Covering nearly 18 000 peer-reviewed journal titles (Elsevier, 2011) as well as book series and conference proceedings, it covers more material than WoS (Falagas *et al.*, 2008), although there is some evidence that the additional material is less well cited (Vieira and Gomes, 2009). The fields of data available via the Scopus web interface are very similar to that in WoS; the bibliographic data and year-on-year citation data are again stored on different screens and retrieved in different downloads. Records can be downloaded in batches of 2000, but consecutive batches cannot currently be easily selected, making the acquisition of larger data sets reliant on complicated filtering of results and thus more difficult and time consuming than on WoS.

Like WoS, Scopus attempts to resolve the issue of author ambiguity through the construction of unique author sets, although again these are sometimes incomplete (Deis and Goodman, 2007). Scopus also provides an institution search, aggregating the articles published by schools, departments and subsidiaries of an institution into one entry. A series of breakdowns by subject area and document type are also available for each institution. Searching is possible by publisher, although the entries sometimes give publisher imprints or out-of-date information, meaning these results are not entirely reliable. Searching by journal title may be less reliable than in WoS, however, as there are some variations in coverage across years, with some journal issues absent from the index (Deis and Goodman, 2007).

Google Scholar

Publishers and institutions must pay for access to WoS and Scopus, but a free alternative exists: Google Scholar (GS) eschews article data provided by publishers in favour of that garnered by automatic crawlers and parsers. The result is a service that theoretically trawls the entire world of online scholarly materials, providing records for journal articles not covered by the other citation indices and creating citation counts for all published researchers.

However, there is a strong case that you get what you pay for with this free service, as problems with data quality have been identified (Falagas *et al.*, 2008). If it lacks a master record for a certain publication, an entry is created from citations to that publication; if these citations appear in different formats or with inconsistent details, multiple entries can be created for the same target article (Jascó, 2009b). This can vastly inflate citation counts for authors and journals. The parser can erroneously create author names from text on a web page (such as Please Login or Payment Options) or can ignore actual author names. Other investigations have shown that pseudo-article generators designed to test journal peer review can fool Google Scholar's crawlers, introducing a new array of inflated article and citation counts (Labbe, 2010).

These problems may affect a relatively small proportion of the GS records, but without any idea of the number of bad records or the total number of GS records available, it is impossible to have confidence in this index. A set of free, independent analysis tools for GS citations called Publish or Perish is available, although these are for personal use only and not commercial use by publishers.

Other indices

In addition to the three main indices, there are a number of other services, including the Chinese Social Science Index, the Asian Science Citation Index and the Indian Citation Index. The creators of these indices often cite low levels of coverage in WoS and Scopus as the reason for their existence. Certainly North American and European articles tend to receive more citations in many subject areas, but whether this is because of a bias against research from the rest of the world or because such research is genuinely and objectively superior has not yet been proven. In any case, the journal metrics currently established or gaining popularity rely on WoS or Scopus.

Journal impact metrics

With the increasing importance of citations in evaluating the impact of research, it was natural that metrics would be devised to measure the citation performance of different journal titles. A great number of metrics of varying degrees of sophistication have now been proposed, with their merits and demerits debated extensively; however, only relatively few have been calculated for a significant proportion of journals and made available over a number of consecutive years. These are the most useful from a publishing perspective as they can be used both for comparative analysis and publicity.

Impact Factor

The first metric to gain currency was the Impact Factor, created by Eugene Garfield (Garfield, 1955), founder of the Institute for Scientific Information (ISI) that created the WoS. Unsurprisingly, this metric is based on WoS data, meaning that only citations from indexed journals are counted. Impact Factors are generated for all of the titles in the Thomson Reuters Science and Social Science indices but not the Arts & Humanities titles. Impact Factors for a given year are released in June of the following year as part of a subscription to the Journal Citation Report (JCR).

The Impact Factor for a given year is calculated as follows:

$$\text{Impact Factor for Year } x = \frac{\text{(Citations from articles published in Year } x \text{ to articles published in Years } x-1 \text{ and } x-2)}{\text{(Number of citable items published in Years } x-1 \text{ and } x-2)}$$

This number, which is given to three decimal places, effectively measures average citations per article for recent publications. There is a disparity between what is counted on the two halves of the ratio. When WoS indexes a journal, the articles in that journal are reclassified according to an internal document type system (which may be entirely different from that used by the journal) as either a citable item, such as an Article, Review or Proceedings Paper, or one of a range of non-citable items, such as Letter, Book Review, Meeting Abstract or Editorial. Citations from any article type to any article type are counted on the numerator, but only 'citable items' are counted on the denominator (McVeigh and Mann, 2009).

A variation on the Impact Factor was recently incorporated into the JCR; the Five Year Impact Factor uses the same calculation, but instead of looking at citations in a given year to articles published in the previous two years, it studies those published in the previous five, with a denominator looking at the same period. This was introduced partly to serve the needs of some subject categories, particularly in the Social Sciences, where a two-year citation window was insufficient to include the core period of citation in the calculation. The JCR gives additional metrics for each title, such as the Immediacy Index (which measures how rapidly a title is cited) and the Cited Half Life (which measures how long after publication issues of a title are being cited).

The Impact Factor is the most widely recognised of the journal metrics (Hoeffel, 1998). It is the metric given as standard on publishers' journal home pages and even low scores are often publicised. As a metric, it has several advantages. Measuring average citations-per-article is easy to understand as a concept and relatively easy to explain as a calculation; furthermore, it can be duplicated, predicted and simulated, rather than being an opaque and inscrutable 'black box'.

However, there are some issues with the metric. Articles only contribute to Impact Factors in the two years following the year of publication; this is too short a window for many subject areas, which take longer to start accruing significant numbers of citations (Jacsó, 2009a). The fact that different subject areas are cited with widely varying frequency and speed also means that the Impact Factors of two similar journals in subtly different fields cannot be fairly compared (Taylor *et al.*, 2008). Veterinary Science provides an excellent example of this; journals within the same subject category, but dealing with different species, have quite different average citation rates.

Furthermore, the metric suffers from 'inflation'; with more journals being published each year, more articles per issue and more references per article, the pool of citations from which the Impact Factors are calculated is continually growing (Althouse *et al.*, 2009). This means there has been inflation in the metric and that an Impact Factor of 5 now is 'worth' less than it was a decade ago.

Some Editors might be tempted to pressure authors to insert citations to their journal into submitted articles before they would be accepted for publication, or publishing editorials citing all of the previous year's articles, in an attempt to artificially inflate citation counts (Brumback, 2009). ISI does exclude journals where the proportion of such self-citations contributing to an Impact Factor is beyond a certain threshold, but it is unclear what this threshold is.

Scimago Journal Rank

The Scimago Journal Rank (SJR) is one alternative to the Impact Factor. SJRs are released biannually, based on half- and then full-year figures for the previous year, by the Scimago Journal Group (Elsevier, 2010). This group consists of academics based in Spain who were closely involved with the creation of Scopus but are not formally affiliated with Elsevier.

A detailed version of the equation is available (Scimago Research Group, 2007), but calculation outlined on the Scimago Journal Rank homepage for the full-year SJR of a given year is:

$$\text{SJR for Year } x = \frac{\text{(Weighted citations from articles published in Year } x \text{ to articles published in Years } x-1, x-2 \text{ and } x-3 \text{ less self-citations)}}{\text{(Number of citable items published in Years } x-1, x-2 \text{ and } x-3\text{)}}$$

There are a few key differences between this metric and the Impact Factor. Citable items are still defined as articles, reviews or proceedings papers, although the classification system employed by Scopus is not the same as that used by ISI. Any journal self-citation above 33 per cent of the citations received during the census period is excluded and the calculation window is extended from looking at the previous two years to the previous three (Anegon, no date).

More significant still is the introduction of weighted citations, where a citation from a high-impact title is worth more than a citation from a low-impact title. The performance of a journal is modified by the performance of those titles that cite it in an iterative process, with the high-impact journals accumulating more of the total prestige with each iteration, until the variation between iterations falls below a certain threshold. The weighting approach is very similar to the PageRank algorithm used by Google to rank pages in search results, although it is still under debate whether this increases the usefulness of the metric.

The metric has strengths and weaknesses. On the one hand, the self-citation limit reduces the chance that the rare unscrupulous journal Editor would seek to manipulate their result. The SJR is entirely free to access and is based on more journals than the Impact Factor, theoretically representing a larger proportion of the scientific community. It also looks at a three-year rather than two-year window, covering more of the core period of article citation. SJRs are also recalculated annually, meaning that they are not affected by citation inflation.

However, some of the innovative solutions applied in the SJR bring new problems. Because the impact of a journal is based on an iterative weighting process, it is impossible to calculate a journal's SJR without knowing the impact of all the other journals in the set. This weighting data for the 18 000 titles in Scopus is not available, meaning the SJR cannot be checked, predicted or replicated for non-indexed titles. This is not ideal from the point of view of publishers wishing to confirm or improve their titles' performance; nor is the metric's annual recalculation, which means that a journal's historical performance may change over time. Finally, like the Impact Factor, the SJR is very much dependent on subject area, meaning the values of two titles in different fields cannot be meaningfully compared.

EigenFactor

Proposed by Carl Bergstrom (Bergstrom, 2007), the EigenFactor (EF) first entered currency in 2007 when it and Article Influence, a related measure, were incorporated into the JCR and released annually along with the Impact Factor. Following the same notation as the two previous examples, it would be represented as:

$$\text{EF for Year } x = \begin{array}{c}\text{Proportion of weighted citations from articles}\\ \text{published in Year } x \text{ to articles published in Years}\\ x-1,\ x-2,\ x-3,\ x-4 \text{ and } x-5 \text{ less self-citations}\end{array}$$

The most notable difference between this metric and the previous two is that it has no denominator; it does not represent an average number of citations but rather the proportion of all available citations that a given journal attracts. So if two journals were to have the same Impact Factor, the larger of them would have a higher EigenFactor because it would attract a higher proportion of all cites. The EigenFactor is also based on a five-year target period rather than two for the Impact Factor or three for the SJR. It shares some similar properties with the SJR in that it ignores self-citations and weights citations received according to the impact of the citing journal, using a similar methodology.

The EigenFactor is complemented by the Article Influence measure. This is more similar to the Impact Factor, in that it takes account of the size of a journal, but it is still not an average cites-per-article. To calculate the Article Influence, the EigenFactor is normalised by the proportion of all articles in the JCR that appear in the journal under study. So if two journals had the same EigenFactor, the smaller of them would have the higher Article Influence.

The EigenFactor has advantages. Looking at a five-year window, it certainly includes the core citation period for most subject areas in the

Science and Social Science citation indices, and again eliminates any possible manipulation through self-citation. It is also fixed, like the Impact Factor. Moreover, because they represent a proportion of citations rather than an average citation count, EigenFactors are not subject to citation inflation, making them comparable across years.

Unlike the SJR, it is theoretically possible to replicate the EigenFactor calculations (West and Bergstrom, 2008), although this requires the CD-ROM version of the JCR and would be computationally intensive. An EigenFactor can be simulated for a non-indexed title too, although clearly citations from such a title could not be included in the citation matrix used to determine the EigenFactors of indexed titles, resulting in an inaccurate simulation. The EigenFactor is therefore far more of a closed box than the Impact Factor. Like the IF and SJR, the EigenFactor and Article Influence are strongly influenced by the subject area of a journal. Additionally, it has been suggested that the weighting of citations does not provide a substantially different result from citation counts without weighting (Davis, 2008a).

Source Normalised Impact per Paper

The Source Normalised Impact per Paper (SNIP) was created by Henk Moed (Moed, 2010), is based on data from Scopus and is released along with the SJR on JournalMetrics.com. It is the first metric to be calculated for the whole journal list that seeks to take account of the varying frequency and speed of citation between different subject areas.

Like the SJR and EigenFactor, it is not easily reduced to a simple equation, but can be expressed as follows:

$$\text{SNIP for Year } x = \frac{\left[\begin{array}{c}\text{(Citations from citable items}\\ \text{published in Year } x \text{ to citable}\\ \text{items published in Years } x-1,\\ x-2 \text{ and } x-3)\end{array}\right.}{\left.\begin{array}{c}\text{(Number of citable items}\\ \text{published in Years}\\ x-1, x-2 \text{ and } x-3)\end{array}\right]} \div \begin{array}{c}\text{Relative Database}\\ \text{Citation Potential}\end{array}$$

It is therefore a two-stage process. First, an average citations-per-paper is calculated for a journal, looking only at citations to and from citable items (articles, reviews and proceedings papers) appearing in journals only, from a three-year target window. This is then normalised by the relative database citation potential, which measures how likely it is that the journal should be cited, given how many citations are made by articles in the journals that cite it. Effectively, every journal has its own subject area, made up only of the journals from which it receives citations. Its raw average citations-per-article is adjusted for the average citations it would be expected to receive.

The major advantage of the SNIP is that it appears to eliminate citation differences between subject areas. Metrics have been theorised that normalise citation performance by subject area, but these are often based on grouping journals by field – this causes difficulties, as noted, for clinical or applied journals, or subject areas with internal variation, such as Veterinary Sciences. By defining subject areas uniquely for each journal, the SNIP avoids this. It also has the strength of ignoring citations to and from non-citable items, making manipulation through game-playing with document type classification far less likely.

It does suffer from drawbacks, however. Clearly, it is complicated to calculate even with all the required data. Getting the required data is no easy task either, because one must know how many times every citing article in the dataset has cited each journal in the dataset. Although it is possible to calculate the Database Citation Potential (DCP) for a single title, one would also need to know the DCP for all titles in a dataset. At present, the SNIP is therefore as much of a 'black box' as the SJR or EigenFactor and cannot be checked, predicted or simulated for non-indexed titles. It is still a very new metric and further debate will probably establish the degree of its usefulness, although it has been suggested that the SNIP methodology does not account for differences in citation between fields (Leydesdorff and Opthof, 2010).

Backlash against citation metrics

As the application of journal citation metrics has grown, so too has opposition to the practice. It is held by some that, far from providing a useful guide, the chasing of high impact has begun to damage research itself.

In some cases, objections are made to specific attributes of the metrics, which make them unsuitable for measuring science. For example, journals publishing a large number of non-citable items, or a small number of very long citable items, may have an unrepresentatively high numerator and a low denominator in metrics that look at average citations (Campbell, 2008). Journals in fields with lower average numbers of citations, such as mathematics or social sciences, can be unfairly discriminated against if funding decisions are based on one of the majority of metrics that do not account for variations in subject area.

Some criticism has been levelled at editors and publishers; for example, it has been suggested that focusing on big-name authors to attract citation creates a barrier to up-and-coming researchers (Tsikliras, 2008). Another criticism argues that clinical articles and case studies, which tend to receive fewer citations (Oh and Lim, 2009), might be avoided despite their importance to a journal's community.

Other issues have been raised with the application of the metrics. Chinese science authors have been instructed to publish articles only in journals appearing in the Science Citation Index, and which therefore receive an Impact Factor (Al-Awqati, 2007). Authors from Imperial College London have had the Impact Factor of the journals in which they publish incorporated into a Publication Score (Colquhoun, 2007). In Brazil, Impact Factors are used to evaluate graduate programmes (de Albuquerque, 2010). There are similar reports of the Impact Factor being used in Italy, Japan and Spain in a similar fashion (Cameron, 2005).

This is particularly problematic; the impact of a journal cannot be used to generalise about the impact of the authors publishing in it because the distribution of citation strength within a journal is highly skewed. In some samples, the most cited 15 per cent of the articles account for 50 per cent of the citations, and the most cited 50 per cent of the articles account for 90 per cent of the citations (Seglen, 1997); in some cases, the skew is even greater (Campbell, 2008).

These concerns have been part of the driving force behind innovations in article-level metrics. Some publishers have begun giving the usage and citation counts for individual articles, allowing authors to report these rather than focusing on journals. Although usage data are incomparable between publishers, owing to variations in what is counted and how, the citation data supplied by CrossRef allow meaningful comparison of citation impact at an article level.

Strategic journal development

From a publisher's perspective, it is crucial to maximise a journal's impact, whichever metric is used to measure it. Authors will often consider Impact Factors when deciding where to publish their work and citation performance may well be one of the elements in a librarian's decision over whether to subscribe to a publication. When working with society-owned titles, retention of contracts may depend heavily on maintaining a strong citation performance. Publishers are therefore compelled to maximise the impact of their publications as much as authors and institutions.

Journal Editors may, of course, have other priorities for a title than maximising its Impact Factor, such as service to the subject community. Moreover, as already noted, some of the tactics used to maximise impact can end up unduly influencing the format or focus of research. Publishers should be sensitive to these considerations and seek to increase impact through citation analysis only when their efforts do not debase the knowledge they seek to make available.

In the future, the metrics that weight citations by the impact of the citing journal may become more popular, in which case it will be important both to attract a high volume of citations and that these citations come from high-impact journals. Currently, however, the Impact Factor is the most widely recognised and prioritised measure, so the key aim of publisher citation analysis is to attract more citations per article for the journal.

Before this is possible, there are some technical constraints to overcome. As previously noted, WoS and Scopus both provide two sets of data, one with bibliographic information and the other with citation counts by year. It may therefore be necessary to join the two sets of data using a database or a program like Microsoft Excel. Address data are also usually combined into one field, so it may be worthwhile separating out the different lines to enable study of institutions, countries and world regions. Some publishers have created tools to automate these processes, which saves a great deal of manual work.

When studying the performance of a journal and working to improve it, it is often best to download several years of articles and their associated citation data, so that trends over time can be established. It is also advisable to acquire records for similar or competitor titles, so that strengths, weaknesses, opportunities and threats can be identified and results can be viewed in proper context.

There are numerous ways to break down and study article data. While a top article list may allow someone familiar with the subject area to spot patterns in what is best cited, more transparent approaches are often effective. Aggregating the articles by author can allow identification of the top names in a field. Articles or reviews could then be commissioned from these individuals or they could be recruited to a journal Editorial Board, to attract papers from their networks. The same can be done for author affiliation, identifying institutions with strong publishing records in certain areas. It should be noted, however, that there will usually be only a few articles for each author or institution, and care should be taken to avoid reaching strong conclusions based on a small sample size.

If country and region data can be extracted from the bibliographic records, these can often provide useful guidance. While all research from a certain country in a field will not be of a similar level of citation strength, analysis by country can allow the identification of areas where publication frequency is growing or where citation strength is trending upwards. Extending a journal's scope or Editorial Board to draw in more papers from other countries can increase the chances that a high-impact article will be submitted to the journal.

More simply, journal strengths and opportunities can be identified through a breakdown of the document types published. It may become apparent that a journal's articles are well cited but its proceedings papers are not; or that a great many citations are attracted by editorials and relatively few by reviews, in comparison with competitor titles. The decision could then be taken whether to decrease the numbers of weak document type articles published, or to try to improve them by looking at what makes a certain document type successful for other journals. This approach can also work when comparing special issues with normal issues; because each citable item contributes to the denominator of an Impact Factor, it is important to ensure that special issues, if published, are attracting as many citations per article as normal issues.

One of the more useful but commensurately difficult analyses often requested is a study of which topics within a field are more or less cited. Although some subject areas, such as chemistry, have an existing taxonomy of subjects with the tagging of indexed articles to allow easier analysis, this is rare. It is tempting simply to look up the citations for a single keyword, but the citation performance of a single keyword is unlikely to be representative of a topic; it is more reliable to aggregate keywords describing topics into clusters and then study the average citation performance of these clusters. Without degree-level experience of the journal topic, however, the assistance of a journal's Editorial Board may be required in establishing topic keyword lists.

There are some simpler tricks to improving Impact Factor performance that do not involve debasing the research presented. Citations count towards metrics like the Impact Factor on a calendar year basis, so that a 2012 article would contribute to the 2013 and 2014 Impact Factors regardless of publication month. However, publishing an issue in January 2011 rather than December 2012 will mean its articles have 36 rather than 24 months before the end of this 'citation window'. These extra 12 months can increase average citation levels significantly. For this reason, publishers often load the early issues of a year with more papers, or fill them with articles written by well-respected authors who are more likely to be cited. However, the most honest, the most effective and the least damaging way to increase an Impact Factor is to identify and publish better research with a higher potential for citation.

WoS additionally allows users to search for and download the citations themselves, along with the data of the articles that made them. This can allow analysis of which authors, institutions and countries cite a particular journal most frequently, which can feed into marketing and sales efforts. More usefully still, it is possible to use these data to check, predict and simulate Impact Factors ahead of their formal release. In the rare case that citations have been missed from the JCR calculations, it is possible to alert Thomson Reuters to the issue and request correction in the September re-release of the JCR. Impact Factor simulation for non-indexed titles also provides a useful guide when applying for coverage in WoS, as a basic level of citation activity is required for admission.

The 'early view' effect

Most major publishers now make copies of their articles available online before they are incorporated into an issue and given page numbers. Certain subjects also have preprint online repositories where the text of an article accepted for publication (but prior to formatting by a publisher) can be hosted; one example of this is the arXiv.org repository for Physics, Mathematics and Computing. Making a version of an article available online ahead of print publication in this way may increase the citations received by those papers before a certain deadline; they are online earlier, more likely to be read and therefore more likely to be cited. The citations are, in essence, brought forward and made sooner (Moed, 2007); this is the early view effect.

Citations from these papers are only counted by WoS when the final paginated version is indexed, but citations to these papers made before that date can theoretically be recorded and added to the article record when it appears in an index. For such a citation to be counted on WoS, it must contain the DOI for the cited work.

However, even if the CrossRef DOI is not given and the citation is consequently not attached to an article's entry on WoS, the citation may still be counted as part of an Impact Factor calculation. This is because the only information sought when identifying citations for the Impact Factor are the cited journal title and the year of the cited article. No attempt is made to verify that the target article has been published in the given year. This means that the effect of making an article available online early is, ideally, to extend the window of citation for that article by the duration of the lag between the early view version becoming available and the paginated version being published.

For example, citations to an article published in December 2011 will be counted towards the 2012 and 2013 Impact Factors. That means a citing article must be written and published within 24 months of the target article becoming available in December or the citation will not contribute to an Impact Factor. In many subject areas, this is too short a window and citations are 'lost'. However, if the target article was made available for early view in December 2010, the 'window' during which citations will count is extended to 36 months, theoretically increasing the likelihood that the target article will be cited.

There are arguments against this theory. It relies on taking an article in isolation; if the target article was available 12 months earlier, there may have been other articles available then that citing authors would have chosen in preference to it. Citations exist as part of a network of knowledge and altering one element may change the whole. It is also possible that citations to the article will be given as 'In Press' or that authors will continue to cite the version under the early view date (2010). Moreover, it is very difficult to test the early view effect, because it is impossible to know how many citations an article would have received if it had not been available for early view. Work on arXiv has found both an early view effect and a strong quality bias in what was submitted to the repository (Moed, 2007). Only through a controlled trial, with articles randomly made available online early or not, would it be possible to test scientifically whether early view increases citation counts; we can, however, be reasonably confident that it does not lower them.

Open Access (OA) and citations

One hotly debated issue in citation analysis is whether making articles freely available increases the numbers of citations made to them. The theory goes that if an article is available to any reader online, the pool of potential citing authors will be larger and that a proportion of these additional citations will be indexed, benefiting authors and the journals in which they publish. Indeed, early studies (Antelman, 2004; Hajjem *et al.*, 2005) showed a correlation between articles being freely available and higher levels of citation; the authors of some of these studies held that there was a causal link between an article being free and receiving more citations (Harnad and Brody, 2004).

Subsequent examinations of the subject found methodological problems with the early studies, such as imbalances in the size of OA and non-OA samples and the use of inconsistent windows for citation counting (Craig *et al.*, 2007). Moreover, higher levels of citation could have been caused by other factors, such as the aforementioned early view effect or selection bias – that authors would only make their best work freely available online or that better authors tended to self-archive (Moed, 2007). Another study, by Davis (2008b), sought to eliminate selection bias by randomly selecting which articles were made available via OA and then checking citation counts over time to see if there was a difference between the two groups; this study found that there was no OA advantage after one year.

Further research by proponents of OA citation advantage compared articles that were made available online by choice of the author with those that were mandatorily made free, for example as part of requirements by a funding agency, but did not randomly select which articles were made OA (Gargouri *et al.*, 2010). Criticism had also been levelled at the Davis study that one year was too short a time for OA advantage to become apparent (Harnad, 2008).

Davis has recently updated his results to show that there is still no OA advantage three years after publication (Davis, 2010), but this has not been accepted by the proponents of OA, whose results suggest there is an OA advantage for both mandated and self-selected OA articles (Harnad, 2010). The two conclusions seem contradictory, although there is a difference between institution- or funding body-mandated OA and random selection; it could be argued still that articles published as a result of funding body grants are more likely to contain significant and citable conclusions. While neutral parties seem to be satisfied with Davis' approach, it has not been suggested that his results can be generalized to the entire journal population. It would take a wide range of large samples for one to be confident that any result could be generalised to all journals. However, the approach of randomly assigning OA status gives a view of the data that is the most free from confounding variables so far. While OA citation advantage cannot be considered to have been comprehensively disproved, it has now been called seriously into doubt.

Author metrics

Although publishers are primarily concerned with metrics relating to journals, many key stakeholders are also authors. As journal metrics have grown in importance over recent years, so too have author metrics. The first metric to gain significant currency was the H-Index, proposed by Jorge Hirsch (Hirsch, 2007). An author has an H-Index of 3 if, from all the articles they have published, there are 3 that have at least 3 citations each; they have an H-Index of 5 if there are 5 articles with at least 5 citations each; 10 if there are 10 articles with at least 10 citations each, and so on (Figure 10.1). The H-Index is therefore a measurement of both quantity of publications and their quality.

H-indices have not been calculated and released in the same way that Impact Factors are because they may change every time a citation is indexed. This is, however, something of a weakness, as there is no definitive version of an author's H-Index. The value will vary depending on whether it is calculated from WoS, Scopus or Google Scholar data. Even the automatic calculations on WoS and Scopus may give inaccurate

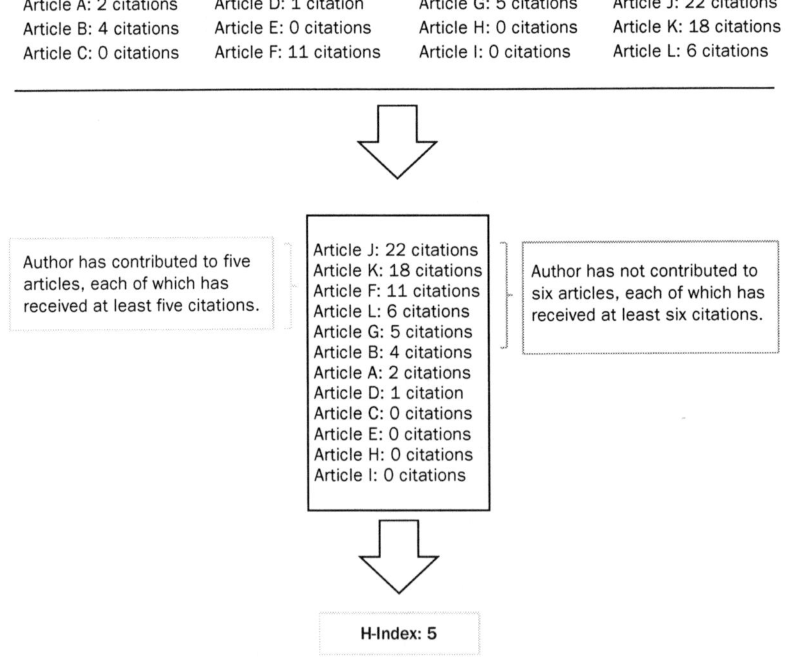

Figure 10.1 Illustration of an author's H-Index calculation

results if based on incomplete unique author article sets. But there are problems with the metric beyond calculation (Bornmann and Daniel, 2007). It is, like the Impact Factor, strongly affected by differences in citation frequency between different subject areas. It is also insensitive to time, in that it can never fall; long-dead researchers may well have higher H-Indices than their living counterparts. Researchers who co-author in large groups tend to receive more citations and so have higher H-Indices, a pattern leading to increasing levels of co-authorship (Ioannidis, 2008). The metric can also be manipulated by publishing a large number of weaker articles that cite each other and would fail to properly rank those authors who publish a very few but critically important articles.

A number of variations on the basic H-Index have been proposed (Bornmann *et al.*, 2008). Alternatives include the AR-Index (Jin *et al.*, 2007), which takes into account the age of the citations, or the Individual H-Index (Batista *et al.*, 2006), which aims to eliminate the effect of co-authorship. None of these deals satisfactorily with gulfs in citation levels between different subject areas that skew as a result of which index is used.

The future of research performance metrics

The next several years will probably see the emergence of some new metrics and the consolidation of some existing ones. At a journal level, the Impact Factor, misused as it sometimes is, will most likely remain the most accepted metric. It took decades for the Impact Factor to reach this position, so we should not expect any of the competitor metrics to replace it imminently, particularly given the complexity of their calculation. It is more likely that we will see the emergence of new approaches to measuring research performance at a journal level. As previously mentioned, the Usage Factor is still in development, and although it may be as prone to manipulation as the Impact Factor, if not more so, it will add a new dimension to the tools we have available. Time will tell whether it is accepted.

Work continues on developing new approaches to research performance evaluation. Grant information could theoretically be used to evaluate research, but the funding a project receives and its eventual usefulness are disconnected. The RAND corporation recently reported on novel efforts to evaluate research using systematically collected 'atoms' of data (Wooding, 2011) but these would seem to be too subject-specific to apply to the entire gamut of journal fields. Given the difficulties encountered in fairly comparing journals from different subject areas, it is even conceivable that field-specific metrics will evolve, but there has been little movement in this direction so far.

The continued development of metrics at other levels is a certainty. The major publishers are investing heavily in usage, citation and social media metrics at an article level, and the sophistication of these is only likely to increase. With the increased adoption of unique researcher identification, the use of author-level metrics should become easier and more reliable; all that remains is to find a strong metric to which author data can be applied (Finch, 2010).

Governments are also making the measurement of research performance a priority at an institutional and subject level. In the US, the National Institutes of Health, National Science Foundation and White House Office of Science and Technology policy has launched STAR METRICS, the first phase of which has looked at job creation resultant from research funding. The second phase plans to look at publications and citations but also social and environmental outcomes, patent grants and company start-ups based on the application of research innovations. In Australia, the ERA (Excellence in Research for Australia) initiative continues to develop its bibliometric indicators as one element of research performance evaluation.

The path and destination of the road ahead are quite uncertain; if only one thing is for sure, it is that publishers' bibliometricians will need to know about far more than just the Impact Factor.

References

Al-Awqati, Q. (2007) Impact Factors and prestige. *Kidney International*, 71: 183–5.

de Albuquerque, U.P. (2010) The tyranny of the impact factor: why do we still want to be subjugated? *Rodriguésia*, 61(3): 353–8.

Althouse, B.M., West, J.D., Bergstrom, T. and Bergstrom, C.T. (2009) Differences in Impact Factor across fields and over time. *Journal of the American Society for Information Science and Technology*, 60: 27–34.

Anegon, F. d. (no date). Auto-citacao - distribuicao global. Retrieved 29 June 2011, from Portal Eventos BVS: http://www.slideshare.net/fkersten/scopus-journal-metrics-snip-sjr

Antelman, K. (2004) Do Open Access articles have a greater citation impact? *College & Research Libraries*, 65: 372–82.

Batista, P.D., Campiteli, M.G., Kinouchi, O. and Martinez, A.S. (2006) Is it possible to compare researchers with different scientific interests? *Scientometrics*, 68(1): 179–89.

Bergstrom, C.T. (2007) Eigenfactor: measuring the value and prestige of scholarly journals. *College & Research Libraries News*, 68(5).

Bollen, J., Van de Sompel, H., Hagberg, A., *et al.* (2009) Clickstream data yields high-resolution maps of science. *PLoS One*, 4(3): e4803.

Bornmann, L. and Daniel, H. D. (2007) What do we know about the H-Index? *Journal of the American Society for Information Science and Technology*, 58: 1381–5.

Bornmann, L., Mutz, R. and Daniel, H.-D. (2008) Are there better indices for evaluation purposes than the h index? A comparison of nine different variants of the h index using data from biomedicine. *Journal of the American Society for Information Science and Technology*, 59(5): 830–7.

Brumback, R. A. (2009) Impact Factor Wars: Episode V - The Empire Strikes Back. *Journal of Child Neurology*, 24(3): 260–2.

Butler, D. (2009) *Web usage data outline map of knowledge*. Retrieved 21 June 2011, from Nature News: http://www.nature.com/news/2009/090309/full/458135a.html

Cameron, B.D. (2005) Trends in the usage of ISI bibliometric data: uses, abuses, and implications. *Librarian and Staff*, Paper 3.

Campbell, P. (2008) Escape from the Impact Factor. *Ethics in Science and Environmental Politics*, 8: 5–7.

Colquhoun, D. (2007) How to get good science. Retrieved 20 June 2011, from DCScience.net: http://www.dcscience.net/goodscience.pdf

Craig, I.D., Plume, A.M., McVeigh, M.E., Pringle, J. and Amin, M. (2007) Do open access articles have greater citation impact? A critical review of the literature. *Journal of Informetrics*, 1(3): 239–48.

Davis, P.M. (2008a) Eigenfactor: does the principle of repeated improvement result in better journal impact estimates than raw citation counts? *Journal of the American Society for Information Science and Technology*, 59(13): 2186–8.

Davis, P.M. (2008b) Open access publishing, article downloads, and citations: randomised controlled trial. *British Medical Journal.*

Davis, P.M. (2010) Does Open Access lead to increased readership and citations? A randomised controlled trial of articles published in the APS journals. *The Physiologist*, 53: 197–201.

Deis, L.F. and Goodman, D. (2007). Update on Scopus and Web of Science. *The Charleston Advisor*, 8(3): 15–15(1).

Elsevier. (2010) *Journal Ranking Metrics - SNIP & SJR: A New Perspective in Journal Performance Management*. Retrieved 29 June 2011, from SlideShare. Net: http://www.slideshare.net/fkersten/scopus-journal-metrics-snip-sjr

Elsevier. (2011) *About Scopus*. Retrieved 29 June 2011, from SciVerse: http://www.info.sciverse.com/scopus/about

Falagas, M.E., Pitsouni, E.I., Malietzis, G.A. and Pappas, G. (2008) Comparison of PubMed, Scopus, Web of Science, and Google Scholar: strengths and weaknesses. *The FASEB Journal*, 22(2): 338–42.

Finch, A.T. (2010) Can we do better than existing author citation metrics? *BioEssays*, 32(9): 744–7.

Gargouri, Y., Hajjem, C., Lariviere, V., *et al.* (2010) Self-selected or mandated, open access increases citation impact for higher quality research. *PLoS One*, 10(5): e13636.

Garfield, E. (1955) Citation indexes to science: a new dimension in documentation through association of ideas. *Science*, 122: 108–11.

Gross, P.L. and Gross, E.M. (1927) College libraries and chemical education. *Science*, 66: 385–9.

Hajjem, C., Harnad, S. and Gingras, Y. (2005) Ten-year cross-disciplinary comparison of the growth of open access and how it increases research citation impact. *Bulletin of the IEEE Computer Society Technical Committee on Data Engineering*, 28: 39–47.

Haak, D.L. (2011) *Perspectives on Metrics-Based Research Evaluation*. Retrieved 27 June 2011, from University of Queensland: http://www.library.uq.edu.au/metrics2011/presentations/Haak per cent2017 per cent20May per cent20am.pdf

Harnad, S. (2008) *Davis et al's 1-year Study of Self-Selection Bias: No Self-Archiving Control, No OA Effect, No Conclusion*. Retrieved 21 June 2011, from Open Access Archivangelism: http://openaccess.eprints.org/index.php?/archives/441-guid.html

Harnad, S. (2010) *Correlation, Causation, and the Weight of Evidence*. Retrieved 21 June 2011, from Open Access Archivangelism: http://openaccess.eprints.org/index.php?/archives/772-Correlation,-Causation,-and-the-Weight-of-Evidence.html

Harnad, S. and Brody, T. (2004) Comparing the impact of Open Access (OA) vs. non-OA articles in the same journals. *D-Lib Magazine*, 10.

Harzing, A. and van der Wal, R. (2008) Google Scholar as a new source for citation analysis. *Ethics in Science and Environmental Politics*, 2008, 61–73.

Hirsch, J.E. (2007) An index to quantify an individual's scientific research output. *Proceedings of the National Academy of Science*, 102: 16569–72.

Hoeffel, C. (1998) Journal impact factors. *Allergy*, 53, 1225.

Ioannidis, J.P. (2008) Measuring co-authorship and networking-adjusted scientific impact. *PLoS One*, 3(7): e2778.

Jacsó, P. (2009a) Five-year impact factor data in the Journal Citation Reports. *Online Information Review*, 33(3): 603–14.

Jascó, P. (2009b) *Newswire Analysis: Google Scholar's Ghost Authors, Lost Authors, and Other Problems*. Retrieved 21 June 2011, from LibraryJournal.com: http://www.libraryjournal.com/article/CA6698580.html?nid=2673&rid=528369845&source=title

Jin, B., Liang, L.M., Rousseau, R. and Egghe, L. (2007) The R- and AR- Indices: complementing the H Index. *Chinese Science Bulletin*, 52: 855–63.

Labbe, C. (2010) Ike Antkare, one of the great stars in the scientific firmament. *ISSI Newsletter*, 6(2): 48–52.

Leydesdorff, L. and Opthof, T. (2010) Scopus's Source Normalized Impact per Paper (SNIP) versus a journal impact factor based on fractional counting of citations. *Journal of the American Society for Information Science and Technology*, 61(11): 2365–9.

McVeigh, M.E. and Mann, S.J. (2009) The journal impact factor denominator: defining citable (counted) items. *Journal of the American Medical Association*, 302(10): 1107–9.

Moed, H. (2007) The effect of 'open access' on citation impact: an analysis of ArXiv's condensed matter section. *Journal of the American Society for Information Science and Technology*, 58(13): 2047–54.

Moed, H.F. (2010) Measuring contextual citation impact of scientific journals. *Journal of Informetrics*, 3(2): 265–77.

Oh, H.C. and Lim, J.F. (2009) Is the journal impact factor a valid indicator of scientific value? *Singapore Medical Journal*, 50: 749–51.

PLoS One. (2009) *Article-Level Metrics Information*. Retrieved 18 July 2011, from PLoS One: http://www.plosone.org/static/almInfo.action

Scimago Research Group. (2007) *Description of SCImago Journal Rank Indicator*. Retrieved 21 June 2011, from SJR - SCImago Journal & Country Rank: http://www.scimagojr.com/SCImagoJournalRank.pdf

Seglen, P.O. (1997) Why the impact factor of journals should not be used for evaluating research. *British Medical Journal*, 314(7079): 498–502.

Shepherd, P.T. (2002) *COUNTER Code of Practice*. Retrieved 21 June 2010, from COUNTER (Counting Online Usage of NeTworked Electronic Resources): http://www.projectcounter.org/code_practice_r1.html

Simkin, M.V. and Roychowdhury, V.P. (2003) Read before you cite! *Complex Systems*, 14: 269–74.

Taylor, M., Perakakis, P. and Trachana, V. (2008) The siege of science. Ethics in Science and Environmental Politics, 8: 17–40.

Thomson Reuters. (2011a) *Discovery Starts Here*. Retrieved 29 June 2011, from Web of Knowledge: http://isiwebofknowledge.com/about/newwok/

Thomson Reuters. (2011b) *Quick Facts*. Retrieved 29 June 2011, from Web of Knowledge: http://wokinfo.com/about/facts/

Thomson Reuters. (2011c) *Quick Reference Guide*. Retrieved 29 June 2011, from Web of Science: http://thomsonreuters.com/content/science/pdf/ssr/training/wok5_wos_qrc_en.pdf

Todd, P.A. and Ladle, R.J. (2008) Hidden dangers of a 'citation culture'. *Ethics in Science and Environmental Politics*, 8: 13–16.

Tsikliras, A.C. (2008) Chasing after the high impact. *Ethics in Science and Environmental Politics*, 8: 45–7.

Usage Factors. (2010) Retrieved 21 June 2011, from UKSG Website: http://www.uksg.org/usagefactors

Van Raan, A.F. (2008) Self-citation as an impact-reinforcing mechanism in the science system. *Journal of the American Society for Information Science*, 59(10): 1631–43.

Vieira, E.S. and Gomes, J.A. (2009) A comparison of Scopus and Web of Science for a typical university. *Scientometrics*, 81(2), 587–600.

West, J. and Bergstrom, C.T. (2008) *Pseudocode for calculating Eigenfactor score and Article influence score using data from Thomson-Reuters Journal Citation Reports*. Retrieved 21 June 2011, from Eigenfactor.org: http://www.eigenfactor.org/EF_pseudocode.pdf

Wooding, S. (2011) Surveying the scene – the RAISS tool for mapping the impact of research portfolios; Perspectives on Metrics-Based Research Evaluation, Brisbane, 16 May 2011.

11

Relating content to the user

Joy van Baren

Abstract: This chapter introduces User Experience and explains its importance to the future of academic and professional publishing. The latest insights into information-seeking behaviour of researchers are presented along with their implications for information solutions. The chapter proceeds to discuss various approaches to relate content to the user including interactivity, personalisation, text mining, and interoperability and workflow support. New challenges facing the industry related to versioning and trust are described as well as proposed initiatives to address them, such as the CrossMark service.

Key words: User experience, user-centred design, researcher workflow, information-seeking behaviour, personalisation, text mining, information extraction, data mining, interoperability, APIs, CrossMark.

Introduction: user experience in the publishing industry

The Digital Revolution has dramatically changed the way in which academic and professional audiences access and use information. In their competition for online readership information providers try to increase the discoverability of their content, present it in an attractive format, and surround it with useful features and services to lure readers back to their sites. For the first time in the history of publishing, publishers truly need to understand the needs, motivations, expectations, and behaviour of their customers and users in order to successfully address them online.

Donald Norman first coined the phrase 'User Experience' in the mid 1990s to refer to the range of psychological and behavioural responses surrounding human–system interactions. The International Organization for Standardization (2009) defines User Experience as 'A person's perceptions and responses that result from the use and/or anticipated use of a product, system or service.' A related but somewhat narrower term, usability, is defined as 'The extent to which a system, product or service can be used by specified users to achieve specified goals with effectiveness, efficiency and satisfaction in a specified context of use.' The invention and subsequent uptake of these terms, accelerated by the widespread adoption of the Internet, signals the realisation by various industries of the need to change product development processes to encompass an increasingly user-centred design philosophy.

A user-centred design process comprises three distinct stages:

- *Understand*: explore the users, their needs and their workflow. Research methods for understanding users include direct observation, diary studies, interviews and surveys.
- *Design*: translate insight from the understanding process into an information architecture, a range of functionalities and a look and feel. This can be achieved through applying interaction design, information architecture and visual design.
- *Evaluate*: validate design assumptions and assess whether the proposed solution successfully addresses user needs and adheres to usability standards. Evaluation methods include formal usability testing, heuristic analysis and cognitive walkthrough.

The user-centred design process is iterative in nature, meaning that the three stages are repeated to optimise different aspects of the product, or to progressively adapt the design until its User Experience is deemed optimal.

Adherence to a user-centred design process results in a User Experience that enables orientation, transparency, consistency and accessibility. Questions such as 'where am I?', 'what can I do?' and 'what will happen next?' should at all times be easy to answer for different types of users. As a result, users can accomplish their tasks in an efficient and effective manner, and will feel comfortable using the system. Various studies have found correlations between user experience and customer loyalty (Temkin *et al.*, 2009; Garrett, 2006). There is also evidence pointing to savings in development spend that can be realised through 'getting it right' the first time around, as well as savings in training and support services realised through better usability. Pressman (1992) and Gilb (1998) investigated studies across different industries showing that every dollar invested in User Experience brings between 2 and 100 dollars in return; IBM (2011) uses the rule of thumb that every dollar invested returns 10–100 dollars.

The publishing industry has been relatively slow to embrace User Experience, perhaps because it was never at the heart of traditional print processes. In a recent article on digital publishing, Brett Sandusky (2011) stated that 'the publishing industry has a history of creating products for a "customer" that they never speak to, speak of, see, interact with, or consider'. In their haste to migrate content from the print into the digital realm, publishers have typically not strayed far from traditional print format. When comparing an eBook with a print book, or a PDF to a print article, one is struck by how similar they look. Not only does this approach make for a suboptimal User Experience by not taking into account the limitations of the medium, it also fails to take advantage of the possibilities to make digital content more attractive to and relevant for users.

An additional cause of the publishing industry not utilising user-centred design processes to their full potential is that the customer and the user are often not the same person. Conversations primarily if not exclusively focus on librarians and information managers who are responsible for the acquisition and roll out of content and workflow solutions. Their needs and level of understanding with regard to online content and systems are different from those eventually using the content in their daily work: the researchers. Although publishers are well acquainted with researchers in the capacity of authors, they are less well informed on their needs as consumers of content.

A final reason for the somewhat unhappy marriage between publishing and User Experience is that content is not a traditional area of focus for User Experience. Design tends to concentrate on the presentation, the interface, rather than its content. In publishing, content is of course the main asset offered to the customer, and therefore needs to be part of the User Experience equation. In light of the progressive commoditisation of content, future solutions will be expected to provide added value by relating content to the end-users and enabling them to efficiently and effectively apply it in the context of their daily work.

This chapter will investigate findings from market and user research providing insight into the workflow and online behaviour of researchers. It then explores characteristics of digital content and electronic environments that can contribute to relating content to the user, as well as challenges that must be addressed in this endeavour.

Researcher workflow: insights from market and user research

Academics and professionals seek to find and consume content not for leisure but to enable the successful performance of their jobs. For knowledge workers in academia and industry, missing a relevant article may mean the difference between acceptance and rejection of an article or grant proposal, or delay in the solving of a critical problem. Researchers have developed a structural process of systematic investigation that has remained fundamentally unchanged through the centuries. Although new media have the capability to change aspects of this process, they can only do so by providing added value. Users are typically unwilling to adapt their behaviour for the sake of using a new tool, unless it allows them to perform an activity faster or better than before.

Industry research and consultancy firms have emphasised the importance of integrating with customer workflow. In an Electronic Publishing Services report, Worlock and Evans (2003) presented five case studies of information providers who managed to deliver significant end-user benefits by adapting existing solutions or developing new web-based solutions based on workflow research and ongoing discussions with their customer base. Brunelle (2006) urged publishers to 'be the scientific user' and to directly tie potential product features to specific and explicit user needs. To follow this advice one must of course first become intimately acquainted with the workflow and information needs of researchers.

Brunelle surveyed information use by academics and professionals reaching 260 respondents in the scientific domain. Perhaps unsurprisingly, nearly all respondents (98 per cent) indicated that they use external information for their jobs. In the majority of cases (77 per cent) they find this information themselves, without the help of others. The physical library has clearly fallen from grace as a valued resource, with only 3 per cent mentioning it as a go-to place for information.

The total amount of time spent on information averaged a significant 11 hours, a 22 per cent increase since 2001. A notable finding is that almost as much time is spent on gathering the information (45 per cent) as on reading and applying it (55 per cent). In nearly one-third of cases the information-seeking process fails, and the scientist has nothing to show for the time invested.

In an ethnographic field study, Jones (2005) examined life scientists' use of information resources, analysing information activity in the context of real-life research projects. He found that in spite of the abundance of information sources available through the library, life scientists typically adopted a small number of simple tools such as Google or PubMed, chosen for transparent interfaces and high expected utility.

Jones also looked at varying information need in the different stages of the scientific workflow, as illustrated in Figure 11.1. He found that information seeking and usage is highest during literature review, and second highest during manuscript writing. Not only the required amount of information but also the nature of the question varies in different stages of the workflow. In addition to different users having distinct strategies for finding information, the same user may have different needs according to the eventual purpose of the information and the broader task they are trying to accomplish. For example, the search behaviours of a scientist trying to find the exact article information to use in a reference and that same scientist conducting a broad search to find new information in the field are very different.

In a series of studies focusing on information-seeking behavior carried out between 2002 and 2012 the Elsevier User Centered Design team interviewed and surveyed hundreds of scientific researchers. The following key recurring challenges were most frequently mentioned as hindering the effective gathering of knowledge.

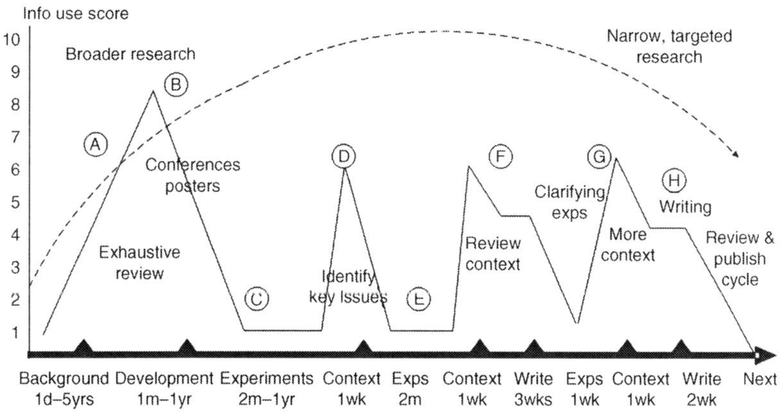

Figure 11.1 **Composite of information activity in research life cycle: A, exhaustive literature review; B, organise, discuss, and share findings; C, initial experiments; D, additional literature review to establish context for initial findings; E, further experiments; F, write draft manuscript; G, additional literature review to establish context for writing; H, write final manuscript**

Information overload

The challenge most frequently mentioned by scientific researchers is that of information overload. With a steep increase in the number of researchers and articles published it has become challenging to filter out irrelevant information. Combined with increased pressure to spend time on research management activities such as grant writing, information overload contributes to the high workload of scientific researchers.

Many different sources

Modern scientists have a great number of different content sources available to them, such as abstract and indexing databases, journal websites, web search engines, institutional repositories, library catalogues, blogs, eBooks and so on. An often heard frustration is the need to repeat the same search in multiple information sources, and more or less manually deduplicate the results.

Need for comprehensiveness

As mentioned in the Introduction, the consequences of not finding relevant content in a timely manner can be severe. Many researchers describe their fear of missing the one article that could have helped win a grant, get their research published or inspire a new idea. Although the need for comprehensiveness has always been present, it is compounded by information overload and the time and effort involved in going to multiple sources.

Finding the right unit of information

Scientific information is contained in documents: articles and books. Although finding a document may in some situations be the ultimate purpose of an online search, in many cases it is not. The primary goal of the searching scientist is to find facts, answers and ideas. Some facts are buried deep in the details of a document, and some patterns may only be discovered through reading multiple documents. Because of this mismatch between information need and information granularity, a lot of time is associated with finding answers, and sometimes they are not found at all.

Workflow support

Once the right information is found, there is still the issue of applying it in the context of one's workflow. Researchers often spend distinct timeslots on finding multiple relevant articles and then use them during subsequent work, sometimes months or even years later. Scientists indicate that the storing, managing and retrieving of this information is far from smooth. Integration between the different tools used along the scientific workflow is a pain point, and disproportionate amounts of effort can be required for simple actions to port information from one tool into the next, such as citing an article found online in a text editor, sharing it with a colleague through an email client or saving the PDF whilst retaining the appropriate metadata to efficiently retrieve it later on.

Quality and authority of information

A final problem that has increased with the growing amount of information available online is establishing the quality of the information and its source. Peer review is of course a traditional quality distinction, but most search engines do not distinguish between published and non-published content. Yet, they are the primary source used by many students and early career academics. How can academics verify that they are dealing with information that is reliable, accurate and current?

The implications of these findings are clear: the process of finding, consuming and utilising content is imperfect, and the available tools fail to cater to the specific information needs along the academic workflow.

The role of the publisher traditionally has been to select the highest quality content for publication without considering how it will be used. To successfully compete in the current market this role will have to expand to ensure the discovery and successful application of the knowledge communicated in the published content. In the next four sections we will look at several technologies that have the potential to contribute to addressing these critical user needs.

Interactivity, personalization and dialogue

The Introduction noted that there are often not many differences between print articles or books and their digital equivalents. A common pitfall when transitioning from print to electronic is to merely repurpose print content, thereby enforcing the limitations of the original print container. Characteristics of electronic environments such as interactivity, personalisation and dialogue can become critical assets for creating a compelling online user experience.

Paper is a static medium that at best can present different versions of a publication at different moments in time and point to other documents through text references. The instant interaction enabled on the web opens up a new range of possibilities for preserving context, presenting multimedia and allowing users to play around with the content presented. Experimental data can not only be looked at, but can be downloaded. Movies or audio fragments can be presented and viewed in context, without leaving the page. Embedded interactive components let readers manipulate images or charts, for example by rotating them, zooming and even adding or removing data. On paper a reference list is just a list, but electronically it can be sorted according to characteristics such as publication date or number of citations, making it easier to explore and scan.

A publication never stands alone: it cites a set of previously published documents as references and is in turn cited by a number of documents published later. Whereas in the past accessing this related content required another walk to the library, it can now be instantly accessed through linking between online documents. Interlinking between different content types can help to further enhance contextualisation and interpretation of content. An example of this is linking from detailed technical publications to subject-specific encyclopaedias or dictionaries that help explain the terminology used in those publications and provide the background information required for understanding them. Significant efficiency gains can be introduced into the user workflow by providing this information in the context of the original article, at the push of a button.

A unique asset of electronic environments is that end-users can customise them according to their needs and preferences. At the most basic level the way the content is presented can be adapted. Interface colours, font sizes and page layout are increasingly subject to customisation. In some cases users can modify the location of features and information elements on the page, for example through 'drag and drop'. They can specify which content is most relevant to them, thereby influencing what shows up, or in which order. The system should of course remember all of these preferences and automatically apply them for future viewing of content. Tools such as iGoogle (http://www.google.com/ig) and NetVibes (www.netvibes.com) enable users to set up a personal information dashboard in which they can customise content, layout and appearance according to their preferences.

In addition to the user manually providing information about their preferences, systems can personalise content and user experience based on implicit data. Online behaviour such as items viewed, search history and features utilised can provide the basis for automatic content recommendations and optimisation of the interface. The system can also look at the choices of users with similar characteristics and online behaviour and content preferences and proactively recommend content based on this analysis; Amazon (www.amazon.com), for example, has successfully used this approach in their 'people who bought this book also bought...' feature.

Scholarly publications aim to contribute to an ongoing conversation. This dialogue has traditionally taken place on paper, at conferences and in offices or labs. Although social media will never replace these interactions, they have the potential to capture at least some aspects of them. Users can share, tag, recommend or rate online content. They can review publications and provide responses through commenting features or on blogs, wikis and discussion forums. Thus, the digital article becomes a living document reflecting not only the thoughts of the author(s) but also the reactions of its readership.

Aggregators such as FriendFeed (http://friendfeed.com) provide customised feeds containing content shared by friends or colleagues, and facilitate discussion around this content. Faculty of 1000 (http://f1000.com) is a website for researchers and clinicians that provides ratings and reviews of research papers by a panel of peer-nominated experts in the field. These examples illustrate how online social or professional networks can be used as a filter for finding relevant information, and finding it fast.

Although the options described here do not fundamentally change content, they do empower users to interact with content in a way that is relevant to their unique needs and preferences, thereby offering an experience far superior to print.

Metadata and text mining

The proliferation of scholarly literature makes it more and more challenging for researchers to stay current in their field. The push for interdisciplinarity further increases pressure on the individual, who has to stay abreast of relevant developments in adjacent fields as well as their own. A simple keyword search generates thousands if not ten thousands of hits in scientific databases or web search engines. It would be an impossible feat to scan through all of these results manually, let alone read and interpret them.

Publication metadata (e.g. title, source, authors and references) can be utilised as a framework for discovery. First, metadata are a key enabler for online search. In addition to making searches more precise by searching in specific metadata elements, metadata can be used in faceted search. In faceted search, sometimes also referred to as faceted navigation, a collection of documents is analysed by a number of discrete attributes or facets. For scholarly content, these facets often include author name, subject area, publication year, journal and affiliation. Values in each of these facets are presented in order of occurrence frequency, and provide the user with a contextual framework for understanding the scope of their search as well as intuitive options for further refining it.

Metadata can also be used for interlinking content: once an interesting article has been found it becomes possible to follow a variety of trails to find related information. In most literature databases documents by the same author, documents citing the current document or other documents citing the same references are only a mouse click away. This capacity greatly promotes the discoverability of 'hidden gems' and helps users find multiple inroads into the abundance of information available for a given topic.

A technology that goes several steps further than the analysis of simple metadata is text mining. Text mining refers to a range of interdisciplinary methods and technologies used to extract information from a collection of free (unstructured) text documents and identify patterns in that information, leading to the discovery of new knowledge (http://www.nactem.ac.uk). Text mining employs methodologies from data mining, information retrieval, machine learning, statistics and natural language processing.

The text mining process can be characterized by three main stages, as follows: *Information Retrieval* refers to the selection of a subset of relevant documents from a larger collection, based on a user- or system-generated query. It can happen based on searching through document metadata, but is increasingly based on full text search. Information Retrieval in this context is a pre-processing step to gather a relevant body of documents for further analysis, but developments in this field can also be used to improve the quality of search for end-users.

Information Extraction transforms unstructured text into structured information by locating specific pieces of data in text documents and extracting them as entities. Simple examples of entities are people, companies, dates or locations. As a next step, relationships between extracted entities can be elicited. For example, a company can be located in a country, or an event linked to a date. Natural language processing principles such as part-of-speech tagging (classifying words in a sentence as verbs, nouns, adjectives, etc.) and word sense disambiguation (selecting the most appropriate of possible meanings) are used to help make sense of the text and structure the information extracted from it. Figure 11.2 shows an example of entities and their relationships extracted from text and placed into a structured representation called a template. Extracting entities and analysing the relationships and interactions between extracted entities enables advanced semantic applications that reveal patterns in content.

Data Mining refers to the computational process of analysing patterns in large sets of data in order to discover new knowledge. Once text has been transformed into structured data, the data can be compared with those extracted from other documents to find similarities and patterns. Examples of frequently analysed entities and relationships in the scientific domain are interactions between proteins and associations between genes and diseases (Ananiadou *et al.*, 2006).

The three stages of text mining to some extent mimic the process that humans follow when searching, reading and analysing literature. The human brain is an impressive but imperfect analytical tool; it simply cannot process the vast amounts of data that computers are capable of. Relationships that are buried in the literature, hidden from the human eye, may be

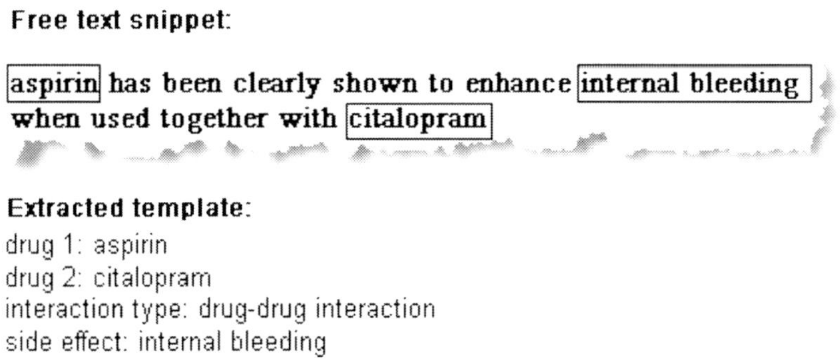

Free text snippet:

aspirin has been clearly shown to enhance internal bleeding when used together with citalopram

Extracted template:

drug 1: aspirin
drug 2: citalopram
interaction type: drug-drug interaction
side effect: internal bleeding

Figure 11.2 Information extraction: from free text to structured template

discovered through the application of text mining technology. Another difference is that whereas humans are subjective computers are objective; unburdened by prior knowledge and expectations they are less prone to selection bias. In a way, text mining allows the data to speak for itself.

Text and data mining are frequently coupled with visualisation techniques to facilitate the discovery of patterns in information. Visualisation techniques such as tag clouds, heat maps, tree maps, (geographical) scatter plots, stream graphs and time series can all be used to expose relationships between entities.

In addition to detecting patterns, text mining can be utilised to automatically assign documents to groups without human judgment or intervention. Two approaches in this area are categorisation and clustering. Categorisation refers to the automated classification of documents into predefined categories, for example scientific subject areas or disciplines, similar to traditional manual indexing systems. Clustering relates to the grouping of documents into organic groups or clusters based on statistical, lexical and semantic analysis. In this latter case it is not only the grouped documents that are of interest, but also the derivation of the themes emerging from this bottom-up process.

Geißler (2008) has explored the diverse scenarios through which these approaches have been adopted by publishing companies through cases studies involving Thomson Scientific, Elsevier, Springer Science & Business Media and LexisNexis. In addition to these applications by major publishers, it is remarkable how many examples of text mining can be found in the academic domain in the form of solutions created by scientists, for scientists. Many of these applications stem from the field of bioinformatics, which by nature deals with enormous amounts of data. Krallinger *et al.* (2008) maintain an excellent compendium reviewing the many available text mining applications.

Text mining is a rapidly evolving field with applications that are becoming increasingly used and valued. Increasing computational capabilities coupled with the availability of digital content hold the promise for further growth and experimentation, allowing the field to reach maturity. However, there are several difficulties that have yet to be addressed. Natural language is characterised by ambiguities, which complicates the accurate extraction of entities and relations. Scientists use many acronyms and abbreviations, which can have different meanings in different disciplines. Scientific terminology can be inconsistent or imprecise, and is subject to constant evolution. Words can have different meanings, and names many variants. Developing systems capable of resolving such ambiguities is far from trivial. They require hand-annotated training data or manually constructed semantic lexicons, and their output needs to be reviewed and revised. There is no 'one size fits all' text mining solution, as different communities have different information needs, and different questions may require different levels of accuracy.

In a study commissioned by the Publishing Research Consortium, Smit and Van der Graaf (2011) interviewed 29 experts and surveyed 190 representatives of scholarly publishers. The results confirm expectations of a continued upwards trend in journal article mining by both publishers and third parties. Several scenarios for responding to increasing content mining demands were explored. More standardised mining-friendly content formats, a shared content mining platform and commonly agreed permission rules for content mining were viewed as the most promising common solutions, with most universal support for the first scenario.

Challenges facing researchers as discussed include being overwhelmed by the amount of available information as well as difficulties arising from a mismatch between the granularity of information and the type of questions that need answering. Text mining can help end-users manage their information overload and discover information which might otherwise only be found by reading many documents – or not at all – and generate new insights by making connections between previously unrelated concepts. It therefore has the potential to accelerate the discovery process for the individual researcher as well as for science in general.

Interoperability and workflow support

We have observed that scientists use many different tools to address the information needs occurring across their workflow. These tools include different content sources, internal data repositories, reference management applications, text editing software, email clients and many more. Some of those tools work well, others work less well – but most of them do not integrate well with each other. Designing and implementing a one-stop shop serving different audiences across different scholarly fields and activities resembles the pursuit of the Holy Grail! Integration is the key; instead of reinventing the wheel, publishers need to ensure that their content and solutions can be integrated with applications widely used among researchers.

Perhaps the most effective way to relate content to users is by making it directly available to them outside of the boundaries of physical or digital containers, because it allows them to flexibly integrate it with other applications. In other words: 'your data, my way'. Structured and open dissemination of data can be achieved through Application Programming Interfaces (APIs), as most commonly used for websites and web-based technologies. APIs make data available to third parties so that software developers can build their own solutions on top of it. The underlying philosophy is that no one knows the needs and problems of scientists as well as scientists themselves. By utilising APIs developers can combine content from different sources and use it in the context of existing applications through mashups, thereby creating powerful productivity-enhancing applications.

The New York Times and the UK Guardian Media Group were among the first content providers to adopt this approach. In the scientific domain, Elsevier, Springer and Public Library of Science are amongst those who have created APIs and have facilitated app contests and hackathons in which developers are invited to package and use their content in innovative solutions of their own design. The developed apps are made available through application galleries and marketplaces. This model allows publishers to more effectively partner with their academic and professional communities, and to provide a platform for collaboration.

Authority, versioning and trust

The Internet has given the term 'authority' a new meaning. Blog search engine Technorati (http://technorati.com), for example, provides the following definition:

> 'Technorati Authority measures a site's standing and influence in the blogosphere. Authority is calculated based on a site's linking behavior, categorization and other associated data over a short, finite period of time. A site's authority may rapidly rise and fall depending on what the blogosphere is discussing at the moment, and how often a site produces content being referenced by other sites.'

Similar to Google's PageRank, this definition reflects the idea that quality and relevance can be predicted based on popularity, thereby relying on the 'wisdom of the crowd'.

In a way, this approach is not very different from using citations, the number of times a document is mentioned in the bibliographic references of other publications, as an indication of quality and impact. Citations have long been used as measures of relative importance of publications and constitute the building blocks of journal ranking indicators such as the Impact Factor (http://thomsonreuters.com/products_services/science/academic/impact_factor/) and more recently SJR and SNIP (Colledge *et al.*, 2010) as well as performance metrics for individuals such as the h-Index (Hirsch, 2005) (see Chapter 10). These indicators can help researchers manage information overload by guiding their decisions on which articles, books or journals to select as primary sources from the large volume of potentially relevant literature.

The notion of authority in academia and scholarship is traditionally associated with the process of peer review. Prior to publication, the work of an author is subjected to the scrutiny of domain experts appointed as reviewers. The aim of this quality control is to enhance scientific merit of published literature by ensuring originality, theoretical foundation, transparency of scientific methods and the validity of conclusions (see Chapter 2).

Web search engines typically do not distinguish between peer-reviewed and non-peer-reviewed content, yet they are often the first source used. Multiple versions of the same publications are often available on the web. Uncorrected manuscripts may be available on author homepages, institutional repositories or preprint servers. The final published versions reside in scientific literature databases or can be found through publisher websites. Students or early career researchers may not be aware of why this distinction matters, and of the potential implications of including references in their own work that are not part of the established, trusted literature. Even for experienced scholars it can be difficult to differentiate between the available alternatives and choose the authoritative copy as a foundation for their research.

To address this challenge and enhance transparency of online scholarly publications, CrossRef (www.crossref.org) introduced the CrossMark service. The CrossMark Service is made up of a logo and associated metadata. The CrossMark logo is placed on a PDF or HTML document or abstract page in order to communicate to readers that they are looking at a publisher-maintained copy of the publication. Articles in press can have a CrossMark, but not preprints. Clicking on the logo will bring up metadata provided by the publisher about the current status of the article and other useful information such as the CrossRef DOI, the location of associated data, publication history, agencies that funded the research and the nature of the peer-review process used to evaluate the content.

In addition to making it easier for researchers to discern the peer-reviewed version from manuscripts and preprints, CrossMark serves as a record of updates occurring post-publication. Scientific content is subject to change, and hence publications can never be considered final. Examples of changes are errata, corrections, enhancements, updates or new editions, while in some cases publications may even be withdrawn or retracted. The CrossMark metadata include status information indicating whether the published content has undergone any changes. Thus, readers can rest assured that they are utilising information that is both accurate and current.

A pilot of the CrossMark service launched in 2011 and is scheduled to go live in 2012. Publishers participating in this pilot include Elsevier, Wiley, OUP and the Royal Society. Participation involves displaying the CrossMark logo in online solutions, depositing CrossMark metadata with CrossRef, and of course keeping this information up to date.

Conclusion and outlook

Over the centuries, publishers have built up excellence in the creation and evaluation of content. In the current age, where the value of content in itself is no longer a certainty, these core competencies need to be extended. Understanding how users need to access and interact with content in their daily work and taking advantage of the capabilities of digital content as well as the environment in which it is presented are critical success factors.

Semantic technologies such as text mining can help to address challenges of information overload, the need for comprehensiveness and granularity of information. As these technologies come of age, they will change the way in which researchers engage with content and speed up the process of scientific discovery.

The structure of the scholarly article has remained relatively unchanged. Its linear, static representation is very suitable for print, but less so for online reading. When will authors truly start writing for the web? New and different structuring approaches could be aimed towards taking full advantage of the interactivity of the web, as well as optimising content for semantic analysis.

APIs allow publishers to open up their data to third parties and individual developers to build their own applications on top of published content. This is expected to result in less product-centric and more modular approaches to product development, in which content sources, applications and platforms can be combined into custom solutions with relative ease.

Publishers will have to find ways to deal with new challenges introduced by the proliferation of information online, such as the availability of multiple versions of documents and the fading distinction between peer-reviewed and non-peer-reviewed. Although initiatives such as CrossMark attempt to rise to this challenge, their adoption and eventual effectiveness remain to be seen.

To take full advantage of the possibilities of presenting content electronically and to rise to the challenges outlined here, publishers will have to develop new skills. They will need user-centred research capabilities to gain insight into customer needs and workflows, design skills to translate those insights into an effective User Experience, and the technology expertise to successfully implement this while utilising the capabilities of online environments. Whereas large publishers may develop or gain access to such skills with relative ease, smaller publishers may have to rely on collective platforms or partnerships with subject matter experts to take the next step in presenting their content to online audiences.

Sources of further information

User experience

Krug, S. (2006) *Don't Make Me Think! A Common Sense Approach to Web Usability*, 2nd edn. Berkeley, CA: New Riders Publishers.

Spool, J., Perfetti, C. and Brittan, D. (2004) *Designing for the Scent of Information*. Retrieved from http://www.uie.com/reports/scent_of_information/

UX Magazine, http://uxmag.com

Researcher workflow and information seeking behavior

Anderson, C., Glassman, M., McAfee, R. and Pinelli, T. (2001) An investigation of factors affecting how engineers and scientists seek information. *Journal of Engineering and Technology Management*, 18(2), 131–55.

Hine, C. (2006) Databases as scientific instruments and their role in the ordering of scientific work. *Social Studies of Science*, 36(2), 269–98.

Inger, S. and Gardner, T., 2008. *How readers navigate so scholarly content.* Retrieved from http://www.sic.ox14.com/howreadersnavigatetoscholarlycontent.pdf

Journal metrics

http://www.journalmetrics.com/

Text mining

Cohen, K.B. and Hunter, L. (2008) Getting started in text mining. *PLoS Computational Biology*, 4(1), 0001–0003.

Jackson. P. and Moulinier, I. (2007) *Natural Language Processing for Online Applications: Text Retrieval, Extraction, and Classification*, 2nd edn. Herndon, VA: John Benjamins Publishing Company.

National Centre for Text Mining, University of Manchester. http://www.nactem.ac.uk.

Rzhetsky, A., Seringhaus, M. and Gerstein, M.B. (2009) Getting started in text mining: Part two. *PLoS Computational Biology*, 5(7).

CrossMark

http://www.crossref.org/crossmark/

References

Ananiadou, S., Kell, D.B. (2006) Text mining and its potential applications in systems biology. *Trends in Biotechnology*, 24(12), 571–9.

Colledge, L., De Moya-Anegón, F., Guerrero-Bote, V., López-Illescas, C., El Aisati, M., Moed, H. (2010) SJR and SNIP: two new journal metrics in Elsevier's Scopus. *Serials: The Journal for the Serials Community*, 23(3), 215–21.

Brunelle, B. (2006) *Scientists As Information Users — Product Innovation is the Name of the Game*. London: Outsell Inc.

Garrett, J.J. (2006) Customer loyalty and the elements of user experience. *Design Management Review*, 17(1). http://www.dmi.org/dmi/html/interests/strategy/06171GAR35.pdf

Geißler, S. (2008) New methods to access scientific content. *Information Services and Use*, 28(2): 141–6.

Gilb, T. (1988) *Principles of Software Engineering Management*. Reading, MA: Addison Wesley.

IBM (2007) *Cost Justifying Ease of Use*. http://www.cim.mcgill.ca/~jer/courses/hci/ref/IBM_ease_of_use.pdf

International Organization for Standardization (ISO) (2009) *ISO FDIS 9241-210. Human-centred design process for interactive systems*. Gland, Switzerland: ISO.

Hirsch, J.E. (2005) An index to quantify an individual's scientific research output. *Proceedings of the National Academy of Sciences USA*, 102(46): 16569–72.

Jones, P.H. (2005) Information practices and cognitive artifacts in scientific research. *Cognition, Technology & Work*, 2005: 88–100.

Krallinger, M., Hirschman, L. and Valencia, A. (2008) Linking genes to literature: text mining, information extraction, and retrieval applications for biology. *Genome Biology* 9: S8. http://zope.bioinfo.cnio.es/bionlp_tools/

Pressman, R.S. (1992) *Software Engineering: A Practitioner's Approach*. New York: McGraw-Hill.

Sandusky, B. (2011) Portraits of an industry in flux: digital publishing and UX. *UX Magazine*, article no. 601. http://uxmag.com/strategy/portraits-of-an-industry-in-flux

Smit, E. & Van der Graaf, M. (2011) *Journal article mining: a research study into practices, policies, plans…and promises*. Publishing Research Consortium. http://www.publishingresearch.net/documents/PRCSmitJAMreport20June2011VersionofRecord.pdf

Temkin, B.D., Chu, W. and Geller, S. (2009) *Customer Experience And Loyalty: A Closer Look. Impact Of Usefulness, Ease Of Use, And Enjoyability Differs Across Industries*. Forrester Research.

Worlock, K. and Evans, N. (2011) *Integrating Content With Workflow: Learning from the pioneers*. London: Electronic Publishing Services Ltd (now part of Outsell).

12

Sales, licensing and marketing

Tony O'Rourke

Abstract: This chapter reviews the sales, licensing and marketing activities undertaken by publishers, and highlights the value the publisher brings to the process of scholarly communication through these activities. It looks at the fundamental and emerging approaches to sales, licensing and marketing of academic content, and considers some of the metrics being used to evaluate the use of content, the development of pricing models and the efforts which the publisher makes to engage and retain customers.

Key words: Sales and licensing, researchers, libraries, consortia, purchasing decision, metrics, marketing, customer retention, pricing models, brand.

Introduction

The market for scholarly and professional publishing is changing at a rate faster than ever previously experienced. The publisher adapts and reinvents its business models in order to survive (and thrive) and there is increased complexity in how content is licensed. At the same time, libraries are re-engineering their services to remain relevant to their research communities.

This chapter focuses primarily on journals rather than books. However, much of what is described below, such as pricing and customer engagement, applies to books and serials in equal measure. I make no attempt to recommend a way forward or best practice, but rather try to explain the options, the pitfalls and also the opportunities which a publisher faces if it adapts its approaches and business models in this ever changing environment.

Fundamentals of a publishing business

Regardless of the nature of the organisation every publisher requires a sustainable revenue stream, whether it is the commercial publisher providing an annual dividend for their shareholders, or the learned society or university press looking at least to break even on the cost of publishing and to reinvest any surplus to produce more and better content and to continue to provide a publishing service for their community. The principle is the same.

Any publisher needs to focus its commercial activities to answer the following questions:

1. What is my product offering?
2. How do I maximise the visibility of my content and provide a return for my stakeholders?
3. What do I need to know about my customer in order to supply more relevant content?
4. How is my brand (article, journal, book, company) perceived by customers (existing, potential) and how does that perception affect 2 and 3 above?
5. What can I do to influence brand perception and thereby increase sales, market share and improve market position?

There is growing competition for the attention of the reader. Content, which until recently could only be read in the publisher's publications, can now be accessed elsewhere – the author's personal repository, a subject repository, an institutional repository or via an e-print server (for example, the arXiv server, hosted at Cornell University, where authors post preprints of papers in the physical sciences).

The publisher needs to consider what value it adds to the content and how best to enhance and maximise that value for the author, the referee, the library and even the funding agency. This entails three key questions this chapter will review:

- Does the publisher know and understand what drives their community (authors, referees, readers)?
- Is the publisher using intelligent pricing to maximise access to content?
- How can the publisher differentiate its version of content from another freely available?

Understanding the market

The scholarly ecosystem

As in any business, it is critical to understand the needs of stakeholders and dynamics of the market, and this is no different for academic and professional publishers. While the ecosystem for scholarly content is highly complex, comprising a wide range of established and emerging fields of study, at its core it is very simple:

- Researchers want their research to be recognised by their peers and therefore further their reputation and career.
- By publishing the research and helping researchers to be recognised, the publisher generates revenue.
- The library serves its community by providing cost-effective access to relevant teaching and research materials.

From the starting point in the late 17th century of only a handful of research papers, it is estimated that researchers from 218 different countries now produce over 1.5 million research papers per year (Royal Society, 2011), and the number of research papers produced grows annually. Researchers bemoan their inability to keep pace with all the relevant research. This complaint is not exclusive to the 21st century. For example, Sir Michael Faraday (1827) complained that, 'it is certainly impossible for any person who wishes to devote a portion of his time to chemical experiment, to read all the books and papers that are published in connection with his pursuit'. One can only speculate what Faraday might say if he were a scientist active in the 21st century.

While scholarly communication is usually analysed along the author–researcher axis, much of the usage comes from students, particularly those taking higher degrees and those training for professional qualifications. As these students do not usually publish they will do little for the citation of articles (and hence for the Impact Factor, as described below), but their usage might ensure renewal of the subscription. Similarly, professional journals aimed at the practitioner or someone training for professional qualifications may be widely read but score low in any citation ratings.

The publisher wants to select articles which attract both citations and readership. One factor is often as important as the other, particularly in the case of a new journal which needs to establish its credentials within its respective community of readers and authors. However, the publisher does not always have the luxury, in terms of production budget, to choose papers based on both merits. As usage becomes increasingly important as a factor to assess the value of a publication to teaching, training and research-intensive institutions, more highly utilised publications will benefit.

The library performs a number of important functions in supporting researchers (many of which mirror the functions of the publisher):

- *Knowledge of the content.* The library wants to know what content is available in order to best serve its community.
- *Support research.* The library wants to offer content which will reinforce the research interests of its community.
- *Value.* The library wants any acquisition to be cost-effective and provide its community with the best and most comprehensive service it can afford.
- *Cost-effective.* The library wants to be able to justify its investments with evidence-based data:
  - how many users?
  - how much usage is being made?
  - how is the content being used?
  - who is using the content?
- *Quality.* The library cares about brand and the values associated with the brand. The reputation of the brand (publisher, journal) and previous purchase, user experiences may be taken into account when considering the next purchase.

In fulfilling its role, the library often struggles to provide access to all the materials required by the researcher, but this is no recent phenomenon. Earlier in this book, Robert Campbell provides an example from the 1920s of a large university library (Cornell), 'suffering because of the increasing volume of publications and rapidly rising prices', and their inability to keep up with demand from researchers (Okerson, 1986).

When an institution complains it has no budget, it does not mean there is no funding. A typical university library in a developed economy has an annual acquisitions fund in the millions of dollars. However, it may not have enough to acquire everything requested by the researchers. One of the roles of the publisher in working with libraries is to help satisfy researchers' demand for content whilst maintaining a sustainable business.

How academic and professional content is purchased

Scholarly content is purchased in a variety of ways by research institutions.

Private use

The researcher acquires content (print, electronic) for their own personal consumption.

Departmental library

Departmental libraries specialise in purchasing content around a particular discipline. In universities, it is not uncommon for library services to be distributed around faculty or even departmental libraries with a central library responsible for acquiring multi-disciplinary works, content which faculties cannot fund by themselves. This parallel library process, often referred to as the two-track library system, still prevails in older research institutions.

For example, the Ludwig Maximillian University is one of Germany's oldest universities, established in Bavaria in 1472. The university library system operates more than 100 libraries, consisting of a central library, a small number of centralised faculty libraries and more than 80 'student libraries' supporting every discipline taught at the university. Funding is distributed across all 100+ faculty and student libraries, leaving each library with a relatively small acquisitions fund, even though cumulatively it has one of the largest acquisition budgets in Germany.

Central library

The central library comprises either a single library or a small number of large departmental libraries centrally managing acquisitions for the entire institution.

The level of purchasing authority delegated to the Central Library can vary depending on geographical location. Typically an academic library in North America has more freedom to act than its counterparts in Europe and more again than those in Asia.

Library consortia

Consortia license content on behalf of multiple institutions within a region, country or even across borders. There are more than 350 purchasing consortia in 98 countries, acquiring e-books, journals and databases. (Source: Consortium Directory Online, 2011). Consortia fall into several types:

- The first type is centrally funded, where funds are typically set aside or removed from existing library budgets to fund access for all institutions in the licence. The consortium pays the entire licence fee, including (a) the value of pre-existing subscriptions, (b) fees for new members and (c) the access fee for all additional content. These three elements comprise the Annual Licence Fee.
- The second type is where the access fee for additional content is funded centrally and previously held subscriptions remain the responsibility of the individual institutions.
- The third type of consortium simply acts as a negotiating agent. No new funding is made available and the licence is negotiated centrally. Fees are payable from existing budgets by individual institutions and membership is optional.

It is notable that funding agencies are creating their own central purchasing services, in order to acquire content directly from the publisher on behalf of member institutions. For example, JISC Collections was established by the UK Higher and Further Education funding councils to support the procurement of digital content for education and research in the UK. Since the 1990s, JISC Collections (and its predecessors) has acquired rights for databases, e-books and journal archives and has pioneered the introduction of electronic national site licences for journal content for universities and colleges in the UK.

Use of metrics in the purchasing decision

An increasing number of metrics are being used to support/inform the library purchasing decision:

- What to buy?
- What to cancel?
- Which publication should the institution support?

The decision regarding which journal to purchase or maintain within a research institution is linked (normally) to the interests of the community being served. When evaluating the addition or removal of a journal or e-Book the library needs to consider how the content is being used, in terms of demand for the content (full-text downloads) but also in terms of research support for the journal. The purchasing institution requires the tools by which it is able to assess the real value and impact of the content.

Usage

One important trend in trying to evaluate value between publishers is to assess the comparative cost per download (CpD) of the publisher's entire content and of all library holdings. CpD can be defined as the cost of purchasing the content divided by the total number of full-text downloads.

As it is important to be clear what 'usage' is being measured when basing one's purchasing decisions on usage data – downloading or viewing the PDF or XML file of the article or book chapter; downloading the abstract or perhaps just the references – stakeholders have worked together to address this issue, through such initiatives as:

- Project COUNTER (Counting Online Usage of Networked Electronic Resources) was established as a cross industry initiative for libraries, publishers and funders to understand usage across all content types – books, journals, databases and multimedia. COUNTER provides codes of practice for standards and protocols to be used by publishers and libraries when counting usage.
- SUSHI (Standardized Usage Statistics Harvesting Initiative Protocol ANSI/NISO Z39.93-2007) is a model for the harvesting of electronic resource usage data, and is intended to replace the time-consuming process of manually collecting and compiling usage data reports. For example, one recent (2011) implementation of the SUSHI Protocol is JUSP, JISC's (UK) Usage Statistics Portal, which aims to provide a 'one-stop shop' for UK university libraries to use publisher download usage reports.

The existence of Project COUNTER protocols and the SUSHI standard for harvesting usage data realises what Franklin (2005) could only dream of – 'the ability to reduce variation in different vendor usage reports by applying a standard protocol and harvesting that data systematically, making it possible to accurately compare cost per use for electronic resources across vendors and publisher'. Funding agencies and their bodies [e.g. Higher Education Funding Council for England (HEFCE) and Joint Information Systems Committee of the Higher Education Funding Councils (JISC) in the UK] are already moving away from simply measuring quantitative measures such as CpD towards a more sophisticated and informative analysis of 'return on investment' relating to content purchases.

Impact

Although it has been subject to some criticism, the Impact Factor (Thomson Reuters) is still widely regarded as the standard measure for quality and importance for any research journal, influencing not only where to publish but also what to buy. The Impact Factor, first developed by Eugene Garfield in the early 1960s, today indexes more than 8000 journals across all disciplines in order to calculate the average number of times a paper in a journal is cited.

The publisher, hoping to persuade the library to add a journal, must understand the perceived value of the Impact Factor, how long it can take for a new journal to receive an Impact Factor and the variation depending on subject matter (the temporal distribution of citations in Mathematics tends to be longer than in other, related disciplines), and the type of content in the publication. When compared with research papers and letters, review articles receive more citations. A new journal may require several years of citations before receiving its first Impact Factor and the resulting lack of Impact Factor can make any acquisition decision difficult for a library to justify.

Usage is not the sole factor, or even at times the most important factor, when it comes to deciding what to purchase, retain or cancel. During a workshop at a US library conference in 2010, I asked a number of university librarians to make a choice of cancelling one of the following journals:

a. A broad subject journal which has a low CpD and is used extensively by the graduate and undergraduate community

b. A specialist journal with a very high CpD and much lower use by a limited research group within the university but one of the researchers happens to be the institution's sole Nobel Prize winning scientist.

Regardless of the low cost per download, each of the librarians asked chose to retain journal b) and cancel a) the broad-subject, high-use journal in favour of the specialist journal, but emphasising that the publisher and library must consider a variety of options when determining on the continued use of an electronic resource within that institution: what to retain (high usage), what to cancel (low usage – but not always) and what to add or reinstate.

The development of pricing models

Licensing and the Big Deal

In scholarly publishing, *licensing* can mean many things. Content can be licensed in different ways – to copyright agencies, individual libraries and consortia, for teaching purposes and to be made available in new technologies. Later in this book, Mark Seeley and Lois Wasoff look at copyright and matters pertaining to copyright licensing. This section will therefore focus on the challenges and opportunities of licensing content to libraries and consortia.

Emergence of the Big Deal

Shortly after journals became available on the internet, publishers began to offer bundled packages of content. These bundles are referred to as the 'Big Deal'. The publisher offers the library a large volume of content at a substantial discount and in return the library commits to maintaining its print and electronic holdings with the publisher. Many would assume that the Big Deal applies only to the very large content collections offered by a small number of large, commercial publishers, but by definition the Big Deal can apply to any aggregation of content, usually from a single publisher and regardless of the number of titles. There are big deals and there are bigger deals, it is simply a matter of scale. The first Big Deals date back to the late 1990s with the licences offered by Academic Press (now part of Elsevier) and Science Direct (also Elsevier).

When licensing content in a Big Deal, the purchasing institution wants to assure that:

- usage is extended to as many users as possible
- the CpD is within acceptable parameters
- access will be maintained after cancellation
- statistics can be provided to support the purchase decision
- where possible, there is training provision
- future pricing is capped at a manageable level

The CpD level quoted can be a key metric in agreeing this kind of licensing deal, depending on whether it is used simply for validation purposes, or as a comparison against other costs of accessing the same version of the content (such as pay-per-view), or as a stick to negotiate on price (when the target CpD can be as high or low as the purchasing negotiator wants it to be).

Model licences

Since the arrival of electronic journals in the mid-1990s, licences have become an essential part of defining the rights and duties of the buyer and seller in relation to electronic content. The original model licences were sponsored and developed in the 1990s by subscription agents preparing for the anticipated shift from print to electronic.

The publishing industry consultant John Cox has produced six different model licences covering a variety of scenarios, including Single Academic Institution, Academic Consortia, Public Libraries, Corporate and other special libraries, and E-book and journal archive purchases (Cox, 2009).

This was in addition to the considerable work done in defining a possible model licence by the UK Publishers Association together with the JISC, by the American Library Association to establish principles to license electronic journals, and by the International Coalition of Library Consortia (ICOLC) in defining the early versions of the academic consortium licence.

These licences have since developed and extended their scope beyond simply journals, covering databases, book and journal archives, backsets, reference books and other e-books. They continue to evolve to reflect changes in the technology and changing methods of teaching, the increased internationalisation and distribution of higher education and increasing demands for text or data mining and negotiated open access rights as part of their content purchasing agreements.

The work done by Cox and others has facilitated a growth in content licensing to consortia, such that today revenue from consortia sales (the Big Deal) forms a large proportion of many academic and professional publishers' revenue streams. There has also been considerable discussion on the future of the Big Deal. Some argue that ending the (large publisher) packages is the only way for a library to save costs in an increasingly challenging economic environment, while others insist that the sheer scale of content licensed and the ability to predict pricing are too important to discard.

Tiered pricing

Publishers have placed strong reliance on subscription income, the model for which has remained largely unchanged for over 300 years. A publisher would typically set two prices for a journal: (a) the institutional price and (b) the discounted price for society members or other private individuals. This very simple model applied perfectly well in a print world with no electronic access.

As soon as journals went online, the publisher witnessed a threat to their traditional income as institutions cancelled multiple copies of journals held in libraries and departments. As long as the content was available for the entire organisation (multiple sites, international locations) one licence would therefore suffice.

Tiered pricing was seen as a way of establishing a fair price for the use of the electronic version of the publication. For example, in 2001, the American Physical Society (APS) was among the earliest publishers to adopt a tiered pricing model. APS saw changes in their revenue streams; article charges had recently been eliminated and the availability of electronic journals led to cancellations of multiple subscriptions. In order to establish a fair pricing method, APS introduced a five-tier system based on the research size of the subscribing institutions, with large government research establishments, large corporate organisations and research-intensive post-doctoral institutions at one end of the pricing scale, and small undergraduate teaching colleges at the other.

Publishers selling to libraries in the US benefit from the US Carnegie Classification, which categorises institutions by research size and uses publicly available and audited data to group institutions. Although there are similar classification schemes in place elsewhere (e.g. JISC bands in the UK) they remain few and far between. Consequently, it is left to the publishing and research community to establish new, equitable and, importantly, fully justifiable ways to tier customer pricing.

Chesler and King (2009) describe the 'guiding principles' which the American Chemical Society (ACS) used to introduce a populated tiered pricing model. The absence of any Carnegie-type classification outside the US, and the fact that even in the US the Carnegie classifications had 'variations in institutional demographics', meant that ACS had to consider a number of additional factors in order to classify customers into their respective and appropriate bands:

- Relevance, as measured by demand for the Journal (including relative usage patterns).
- The type of research institution.

- Economic strength of the country, using World Bank Classifications for each country, ranging from high to low income.
- Costs and institutional budget, as suggested by an institution's article output. The more papers published, the more resources required in that institution.
- Utility, as measured by Impact Factor, with the assumption that the higher the Impact Factor, the greater the demand and usage of the content and of the research generated.

However, the path to establishing tiered pricing is not always without danger. Rapple (2011) explains the phases which a publisher must go through to transition to a tiered pricing model, which include:

- Data audit – to place the customer in the correct tier, one needs to understand the customer data.
- Market research – what is happening elsewhere in the competitive space.
- Data cleansing – Chesler and King refer to this as 'data hygiene'. It becomes a business process rather than simply a one-off activity completed in preparation for a tiered pricing model.
- Data modelling – testing different options.
- Applying the model.
- Communicating the change to customers.

These responsibilities need careful consideration by publishers, given the need to review pricing tiers in line over time due to changes in the market and at an institution. The publisher must ensure that the pricing tiers are reviewed regularly, adjusting the institution bands where necessary both up and down, particularly if there is a major change in research interests. Publishers operating a tiered pricing policy must also maintain a data infrastructure (such as acquiring relevant content, market research, analytical tools and staff) to facilitate the assessment of bands. The publisher must instill confidence that sufficient consideration has gone into the methodology used to calculate the price bands in an open and equitable manner.

Open Access business models

Open Access (OA) has only existed as a concept in academic and professional publishing for a relatively short period of time, but despite this fact a total of 7036 peer-reviewed journals or nearly one-quarter of all published journals were categorized as OA at the end of 2011 [according to the Directory of Open Access Journals (DOAJ), Lund University Libraries].

Many different business models have started to evolve:

- Fully OA, with article processing charges and no journal subscription fees, where 100 per cent of journal revenue is funded by author charges.
- Hybrid OA, which enables a journal with content behind a pay-wall to make certain articles free to read.
- Open Access Consortium, which negotiates publication charges on behalf of a larger community. This is referred to also as a Collaborative Purchasing Model. An example of this is the SCOAP3 (*Sponsoring Consortium for Open Access Publishing in Particle Physics*) consortium managed by CERN, which aims to re-direct library funding from traditional journal subscriptions towards the payment of OA charges in certain subscription-based journals. To fund author charges, SCOAP3 members are expected to reduce existing subscription expenditure either by cancelling titles or through publishers reducing subscription prices.
- Institutional Membership Schemes, such as those offered by BioMed Central and the Public Library of Science (PLoS), which enable institutions to anticipate publication in particular journals by pre-paying or offering discounts on the publication charges. The scheme acts like a membership subscription and is re-assessed every one or two years.
- Funding agency-supported OA journals, where funding agencies create their own journal for their funded research to appear. For example, the journal *eLife*, announced in November 2011, has been established as a 'top tier, open access research journal' supported by three funding organisations – the Howard Hughes Medical Institute (USA), the Max Planck Society (Germany) and The Wellcome Trust (UK). It is expected that once the journal is established, funding will switch away from the seed funding provided by the three funding agencies towards an author pays model.
- Advertising or sponsorship-based journals, more likely in well-funded areas such as medicine or pharmaceutical science.
- Institutional subsidy, where an institution financially supports the publishing activity carried out by either the library or a group of researchers.

- Hard copy sales used to fund publication charges, where the journal is available online free of charge but charges are made for printed copies. For example, the *British Medical Journal* has made research articles free online whereas it still charges for the print version.

Publishers, as well as funding agencies and researchers, want a model which is sustainable. Few publishers oppose the principle of funded open access (Gold OA) and most expect to see an increase in the number of OA papers published. Although OA may be requested by authors and their funding agencies, it is far from being a simpler model and the transition to a more OA-based business model can impact on the publisher's cash flow and cost base, particularly in smaller, more niche publications.

While subscriptions are traditionally pre-paid at the beginning of a year and processed en masse, the cost of processing and supporting article charges can be significantly greater. A single article may require partial invoices to be sent to multiple authors, not unusual in papers from large collaborations, while article fees are not pre-paid so an element of credit control is required. Moreover, the article charge is often an ad-hoc, one-time transaction with the full value taken only once the article is published. The subscription relationship, on the other hand (assuming the quality of publication is appropriately high), can last many years with a predictable proportion of subscription revenue taken each month. By operating an Institutional Membership scheme and allowing institutions to prepay author charges, it affords the publisher an element of predictability and stability from OA revenue, if only for the period during which the licence is in place.

It is too soon to say whether OA publishing models will become dominant in academic and professional publishing. Much has been written in recent years on the economics of OA publishing. Houghton and Oppenheim (2010) and Hall (2010) assess the financial merits and impact of OA publishing and take contrary positions in determining the economics of OAs and its long-term viability. Withey *et al.* (2011) review the economics for a university press to sustain scholarly publishing in an increasingly open environment.

The role of the publisher in adding value

Earlier in this book, Green and Cookson explain the services which the publisher needs to provide in order to succeed in an increasingly competitive environment. We should assess some of the commercial services which the publisher can provide. Before addressing the topic further, let us review what 'marketing' means in the process of scholarly communication.

Marketing and brand

The marketing function for academic and professional publishing is not just a department with a 'Marketing' label; rather, marketing *is* its core business. Each piece of communication reinforces the brand, whether it is the publisher's own (corporate) brand, the journal, the book series or the book itself, even the journal article or book chapter (the product brand). Each communication is an engagement to action – submit a paper, commission a new book, act as a referee, become an expert consultant (e.g. journal board member) to support the brand, sample the content and then buy it.

Marketing in an academic and professional publishing context consists typically of the following functions:

- Sales and customer support – global reach, in-house sales staff, sales channel management, pre- and post-sales customer support, pricing, licence management.
- Library- or institution-facing marketing – libraries, consortia, funding agencies.
- Author-facing marketing – board members, authors, referees, funding agencies. Goals can vary from attracting more papers, or encouraging referee engagement, to encouraging adoption and support of content offered (journal champion, textbook adoption).
- Corporate marketing – a cross disciplinary service which supports the corporate, journal and article brands. The PR service (public or press relations) is an important function of any corporate marketing service. Good press, and by good I mean appropriate, relevant and targeted press coverage, can increase awareness for the author and their work. The researcher wants to be recognised by the respective research community. An effective PR activity will accelerate the process of awareness and recognition.
- Data marketing – understanding the customer and all engagements with the publisher. The publisher ensures that it has the appropriate systems and processes in place to capture customer data, manage

rights correctly and adhere to any Data Protection rules which might apply in that market (e.g. opt-in, opt-outs). The data marketing function will ensure that data quality is maintained, thus reducing any wastage or failure in communication.

- Usage marketing – the publisher wants to ensure that content usage is as high as possible and that purchasing institutions are able to extract the maximum value from the content. This may not necessarily be a department or responsibility of an individual but a maxim for the organisation. For example, enhancing the technology used to deliver content is a direct attempt by the publisher to improve usage. The publisher wants 'stickability' of content, particularly for the reader referred from a search engine such as Google. Once the reader reaches the site, the publisher needs to find ways of keeping that user, and increasing usage for other content. Recent developments on the Web have enabled the use of 'semantic technologies', which allow the publisher and reader to better describe the content and link the content more accurately with other similar content elsewhere on the site. By making the technology more interesting or attractive for the reader it can positively affect usage in the same way that a reader awareness campaign, PR campaign or referral campaign might.
- Market research – the publisher, regardless of size, needs to support investment decisions with evidence or relating to their customer requirement and to the markets in which it operates.
- Social media – without doubt, social media tools are starting to have an impact on the scientific workflow. Rowlands *et al.* (2011) produced the results of an extensive survey of 2000 researchers which investigated the use of social media in the scientific workflow. This 2011 report highlights how quickly social media tools (such as Facebook, Twitter, blogging, YouTube) have been embraced by researchers to disseminate and discover research results. The publisher has had to quickly acquire the skills and techniques to make best use of these new media, promoting scholarly content using videos on video management sites such as YouTube, creating Facebook profiles for certain types of content or communities, encouraging or even commissioning the use of blogs to draw attention to certain disciplines and content types, and the creation of community portals to promote content in a given discipline or geographical sector.

Managing sales, licensing and marketing activities

Larger (commercial and society) publishers tend to have economy of scale, global reach, negotiating skills and general commercial expertise. They employ staff with specialist knowledge of licence negotiation and detailed knowledge of the library market to manage the consortia and library licensing process. They also ensure that any third-party content represented by them is sold in exactly the same manner as their own.

Smaller publishers are generally unable to employ similar levels of sales and marketing expertise, and so they tend not to have the internal capacity or commercial capability required to license content effectively to consortia, or to deal with the end-users directly. Contract publishing organisations offer the small to medium-sized publisher the kind of global reach and marketing resource which they would struggle to achieve without significant investment in staff and expertise. Small publishers may also require a subscription agent to manage the library engagement on their behalf.

One notable approach to addressing the imbalance in consortia negotiations is The ALPSP Learned Journals Collection (ALJC), which acts as a consortium club to help smaller publishers to sell content licences. This initiative enables a group of publishers to aggregate their content and, via an intermediary, sell a combined package to consortia and libraries. As of December 2011, ALJC contained 1070 journals in nine subject disciplines from 47 publishers.

Securing sustainable income

For a publisher to maintain or grow a customer base, it needs to invest in resources which can maintain and even increase sales, market presence, visibility, etc. Although the investment in acquiring a subscription can be high compared with the cost of the journal product, the subscription relationship can last many years and provide a very positive return to the publisher and stability of income. Therefore, as long as one takes a medium- to long-term view, the investment required to acquire a new subscription or indeed to maintain a subscription can be fully justified.

Let us consider some of the factors which will give the publisher the best possible chance of reaching the target audience, acquiring and retaining the subscription or licence.

Global reach

Academic and professional publishing is a global business so the publisher must provide the infrastructure and international channels to ensure the content and service is available as widely as possible. For example, in the case of IOP Publishing, UK, there are customers – including libraries, readers, authors, referees – in more than 120 countries (as of December 2011) and thanks to '*subscription aid*' initiatives such as Research4Life, INASP and eIFL, readership extends to more than 150 countries. The UK, despite being the home market for the Institute of Physics, represents a small proportion of revenue, readership and author/referee base. This is typical for most medium- to large-sized society and commercial professional and academic publishers.

Discoverability

The publisher ensures that the metadata describe the content accurately and are interoperable across a variety of platforms, making their content as easily and widely discoverable as possible.

Distribution and dissemination

Not only must the content be discoverable, it must be accessible. The publisher needs to invest in content delivery systems (journal or e-book platforms) or outsource the content to external providers (e.g. High Wire, Metapress, Ingenta, Silverchair and Atypon).

New markets and new customers

The publisher needs to ensure that the content is available in whatever form the reader may want to access it, including PDF, HTML, XML and EPUB. Book publishers need to produce content in multiple formats depending on the target user – MOBI for Kindle, HTML for search engines, ONIX for book distributors and NLM XML for future reading devices.

In order to reach the largest possible market, the publisher needs to consider how to make content available and to determine the value of offering content via third-party platforms. The publisher may choose to be platform-agnostic as to the location of the final article as long as the content is discoverable and any citation is credited back to the publication. Aggregation service providers would argue that they serve a different community from the publisher and therefore the risk of possible cannibalisation is low.

Customer engagement and retention

Here we address the challenge of understanding and attracting readership, what has been referred to as 'attention marketing' (Esposito, 2010).

Market research and customer insight

Industry and customer data come in many forms and sources:

- The Publisher may choose to commission its own research to determine its market share, its market perception or simply gain an understanding of how its content or its service is used. To develop its products and services, the publisher must first determine how it is being used – what is the user experience and what can be done to enhance the experience.
- Shared research data. As part of their services to support member publishers, trade associations (such as ALPSP, STM, SSP) conduct regular research studies on different aspects of academic and professional publishing, the findings for which are then distributed to member organisations as part of their membership. (Research reports can also form a useful revenue stream for the trade association by selling reports to non-members.)
- More general research reports are published by specialist research organisations such as EPS Outsell, Key Perspectives and Publishing Research Consortium. These organisations produce reports ranging from broad industry surveys to specialist analysis and comment on particular aspects of professional and scholarly publishing.
- Governmental and intergovernmental organisations such as UNESCO, OECD and National Science Foundation (NSF) produce annual reports containing detailed statistics on the size of the research marketplace, including total numbers of researchers and growth trends by country/region.

The publisher needs to invest time and money to engage with the customer, researching the customer's current and future requirements, understanding research workflows and identifying a role for itself in that process.

Larger publishers have the benefit of economy of scale – expert staff, Customer Relationship Management (CRM) systems, funding for resources, marketing collateral and general promotion. However, the smaller publisher, in particular the smaller society publisher, knows how to serve their community, which may gravitate around their respective society. This can be achieved by offering a focused suite of products and services that the community will consume, such as in-house publications, member magazines and web pages, society meetings such as conferences and workshops, and subject working groups and by representing the society itself, acting on its Council or other governing bodies. The smaller society (and publisher) is also well positioned to identify new research areas, current and future trends in their particular discipline and to produce new services to support these new research areas.

Bringing all relevant customer data together in one place, typically using CRM-type systems to establish a 'data warehouse', facilitates a detailed analysis of the customer's engagement with the publisher, analysing trends, identifying any opportunities or gaps in the service provided. Important criteria for a particular institution include:

- How many papers does the publisher receive from the institution?
- Which content does the institution have access to and what are researchers trying to use?
- How many authors, referees, board members, librarian advisors?
- What is the usage/submission rate compared with similar institutions – size, geography, research interests?

This kind of CRM functionality is no longer the exclusive domain of the larger publisher. Services exist which the small to medium-sized publisher may be able to exploit with their otherwise limited budgets. For example, Mastervision (from Datasalon) provides insight into a Publisher/Customer relationship by collating data on publishing transactions, including: marketing campaigns; article views; alerts; member data; author data; referees and board members; subscription data; user registration data; consortia membership data; and any other structured data. Mastervision's search tools then look for relationships within the data to identify segments and trends.

Data hygiene

One particular problem which the publisher must face when trying to understand its customer relationships is ambiguity. When trying to understand how many authors, referees, subscriptions and board members which the publisher has from any given institution it needs to know how that institution is described, which naming conventions are used and which department belongs to which institution.

One often sees the following affiliation on a journal paper: 'Department of Physics, Cambridge'. How can the researcher be sure this is Cambridge in the UK and not say MIT or Harvard, both located in Cambridge, Massachusetts?

Tools and standards are being developed to resolve (or at least reduce) this institutional identity problem. For example, the Ringgold database (http://www.ringgold.com) was created to help with the process of institutional disambiguation. The publisher assigns the relevant Ringgold master name to any given 'transaction' in order to track relationships more accurately.

Similar services utilising improvements in web technology have been developed by publishers for use by researchers to engage with their respective research communities. For example, in 2010, the American Institute of Physics launched AIP UniPHY, a website which enables researchers from the physical sciences to identify possible connections within their scientific community, identifying researchers who may possess the expertise required for future collaborations. Another example, pre-dating AIP UniPHY, is BiomedExperts (Collexis Holdings, now part of Elsevier) which uses the PubMed database to connect nearly 1.8 million researchers worldwide according to publication profiles and research interests.

The problem of author ambiguity is, however, even greater than that of institutional ambiguity. According to Elsevier's Scopus database (June 2011) there is a global community of 6.2 million active researchers in 16 000 organisations and 27 million researchers globally (excluding undergraduate students). Many commercial publishers have created proprietary systems to help with author identification, such as Scopus Author Identifier (Elsevier), Wiley-Blackwell Author Services, Distinct Author Identification System (Thomson Reuters) and Scholar Universe (ProQuest).

In order to better identify more exactly who the author is, and to ensure interoperability, new services and standards are being developed to address author disambiguation, including:

- ORCID (http://www.orcid.org), which aims to remove any author/contributor name ambiguity in scholarly communications by creating a central registry of unique identifiers for individual researchers which the researcher uses during their career.
- The International Standard Name Identifier (ISNI) Agency, which has created an ISO standard (Draft ISO Standard – ISO 27729) to connect research information to the individual.

These new, cross-industry initiatives should allow publishers and researchers alike to forge better relationships. By embracing standards such as ORCID the author ensures that their work is correctly attributed now and in the future and the publisher has the data to better understand the author and their work.

The ecosystem for scholarly publishing binds the researcher with the publisher in a very real way. The benefits of the publishing process are mutual. The researcher needs visibility and the publisher needs revenue to achieve whatever commercial or altruistic goals it may have. In scholarly and academic publishing, the researcher is the producer and the publisher is the diffuser – the system does not work if either party is missing.

The evolving role of the sales intermediary

Another key player in publisher–customer relationships is the sales intermediary (subscription agent), who typically performs many functions on behalf of publishers and customers, for example:

- As the publisher's official representative acting in matters relating to content sales, negotiation, invoicing, debt collection, business development and customer support.
- Sales only but no invoicing. This is what was typically referred to as the 'Publisher's Agent' in the old print world. This agent is remunerated on the basis of sales generated. Costs may include an optional retainer fee to cover upfront costs. This intermediary would not engage in either invoicing or debt collection and the customer decides on the appropriate method of being invoiced – e.g. via a subscription agent or directly by the publisher.

Whereas the role of the subscription agent was clearly defined in the print-only world ('buying intermediary', with improved processing and administering of print orders), the arrival of electronic-only content changed the market dynamic.

This opens up questions of what role a subscription service can play when the library can license all content electronically directly from the publisher, or indeed of whether traditional subscription services (such as cataloguing, print consolidation and managing claims) are still relevant when the *content* is supplied electronically?

Managing e-collections and providing access for the research community generates a lot of administrative effort. As more content is born electronic or retro-converted, it becomes difficult for library staff to know precisely which titles are available to them. They may know which journal or book titles are included in a particular package but not necessarily to which years they have an entitlement. It can become difficult therefore for a library to provide services which assist in linking and discovery of content when they are unable to inform users as to which content is available if they are not always sure themselves. There are still thousands of publishers with thousands of products to sell. Only the format – electronic as opposed to print – has changed.

Hence, subscription agents can still provide an important role for the library, but it is a role which continues to evolve. The subscription agent, if engaged correctly, can provide an important service to institutions by:

- managing their e-collections and entitlements – helping with processing new orders, renewals and claims;
- providing accurate and timely pricing information;
- providing usage data (SUSHI/COUNTER-compliant);
- providing assistance with publisher negotiations, cost comparison calculations and sophisticated, pre-populated ERM services (Source: The Association for Subscription Agents: Library Choice http://www.subscription-agents.org/library-choice).

There is also still a market for the specialist sales agent, particularly for the smaller publisher unable to justify the cost of recruiting in-house. Geographically distributed sales agents will have specialist knowledge of their respective markets. If the agent agrees to operate on a commission-based sales basis, then the risk is minimised.

Conclusion and outlook

There is no crystal ball to predict the future, but there are certain truths which remain with us:

1. The author still wants recognition for their work.
2. The researcher wants to further their career.
3. There is still a role for peer review and quality associated with journal brands, regardless of the business model applied.
4. Funding agencies fund research and want their efforts to be recognised.
5. There is still a requirement for content distribution and quality control.

6. Research output is growing at a faster rate than scientists can absorb.
7. Even the largest research libraries are unable to acquire all the content its researchers require.
8. The subscription model will continue to exist, albeit in a different form from previously.

These truths apply today as much as they have at any time in the past. The Web has just changed expectations among the respective stakeholders.

New methods of accessing content will continue to emerge (e.g. DeepDyve, which has been described as the iTunes for academic and professional content) and successful publishers must find ways to engage more closely with their researchers, to develop business models that provide the level of global visibility researchers and their funding institutions require, and to adapt their business practices to embrace changing business models (such as OA) in a way which is sustainable in the long term.

Acknowledgments and sources of further information

I would like to thank Mark Ware, Lead Analyst, Outsell Inc., and Bob Campbell (Co-Editor of this book) for their assistance in providing references and other source material for this chapter. I would also like to acknowledge the publishing industry consultant John Cox on his invaluable work in developing Model Licences for academic and professional content and for the countless hours saved by publishers not having to reinvent the licensing wheel *ad infinitum*.

General sources

Consortium Directory Online http://www.frontlinegms.com/6.html
General overview of scholarly publishing practice by John Cox: http://www.alpsp.org/Ebusiness/ProductCatalog/Product.aspx?ID=44
List of 110 libraries found at the Ludwig-Maximillian-Universität München: http://www.ub.uni-muenchen.de/bibliotheken/
Model Licences: http://www.licensingmodels.org/
The Scholarly Kitchen (from the Society for Scholarly Publishing) provides a very useful and regular commentary on the latest trends in scholarly publishing: http://scholarlykitchen.sspnet.org/

Upshall, M. (2009) *Content Licensing: Buying and Selling Digital Resources.* Oxford: Chandos Publishing.

Market reports

National Science Foundation (NSF) Science and Engineering Indicators (2010): http://www.nsf.gov/statistics/seind10/
OECD Key Figures on researcher numbers and growth trends by country/region (2009): http://www.oecd.org/dataoecd/27/52/47406944.pdf
The UNESCO Science Report on research market size: http://unesdoc.unesco.org/images/0018/001898/189883E.pdf
Ware, M. and Mabe, M. (2009) *The STM Report*, STM Association report; http://www.stm-assoc.org/news.php?id=255

Long-term preservation archival services

CLOCKSS: http://www.clockss.org
Portico: http://www.portico.org/digital-preservation/services/
Bone, D. and Burns, P. (2011) *An Overview of Content Archiving Services in Scholarly Publishing* (Allen Press): http://allenpress.com/system/files/pdfs/library/archiving-whitepaper.pdf

Useful sites relating to measuring usage and emerging standards

A list of emerging international standards for naming conventions: https://repinf.pbworks.com/w/page/13779410/Authorpercent20identification
Project COUNTER: http://www.projectcounter.org
SUSHI Protocol: http://www.niso.org/workrooms/sushi
JISC Usage Statistics Portal: http://jusp.mimas.ac.uk/

Open access business models

For anyone interested in the variety of Open Access business models, I would refer you Raym Crow's comprehensive review of various income models: http://www.arl.org/sparc/bm~doc/incomemodels_v1.pdf
Directory of Open Access Journals is a comprehensive database of OA journals: http://www.doaj.org/
Open access case studies: OUP have been very open with information relating to their open access publishing activities, e.g. Bird, C. (2010) Continued adventures in open access, *Learned Publishing*, 23: 107–16 http://dx.doi.org/10.1087/20100205

Withey, L. *et al.* (2011) *Sustaining Scholarly Publishing: New Business Models for University Presses; A Report of the AAUP Task Force on Economic Models for Scholarly Publishing.* Lynne Withey from the University of California Press and her colleagues produced a very useful report on the economics of publishing primarily for university presses. However, much of the report's findings can be applied to other types of publishing organisation. http://www.aaupnet.org/images/stories/documents/aaupbusinessmodels2011.pdf

References

Chesler, A. and King, S. (2009) Tier-based pricing for institutions: a new, e-based pricing model. *Learned Publishing*, 21: 42–9, doi:10.1087/095315108X378767.

Cox, J. (2009) *Model standard licenses for use by publisher, librarians and subscription agents for electronic resources*: http://www.licensingmodels.org/

Esposito, J. (2010) What's for sale? Moving from selling content to monetizing attention. *The Scholarly Kitchen*, 2 June: http://scholarlykitchen.sspnet.org/2011/06/02/whats-for-sale-moving-from-selling-content-to-monetizing-attention/

Faraday, M. (1827) Experimental researches in chemistry and physics. *Philosophical Transactions.*

Franklin, B. (2005) Managing the electronic collection with cost per use data. *IFLA Journal* 31: 241, doi: 10.1177/0340035205058809.

Hall, S. (2010) A commentary on 'The economic implications of alternative publishing models'. *Prometheus* 28(1): 73–84: http://www.tandfonline.com/doi/abs/10.1080/08109021003676383

Houghton, J. and Oppenheim, C. (2010) The economic implications of alternative publishing models. *Prometheus* 28(1): 41–54: http://dx.doi.org/10.1080/08109021003676359.

Okerson, A. (1986) Periodical prices, a history and discussion. *Advances in Serials Management* 1: 101–34: http://www.library.yale.edu/~okerson/pricing.html#fn0

Rowlands, I., Nicholas, D., Russell, B., Canty, N. and Watkinson, A. (2011) Social media use in the research workflow. *Learned Publishing*, 24: 183–95, doi:10.1087/20110306.

Rapple, C. (2011) Researching and implementing a new tiered pricing model. *Learned Publishing*, 24(1): 9–13.

The Royal Society (2011) *Knowledge, Networks and Nations: Global scientific collaboration in the 21st century*: http://royalsociety.org/uploadedFiles/Royal_Society_Content/Influencing_Policy/Reports/2011-03-28-Knowledge-networks-nations.pdf

Withey, L. *et al.* (2011) *Sustaining Scholarly Publishing: New Business Models for University Presses*; A Report of the AAUP Task Force on Economic Models for Scholarly Publishing; http://www.aaupnet.org/images/stories/documents/aaupbusinessmodels2011.pdf

13

The evolving role of libraries in the scholarly ecosystem

Keith Webster

Abstract: This chapter outlines the ways in which libraries have been transformed by advances in scholarly publishing, by new patterns of student and researcher information behaviour, and by the emergence of new approaches to scholarly communication. It reviews the development of research collections over the past 20 years, and the emergence of online journals and books. The impact of government and research funder policies on libraries is discussed, with specific reference to research assessment, open access and data curation. Finally, consideration is given to the impact of new players in the scholarly information landscape.

Key words: Open access; online journals; the Big Deal; institutional repositories; learning spaces; research assessment; libraries

Introduction

University and research libraries have long served a diverse client base: students, teachers, researchers, alumni and the wider community of which their parent institution is part. In the context of a book addressing the broad sphere of scholarly publishing, this chapter will focus upon the relationships between libraries and researchers, and, particularly, the part played by the former in supporting the broad pattern of information-related activity of the latter.

The traditional role of the library in supporting research involved identifying, selecting and acquiring books and journals, making them available and providing assistance to the researcher. In a specialist research environment (such as a government laboratory) this might represent the dominant picture of a library's activity; in a broader university environment, the needs of the research community had to be balanced against the demands made by students and resource allocation optimised to provide the best overall service model. As libraries have made the shift to predominantly digital collections, those needs and demands have moved, offering libraries unprecedented opportunities to transform their portfolio of services. One view that can emerge from changes of the past decade is that libraries are better placed now to serve the often competing demands of different clients, and are able more fully to meet the heavier demands placed upon them by the research community.

The move to digital collections

In the print era, libraries supported research primarily through building collections of relevant materials and providing specialist support in their use. Collections of books and journals were selected, acquired and maintained, and were augmented by special collections relevant to institutional needs. Such collections would often take the form of archives and manuscripts, slides and, especially in engineering and scientific fields, grey literature in the form of technical reports, working papers and unpublished conference proceedings.

Many libraries, especially those in research-intensive settings, employed subject-specialist librarians to provide disciplinary-specific support to researchers. These librarians would work closely with their clients, ensuring that collections continued to be developed in response to information needs, and promoting the library's existing services and collections. In the 1980s, this represented one of the fundamental roles of the research librarian, as researchers coped to struggle with an explosion in the volume of information available, coupled with imperfect discovery and retrieval systems. Concern was expressed at the volume of publicly funded research conducted in the UK which unnecessarily replicated work that had already been reported in the literature, but was not discovered by researchers (Martyn, 1987).

The widespread availability of online networks in the mid-1990s heralded new opportunities for the discovery and dissemination of scholarly publications. Publishers were alert to the opportunities to distribute content in electronic format, and their customers were equally receptive to testing the possibilities of new approaches to delivery. In 1995, the Higher Education Funding Councils in the UK had established a Pilot Site Licence Initiative (PSLI) through which funding was provided in order that materials from four publishers could be made available to participating universities. This central approach meant that British university libraries and researchers were early adopters of electronic journals. A review of the PSLI concluded that there was overwhelming support for ongoing access, and recommended bringing a much wider range of publishers into the fold (HEFCE, 1998).

Early acceptance and use of electronic journals was more widespread amongst academics in the sciences and engineering. This was considered inevitable: much early content was from those fields, and it was perceived that academics in the humanities and social sciences were less comfortable in using computerised technology. Other concerns were associated with archival access to journal content (in the event of a publisher going out of business or the loss of online journal access), the poor availability of usage statistics, the imposition of VAT on electronic content[1] and the quality of photographic images and illustrations. However, the general view from librarians, academics and publishers was one of great support for provision of journal articles online. Against this backdrop of enthusiastic reception for electronic journals, publishers were quick to innovate, in terms of both the platforms through which their content was accessed and the business models through which libraries purchased content.

In 1996, Academic Press became the first publisher to offer academic libraries a subscription model which has become known as the Big Deal, and which now represents the dominant approach used between large publishers and major university libraries and consortia to license access to journal content. In essence, the Big Deal offers libraries the opportunity to subscribe, in electronic form, to large bundles of journal titles. This subscription model was widely welcomed at first: it offered an elegant response to the serials crisis of the early 1990s, and took advantage of the development of computer networks across many higher education systems.

The serials crisis had been brought about by the imposition of high annual price increases for scholarly journals coupled with stagnant library budgets. Until the late 1990s, academic libraries predominantly acquired collections in print form. Whilst practice varied from one library to another, broadly, subject or liaison librarians, in consultation with their academic clients, identified materials to be added to the collection. Journal collections represented titles which were subscribed to on an ongoing basis, with little change from year to year. Many libraries chose to constrain expenditure by creating separate funds for one-off purchases, such as books, and funds for recurring expenditure such as journals, abstracts and indexing services. A combination of constrained budgets and high price increases for journals in the 1980s and 1990s, however, forced many to cancel titles (Blake, 1986). Such cancellations were the focus of heated debate inside universities, and in many institutions academic staff voted on titles to be deleted. In such a climate, the addition of new titles to a library's holdings was difficult to accommodate, and often was achieved only through agreement to cancel existing titles of the same subscription cost. Recognition of the impact of reduced numbers of subscriptions was exacerbated by a continued increase in the number of new journal titles being produced, in part to accommodate a growing volume of journal literature being produced in research institutions and universities.

Almost every academic library worked with one or more serials agents to help manage their subscriptions. Instead of dealing directly with many individual publishers, libraries would appoint a small number of intermediaries, companies such as Swets and Faxon, to act on their behalf. Agents would, in turn, deal with publishers, and invoice libraries, manage the subscription and cancellation cycle, and deal with the regular 'claims' process associated with locating or replacing missing issues of titles.

In this climate of financial constraint, and cumbersome serials management systems, the concept of a Big Deal was perceived as bringing great benefit to libraries. Generally offered to library consortia, publishers would make available to each member institution access to an extensive range of content, frequently the entire journal list, online, in exchange, typically, for the price of original print subscriptions plus an electronic premium (commonly known as p+e) of around 10 per cent. Such licences were often multi-year and provided for an annual price increase. In the early years of the Big Deal, these increases were generally around 6 per cent per annum.

The Big Deal was received enthusiastically by librarians and academics alike. Libraries, as we have noted, are in the business of providing access to scholarly publications, and the Big Deal reversed the trend of journal cancellations at a stroke. Many smaller libraries, historically able to provide a relatively small selection of titles, were now able to offer access to the same content as their research-intensive colleagues.

Researchers in particular were winners, because they wanted to access as much literature as possible, and as writers they welcomed an extension of the potential readership of their works. In the ten-year period to 2009, it was estimated that the number of journals available through academic libraries more than doubled.

Despite these evident gains, during the same period, librarians in particular began to challenge the operation of the Big Deal. As the cost of annual licences grew, almost always above the rate of growth of library budgets, library funding became squeezed. Almost all of a library's serials budget could be spent on a small number of Big Deal licences, and in many cases, expenditure on books was reduced to ensure continued payment of Big Deal licences. This proved especially challenging for the humanities and social sciences, where traditionally book-reliant disciplines saw 'their' collection funds cut, ostensibly to maintain access to Big Deals which primarily served the sciences.

Librarians also recognised that bundles of journals would contain titles which received little or no usage, but with no opportunity to remove subscriptions to these to save money. In the title-by-title subscription model common in the print era, titles which were not used would be cancelled and funds released for higher priority needs, but the Big Deal precludes easy implementation of such an approach.

For much of the past ten years, libraries have coped through a combination of cost-cutting, and the cancellation of lesser used products, often indexing and abstracting services. They have also sought to secure discounts from publishers, for example by providing early payment for a subscription period, or by joining together in consortia to secure favourable pricing for large-volume purchasing. Such approaches have offered some relief, but the global financial crisis of 2008 has intensified scrutiny of the sustainability of the Big Deal. A number of studies have reported the impact of the crisis on public-sector funding, which has had a profoundly severe impact on many library budgets, and on investment returns, which has hit those libraries reliant on endowment income to provide some of their annual funding (CIBER, 2009; Research Information Network, 2010a). The Association of Research Libraries in the US (ARL, 2009) and the International Coalition of Library Consortia (ICOLC, 2009) were prominent in bringing the library funding shortfall to the attention of publishers, and seeking relief from the severe financial situation whilst maintaining access to essential research content.

By comparison, the acquisition of books appeared much more straightforward. Many libraries allocated their book fund by subject or academic department, and selection was seen as a shared responsibility between librarians and academic staff. Approval programmes were common: a bookseller would supply a selection of new publications 'on approval'. Selectors would make choices with the advantage of being able to see the whole item, rather than brief details in a glossy catalogue.

Those books to be purchased were retained, and others returned to the bookseller. In other cases, publishers' marketing materials, book reviews and word of mouth, often from academics, would inform the selection process. However, there remained concern that many books were acquired, but never used: a recent study at Cornell (Collection Development Executive Committee, 2010) revealed that 55 per cent of books in the collection published since 1990 have never circulated. However, some libraries, often national libraries and highly prestigious academic libraries, have a responsibility to build collections irrespective of active usage, seeking to preserve the development of knowledge for future generations of scholars. That role is fundamental.

For many libraries, though, budget and space constraints mean that selection has to be more focused on what is actively in demand, complemented by judicious and informed selection to arrive at a rounded collection. In some instances that has meant a greater focus being placed on acquiring materials recommended by a library's clients. In others, it has been informed by monitoring requests for inter-library loans (a mechanism by which a library will obtain a requested book from the collection of another institution) and acquiring rather than borrowing those titles in print (Allen *et al.*, 2003).

With the advent of e-books, the involvement of library clients in collection development has taken on a new focus, through the advent of patron-driven acquisition models offered by aggregator services such as ebrary and Ebook Library. Through these models, a library is able to upload details of a wide range of books into the local catalogue (the books can represent all, or subsets of, the aggregator's offerings). Library clients can access the full e-book through the service, and the library only pays for, and adds to its ongoing collections, a title when it has been viewed on a certain number of occasions – the number of views which triggers purchase can be determined by the library, with the purchase price varying accordingly. Many have welcomed this approach as an antidote to the perception that Big Deal bundles of journals contain much that is unread. A library's clients can look at anything that might be of interest, but only repeated viewing will lead to addition to the ongoing collection. Variations on the model are also offered, notably in the student textbook market, for example through short-term rental of access to an item, paid for by the library, and rental of e-books, paid for by the student, from commercial services such as Amazon, and in print from booksellers such as Barnes and Noble. These solutions are better developed in the US, where there is a culture of student purchasing of textbooks, than in the UK, where libraries have traditionally played a stronger role.

At the time of writing, the immediate future for library acquisition models is unclear. Funding shortfalls are very real, but so too is the demand for content from major publishers. The sustainability of the Big Deal in the long term will be a particular focus over the next few years. One certainty is that the Big Deal, and models of scholarly communication, form only one part of significant change affecting university libraries. It is therefore pertinent to reflect upon some of the broader changes, to understand their interconnectedness, and how each element might support the other.

The changing role of libraries[2]

In recent years, numerous changes in the 'leisure' information world have transformed high streets across much of the western world. Leading brands in the book, movie and music distribution business – for example Borders, Blockbuster and HMV – have closed stores in response to two broad phenomena. The first of these is competition from online retailers, who are able to offer deep discounts through efficient warehouse and distribution models and massive sales volumes. But increasingly, consumers choose also to acquire their books, music or movies in digital form, taking advantage of vastly improved computer network speeds. Affordable handheld devices such as Amazon's Kindle and Apple's iPad have allowed people to access and enjoy content largely independent of location.

In large part, this shift has brought little change to the academic information landscape – most scholarly material continues to be accessed primarily, albeit in electronic form, through university and other research libraries. However, the virtual access that has underpinned the transformation of scholarly publishing over the past 15 years has brought profound and enduring change to academic libraries, one of the key players in the distribution channel of research publications.

For almost the whole of the 20th century, interactions between students, researchers and teachers and library staff and collections have taken place within the physical boundaries of the library. The constraints of the print environment necessitated the construction of libraries which served as substantial warehouses of print materials and provided a place dedicated to the quiet and private study of books and journals. Service points were constructed to provide access to library staff for support in the use of library materials and to facilitate the borrowing of items that could be taken away from the confines of the library building. The nature of university teaching required little else, as it embraced a model where students attended lectures and tutorials, but demonstrated their learning outcomes in an assessment model that embraced solitary learning. The essay and the examination were the products of individual achievement.

In that era, access to information largely depended upon a visit to the Library, with hours spent copying or note-taking from print volumes. The Library loomed large as a physical presence at the heart of many campuses, with space pressures mounting in response to a growing output each year of scholarly books and journals. The introduction of computer facilities initially exacerbated space demands – print collections continued to grow, and were coupled with demand for space for online catalogue terminals in the 1980s, followed by end-user CD-ROM search workstations at the end of that decade. By the mid-1990s, student demand for library-based, general-use computer laboratories had grown immensely. In the UK, following the publication of the Follett Report (1993), substantial funds were made available for the construction, extension and modernisation of library buildings. This scheme was intended to allow libraries to respond to the opportunities brought about by new technology, and represented the first substantial investment in university libraries since the Parry Report in the 1960s (University Grants Committee, 1967). Almost simultaneously, academic libraries began to have access to substantial online collections of scholarly journals, bringing to mainstream academe the first real evidence of the digital library.

The arrival of electronic forms of scholarly information resources over the past 15 years, coupled with changes in teaching practices and comfort with technology, has brought rapid and significant change. Many libraries are full of increasingly unused print collections, and traditional activity such as the lending of books and answering of reference questions has declined rapidly. Meanwhile, all library clients have come to demand instant access, online, to all forms of academic information content. Students seek a wide range of study and social spaces inside libraries, coupled with access to technology to support information use. These broad trends have been seen as presaging a fundamental reinvention of the academic library (Lewis, 2007; Webster, 2010).

The challenge for libraries is inextricably linked at this moment in time with the need to make hard decisions about the future of legacy collections and the securing of sufficient funds to repurpose library space to meet the expectations of teachers and students operating in an academic world very different from that seen only a generation ago.

Library generations

It is worth reflecting briefly upon a generational model of library space design which maps out the movement in the concept of the library as place over the past 30 years (Webster, 2008).

In the Generation 1 research library the physical space can be considered collection-centric: all design was focused upon the building as a physical repository of library collections. Space was provided in which library clients could consult and work with collections, but the notable design features were very much structured to support the storage of printed materials. This is most instantly recognised by the appearance of many mid-20th century library buildings with narrow windows, designed to keep out light which might damage the collections, irrespective of the wishes of library clients.

The second-generation library coincides with the emergence of electronic information resources in the early 1990s, and a growth in customer care and quality initiatives which promoted a stronger focus upon and engagement with clients. The arrival of computers and CD-ROMs brought a degree of technological sophistication into the Library which was often ahead of the ability of library clients. Inviting spaces were created in which librarians and clients could work together, facilitating teaching and training and supportive exploration of new forms of electronic resources.

The third-generation library recognises the different forms of learning expected of students in the 21st century university and also acknowledges the different behaviours and learning styles of new generations of students. Whilst provision for 'formal', quiet study continues, it has been complemented, and occasionally supplanted, by group study facilities, open discussion spaces and social networking environments.

Finally, a fourth-generation library can be envisaged, one in which the Library forms part of a campus-wide learning environment and which is designed predominantly upon pedagogical principles.

The changing environment

As foreshadowed above, the nature of pedagogy in the university has shifted. A growing emphasis has been placed upon student-centred learning, and upon group work and collaborative forms of assessment. These changes have driven a vast demand for spaces which foster and support emerging forms of learning activity. It is worth noting that this shift has not replaced, but has generally supplemented conventional forms of student learning.

Secondly, the nature of the student body has shifted, with the arrival at university of students frequently characterised as the net generation or Generation Y. These students have grown up surrounded by technology – most will have been born several years after the popularisation of personal computing and will have started school after the emergence of the Internet. They use technology to maintain contact with friends, are inquisitive and multi-tasking. The notion of sitting quietly in a Library for prolonged periods of time, reading and taking notes is as alien a concept as sitting motionless in a lecture listening and taking notes! As the environment in secondary schools shifts towards one which reflects the nature of today's students, expectations of the provision of learning facilities in post-compulsory education will also shift.

We cannot ignore, either, the changing nature of library use. Conventionally, the Library existed to house printed collections and to make them available for consultation and borrowing. This mission was enhanced by the work of reference librarians who aided clients in the use of these collections. Such activity was conventionally measured by libraries in terms of numbers of loans per annum, numbers of reference questions answered and the numbers of visits to libraries per annum.

For many years, the library has been regarded as a core part of a university's research infrastructure. At the heart of the university, a library with extensive collections built up over time and reflecting both a breadth and a depth of scholarship is regarded as a symbol of research excellence.

The research library as learning space

Whilst there are many great libraries in modest institutions, no great university is without an outstanding library. That status remains of tremendous importance, and few researchers would dispute the need for extensive collections of scholarly information and the support of experienced librarians in their scholarly endeavours, although with a strong preference for that support to be delivered in the school or laboratory rather than in the library. However, the notion of library as place in that dynamic has shifted. Academics report fewer visits to the library than was the case only a few years ago, and many predict a continued decline in years to come (Research Information Network, 2007). The importance of the library's print collections is also diminishing, with desktop delivery of electronic information seen as a fundamental requirement (British Academy, 2005). Many report a reluctance to visit the library to copy a journal article held on the library's shelves: the effort required is seen as disproportionate to the likely academic benefit (Research Information Network, 2007).

All of these strands can be brought together to form a hypothesis. We see lowered patterns of demand for conventional library services and collections, and a stronger emphasis upon the provision of information in electronic form.

However, we can also see a real need for a place on campus which offers a forum for student interaction with technology, information and their peers. On occasion, these interactions might be strengthened by the support of librarians, offering guidance on information searching and evaluation, and by learning advisers skilled in strengthening student academic skills.

I would argue that the path is clear: librarians need to take a long, hard look at the disposition of their collections, working collaboratively with colleagues to share the responsibility for maintaining lesser used material, much of which is available in electronic form. For example, The University of Queensland is part of an initiative of major university research libraries in Australia seeking to manage back runs of journals, electronic equivalents of which have also been purchased by those libraries. The project aims to identify a single print run of each journal title to be managed by a participating library, with each library looking after their fair share of titles. In turn, they will be able to remove from their collections those titles which are the responsibility of other libraries. Through this approach, a complete print archive will be maintained onshore for preservation purposes, but with library clients having access to the electronic version of the same titles. Initiatives such as this will provide an opportunity for libraries to reduce the storage space in library buildings, and redevelop the space released to provide support for learning activities. Whilst an approach of this sort might be less straightforward for monograph collections, immediate savings through responsible management of journal collections will yield considerable opportunities. As book digitisation projects, such as that managed by Google, come to maturity over the next decade, there can be little doubt that similar approaches will be adopted.

Although numerous studies show an irrefutable demand for library-provided learning space, what is not clear is how best to make this available. In many universities, campus space is at a premium and libraries are required to meet client needs from a static footprint. Library staff accommodation apart, that space is normally allocated to study facilities and teaching rooms, and to storage for print collections. Can librarians reasonably adjust that balance, by retiring legacy collections in favour of learning space provision? What part does the Library play in meeting the needs of its other core constituency, the research and faculty community?

The needs and opinions of researchers were addressed in part through a collaborative study conducted by Outsell Consultants on behalf of the Group of 8 (Go8, Australia's eight leading research-intensive universities) university libraries, with support from the Council of Australian University Librarians.[3]

The focus of that study was to understand the benefits to academic research of the free provision at the point of use of information resources. In formulating a response to that broad question, the study (which was conducted at three of the Go8 member universities) sought to understand how libraries and their collections are used by researchers.

The survey was conducted using a web-based survey instrument, and attracted responses from all broad academic disciplines. Overall, 30 per cent of those surveyed were located off-campus more often than on-campus, and relied upon access to electronic resources to meet their needs. Journal articles were the most heavily used from of content, with 95 per cent of respondents using these in electronic form. On average, respondents spent 4.5 hours per week using print resources and 11.2 hours consulting electronic resources. There was overwhelming agreement that provision of information resources enabled researchers to access materials indispensible for research and to maintain a comprehensive overview of developments in their fields.

In general, there was clear signal of reliance on electronic resources, and whilst those in the arts and humanities made greater use of print materials than their colleagues in other fields, their use of electronic resources was at a similar level to those in the life and physical sciences. What emerged, overall, was a situation that supported evidence emerging from library use statistics, client surveys and other studies. These all depicted a pattern of information resources use by researchers and faculty members that was overwhelmingly electronic in nature, frequently off-campus and of immense value.

The triple helix, research funding and libraries

Over the past 20 years, academic research has been increasingly directed by the needs of government and by research funders more generally. The complexity of these relationships has been captured in the triple helix concept (Leydesdorff and Etzkowitz, 1996) which serves to depict the influence each has over the other. Research funders have been keen to target their limited resources towards high-impact research. Increasingly, this has been directed towards very large-scale problems, demanding inter-disciplinary and international collaboration. The very nature of this research has brought increased demands on libraries, in terms of both the spread of collection development and the need to provide access to their immediate clients' collaborators elsewhere, and to help researchers navigate the information landscape of adjacent disciplinary domains.

Research funders have also introduced policies which have brought fresh demands upon researchers, and two of those have had profound impacts upon many libraries and their place in the scholarly publishing arena. The first has been the assessment of research quality, as seen in the British Research Assessment Exercise and the Excellence in Research for Australia initiative. The second has been the growth in mandates from research funders and governments recognising the importance of easy access to the data and publications arising from funded research.

Research assessment

In the UK the first Research Assessment Exercise (RAE) was conducted in 1986, and has been followed by a further six cycles, the most recent in 2008. In 2014, the RAE will be replaced by the new Research Excellence Framework (REF) intended to shape funding of research in universities, provide for benchmarking and impact assessment, and provide public accountability for the expenditure of public funds on academic research. Similar schemes now operate in a number of countries, including the Performance Based Research Fund (PBRF) in New Zealand and the Excellence in Research for Australia (ERA) scheme which commenced in 2010.

The Australian scheme endeavours to be comprehensive in its approach – all researchers employed on a given census date are eligible for assessment, and all of their publications in a six-year window are to be notified for this purpose. In the 2010 exercise, the Australian Research Council (ARC), which oversaw ERA, produced ranked journal and conference lists, deployed a range of bibliometric indicators and conducted peer review of a number of publications, especially those in the humanities and social sciences.

Although I have worked in university libraries during cycles of each of the RAE, PBRF and ERA, my most recent experience is with the Australian scheme, and it is used as a reference point for the impact on scholarly publishing and library provision in support of research. It is worth noting that there has been close contact between the agencies responsible for the Australian ERA and the new British REF. Experiences from Australia may therefore have particular relevance to those preparing for the REF in the UK.

At its simplest level, ERA was conducted on the basis of reviewing the research work of staff employed in Australian universities (and some other agencies) on a particular census date – for the 2010 exercise the census date was 31 March 2009. A range of factors were taken into account – research income, academic esteem and research outputs. It is in the area of research outputs that libraries felt the greatest impact, and which will be reviewed here. Those interested in the broader conduct of ERA will find relevant documents on the ARC website (www.arc.gov.au/era/era_2010/era_2010.htm). For the purpose of reviewing research outputs, all publications by researchers employed on the census date and published during the six-year period ending on 31 December 2008 had to be notified to the ARC. This reporting requirement applied to publications irrespective of the institution in which the research had been conducted.

The ARC procedures for assessing publications fell into two categories: most fields in the sciences were reviewed in part using citation metrics; in the humanities and social sciences there was a greater reliance upon peer review. A number of disciplinary panels, comprising Australian and international reviewers, were established to oversee the assessment and allocation of ratings to each field of research for each institution. There were minimum publication thresholds which meant that the number of research areas considered in each institution varied.

The impact on libraries was two-fold – helping to identify and gather publications for reporting, and advising on the metrics profile for different disciplines in their institution. In the largest research intensive universities in particular, the process of identifying all relevant publications was a mammoth undertaking, and the deficiencies of searching proprietary bibliographic databases by institutional affiliation became readily apparent. Instead, much work depended upon contact with individual researchers, especially those who had joined the institution during the six-year window and whose publications from previous institutions had to be identified and recorded, and where likely to be offered for peer review, copies of the publication obtained.

The ARC required that around 20 per cent of outputs in each field of research subject to peer review be made available for assessment. Where possible, publications were to be placed in an institutional repository, and libraries were allocated government funding to allow for the creation of suitable repositories. The government relied upon provisions under the Copyright Act to allow universities to make and deposit copies in a 'dark archive', accessible only to ARC reviewers. Whilst the primary focus was on deploying repositories to support ERA, the government indicated that it saw this activity as providing the infrastructure to support a wider move towards open access through institutional repositories.

One of the most controversial features of ERA 2010 was the creation of a *ranked* list of peer-reviewed journals. In excess of 20 000 titles were included on the list, with each being allocated to up to three disciplinary codes, and a rating on a four-point scale (A*, A, B or C). Although the list had been developed in consultation with learned academies and disciplinary bodies, the ranking of each journal, intended to represent the overall quality of the journal, provoked considerable debate and seemed set to shape academics' publishing behaviours quite markedly. However, partly in response to criticism from the research community, the government announced that for future ERA rounds, the ranking element would be removed from the list.

Another, perhaps unintended, consequence of the journal list was the allocation of up to three disciplinary codes against each journal title [the coding system was the ANZ Fields of Research (FoR) scheme]. Publications are assessed at a disciplinary level, and the allocation into these groupings is pre-determined by the FoR code. In fields where assessment is based upon citation counts, there may be some scope for marginal gains to be made by seeking to publish multidisciplinary articles in journals where average citation counts are lower. For example, an article on the quality of research in genetics might better be served by being published in an information science journal than in a genetics title.

Open access and public access

One response by sections of the academic and library communities to the 'crisis' in scholarly journal publishing has been the evolution of open access forms of dissemination. The open access movement has emerged from the belief that the products of publicly funded research should be freely available, and the opportunities afforded by the Internet for such access to be made possible. Broadly, open access is achieved through one of two routes: articles are published in open access journals, or they are deposited in research repositories, freely accessible stores of articles maintained by universities or on behalf of disciplinary groups.

As noted above, research funders and universities have increasingly introduced expectations – and in some cases mandates (http://roarmap.eprints.org/) – that data and research results from the work they fund should be made publicly accessible. Numerous studies have pointed to the gaps between those who are able to access subscription content and those who are able to access freely available content. It is worth noting that the gap has for some been widened by the shift from print journals to electronic access which is typically restricted to those with login credentials. Members of the public could, in some cases, visit university libraries to consult print collections held on open shelves, although libraries, especially in the UK, have restricted entry to those with university identity cards. It should be noted that publishers have generally allowed libraries to provide 'walk-in' access through which anyone can view electronic resources on computers inside the library's premises. Some libraries have not taken advantage of this, either due to limited facilities or institutional policy towards authentication.

One of the most prominent examples of a funder mandate is that of the National Institutes of Health, which in a 2008 appropriations bill secured the following:

> The Director of the National Institutes of Health shall require that all investigators funded by the NIH submit or have submitted for them to the National Library of Medicine's PubMed Central an electronic version of their final, peer-reviewed manuscripts upon acceptance for publication, to be made publicly available no later than 12 months after the official date of publication.

We can distinguish between expanding access to support active researchers and those who require research results in the course of their employment, including policy-makers and professionals such as engineers and doctors, which we shall describe as open access, and that intended to reach a wider audience, for example interested citizens, patients and students, which can be referred to as public access. The mechanisms for satisfying the needs of both categories can be the same: a research output or report (subject to copyright provisions) can be made accessible through one of the open access channels mentioned above. However, the need for research to be made understandable to the lay reader is becoming increasingly important. The *Patients Participate!* Project, funded by the JISC, UK, is one example of an approach to overcoming barriers to understanding. The project recommended the publication of lay summaries for articles included in the UK PubMed Central archive, and noted the role that social media can play in the wider dissemination of research outside the traditional scholarly community.

Open access journals are very similar in form to paid-for titles: articles are frequently brought together into issues, are subject to peer review, have ISSNs, are indexed in citation and bibliographic databases, and are seen as a core element of the scholarly communication landscape. They are predominantly made available online, although some offer a print version, but the key distinction is that they are freely accessible at the point of readership. The Directory of Open Access Journals (www.doaj.org) lists, at the time of writing, considerably more than 7000 journal titles, subject to peer review or editorial quality control. The Web of Science, one of the leading citation indexing databases, published by Thomson Reuters, indexes around 500 open access journals, allowing them to attract impact factors which in turn can serve to attract a higher selection of better quality articles.

Whilst many open access journals have adopted an article rate, acceptance policy and publication pattern similar to subscription titles, some have adopted a more transformative approach. The Public Library of Science (PLoS), for example, makes publication decisions in its *PLoS One* title on the basis of the technical soundness of an article, allowing it to accept and publish a higher quantity of items than conventional journals. After verification of a paper's soundness, articles are published and exposed for wider discussion by the broader scientific community. *PLoS One* published 6800 articles during 2010.

Although early open access journal initiatives frequently came from the not-for-profit arena, commercial publishers have become increasingly active in the production of open access journals, either as standalone titles, or in association with learned societies whose subscription titles are produced by the same publisher.

Naturally, open access journals cannot exist without any income to support the costs of editorial work, page preparation, technology platforms and other expenses. In many cases, in the absence of readers' subscription revenues, journals turn to authors to cover the costs through the payment of a publication fee. Fees vary, not only between publishers, but across journals in the same portfolio. In 2011, for example, an article in *PLoS One* will attract an author fee of \$1350, whilst *PLoS Biology* and *PLoS Medicine* can command \$2900 per article. Springer, one of the most active commercial publishers in the open access field, charges article processing fees ranging from $680 to $1695, with discounts and waivers for those authors whose institutions are members of SpringerOpen. Waivers are also granted to authors from many low-income countries.

Libraries have seen involvement in the open access journal space, both through promoting readership and in advising authors. Many have chosen to harvest records from The Directory of Open Access Journals for addition to local catalogues and search engines, seeking to ensure that open journal content is as prominent as subscription material. They have also sought to raise awareness of open access journals amongst their clients, highlighting the growing impact factors and academic standing of many titles. This has been particularly evident when reaching out to authors who will be bound by open access mandates imposed by research funders.

An alternative approach to open access is the deposit of publications in an institutional or disciplinary repository. In this situation, a variant of a publication from a subscription journal may be made freely available, typically based upon permission granted by a publisher. This permission may provide for the author's manuscript to be deposited in a repository, before or in some cases after peer review. Publishers' policies are helpfully collated by the RoMEO service (http://www.sherpa.ac.uk/romeo/). The RoMEO service developed a colour-coding system to categorise publishers, indicating which archiving policy was adopted: for example, green indicated that a publisher permitted deposit of articles both before and after peer review, and in some cases the publisher's version.

Another adoption of colour coding, independent of RoMEO, has been that of gold open access, used to signify an article or journal that allows full open access to the published version. This may refer to open access journals, described above, but also to articles published in subscription journals, but for which the author or their institution or funder has paid an open access fee. Wiley's Online Open and Taylor and Francis's iOpenAccess are examples of this approach.

The management of an institutional repository typically rests with a University Library. Platforms such as DSpace, Fedora and Fez provide the architecture for the organisation and management of the repository and its front end. Repositories are also harvested by search services such as Google and OAIster, providing an additional layer of discoverability. Many libraries have received special funding to establish or enhance their institutional repositories, for example through the ASHER scheme in Australia. The long-term costs and sustainability of institutional repositories is of concern, although as they become established as part of an institution's enterprise system architecture, they will be seen as deserving of continued support. At The University of Queensland, for example, the institutional repository, UQ eSpace (http://espace.library.uq.edu.au/), which is ranked amongst the top ten world repositories,[4] served not only as an archive of publications deposited by academic staff, but also as the university system for the deposit of PhD thesis manuscripts for assessment. It also housed bibliographic information about all academic publications (even if the full publication was not present) for the purpose of annual returns to the government, and for the ERA research assessment exercise referred to above.

Many universities are now looking also to deploy their institutional repositories as part of their approach to data curation. Research funders and institutions have recognised that access to research data is increasingly important, and as with research outputs, many are requiring researchers to make data sets arising from research available for access by other members of the research community. The library is a natural participant in the process of data curation. Whilst many data sets require specialist storage, beyond the capacity of many repositories, librarians are able to argue effectively that their professional skills lie firmly in the curation space. They can advise on storage and access mechanisms, and many have used repositories as data registers or catalogues.

Where next? Discovery and the role of libraries

Studies have shown that researchers have turned almost exclusively to large search engines and portals such as Google and PubMed Central to discover journal content, bypassing conventional tools such as abstracting and indexing services, and ignoring, to a large extent, publishers' own platforms (Nicholas *et al.*, 2011). Many libraries have felt increasingly isolated from information discovery by their core client groups, and have adopted numerous responses. Some have chosen to support the move to Google, exposing details of their licensed journal subscriptions to allow direct linking to licensed articles. Others have chosen to implement an aggregator search system such as Summon from Serials Solutions and Primo from Ex Libris, allowing for the easy discovery of book chapters and journal articles, and easy links to online full text where available. Community initiatives have also been announced, such as the eCollections service developed by JISC in the UK (www.jiscecollections.ac.uk).

These developments all serve to support greater end-user access to scholarly content, and reinforce a common observation that academic readers are seeking an interface that promotes the most straightforward access to the highest quality content. Whilst librarians on occasion take issue with the inadequacies of 'popular' tools such as Google, they have failed to deliver large-scale services that integrate seamlessly into the academic workflow. Those who work with – rather than against – new players are most likely to remain visible and viable partners in the research process.

Some libraries have sought to embrace Web 2.0 technologies, building services either in the hope of new forms of client engagement or as proof of concept. At this stage, there is little evidence to support widespread adoption by researchers (Research Information Network, 2010b).

Competition is not exclusively found in the discovery space, but also in the domain of information sharing and delivery. Services such as Mendeley, PubGet and DeepDyve are all offering low-cost, and often free, alternatives to academic libraries. Publishers and societies are launching mobile device apps, often with value-added content to supplement traditional content. And publishers are experimenting with new forms of journal articles, recognising that technology can offer much richer reader experiences than a PDF surrogate of a traditional printed article. All of these offer the potential for great advances in information delivery, and libraries must look to these if they are to develop sustainable service models.

In many areas mentioned above, for example in data curation, but also in the information landscape more broadly, there is a growing disconnect between librarians and researchers. Reports by the Research Information Network (2006, 2007) have shown that many researchers do not appreciate the skills that librarians can bring to the research process. Conversely, many librarians feel isolated and removed from their researcher clients. As researchers have moved online for almost all of their information needs, their presence in the library has declined greatly.

This must be of some concern to all concerned with scholarly publishing and communication. The tools and technologies of the digital age offer unprecedented opportunities to enhance research. But the advances they bring add a layer of complexity to the environment. Librarians have the skills and knowledge to help navigate this arena most effectively, but to do so, they need to leave the library and enter the laboratory, common room and clinic. Such a move will allow libraries to take their traditional role – set out at the beginning of this chapter – and transform it truly for the digital age. The many who have done so already can point to new relationships and great successes, and to a vibrant future at the core of research.

Notes

1. In the UK, print materials are zero-rated for VAT, but electronic publications are taxed at the full rate.
2. Elements of this section are drawn from Webster (2008, 2010).
3. Outsell Consultants, Australian Go8 libraries cost-benefit study. Further details and a summary presentation are available at http://www.caul.edu.au/caul-programs/best-practice
4. Ranking of World Repositories, July 2011, http://repositories.webometrics.info/toprep_inst.asp

References

Allen, M., Ward, S.M., Wray, T. and Debus-Lopez, K. (2003) Collection Development Based on Patron Requests: Collaboration between Interlibrary Loan and Acquisition. *Libraries Research Publications*, Paper 37. http://docs.lib.purdue.edu/lib_research/37

ARL (Association of Research Libraries) (2009) *ARL statement to scholarly publishers on the global economic crisis.* http://www.arl.org/bm~doc/economic-statement-2009.pdf

Blake, M. (1986) Journal cancellations in university libraries. *The Serials Librarian*, 10(4): 73–80.

British Academy (2005) *E-resources for research in the humanities and social sciences*. London: British Academy.

CIBER (2009) *The economic downturn and libraries: survey findings*. London: UCL.

Collection Development Executive Committee (2010) *Report of the Collection Development Executive Committee Task Force on Print Collection Usage.* Ithaca, NY: Cornell University Library.

Follett Report (1993) *Joint Funding Council's Libraries Review Group Report.* Bristol: HEFCE.

HEFCE (1998) *Evaluation of the UK Pilot Site Licence Initiative – Phase II.* Bristol: HEFCE.

ICOLC (International Coalition of Library Consortia) (2009) *Statement on the Global Economic Crisis and Its Impact on Consortial Licenses.* http://www.library.yale.edu/consortia/icolc-econcrisis-0109.htm

Lewis, D.W. (2007) A strategy for academic libraries in the first quarter of the 21st century. *College & Research Libraries* 68(5): 418–34.

Leydesdorff, L. and Etzkowitz, H. (1996) Emergence of a triple helix of university-industry-government relations. *Science and Public Policy* 23: 279–86.

Martyn, J. (1987) *Literature Searching Habits and Attitudes of Research Scientists*. London: BLRD.

Nicholas, D., Rowlands, I. and Williams, P. (2011) E-journals, researchers – and the new librarians. *Learned Publishing*, 24(1): 15–27.

Research Information Network (2006) *Researchers and Discovery Services: Behaviour, Perceptions and Needs*. London: RIN.

Research Information Network (2007) *Researchers' Use of Academic Libraries and Their Services*. London: RIN.

Research Information Network (2010a) *Challenges for Academic Libraries in Difficult Economic Times*. London: RIN.

Research Information Network (2010b) *If You Build It, Will They Come? How Researchers Perceive and Use Web 2.0*. London: RIN.

University Grants Committee (1967) *Report of the Committee on Libraries* [The Parry Report]. London: HMSO.

Webster, K. (2008) The research library as learning space: new opportunities for campus development. In: *Learning Spaces in Higher Education: Positive Outcomes by Design*. http://www.uq.edu.au/nextgenerationlearningspace/proceedings

Webster, K. (2010) The library space as learning space. *EDUCAUSE Review*, 45(6): 10–11.

Publishing ethics and integrity

Elizabeth Wager

Abstract: Publishers should be concerned about ethics because they carry important responsibilities (shared with editors, authors and reviewers) for the integrity of their publications and because they are professionals. Companies and individuals with long-standing experience of publishing are well placed to develop policies and advise less experienced editors on best practice. Being ethical can also make good business sense, as good policies can prevent serious problems and costly litigation. Successful scholarly publishing involves a skilful juggling act of creating an environment that respects editorial independence yet guards against editorial indiscretion or malpractice, and developing a business strategy that generates both income and a high-quality, well-respected publication. Therefore publishers need a good understanding of both publication and business ethics.

Key words: Ethics, misconduct, integrity, editors, editorial independence, plagiarism.

Introduction: why should publishers be concerned about ethics?

Scholarly publications are influential because they can affect decisions with important consequences for individuals and society. For example, papers in medical journals may influence doctors' decisions about how to treat individual patients or health policy decisions affecting society at large. If the published reports of medical research are unreliable or unclear, patients and society may be hurt. Perhaps because of this, medical publishing has often taken a lead in discussing ethical issues and setting standards, but there is no reason to think that other fields are immune from ethical problems. Publications in disciplines such as engineering, environmental science and agriculture can have important implications for society. Therefore, those who produce scholarly publications, i.e. publishers, carry ethical responsibilities for the integrity of their publications which they share with other players such as editors, peer reviewers and authors.

Peer-reviewed publications can also affect the lives of academics because they are used to measure the productivity of individual researchers and entire departments. Academic appointments and careers therefore depend heavily on publication records. Those who act as editors or reviewers of scholarly journals therefore wield considerable power as they can influence what gets published. Peer review systems should therefore be as fair as possible and designed to minimise bias and ensure consistent treatment for all authors; publishers can play an important role in ensuring that they are.

Another reason why publishers should be concerned about ethics is because they are professionals. Many of the other key players in peer-reviewed publications, whatever their skills or expertise, will be volunteers or amateurs (i.e. not doing this role as their main occupation and very often doing it without any formal training). Most academic editors take on this role on top of other academic commitments and without any specific training. It often therefore falls to the full-time, professional publishing staff to advise on policies and practices and to assist editors when faced with ethical issues.

Because cases of serious misconduct, such as data fabrication, occur infrequently, few academic editors will have experience of handling these issues more than once in their editorial career. However, companies with long-standing experience of publishing are well placed to develop policies and advise editors on best practice on the basis of this experience.

Lastly, following ethical guidelines can make good business sense, as having good policies can prevent many of the costly and time-consuming problems that can arise in scholarly publishing, or make them easier to resolve, and, in extreme cases, may reduce the risk of litigation.

What can go wrong if scholarly publishing is unethical?

Publication ethics is concerned with various types of misconduct and unethical behaviour committed by authors, editors, reviewers and publishers. The worst forms of publication misconduct committed by authors are generally held to be data fabrication, data falsification and major plagiarism (sometimes termed FFP). Other forms of misconduct or questionable practices by authors include failure to disclose conflicts of interest and misleading authorship. Journal editors and peer reviewers may also abuse their positions and commit misconduct, for example by attempting to suppress or delay the work of rivals or inappropriately promoting or publishing their own work or that of their friends or families.

The publication of unreliable (or fraudulent) data can have adverse consequences for researchers, funders and others, such as doctors, who base decisions on the research. It may even pose a risk to members of the public. For example, Potti *et al.* (2006) described a technique for predicting patients' responses to different types of chemotherapy. This technique was used in a clinical trial to determine which treatment cancer patients received. However, while the trial was underway, the research was shown to be unreliable and the trial was stopped (Baggerly and Coombes, 2009). The publication was later retracted (after the work was shown to be fraudulent) but its use as the basis for a clinical trial probably resulted in patients receiving suboptimal treatments, which may have reduced their chances of survival.

Although it is rare to be able to demonstrate serious harm caused directly by a single publication, there is considerable evidence that biases in the published literature can undermine decision-making. For example, national or institutional decisions about which treatment to prescribe for a particular condition are generally based on systematic reviews of the medical literature. If a manufacturer does not publish the less favourable studies of its drug, or suppresses those that suggest harmful effects, the evidence will be incomplete and therefore unreliable. The evidence may be further skewed if manufacturers repeatedly publish positive findings without making it clear that they are presenting the same data several times. Several studies have shown that such publication bias is common and, if undetected, can undermine medical decision-making (Tramèr *et al.*, 1997; Melander *et al.*, 2003; Chan *et al.*, 2004).

Improper behaviour by reviewers can harm other researchers, especially if it goes undetected. In the 1980s, scientists working for Cistron, a US biotechnology company, sequenced the gene for interleukin-1 and submitted the results to *Nature*. Their paper was reviewed by a scientist working for Immunex, a rival company, who recommended rejection. The paper was therefore rejected by *Nature* and submitted to the *Proceedings of the National Academy of Sciences* (*PNAS*) which accepted it. Meanwhile, both companies filed a patent for the gene sequence.

However, the sequence filed by Immunex contained seven errors that had appeared only in the manuscript submitted to *Nature*, and not in the final paper published in *PNAS*, strongly implicating the peer reviewer in stealing the sequence. After a lengthy legal battle, Immunex agreed to pay $21 million to Cistron in an out-of-court settlement (Rennie, 2003). While such extreme misconduct is probably rare, many academics believe their work has been held back by rivals during the peer review process, or their ideas have been stolen.

Ethical issues may have legal implications for journals and therefore for their publishers. If peer review and publication are not handled appropriately there is a risk that the publisher may be sued. In 2006, an authorship dispute that was inappropriately handled by the *British Journal of Obstetrics & Gynaecology* caused the journal to be named in a US court case costing the publisher considerable amounts in legal fees and expenses (Anon., 2006).

What can publishers do to prevent, detect and respond to research and publication misconduct?

Because scholarly journals provide a permanent record of research findings and these findings can influence important decisions affecting individuals and society, publishers and editors have a duty to ensure the integrity of everything they publish. This means they should endeavour to prevent and detect research and publication misconduct such as data fabrication and plagiarism. As prevention is not always possible, and honest errors may also occur, editors and publishers should also have systems in place to minimise the harm caused by the publication of fraudulent or unreliable work.

Journal policies and instructions to contributors may encourage good practice and discourage misconduct. Many journals publish their policies on ethical issues such as plagiarism and authorship in the hope of educating and guiding authors. Journal policies can also have a direct influence on researchers' behaviour. For example, many commentators have expressed concern about the non-publication of negative studies, redundant publication of positive findings and misleading reporting of trial designs and suggested these problems could be reduced if clinical trials were registered at inception. The first proposal for a public trial register was made by Simes (1986) but widespread registration did not occur until the International Committee of Medical Journal Editors announced in 2004 that their journals would not publish findings from clinical trials unless they had been registered (De Angelis *et al.*, 2004). The influence of the journals' policies was clearly shown by the marked rise in registrations around the cut-off date for registering studies that had started before the policy was announced (Zarin *et al.*, 2005).

Journals may actively screen for some forms of publication misconduct. Text-matching software can be used to detect plagiarism and duplicate publication. The usefulness of this technology for scholarly publishing has been greatly enhanced by the CrossCheck initiative which, using the iThenticate® system from iParadigms, enables text to be compared against a large database of academic publications that would not be included in a simple search (such as one using Google™), which is limited to searching for text on publicly available websites and therefore cannot 'see' text from journals that is behind access barriers (http://www.crossref.org/crosscheck/index.html). The creation of the CrossCheck database by CrossRef was only possible due to cooperation between publishers and it works because those that use the system to check submissions also contribute their publications to the database. As well as detecting cases of plagiarism and redundancy before publication, publicising journal screening policies may act as a deterrent (Kleinert, 2011).

Software can also be utilised to detect inappropriately manipulated (i.e. falsified) images. These techniques were pioneered by the *Journal of Cell Biology* (*JCB*) and have been adopted by journals in other disciplines (Rossner and Yamada, 2004). As with other forms of misconduct, routine screening revealed that inappropriate manipulation of images was more common than many editors had imagined, occurring in about 1 per cent of submissions to the *JCB* (Rossner, 2006).

Publishers need to understand methods for preventing and detecting misconduct so that they can advise editors on their use, establish appropriate policies and take decisions about what tools to fund.

Despite editors' and publishers' best efforts, and despite the most stringent peer-review systems, fraudulent or unreliable work will occasionally get published. Therefore, journals need policies for issuing corrections and retractions; these policies will often be guided by the publisher. Journals not only have responsibilities to their readers (to ensure the quality and integrity of what they publish) but also to their authors. Retracting a published article can affect the reputation and career of the author so it is important that retractions are handled fairly and consistently. Following research suggesting that journals' retraction practices were not consistent, and showing that retractions were not always clearly indicated to readers and sometimes failed to distinguish the reasons for the retraction (e.g. whether they were due to misconduct or honest error) (Wager and Williams, 2011), COPE (the Committee on Publication Ethics) produced guidelines on this topic to assist editors and publishers (Wager *et al.*, 2009).

Despite publishers' best efforts, several studies have shown that retracted articles do not disappear but continue to be cited and may therefore continue to mislead (Budd *et al.*, 1998; Steen, 2011). Even when articles are sound they usually undergo various revisions so readers may be confused to find several versions on the Internet, for example on an institutional repository, a pre-print server and a journal website. A new initiative which may help to address these problems is CrossMark (http://www.crossreforg/crossmark/index.html) which will allow publishers to identify the current version of a publication and provide information about its status (e.g. if an article has been corrected or retracted). According to the CrossMark website this is designed to 'Highlight that the scholarly publisher is responsible for both the initial certification of a publication, as well as the ongoing stewardship of said certified publication'. CrossMark builds on CrossRef's application of the DOI (Digital Object Identifier) system, which creates permanent links to online content. It was launched in Spring 2012 and is already being used by several major publishers.

When allegations or suspicions of misconduct arise, journals usually need to liaise with authors' or reviewers' institutions. It is helpful to have policies for handling such allegations and for responding to institutions and research integrity organisations (such as the Office for Research Integrity or the Office of the Inspector General of the National Science Foundation in the US). Again, because these are relatively rare occurrences, publishers can play an important role in setting policies and advising editors on how to handle cases.

How should editors and publishers respond to allegations or suspicions of fraud and misconduct?

Research and publication misconduct, such as data fabrication and plagiarism, often surface at submission or after publication. Therefore editors and publishers may find themselves having to handle suspicions of misconduct (e.g. reviewers saying that findings are 'too good to be true') or allegations of misconduct (e.g. from alert readers or aggrieved researchers). When the concerns relate to published material, there is a clear responsibility to address the issues and, if necessary, correct the record. When they relate to submitted material it may be tempting simply to reject the submission and pass the problem onto somebody else, but the COPE Code of Conduct advises against this (COPE, 2011a).

COPE publishes a series of flowcharts which set out recommended steps for handling most types of misconduct (http://publicationethics.org/resources/flowcharts). In most cases, they recommend that those accused or suspected of misconduct should be contacted, in neutral terms, asking for an explanation. If this proves unsatisfactory, or no response is received, the case should be investigated further. In some cases, such as plagiarism or image manipulation, the available evidence (e.g. from text-matching software) may be sufficient to determine clearly that misconduct has occurred (but it is still important to let the accused give their account, as first appearances can be misleading). However, in other cases, such as data falsification or disputed authorship, it will be necessary to refer the case to the institution where the research was done. In such cases, publishers and editors should not be expected to act as adjudicators or to conduct their own investigation. However, trying to contact research institutions and instigate an appropriate investigation may be challenging as shown by cases presented to COPE (Wager, 2011).

Publishers can support editors in responding to possible misconduct by offering advice, including legal advice, and administrative support (as getting responses can be time-consuming). While editors should be encouraged to take misconduct seriously, publishers may also need to advise editors not to attempt to investigate or resolve contentious cases by themselves. However well-intentioned they may be, editors (often in a different country or even continent) should not attempt to investigate or arbitrate on most types of serious research misconduct but should focus their energies on ensuring that an appropriate investigation is performed and then acting on the outcome. On the other hand, editors may sometimes need to be protected against bullying and unreasonable behaviour by aggrieved or campaigning parties, who may demand retractions and threaten legal action. In each case, working closely with a knowledgeable and helpful publisher can not only make the editor's life easier but is also likely to ensure that a good outcome is reached and further problems, such as litigation, are avoided.

What role should publishers play in setting journal policies?

Publishers can play an important role in ensuring their journals have sound policies and that these policies are put into practice. The relative contributions of publishers, editors and journal owners (e.g. academic societies) to developing such policies varies and probably depends on the history of the journal, the relations between the parties and the degree of individual (or corporate) interest in ethical issues. As publishers normally have more experience of running journals than individual editors, they are well placed to offer advice or propose policy templates. Policies should be revised in the wake of problems, and publishers can ensure that experience gained at one journal is shared with others. While detailed instructions to authors may vary for each journal, many publishers set common ethical policies for all their journals and may provide resources for editors, authors and reviewers to explain and elaborate on these. Examples of some publishers' ethical policies and resources are shown in Table 14.1.

One area in which publishers' policies should provide guidance is the handling and disclosure of competing interests. Most individuals, and especially academic researchers, like to think they are totally objective and therefore uninfluenced by financial or other factors. However, it is important to realise that editors, reviewers, authors and publishers may be subject to competing interests. WAME (the World Association of Medical Editors) notes that: 'Conflict of interest (COI) exists when there is a divergence between an individual's private interests (competing interests) and his or her responsibilities to scientific and publishing activities such that a reasonable observer might wonder if the individual's behaviour or judgment was motivated by considerations of his or her competing interests.' (WAME, 2011a). This definition is helpful because it stresses that conflicts relate to what 'a reasonable observer' might think rather than whether an editor or author believes their actions have actually been affected. In other words, conflict (like beauty) lies 'in the eye of the beholder'. The WAME statement goes on to note: 'Everyone has COIs of some sort. Having a competing interest does not, in itself, imply wrongdoing. However, it constitutes a problem when competing interests could unduly influence one's responsibilities in the publication process (or be reasonably seen to do so).'

To retain confidence in the peer review process, it is important that conflicts of interest are correctly handled. Publishers should work with

Table 14.1 Ethical policies and resources of some publishers

Company/society	Document/resource	URL
American Chemical Society	ACS Ethical Guidelines	http://pubs.acs.org/page/policy/ethics/index.html
American Physiological Society	Ethical Policies and Procedures	http://www.the-aps.org/publications/authorinfo/index.htm (available in English, Chinese, Dutch, French, German, Greek, Japanese, Portuguese, Russian, Spanish and Turkish)
American Society of Plant Biologists	ASPB Ethics in Publishing	http://www.aspb.org/publications/ethics.cfm
BMJ Group	Policies	http://resources.bmj.com/bmj/about-bmj/policies
Elsevier	Publishing ethics resource kit (PERK)	http://www.elsevier.com/wps/find/editorshome.editors/Introduction
Nature Publishing Group	Publication ethics policies	http://www.nature.com/authors/policies/publication.html
Royal Society	Publishing ethics	http://royalsocietypublishing.org/site/authors/policy.xhtml
Springer	Policy on Publishing Integrity	http://www.springer.com/authors/journal+authors?SGWID=0-154202-12-601001-0
Taylor & Francis	Ethical guidelines to publication of scientific research	http://www.tandf.co.uk/journals/pdf/announcements/tmph_guidelines06.pdf
Wiley-Blackwell	Best practice guidelines on publication ethics	http://www.wiley.com/bw/publicationethics/

editors to decide which conflicts of interest are either so serious or so easily avoidable that they should be prevented and which are less serious, or unavoidable, but must be disclosed. For example, editorial board members should never be involved in decisions concerning their own research papers, nor should they handle papers from close colleagues or family members, so journals need to have systems in place to prevent this. However, editors are usually also researchers, so they are likely to be receiving funding for their research (or to have received this in the past) and this may create conflicts of interest. If editors have strong links to a company or organisation which might be affected by a publication, then they should ensure such papers are handled by another editor without such interests. In 2009, the editor of an orthopaedic journal was heavily criticised in the media for failing to disclose that he had received over $20 million in royalties from a medical device company (Fauber, 2011). Some commentators suggested that he should not be a journal editor given his close ties to one company (Lenzer, 2010). Indeed, the Association for Medical Ethics (2011) recommends that editorial board members should not have 'substantive financial interests' in a commercial company (which they define as receiving more than $50 000 in personal compensation).

While having good policies is clearly important, making sure they can be, and are, followed is even more so and this may also depend on publishers. Not only should publishers show leadership in setting high standards for their journals, they will have to decide how much resource to invest in various processes. Actively screening manuscripts for problems such as plagiarised text or inappropriately manipulated images consumes time (usually of paid staff) and may require specialised tools, such as CrossCheck. Therefore, publishers should be involved in decisions about how and when to screen. Training of staff and editors, possibly even of authors and reviewers, may also be needed to ensure that ethical policies are implemented, so publishers should consider funding this. Holding annual meetings for editors from particular disciplines or regions may also provide opportunities for training and raising awareness of ethical issues.

Many publishers pay for their journals to belong to COPE (see www.publicationethics.org and specific documents referenced at the end of the chapter), which provides guidance on all aspects of publication ethics via its public website and advice on specific cases to members.

Another way of increasing compliance with policies is to do an audit. COPE makes audit guidelines available to its members and some publishers have used this for their journals.

While publishers can do much to promote and support initiatives aimed at making their publications ethical, they also need to realise the ethical responsibilities of their own roles. Many of these ethical duties are related to handling conflicts of interest and, in particular, in separating editorial from commercial decision-making as far as possible.

The relationship between publishers and journal editors

The COPE Code of Conduct for Editors notes that 'The relationship of editors to publishers and owners is often complex but should be based firmly on the principle of editorial independence.' It also states that 'Editors should make decisions on which articles to publish based on quality and suitability for the journal and without interference from the journal owner/publisher' and recommends that 'Editors should have a written contract(s) setting out their relationship with the journal's owner and/or publisher'. The COPE Code of Conduct for Publishers (2011b) reiterates this by stating that publishers should 'foster editorial independence'.

The World Association of Medical Editors (WAME, 2011b) notes that 'Owners (whether professional associations or for-profit companies) ... are ultimately responsible for all aspects of publishing the journal, including its staff, budget, and business policies.' However, 'Owners should not interfere in the evaluation, selection or editing of individual articles, either directly or by creating an environment in which editorial decisions are strongly influenced.' Indirect influences might include bonuses paid to editors linked to journal profitability.

Both COPE and WAME recognise that editorial independence is not absolute; for example, a publisher may legitimately refuse to publish something they consider libellous or likely to bring the publication into disrepute. As Richard Smith (former editor of the *BMJ*) has written 'editorial freedom ... cannot be total. I couldn't turn the *BMJ* into a soccer magazine because I'd got bored with medicine. Freedom must be accompanied by accountability.' (Smith, 2004).

The WAME Policy Statement notes that 'The limits of editorial freedom are difficult to define in the general case' and recognises that 'Owners have the right to hire and fire editors-in-chief'.

Smith (2004) also commented that 'everybody supports editorial independence in principle, although it sometimes feels to editors as if the deal is "you can have it so long as you don't use it".' He also quoted a similarly cynical interpretation (attributed to journalist Hannen Swaffer) that 'freedom of the press ... means freedom to print such of the proprietor's prejudices as the advertisers don't object to' (Swaffer, 2002).

For commercial publishers, potential conflicts of interest are most likely to arise from commercial aspects. They should therefore ensure that, as far as possible, activities such as selling advertising space or reprints are not allowed to influence editorial decisions. However, when journals are owned (or published) by academic societies, conflicts can also arise if the editor disagrees with a position taken by the society or wishes to publish something that is critical of the society. Several high-profile disputes between the owners and editors of prominent medical journals, which have resulted in editors being fired or resigning, involved this type of dispute. Commenting on one such well-publicised dismissal (of George Lundberg, editor of the *Journal of the American Medical Association*) two other former editors wrote 'there is an inherent friction between the society's journal editor and its executive officer. The mindset and mission of editors are frequently at odds with the understandable wish of the executive to control the society's affairs and realize as much income as possible for other activities.' (Fletcher and Fletcher, 1999). In a more recent case (in 2006), two senior editors of the *Canadian Medical Association Journal* were fired following a dispute over editorial freedom (Spurgeon, 2006).

Separating commercial and editorial decisions is not always straightforward. The WAME Policy Statement (2011b) reminds publishers that they need to avoid 'creating an environment in which editorial decisions are strongly influenced'. This might include considering how editors are paid or setting up systems to ensure that editors are unaware of any financial implications of publication. For example, if a journal charges authors a publication fee, but waives this for authors who cannot pay, then editorial decisions might be influenced if editors know which authors had requested a waiver. Similarly, reprint transactions (which can be highly lucrative for journals) should be handled separately from editorial discussions – although even if effective 'firewalls' are created, it may still be possible for editors to predict which articles are most likely to generate reprint sales (Lundh *et al.*, 2010).

Similarly, while the timing of publication should normally be a purely editorial decision, uninfluenced by the publisher, in some cases journals may agree to publish a study to coincide with a major meeting at which the results will be presented. Such timing is likely to increase media attention, which may be good for the journal, but may also benefit the study's sponsor, who may also buy reprints to distribute at the meeting. Publishers should endeavour to ensure that the initial editorial decision (i.e. whether or not to publish a particular article) is based solely on the study's importance and validity, and is not influenced by commercial considerations. However, being responsible for running the business side of the journal, it is reasonable for publishers to allow some coordination between editorial and sales departments after an article has been accepted. Likewise, if a journal offers a rapid publication service for a fee, the editor must be aware of which articles fall into this category (as rapid peer review will have to be organised). Because, in this case, it is impossible for the editor to be 'blinded' to the category of submission, it is particularly important that the editor does not have a direct interest (such as a bonus scheme or shareholding) in the journal's profitability in order to minimise bias in the publication decision.

Why being ethical makes commercial sense

Breaking ethical codes and conventions can have either short- or long-term effects on the commercial viability of a publication. The acute (i.e. short-term) problems, especially if they end up in court, receive most attention but occur less often, while insidious (i.e. long-term) problems are less dramatic, but may still cause the demise of a publication. Publishers need to remember that either scenario, be it a sudden, violent and unexpected blow, or a slow, lingering decline, may be fatal to the journal.

Avoiding expensive legal issues

Anything involving lawyers is likely to be expensive, so publishers should try to avoid any entanglement in legal cases. A single court case could bankrupt a small journal and, because they have more resources, it is usually the publisher, rather than the editor or author, who gets sued. Inappropriately handled authorship disputes have landed journals into lengthy and expensive legal battles (Anon., 2006) and, especially in the UK, libel cases can also inflict huge financial damage. Having good policies and following best practice can protect publishers from such events.

Authors may threaten to take legal action if a journal retracts their work, so this needs especially careful handling. As retractions are (mercifully) rare, publishers should ensure they have clear and consistent policies for all their journals to enable editors to retract unreliable material and inform readers of the reason for the retraction while protecting authors from arbitrary or unreasonable retractions (COPE's guidelines on retractions may be useful to guide policy) (Wager *et al.*, 2009).

Sustaining a successful publication

Academic publishing relies, to a considerable extent, on trust, between authors, editors, reviewers and readers. The reputation of a publication depends on a number of factors, but can be damaged rapidly if this trust breaks down. Frank Davidoff, when editor of *Annals of Internal Medicine*, commenting on the firing of George Lundberg from *JAMA*, highlighted 'the pragmatic issue of how hard it is to build a journal, and how easy it is to destroy one' as well as the ethical questions about editorial freedom involved in this case (Davidoff, 1999). Richard Smith (former editor of the *BMJ)* also writing on the topic of editorial freedom, noted 'If readers once hear that important, relevant, and well argued articles are being suppressed or that articles are being published simply to fulfil hidden political agendas, then the credibility of the publication collapses—and everybody loses' and publishers need to remember that this 'everybody' includes them (Smith, 2004).

There is an essential tension built into scholarly and professional publishing as a business (which, to my mind, is one of its attractions and makes it so fascinating). Publishers want their publications to make money, whether for their company/shareholders or for their academic society. A publication that continually loses money will simply not survive. Yet, in order to thrive, publications need a reputation of high scholarly values, impartiality and independence. A publication that is considered biased or over-promotional will rapidly lose readers and authors. Editors and publishers must therefore ensure they have systems in place to deliver fair peer review, handle conflicts of interest, and keep commercial and editorial decisions separate. However, the publisher also has to try to make the business as profitable as possible while working within these constraints.

One complicating factor in academic publishing, unlike other businesses, is that the suppliers (i.e. the authors, editors and peer reviewers) are also, to a large extent, the purchasers (i.e. the readers and subscribers). If a publication loses trust among its authors/readers, they may stop sending their papers there, may cancel personal subscriptions or influence their institutions to stop subscribing, or may even refuse to act as reviewers or editors. Publishers therefore need to guard their journals' reputations fiercely. This will require not only appointing a good editor, and providing the resources needed to do a good job, but also ensuring that business matters do not undermine this work. However, the stereotyped image of editor and publisher described by Richard Smith as the 'pure editor concerned with science and quality and a grasping publisher bothered purely with revenue and profit' is, like most stereotypes, an over-simplification (Smith, 1999). Occasionally, publishers will have to protect their publications against editors who behave inappropriately whether through ignorance, negligence or malice. A biased or unfair editor will lose readers and authors just as rapidly as a publisher's inappropriate business tactic.

Academic publishing therefore involves a skilful juggling act of creating an environment that respects editorial independence yet guards against editorial indiscretion or malpractice, and a business strategy that generates both income and a high-quality, well-respected publication. Flouting principles, of either publication or business ethics, is therefore not a good long-term strategy.

Conclusions and outlook

Publishers need to appreciate the ethical implications of their work. In particular, those producing scholarly (peer-reviewed) publications that report research findings need to consider the responsibilities that this entails. Such responsibility is carried jointly by publishers and editors (and, to some extent also by authors and reviewers). The relationship between publishers and journal editors is, ideally, a close one and should be based on trust and respect, but nevertheless be formalised in a written contract defining the roles and responsibilities of the different parties. Publishers can play an important role in setting journals' policies and enabling these to be followed. They also have an important role in educating editors and providing guidance based on their more extensive experience.

Whether done by a commercial company or a learned society, publishing is usually undertaken as a business designed to make money or at least cover costs. Following ethical practices represents good business, as ethical breaches can damage confidence in publications and, on occasion, threaten the solvency of a journal or publishing company if disputes have to be resolved in court.

While some ethical issues have been present ever since researchers started to publish their work, developments in technology and changes in societal attitudes mean that new issues and challenges continue to emerge. Advances in detecting or preventing misconduct (such as the availability of software for text matching and image screening) offer opportunities to improve publishing practices. Publishers need to be alert to new developments and ensure their policies and practices are up to date and reflect current realities.

Sources of further information

Perhaps because their publications can have a direct effect on healthcare decisions, and may therefore, directly or indirectly, harm patients, many guidelines on ethics come from the editors and publishers of medical journals. Although some ethical considerations (such as the protection of participants in clinical trials) are not relevant to publishers working in other fields, much advice on general issues such as conflict of interest, authorship and editorial independence applies to all areas of academic publishing. Therefore, do not be put off by guidelines that appear to relate to medical journals even if you are working in another field.

COPE, Committee on Publication Ethics
www.publicationethics.org
An international not-for-profit organisation that advises editors and publishers on all aspects of publication ethics and covers all academic disciplines (although it was originally founded by medical editors). It has published a Code of Conduct for publishers as well as guidance and flowcharts on topics such as retractions and how to handle plagiarism, redundant publication, authorship disputes, reviewer misconduct, etc.

ICMJE, International Committee of Medical Journal Editors
www.icmje.org
An influential group of editors of major medical journals who have produced guidance on many aspects of publishing, notably authorship and dealing with the press. Their guidelines have been widely adopted by many journals, including some outside the medical field.

CSE, Council of Science Editors
www.councilscienceeditors.org
A US-based organisation of science editors (with members around the world). It has published thoughtful guidance, including a useful White Paper on Promoting Integrity in Scientific Journal Publications. (http://www.councilscienceeditors.org/i4a/pages/index.cfm?pageid=3313)

WAME, World Association of Medical Editors
www.wame.org
An international organisation of medical editors. It has published useful policy statements on many aspects of publication ethics.

References

Association for Medical Ethics (2011) Ethical rules of disclosure. http://www ethicaldoctororg/Ethical_Rules_of_Disclosure html, accessed 9 May 2011.

Anon. (2006) Statement of disputed authorship. *British Journal of Obstetrics & Gynaecology* 113: i.

Baggerly, K.A. and Coombes, K.R. (2009) Deriving chemosensitivity from cell lines: forensic bioinformatics and reproducible research in high-throughput biology. *Annals of Applied Statistics* 3: 1309–34.

Budd J.M., Sievert, M. and Schultz, T.R. (1998) Phenomena of retraction. Reasons for retraction and citations to the publications. *Journal of the American Medical Associoation* 280: 296–7.

Chan, A.-W., Hrobjartsson, A., Haahr, M.T., Gotzsche, P. and Altman, D.G. (2004) Empirical evidence for selective reporting of outcomes in randomized trials. *Journal of the American Medical Association* 291: 2457–65.

COPE (2011a) Code of conduct and best practice guidelines for journal editors. http://www publicationethics org/resources/guidelines, accessed 8 June 2011.

COPE (2011b) Code of Conduct for Journal Publishers. http://www. publicationethicsorg/files/CodeofconductforpublishersFINAL_1 pdf, accessed 8 June 2011.

Davidoff, F. (1999) The making and unmaking of a journal. *Annals of Internal Medicine* 130: 774–5.

De Angelis, C., Drazen, J.M., Frizelle, F.A., *et al.* (2004) Clinical trial registration: a statement from the International Committee of Medical Journal Editors. *Lancet* 364: 911–12.

Fauber, J. (2011) Journal editor gets royalties as articles favor devices. www.jsonline com/watchdog/watchdogreports/80036277html, accessed 9 May 2011.

Fletcher, S.W. and Fletcher, R.H. (1999) Medical editors, journal owners, and the sacking of George Lundberg. *Journal of General Internal Medicine* 14: 200–2.

Kleinert, S. (2011) Checking for plagiarism, duplicate publication, and text recycling. *Lancet* 377: 281–2.

Lenzer, J. (2010) Journal editor gets $20m in royalties and $2m in fees from device manufacturer. *British Medical Journal* 340: c495.

Lundh, A., Barbateskovic, M., Hrobjartsson, A. and Gotzsche, P. (2010) Conflicts of interest at medical journals: the influence of industry-supported randomised trials on journal impact factor and revenue – cohort study. *PLoS Medicine* 7(10): e1000354.

Melander, H., Ahlqvist-Rastad, J., Meijer, G. and Beermann, B. (2003) Evidence b(i)ased medicine – selective reporting from studies sponsored by pharmaceutical industry: review of studies in new drug applications. *British Medical Journal* 326: 1171–3.

Potti, A., Dressman, H.K., Bild, A., *et al.* (2006) Genomic signatures to guide the use of chemotherapeutics. *Nature Medicine* 12: 1294–300.

Rennie, D. (2003) 'Misconduct and journal peer review', in F. Godlee and T. Jefferson (eds). *Peer Review in Health Sciences*, 2nd edn. London: BMJ Books, pp. 118–29.

Rossner, M. (2006) How to guard against image fraud. *The Scientist* March: 24–25.

Rossner, M. and Yamada, K.M. (2004) What's in a picture? The temptation of image manipulation. *The Journal of Cell Biology* 166(1): 11–15.

Simes, R.J. (1986) Publication bias: the case for an international registry of clinical trials. *Journal of Clinical Oncology* 4: 1529–41.

Smith, R. (1999) Another editor bites the dust. *British Medical Journal* 319: 272.

Smith, R. (2004) Editor's Choice. *British Medical Journal* 329: doi:10.1136/bmj.329.7457.0-g.

Spurgeon, D. (2006) CMA draws criticism for sacking editors. *British Medical Journal* 332: 503.

Steen, R.G. (2011) Retractions in the medical literature: how many patients are put at risk by flawed research? *Journal of Medical Ethics* jme.2011.043133.

Swaffer, H. (2002) cited in *The Oxford Dictionary of Modern Quotations*, 2nd edn. Oxford: Oxford University Press, p. 312.

Tramèr, M.R., Reynolds, D.J.M., Moore, R.A. and McQuay H.J. (1997) Impact of covert duplicate publication on meta-analysis: a case study. *British Medical Journal* 315: 635–40.

Wager, E. (2011) Coping with scientific misconduct. *British Medical Journal* 343: d6586.

Wager, E., Barbour, V., Yentis, S., Kleinert, S. (2009) Retractions: guidance from the Committee on Publication Ethics (COPE). *Croatian Medical Journal* 50: 532–5.

Wager, E. and Williams, P. (2011) Why and how do journals retract articles? An analysis of Medline retractions 1988–2008. *Journal of Medical Ethics*.

WAME Policy Statement (2011a) Conflict of interest in peer-reviewed medical journals. http://www.wame.org/conflict-of-interest-in-peer-reviewed-medical-journals, accessed 22 May 2011.

WAME Policy Statement (2011b) The relationship between journal editors-in-chief and owners. http://www.wameorg/resources/policies#independence, accessed 8 June 2011.

Zarin, D.A., Tse, T. and Ide, N.C. (2005) Trial registration at ClinicalTrials.gov between May and October 2005. *New England Journal of Medicine* 335: 2779–87.

15

Legal aspects and copyright

Mark Seeley and Lois Wasoff

Abstract: This chapter reviews the fundamental relationship between copyright and publishing, including contracts and licences, piracy and enforcement, among other legal issues. Coverage of the management of rights in the digital age and the 'orphan works' question are discussed in depth, alongside publishing agreements, creative commons and other licensing arrangements.

Key words: Copyright, digitisation, orphan works, creative commons, licensing, publishing agreements, piracy, litigation.

Introduction

Publishing is a business of rights. Publishers obtain the legal right to distribute the materials they publish through copyright and contracts, and then use copyright and contracts to manage their relationships with those to whom those works are distributed. The legal principles that apply to copyright and contract are implicated at every step of the publishing process, from the moment a work is created through the time it is in the hands of the researcher, scholar, student, librarian or reader for whom it is intended.

Publishers acquire rights through publishing agreements with and copyright transfers from authors. Distribution of digital works is accomplished through contracts such as subscription access or licence agreements. Other sets of rights are provided, by contract, to local distributors, translators and services that authorise certain activities such as internal distribution or document delivery of individual journal articles.[1] Legal issues such as copyright, contracts and licences, and piracy and enforcement, are fundamental to the enterprise regardless of whether a publisher is a commercial or non-profit organisation. To maintain this business it is necessary to manage rights properly, including on occasion by enforcing rights when there is unauthorised harmful use being made. This chapter will discuss these issues.

There are other legal issues that are relevant and important to publishers, including trade regulation (involving sales into particular countries where there are trade sanctions, even though there are usually exceptions for published content) and other areas of compliance such as bribery protection, labour and employment concerns, and libel and defamation. The last area is often a concern for authors and editors as well as publishers, and has also intruded into considerations of publishing ethics notes and retractions.[2] Concerns have been expressed that libel cases could be used as a tool to interfere with legitimate scientific discussion and inquiry.[3] We will concentrate, however, on publishing agreements and copyright issues in this chapter. Please note that this chapter is by no means a substitute for experienced legal counsel and so it is strongly recommended that anyone looking to implement or analyse any ideas or concerns mentioned in this chapter further should consult with their own lawyers and attorneys with respect to these issues.

Copyright basics

Although publishing and publishers depend on it, there are a surprising number of common misconceptions about copyright in the publishing community. Because of that, a short review of some basic principles may be useful.

Scope of copyright protection

Copyright protects the rights of authors of original[4] works of authorship and of those to whom authors have licensed or assigned those rights. National laws define the included rights, but those laws are subject to some international norms created by treaties. So although there is no such thing as an 'international copyright' it is still possible to make some general statements about what rights and works are covered by copyright.

Copyright protection applies to both published and unpublished works. Although publishers would seem, at first glance, to be concerned only with the first category, the second is of concern as well. Published works often include quotations from or, in the case of images for example, entire copies of other works. Even if those included works were not previously published, they can be protected by a copyright owned by a third party, so their use can have copyright implications.

Copyrights can apply to creative works in various forms, formats and media. Books, articles, photographs and other images, audio-visual works and music, in analog, digital and any other format, can be protected by copyright. There are, however, types of works and aspects of copyrighted works that are *not* protected by copyright. Most importantly, copyright protects the particular *expression* of an idea but not the underlying idea itself. Facts and data are not protected by copyright, although the particular presentation of those facts and data (i.e. a journal article reporting on the results of a study) can and typically will be protected. But that presentation has to have some aspects of originality to it. The classic example of an entirely factual work that may not be eligible for copyright protection is a 'white pages' telephone list, where the work entirely comprises 'facts' (names and associated addresses and phone numbers) and there has been no originality or creativity associated with the selection, organisation or arrangement of those 'facts'.[5]

Copyright has a specified duration, tied in most instances to the life of the author plus a period of years (70 in the US and the UK; 50 in some other countries) or in some circumstances from the date of publication (95 years in both the US and the UK). Works for which the term of copyright has expired are in the 'public domain' and may be freely used by anyone. Works may also be in the public domain for reasons other than their date of creation or publication. Some works were created under circumstances that prevented copyright from being claimed (as is the case in the US for works created by the federal government), or have lost their copyright protection (as is the case for some works published in the US before 1 January 1978, when the US copyright law was changed to eliminate certain formalities that had been a prerequisite to copyright protection).[6]

Copyrights comprise a set of exclusive rights that are then subject to certain exceptions and limitations. The exclusive rights include:

- the right to control the copying and distribution (or communication) of the copyrighted work;
- the right to authorise the creation of works derived or adapted from the original work (e.g. creating a screenplay based on a novel, or a French translation of a work originally published in English); and
- the rights to publicly perform or display the work.

The individual rights covered by copyright are a 'bundle of rights' that can be licensed separately. So, for example, the copyright owner may license a publisher to distribute copies of a work in print and digital form, but may have the rights granted back to do certain kinds of distribution him/herself (for example, when a professor retains the right to post a copy of an article on his or her own website or in an institutional repository). An author may divide the granted rights geographically (permitting a book publisher to publish a novel only in the US and licensing another publisher to publish the work in the UK), and/or may permit the publisher to publish the text of the work, but retain the right to separately license adaptations or derivative works. It is also important to keep in mind that some jurisdictions (including Germany and France) limit by law the extent to which an author can transfer certain exclusive rights to a publisher or other distributor.[7]

Copyright exceptions and limitations

Exceptions or limitations to these exclusive rights are specified in the applicable national law. These exceptions vary from country to country, but must fall within the international norms that are contained in the relevant multi-lateral treaties. The most important of those treaties is the Berne Convention, which is administered by the World Intellectual Property Organization (WIPO). Berne is the oldest (it dates from 1886, although it has been amended many times since) and most widely accepted international treaty dealing with copyright and currently has more than 160 signatories.

The Berne Convention sets out a 'three-step test' (now incorporated into other important treaties and trade agreements) against which exceptions to the exclusive rights of copyright owners must be measured. Exceptions and limitations must relate to 'certain special cases', may not 'conflict with the normal exploitation of the work' and may not 'unreasonably prejudice the legitimate interests of the rights holder'.[8] The types of exceptions with which scholarly publishers will be most familiar are those that deal with certain educational and library uses. In many countries, including throughout the EU, the exceptions apply to specific circumstances and are designed to support public policy goals (such as news reporting and education) and cultural objectives (for example the promotion of literacy and preservation of history through library and archive privileges). In the US, there are some specific exceptions for uses such as in classroom teaching or in digital distance education, by blind and disabled persons, by libraries and archives, and in other special situations. But there is also the general exception set out in the law for the 'fair use' of copyrighted materials for certain purposes.[9] The UK's 'fair dealing' exception, although very similar to the US exception including in its common-law heritage, has been applied primarily to the use of quotations for criticism and news. The laws of other EU members do not have the same general 'fair use' or 'fair dealing' exceptions, but instead include more detailed and specific exceptions for particular uses and users and provide for private copying privileges. The US doctrine of 'fair use' has the advantage of flexibility – because it describes the process by which a determination is to be made rather than specifically describing a particular activity, it can be applied to changing circumstances and in situations involving new technologies. However, that advantage is also a weakness, as outcomes under a 'fair use' analysis are not always clear and users who rely on it are sometimes disappointed when a court disagrees with their understanding of its application. That lack of certainty can be a drawback in many situations.

In addition to the exceptions and limitations provided in national laws, there are in some circumstances forms of non-voluntary or compulsory licences that provide for the payment of remuneration to the copyright holder. These compulsory licensing schemes are generally seen as a way of addressing a 'market failure'. These are typically situations in which it is impractical or logistically difficult for the user and the copyright owner to locate each other and engage in an individual transaction with respect to the particular use. Examples include broadcasting, music recording and (in some countries) photocopying. As a way of both managing those statutory licences and handling permissions for certain other uses that do not fall within exceptions or limitations (including photocopying in many countries where no compulsory licence for such copies exists), the collective management of copyrights has become increasingly common. For text materials in particular, there is a well-established structure built around 'reproduction rights organisations' ('RROs') (sometimes now referred to as 'collective management organisations' or 'CMOs') pursuant to which creators and publishers, either on a voluntary basis (in the US) or through a legislative mandate (in many other countries) authorise an RRO or CMO to act on their behalf in granting permission and collecting payments for certain uses of their works. As will be discussed below, collective management schemes are particularly relevant when considering the impact of digital technologies on copyright generally and scholarly publishing in particular.

Role of copyright in the digital age

Although the law provides that the copyright owner has the exclusive right to make or authorise the making of copies, unauthorised copying has always been an issue for copyright owners.[10] Now that digital technology has made the making and distribution of unlimited numbers of perfect copies simple, seamless and inexpensive, the problems for copyright owners have increased exponentially. But at the same time that digital technology has created problems for rights holders, it has also created enormous opportunities. For some publishers, such as trade publishers seeing the dramatic recent growth in the e-book market, these opportunities have only recently begun to be utilised in a significant way. Others, particularly in the area of scholarly publishing, have been exploring these opportunities for many years and have developed business models and technical infrastructures to help them realise the benefits for themselves and their customers.

Changes in copyright law to address digital technology

The development of digital technology has also had an impact on copyright itself. The law of copyright is generally 'technology neutral'. In other words, the exclusive rights of the copyright owner apply – in the absence of a specific exception – regardless of the format in which the work was created or in which it is being distributed. This concept is sometimes difficult for users to understand and accept. Technical tools make copying and redistribution so simple that the legal implications of the use of those tools are often misunderstood and even resented. Copyright law has been under pressure to adapt to the changing realities of the digital world.

The WIPO Copyright Treaty (WCT, 1996) was a multilateral, treaty-based approach to this issue.[11] It provided, among other things, for computer programs to be protected by copyright as literary works (an approach already taken by many national laws), for the protection of the selection and arrangement of databases (although not for the factual information incorporated into the database), and for the prohibition of both circumvention of technological measures for the protection of works and unauthorised modification of rights management information contained in works. The treaty now has more than 80 signatories including the US and the countries of the EU. It was implemented in the US through the Digital Millennium Copyright Act (DMCA) enacted in 1998[12] and in the EU through several Directives dealing with software copyright, database protection and anti-circumvention measures.[13]

The WCT has been controversial. The debate over the perceived tension between existing copyright law and uses of digital technology is contentious and features in current deliberations in the courts as well as in legislatures. The dispute in the US courts over Google's library scanning project (the Google Books case) is perhaps the most prominent recent example.

Mass digitisation and the Google Library Project

In 2004, Google began the ambitious project of creating a massive digital library by scanning the collections of a number of major academic libraries in the US. In 2005, the Association of American Publishers (AAP) and the Authors' Guild (AG) each sued Google, claiming that Google's inclusion of copyrighted works in its scanning program without having first acquired permission from the copyright owners of those works was infringing. Google's defence to these lawsuits was that its actions were protected under the 'fair use' doctrine. The parties attempted to settle the dispute by entering into an agreement releasing Google (in exchange for payments to rights holders) from liability for its past activities and authorising future uses by Google (through the use of an extensive licensing and collective management mechanism) of the scanned works. The proposed settlement agreement would, through its use of the 'class action' mechanism available under US law, have been binding on many hundreds of thousands of rights holders – from individual authors to large commercial and non-profit entities – from around the world who were not named as parties to the litigation. In March of 2011, Judge Chin, the judge before whom the case is pending, issued an opinion that rejected the proposed settlement agreement. In the opinion, he focused in particular on the forward-looking aspects of the settlement agreement, saying that such extensive future activities could not be authorised in a class action settlement.[14] The judge also, in his decision, discussed some of the policy implications of the proposed settlement agreement, which would have authorised Google to make extensive use of many 'orphan works' (works still in copyright for which the owners had not come forward or could not be found). The judge expressed his view that certain aspects of the settlement – in particular the treatment of 'orphan works' and certain international law issues that had been raised – should be addressed through legislation rather than through judicial approval of a privately negotiated agreement.

The parties in the Google Books case began negotiating a settlement before the court had an opportunity to directly consider the underlying legal issue in the case (that is, whether Google's scanning and subsequent uses of the scanned copies of the works fell within 'fair use'). That legal issue remains open and will presumably be addressed in the case if the parties are unable to agree to an amended settlement agreement that is approved by the court. Although a resolution of the 'fair use' issue would be of interest and could provide guidance for future uses and users of copyrighted material, the core problem highlighted by the Google Books case is the desire by users of digital technology to make broader use of the copyrighted materials that they can now so easily copy and redistribute. These issues are complicated when, as here, the user wishes to reproduce a huge number of works, including those for which licences may not be obtainable because the copyright owner may not be identifiable or locatable. That is the 'orphan works' issue that Judge Chin felt should be addressed by the US Congress rather than the courts.

Legislation and the 'orphan works' question

The US has looked at possible changes to copyright law to address these issues. Orphan works were the subject of a major study completed by the US Copyright Office in 2006; that study resulted in recommended legislation that was introduced in the US Congress in two consecutive terms. The approach taken in that legislation was based on a 'limitation of liability' model, and was focused on individual uses (although nothing would have prevented its application in a mass digitisation context). The proposed legislation applied to circumstances in which a good-faith user could not locate the rights holder after conducting a reasonably diligent search and was applied on a case-by-case basis (meaning users could not designate or rely upon permanent orphan status with respect to any work). If the rights holder ultimately emerged, he or she could collect only reasonable compensation (not damages) from the user.

Despite the failure of this attempted legislative solution in the US, interest in the issue has increased. The Google Books litigation, and in particular the court's rejection of the proposed settlement agreement in part on the basis that the agreement appeared to 'solve' the orphan works problem for the benefit of a single commercial entity, has again focused attention on the problem.

Attention is clearly being paid in the EU, where a proposed draft Orphan Works directive was published in May 2011.[15] The stated purpose of the draft directive is to 'create a legal framework to ensure the lawful, cross-border online access to orphan works contained in the online digital libraries or archives of a variety of institutions ... when such orphan works are used in pursuance of the public interest mission or such institutions.' The approach currently proposed in the draft directive has some elements in common with the US approach, but there are important differences as well. Both would require a diligent search be conducted for the owner, but under the proposed EU Directive a determination that a work is an 'orphan' would benefit subsequent users; in other words, the work would have 'orphan status' unless and until the owner came forward to claim the work. The search would have to be conducted in the country of origin of the work, but the 'orphan status' would apply across the EU, permitting cross-border use within the EU of the work. The 'beneficiaries' of the proposal are different as well. Under the US proposal, uses could be made of the 'orphan work' by either a for-profit or a non-profit entity, so long as the other requirements are met. The EU proposal is directed toward materials 'contained in public libraries, educational establishments, museums and archives' along with certain archives devoted to film and broadcasting. The beneficiary institutions may make the orphan works available to the public as long as the institutions' activities are consistent with their 'public interest missions', including preservation, restoration and 'the provision of cultural and educational access to works contained in their collections'. It is expected that the proposed directive will be submitted for legislative action in autumn 2011.

It is not surprising that libraries are direct beneficiaries of the proposed EU directive on orphan works. Libraries obviously have a critical and important interest in mass digitisation. Libraries served as a convenient source, for Google, of works to be digitised, but the willingness of many major libraries to participate in the Google program was clearly based in those libraries' view of their own interests and goals. The recent rejection of the class action settlement agreement in the Google Books case, coupled with the judge's specific call for legislative action, may help renew interest in addressing some of these issues through legislative changes in the library and archive exceptions in US copyright law.

Orphan works were only one of the issues considered by Professor Ian Hargreaves in the recent report he prepared at the request of the British government. Professor Hargreaves was asked to examine whether the current UK copyright regime is interfering with innovation. The report, released in May 2011,[16] recommended certain changes be made in UK law, including the creation of a 'Digital Copyright Exchange' to facilitate copyright licensing, the enactment of legislation to address 'orphan works' and the expansion of copyright exceptions to cover uses such as format shifting and data mining. Clearly, the impetus behind the preparation of the report and the goals of the recommended changes was to adapt copyright law to facilitate the use of digital technologies.

Possible roles for collective licensing

One important area being debated in discussions about copyright law and digital technologies is that of collective licensing, and in particular 'extended collective licensing'. There are many instances in which a rights holder can directly authorise use of its works through, for example, subscription agreements or individual licences. There are other circumstances in which such direct licensing is unavailable or impractical (for example, if the rights holder is unable to efficiently reach particular users), and RROs can 'fill the gap' in those situations. RROs generally act on behalf of their members or constituents, authorising certain third-party uses on behalf of those individuals and entities that they represent. In the US, where collective licensing for text materials is done on an entirely voluntary basis, the Copyright Clearance Center (CCC) can only offer licences for those works for which the copyright owner has given explicit permission. By contrast, the Scandinavian countries use 'extended collective licensing', under which an RRO is empowered to represent all works in a defined category when a significant number of rights holders in this category have provided authority to the RRO, even if the RRO has not been given specific authority by the copyright owner with respect to a particular work.[17] The owner of a work falling within that category who does not wish to see the work licensed by the RRO would have to specifically 'opt out' of the representation. It has been suggested that the introduction of extended collective licensing could address the issue of orphan works. The pros and cons of that suggestion are outside the scope of this chapter, although it should be noted that the drafters of the proposed EU directive on orphan works explicitly chose not to adopt that mechanism for the time being. Nevertheless, given the success shown by collective licensing organisations generally in facilitating the management of rights, there will be undoubtedly be further discussion of the utility of collective rights management, and perhaps of extended collective licensing, in addressing the copyright and licensing issues raised by digital technology.

Publishing agreements

Publishers sometimes acquire rights from creators by operation of law (for example, the 'work-for-hire' doctrine in the US).[18] But more typically, publishers acquire rights through assignments (which are, of course, a type of contract), or through the specific form of licence agreement known as a publishing agreement. For academic and professional publishing, there are three categories of publishing agreements, the first dealing with authors (for both journal articles and books), another dealing with editors and the final category dealing with third-party publishing services (i.e. society-owned journals).

The publisher usually designates the law that will apply to the contract, typically the law of the country in which the publisher has its principal office. This choice is significant because national laws differ with respect to such critical issues as an author's ability to freely transfer rights and enable their enforcement. In some countries, for example France and Germany, only the right to commercially exploit a work may be transferred. In others, such as the UK, rights can be transferred but issues may arise with respect to 'moral rights', which must be expressly waived if that is the intention of the parties.[19] Differences in national laws also exist with respect to the granting of rights to future technologies. A contract drafted with reference to the law of one country may be able to address these concerns but that structure will not necessarily work if the choice of law is ultimately rejected by a court. For that reason, publishers should consider describing the rights granted as specifically as possible in the agreement.

Author agreements for journal articles

Author agreements for academic and scholarly journals do not have to deal with the service or delivery aspects that arise for book author agreements (see discussion below), given that authors prepare their first drafts of articles prior to and somewhat independent of the submission process. Journal authors are also highly motivated to respond quickly to peer review and other editing requirements, given the general importance to researchers of speedy publication of their work in reputable journals. Journal author agreements, however, must deal with copyright issues (licence or transfer), and often focus on publishing ethics issues as well given the increasing attention to such matters in the research community. The copyright and rights transfer issues, including whether to include specifically enumerated rights as opposed to general references to copyright transfer and the issues about future technologies, apply to journal author (and editor) agreements in precisely the same fashion as noted below for book author agreements, and the reader should review those sections. Journal agreements will generally deal more specifically with the question of rights retained by or transferred back to the authors, in light of the broader use by authors of their journal articles in scholarly pursuits such as their own teaching. Journal authors generally want to use their articles for teaching purposes, in later compilations of their work and to provide copies to research or teaching colleagues. Publishers generally assess and balance whether these needs conflict with normal publishing and distribution rights, and most agreements do provide for such uses provided they are for the personal use by the authors. Agreements generally also reference and incorporate journal publishing ethics codes of conduct, including conflicts of interest statements, double submission issues, and plagiarism. International organisations dealing with publishing ethics issues are now often referenced or included in journal agreements. Many publishers, for example, have joined COPE (the Committee on Publication Ethics)[20] which publishes guidelines and cases and through which some disputes may be mediated, which can be especially useful when the issues require more expertise and experience.

Author agreements for books and reference works

Author and contributor agreements for books and reference works must deal with a number of fundamental issues. These contracts deal with the delivery of services as well as the transfer of rights in the contents. The publisher must be very clear about expectations, the subject matter of the commissioned piece, its contextual connection to and citation of other published works, and potentially painful issues such as remedial steps if the author does not deliver, or does not deliver on time. The publisher has substantial financial risk if a particular book or reference work falls behind schedule, given marketing expectations and production scheduling requirements. Reference work agreements must also deal with long-term 'franchise' issues – reference works in core academic subjects can be extended through many editions and many decades, and may actually be prepared by several generations of editors and authors. However, such works often become known by the identity of the original author, and trademark rights may need to be conveyed (concerning the identification of the work with the original author). Agreements must also deal with warranties of originality, adherence to publishing ethics and often with questions about competitive works.

Well-structured book author agreements will include a clear description of the scope or subject matter of the proposed book or reference work, with an extensive description of the content, orientation and audience, in addition to the more operational issues such as the number of words/pages and language. Schedules must be established for the initial delivery of the manuscript and the speed with which suggested revisions will be considered and provided by the author. Many publishing agreements provide that if revisions are not made in a timely fashion, then the publisher may finalise the revisions, in some cases subtracting any additional costs from author royalty payments. Not all agreements address remedial efforts for complete non-delivery by an author, particularly for new books where the publisher believes there is significant motivation on the part of the author to prepare and submit the initial manuscript, but it may be something for the publisher to consider – should the publisher have a right to terminate, appoint a substitute author, rescind any advance payments or possibly have another form of financial penalty.

The publisher must clarify whether the author or the publisher will be responsible for clearing permissions for previously published third-party information (typically this is about illustrations and charts, although sometimes extensive textual quotations will also be proposed). Authors generally have a more direct relationship with other authors and research colleagues than would the publisher, and may also be in the best position to judge whether a particular illustration is vital to the chapter in the event that that permission proves difficult to clear, or overly expensive. However, the publisher may be in a better position to obtain permissions from other publishers, and may do a more professional and thorough job of clearing permissions and ensuring that electronic rights are properly obtained. As book content is increasingly made available online and through e-book platforms, publishers must ensure that permissions cover electronic distribution. Scholarly publishers should be aware and inform their authors of the STM trade association Permissions Guidelines (see http://www.stm-assoc.org) which provide for certain gratis permissions between member signatories, and mechanisms established for permissions clearances including the CCC's Rightslink service for clearing permissions (see http://www.copyright.com/content/cc3/en/toolbar/productsAndSolutions/rightslink.html).

Contributor agreements are generally brief forms which do not have the degree of formality and 'delivery' requirements that author agreements will have. Contributor agreements are used for short contributions that make up a larger reference work, which are reviewed by the reference work editors (or for multi-volume reference works, by the volume editor and the overall editor-in-chief). These agreements must nonetheless deal with core issues such as the delivery schedule, subject matter and length, copyright and payment. Contributor agreements often have a flat fee structure as opposed to the royalty arrangements which are more typical for author agreements.

Payment mechanisms for book author agreements

Royalty provisions, which are the principal method for payments to book authors, are typically based on a 'net sales' model in academic and professional publishing and therefore contemplate that certain overall costs (usually commissions and other marketing costs) will be deducted before royalty calculations are made. Book author agreements may also contemplate different royalty rates for different types of revenue, for example in dealing with distribution through affiliates, and rights for translation and adaptation. A trend in recent years, however, is towards convergence of royalty rates for these different forms of exploitation. As noted previously, a key issue is the question of repurposed content, where excerpts are used in ways significantly different from the distribution of traditional book content. This has happened for some years in course-pack products, but new products and services are being offered which use sections or one or more chapters of one work along with many other different types of works, excerpts and data. There are several different models to value these different contributions, and indeed some services where the actual fees and payments from consumers are themselves determined 'on the fly'.

Arguments can be made that simple metrics such as usage should be used as the primary measure for the financial value of the individual sections of the work used in a new bundled product or service, although it may be easier to measure volume. Some authors, however, will insist that the inclusion of excerpts from their work will have a significant impact on the value of the new combined product. Given the uncertainty in this area, and the rapid market developments, some publishers are including language in publishing agreements that gives the publisher the right to allocate revenues 'in such manner as it reasonably determines is equitable' while noting that the bases for such determinations may focus on relative value, quantity or usage.

Copyright management

Publishers and authors have a strong common interest in protecting the copyright in their works and recognise that the current online environment presents new risks and challenges, as web sites that encourage the posting of illicit scans and digital copies of popular books proliferate. Publishing agreements need to ensure that all rights in a copyright work that are *needed* by publishers to support traditional and new digital means of distribution are transferred from or licensed by authors. To publish a book or reference work in all appropriate forms and formats, the publisher should be careful to utilise publishing agreements under which it acquires the following rights, on an exclusive basis:

- to produce and publish (editing and publishing);
- to reproduce, transmit, sell and distribute (distribution and marketing);
- to make derivative works, adaptations, abridgements or translations (adaptation); and
- to authorise others to so distribute or adapt (further licensing).

Journal publishers will generally need the same set of rights.[21] An argument can be made that an outright copyright transfer provides all these core publishing and distribution rights (and more) and does not need to be so specifically enumerated. Some jurisdictions, however, are very protective of authors' rights and it may therefore be sensible to enumerate the rights that are being transferred, even if the publishing agreement also specifically notes a transfer of all rights under copyright. Specifically enumerated rights (and perhaps rights retained or granted back to authors for certain non-competitive uses by authors) may help to eliminate arguments about the scope of rights granted for a particular work. For these reasons it is useful to include language making it clear that the rights transferred or licensed include the rights to 'all forms, formats and media, now known or hereafter developed'.

Publishing agreements should also provide for the ability on the part of the publisher to enforce copyright, including by bringing litigation if necessary. Publishers and often authors are monitoring online sites where unauthorised e-book files are being posted (or appear to be posted) and are actively demanding that such materials be taken down from the site. Publishers are active in monitoring sites where unauthorised document delivery services are being provided, with particular concerns for services that facilitate deliveries to commercial entities (as these are important markets for direct publisher services).

Editor agreements

Many multi-volume reference works involve editors who review, revise and edit the work of individual chapter editors or contributors. Indeed, some reference works will include an overall editor plus individual volume editors for different core subject areas, and the 'editor-in-chief' will also review the work of the volume editors in addition to the overall content. These agreements will typically include the delivery service requirements similar to those in book author agreements, but will also describe the editing and review services in some detail. These agreements will often have strict requirements for timely delivery and more ability on the part of the publisher to substitute services in the event of delivery or quality issues. The potential commercial risks in delays to production and distribution of reference works are often significantly higher than for monographs. Although editor agreements are service-oriented contracts, they must nonetheless also include copyright or rights transfer provisions, to ensure that all rights in the final edited work are consolidated with the publisher. Journal editor agreements are service contracts and should identify the services expected by the journal publisher in some detail and with some specificity. A journal's identity, its aims and scope, its editorial stance and orientation, should be identified. Difficult issues such as duration, renewal and termination (for example, how to define 'for cause') must also be addressed. Fees to be paid to editors may also include support for editorial office services. Many journals will have multiple editors (sometimes with an editor-in-chief supervising several regional or deputy editors), and should clarify the hierarchy with some precision. Most journals have editorial advisory boards, and such advisers should be appointed with formal (but short) agreements. As noted, all editor agreements should also address copyright and rights transfer issues. In some cases where a publisher is providing publishing services for a journal-owning entity (often a scientific or medical society which does not have publishing as a core function), the journal owner will not only own the journal title (from a trademark perspective) but will also manage and control the editorial identity of the journal and may be responsible for appointing the editor.

Third-party publishing agreements

Learned societies that own and manage journals in their fields sometimes look to third parties to produce and distribute their journals, on a service basis. In some cases the third-party professional publisher will be another society and in other cases it will be a commercial publisher. The decisions about whether and how to seek such services are complex and will differ from society to society, but it is a strategy often pursued to take advantage of the professionalism that a larger house can offer and to permit the society to concentrate on more 'core' activities. Many such contracts are put out for competitive bids, where publishers will compete in terms of the scope of services to be provided in addition to the financial contributions they are prepared to make to the journal-owning society. There are other arrangements between specialist societies and professional publishers, including 'sponsorship' agreements by which a society becomes associated with a journal owned by another society or publisher. We will concentrate on the first example of a society-owned journal produced and managed by a professional publisher.[22]

Third-party publishing agreements must address core issues such as editorial control and management; distribution and marketing; and the distribution and sharing of financial risk and reward. Clear provisions on term and duration, termination and renewals, are also recommended – the professional publisher will often want a right of first refusal with respect to competing bids for any post-term periods. Most of these agreements note that the society owner sets the aim and scope, is responsible for monitoring the scientific field and changing the editorial policies if appropriate, and often plays the primary role in selecting the Editor-in-Chief (and sometimes other Editorial Board members as well). The professional publisher will want to have some ability to influence the selection and retention of editors, particularly where there might be a performance concern (see discussions above re editor agreements). Highly competitive bidding processes often result in more up-front financial payments for the society owner, as opposed to the more traditional royalty structure (based on 'net sales' revenues).

The third-party professional publisher is often looking for clarity and substantial authority concerning the 'business' issues of distribution and marketing, and indeed one reason that a society owner may select a particular publisher is such marketing ability. A well-established sales force or process, strong relationships with key subscription agents, and an ability to cover new emerging territories and thus expand the reach of the journal will be key competitive differentiators. A professional publisher with a large journal programme, however, will want to manage that programme in as consistent a fashion as possible (using, for example, the same overall online subscription access agreement), and thus will want to exercise considerable discretion in these areas.

Creative commons and similar licences

Prior to the advent of digital distribution of text works, scholarly publishers distributed print publications using a well-defined and straightforward business model. Revenues that came from subscription agreements and sales of tangible copies covered the costs of peer review, printing paper and binding, marketing and distribution, and reinvestment in the company. Licensing was largely limited to rights acquisitions and intra-publisher arrangements. Over the last two decades, the importance of print publication has declined and that decline continues. Costs related to peer review and marketing remain, but certain other costs have been replaced or supplemented by those required to maintain a complex technical infrastructure. Revenues still often come from subscription agreements, but those agreements take the form of licensing agreements providing subscribers with access to digital copies maintained in databases. Some publishers have moved away from, or have never adopted, a subscription-based revenue model, but instead cover the costs of publication through other means (like the 'author pays' – or more typically the 'supporting institution pays' – model) and distribute their works without charge to users. The authors of the materials being published (scholars and researchers) are no longer, in many cases, willing or even able to assign all rights to scholarly publishers, absent an institutional waiver or permission (due to policies adopted at their supporting institutions). Provisions permitting the author to retain the right to include the work (or some version thereof) in, for example, institutional repositories or author-maintained web sites or requiring that articles be made openly available within a fixed period after initial publication are becoming commonplace.

One of the tools increasingly used, in particular by entities using an 'open access' publishing model and by individual authors as well, are licence agreements that explicitly permit reuse and redistribution of a work. By far the most widely used of these types of agreements are the various forms of the Creative Commons licence. Creative Commons was founded in 2001 and, according to the organisation's website,[23] an estimated 350 million works had been distributed under Creative Common's licences by the end of 2009. Creative Commons licences can be and are used for analog works, but their primary, most typical use is in connection with works published online. The creator includes HTML code (generated with the use of a tool available at the Creative Commons web site) with the digital copy of the work that provides notice that the work is being distributed pursuant to a Creative Commons licence and a link to the full text of the licence.

The deployment of a Creative Commons licence is not, as is sometimes mistakenly assumed, the same as a dedication of a work to the public domain.[24] To the contrary, the licence can only be used in connection with a work to which copyright ownership is asserted. The copyright owner chooses between several different versions of the Creative Commons licence, all of which permit downstream sharing of the work to which the licence is applied. The least 'protective' version requires only that subsequent users of the work provide an attribution to the creator. Other versions add other provisions, such as a prohibition on the creation of derivative works and/or a prohibition of commercial uses and/or a requirement that subsequent users license any works incorporating or derived from the original work on the same terms on which the original work was licensed (a 'share-alike' requirement). Creative Commons encourages the use of its licences for copyrighted works in all forms and formats *except* software, recommending that those wishing to distribute software on a similar basis instead consider using licences obtainable through such sources as the Free Software Foundation and the Open Source Initiative.[25]

Factors to consider

In considering whether to use a Creative Commons licence as part of a publishing programme, or whether to use materials previously distributed under a Creative Commons licence as part of a new work, there are several important considerations to keep in mind. The 10-year history and extensive nature of their use has created a presumption that these licences will probably be enforceable in many jurisdictions.[26] By its terms, a Creative Commons licence is not revocable. And, although Creative Commons licences are non-exclusive and require a downstream user to come back to the creator for further permission for uses not covered by the particular licence form (most commonly, perhaps, for permission to make a commercial use of materials licensed for non-commercial use only),[27] it should be kept in mind that once a non-exclusive licence has been granted the potential opportunity to license the same work on an exclusive basis has been lost. It should also be noted that in some jurisdictions, creators and/or publishers are required to assign rights to an RRO so that the RRO can represent the copyright owner in connection with certain uses of the work, and that assignment may complicate the use of a Creative Commons licence for creators from that jurisdiction.[28] However, in many circumstances in which the copyright owner has clearly made the informed decision to permit the use and redistribution of a work on a permanent basis on the terms set forth in a Creative Commons licence, that licence can be a valuable tool for achieving the copyright owner's goals.

The use and reuse by third parties of works distributed under a Creative Commons licence should be approached with similar care. It is important to review and comply with the form of licence applied by the original copyright owner. For example, the applicable Creative Commons licence may limit use of the work to non-commercial purposes. Or, it may permit a subsequent user to redistribute and even adapt and change a work even for commercial purposes, but require (under the 'share-alike' formulation) that the subsequent work be distributed on the same licence terms as the original work, a requirement that may or may not fit the business model of the subsequent user. It should also be kept in mind that Creative Commons licences are explicitly not intended to supersede or replace the exceptions or limitations that apply to copyright works under the relevant laws. So if the particular use of a Creative Commons-licensed work falls within an exception like 'fair use' or 'fair dealing' the factors relevant to a decision to use that work will be no different from those which should be considered if that licence did not apply.

Piracy issues and enforcement routes

A publisher's efforts to properly obtain the rights needed for the journal article or book chapter may be rendered pointless if third parties are providing unauthorised copies or access, without recompense to the author or publisher, and the publisher is not taking, or doesn't have the right or authority to take, legal steps to enforce these rights. Third parties providing unauthorised copies or access have varied their methods to now include offering content online, and in some cases do so for non-commercial reasons.[29]

Forms and types of piracy

Piracy takes many forms, including traditional print piracy involving warehouses and lorries, sometimes enabled by parties involved in legitimate production or distribution services. Some pirated editions are of surprisingly good quality, in terms of the quality and consistency of the production and legibility of images and text, and the quality of paper and binding. The works of international authors and publishers are often highly prized, and some customers are not always careful or concerned enough about quality or legality, especially if the price is significantly lower than for a legitimate product.

Piracy became digital more than a decade ago, with vendors offering CD-ROMs with multiple works on one disk for a low price. In some cases these products were sold in flea and street markets, sometimes through online auctions such as eBay. However, eBay has been generally cooperative with publishers over the last few years in monitoring and disqualifying vendors of such materials. Piracy has migrated to the web in other ways, including to sites that enable or encourage the posting of e-book files by individuals (file sharing sites). Often these sites involve the posting of unauthorised content of all types, including music and films, and are supported by business models involving 'membership' fees or advertising. One of the largest sites, RapidShare, has over recent years been subject to numerous challenges from copyright owners including publishers (most cases have been brought in Germany), and has recently undertaken greater efforts to 'filter' posted files to identify and delete illicit content.

Some of these Internet sites are located in jurisdictions where the lamentable state of the rule of law makes litigation uncertain and even pointless, especially where, as would generally be the case, the plaintiff will be perceived by the court system as the outsider and 'foreigner'. However, even in such instances, the business operations of the site, whether arranged through credit card and other payment systems or supported by advertisers, often have a link to a country where the rule of law is applied more consistently, and the payment providers and advertisers may be subject to legal claims in such countries. Such providers may also respond to social pressure and may not be fully informed about the questionable activities of some of the sites to which they are providing services or support.

Note that many file sharing sites depend on the copying and scanning activities of their members and supporters, whose motives are not always clear.

Litigation formalities and requirements

When bringing formal legal claims, evidence and documentation will be required, both as to the actions and conduct of the defendant and as to the rights of the plaintiff. For traditional print piracy the evidence of conduct may well require cooperation with local authorities on investigations of shipments of pirated goods, and in this area collective investigations done by trade associations such as the Publishers Association (UK) and the Association of American Publishers (AAP) have been indispensable. For digital piracy, evidence in the form of screen shots, downloads from the sites, and careful documentation of the same, will be required, and in some countries the courts will require that such evidence be collected by certain official agents. Copyright litigation in the US in particular will require copyright registration of the works to initiate a suit and to obtain statutory damages (damages set by law that may be available in the absence of or as an alternative to actual damages).[30] Publishers will typically need to provide their author agreements (and in some cases editor agreements) to demonstrate that the rights have been transferred to the publisher (including the right to enforce), and that the publisher has full legal authority to pursue such matters. This applies equally to journal articles and books. In some jurisdictions only the original creator or author will be deemed legally capable of bringing a copyright litigation claim, and therefore approval or participation by authors may be required.

Maintaining proper administration of author and editor agreements, and copyright registration certificates for US enforcement purposes, is therefore an indispensable part of an enforcement programme. Publishers are not always well organised in these areas, and it is likely that any publishing house entering into a significant enforcement programme will need to invest in a fair amount of 'house-cleaning' to pull its records together and to be able to easily find all the relevant documentation for a particular work, an investment of resources that may not be trivial.

Copyright owners often have to consider whether to bring actions themselves in the civil court system, or to coordinate with government prosecutors and agencies (for example, the relevant customs authorities). Government agencies will often have significant resources and investigative and seizure capacities well beyond what is available through the civil court processes. Nonetheless, prosecutors are selective about the cases that they bring, and will probably only bring actions if they feel the targets are significant and their actions are material. Additionally, once the government initiates legal action, the government will be the entity directing the strategies and tactics in a particular case, and will of course aim to secure judgments and seizures. In many instances, rights holders will utilise litigation as a way of encouraging settlement and negotiation, often after previous attempts have not been given serious credence by the defendant, and may therefore want to preserve more control over strategies and outcomes.

Controversies and uncertainties

As noted, not all unauthorised copying and distribution is done for commercial purposes by parties without socially redeeming qualities. Motives may be mixed, and there are individuals who sometimes create a scanned version of a work because they truly believe there are no available alternatives and because they believe the work is important and should be shared. In many of these instances, the suspicion is that individuals have not tested the question of availability with much rigour, given that in the Internet age more and more copyright works have been made more easily discoverable and broadly available through normal commercial channels.

Other parties such as libraries, research institutions and universities play a significant role in informing their user communities about permitted uses under publisher licences, and there has been important and useful work to try to simplify and clarify licence language (for example in the ONIX-PL project[31]).

These same institutions have a heritage and a mission of providing access for educational and research purposes, and understandably wish to embrace digital technologies to enhance their services. The legal basis for some of these actions, an exception to or limitation of local copyright law, may not be clear-cut, and there have in recent years been significant disagreements over issues such as electronic course packs and international supply of copied articles, with rights holders generally supporting a system of permissions and licensing options.[32]

Then there are other actors, including most notoriously Google in connection with its library scanning project, that are testing copyright law in their own ways and for their own purposes.

In these instances, litigation will be a way of testing the limits of copyright law and exceptions and limitations and of settling areas of the laws that legislation has not fully clarified. Such cases are sometimes truly precedent-setting, as in the *Texaco* decision[33] in the US, which established a boundary of commercial use in the corporate environment. Such cases are usually brought by trade associations or groups of publishers given the potential impact of the precedent and likely expense of major litigation.

Conclusion and outlook

There is a strong and fundamental relationship between copyright and publishing. This is not an accident – the origins of copyright law can be traced back to the professional development in past centuries of an independent publishing industry (or at least one independent of religious authorities). Then, as now, copyright law was seen to serve a public purpose by encouraging the broad dissemination of works that might otherwise have had only limited distribution. Public policy considerations also apply in the treatment of certain principles and exceptions from country to country, related to whether certain types of unauthorised copying also serves a public good. These considerations are particularly complex in migrating principles developed for the print environment to the digital.

Copyright law has evolved to deal with technological changes before, and there is no reason to believe that with goodwill and intelligence copyright law cannot evolve again to deal with the Internet age. In fact the laws of most countries have already made significant steps in this direction over the past 10 years.

Advocates for the commoditisation of published information are often strident and sometimes, on a surface level at least, compelling (don't we all want 'information to be free' of constraints?), but generally fall short of offering alternatives with sound financial footings to support the current and critical editing processes and publishing services. Publishers have adapted their business practices to accommodate some of the concerns that have been expressed. For example, certain publishers have begun asking for limited exclusive rights rather than copyright transfers; some are experimenting with or have adopted non-subscription business models such as the 'author pays' mechanism. The process is evolutionary and ongoing.

Public policy analysts should always consider that our world is currently rich, some might say awash, in high-quality published information. That is an enormous social good, and sets the bar high for the advocates of alternative approaches in discussion over whether their suggested approaches can support a similarly vital infrastructure of published content. As legislatures and courts continue to consider how copyright law will evolve in response to the changing digital landscape, publishers and authors must be prepared to carry the burden of demonstrating the value that they provide to knowledge, to learning and to society as a whole.

Sources of further information

Useful books and reference works

Dreier, T. and Hugenholtz, B. (eds) (2006) *Concise European Copyright Law*. The Netherlands: Kluwer Law International.

Goldstein, P. (1992-current) *Goldstein on Copyright*, multi-volume edition. New York: Aspen Publishers.

Kaufman, R. (2008) *Publishing Forms and Contracts*. New York: Oxford University Press.

Nimmer, D. and Nimmer, M. (1978-current) *Nimmer on Copyright: A Treatise on the Law of Literary, Musical and Artistic Property, and the Protection of Ideas*, multi-volume edition. New York: Matthew Bender & Company,

Owen, L. (2008) *Clark's Publishing Agreements: A Book of Precedents*, 8th edn. Haywards Heath, UK: Bloomsbury.

Useful websltes

International Publishers Association (see http://www.internationalpublishers.org/)

The International Assocation of Scientific, Technical & Medical Publishers (see http://www.stm-assoc.org/)

The International Federation of Reproduction Rights Organizations, with useful links to national RRO sites (see http://www.ifrro.org/)

British Copyright Council (see http://www.britishcopyright.org/)

The US Copyright Office, many useful circulars and brochures, also search capacity of the Copyright Office records (see http://www.copyright.gov/)

The EU Information Society directorate, relevant for copyright policy matters (see http://ec.europa.eu/dgs/information_society/index_en.htm)

Notes

1. Contracts dealing with rights acquisition are discussed under 'Publishing agreements'. Other types of contracts, like those entered into between publishers and other publishers (for example, co-publishing, translation and distribution agreements) and between publishers and customers (for example, subscription agreements), are beyond the scope of this chapter.
2. For a useful discussion on libel and defamation, see Jones and Benson (2011).
3. This has been a particularly controversial issue in the UK, where the defendant in a libel case does not have available to it certain defences that apply under, for example, US law. One prominent example of this is the case brought (and subsequently dropped) by the British Chiropractic Association against science writer Simon Singh.
4. 'Originality' in a copyright context does not mean 'novel' or 'unique'. A work is sufficiently 'original' to be eligible for copyright protection if it includes some level of creative expression, which can be very small, that originates with the author.
5. Where a factual compilation is in the form of a database it may, in some jurisdictions, be subject to a form of protection that is somewhat similar to, but not the same as, a copyright. See, for example, the EU database directive (Directive 96/9/EC).
6. It is also possible for a work to be dedicated to the public domain, or for rights under copyright to be waived by contract. See discussion under 'Creative Commons and similar licences'.
7. See 'Publishing agreements'.
8. The text of the Berne Convention can be found at the WIPO web site, at http://www.wipo.int/treaties/en/ip/berne/trtdocs_wo001.html. The 'three-step' test is in Article 9(2), which was added as part of a revision of the treaty done in Stockholm in 1967.
9. The US 'fair use' doctrine was first developed by the courts but is now set out in Section 107 of the US Copyright Act (17 U.S.C. §107). It states that a particular use will be deemed 'fair' (and therefore non-infringing) if it is made 'for purposes such as criticism, comment, news reporting, teaching (including multiple copies for classroom use), scholarship, or research.' A determination of whether a particular use is 'fair' must consider four factors: '(1) the purpose and character of the use, including whether such use is of a commercial nature or is for nonprofit educational purposes; (2) the nature of the copyrighted work; (3) the amount and substantiality of the portion used in relation to the copyrighted work as a whole; and (4) the effect of the use upon the potential market for or value of the copyrighted work.'
10. When the primary format for distribution of scholarly works was print, the relationship between the publisher and the ultimate customer for the work (for example, the library or scholar receiving a copy of the journal) was typically managed through the application of copyright law. The customer got ownership of a tangible copy; the rights (if any) of the owner of that tangible copy to reproduce or redistribute work were determined by applicable copyright laws. Digital distribution has changed things dramatically.

11. Information about the WIPO Copyright Treaty, including a link to the full text of the treaty, can be found at http://www.wipo.int/treaties/en/ip/wct/.
12. The DMCA was an amendment to the US Copyright Act. It can be found at 17 U.S.C. §1201 et. seq.
13. There are several EU Directives that deal with the subjects covered in the WCT. They include: Directive 91/250/EC (copyright protection for software), Directive 96/9/EC (database protection), and Directive 2001/29/EC (prohibiting devices for circumventing technical protection measures).
14. A copy of the decision rejecting the settlement in the Google Books case can be downloaded by clicking on the specified link at http://www.publicindex.org.
15. A copy of the proposed Orphan Works directive can be found at http://ec.europa.eu/internal_market/copyright/docs/orphan-works/proposal_en.pdf.
16. A copy of the Hargreaves Report can be found at http://www.ipo.gov.uk/ipreview-finalreport.pdf
17. In this respect, extended collective licensing has some aspects in common with the class action mechanism adopted by the proponents of the Google Books settlement, and thus far rejected by the court. Both approaches contemplate that licences could be granted on behalf of a rights holder without explicit authorization *unless* the rights holder has expressly 'opted out'. The judge in the Google Books case expressed concern that this 'opt-out' approach was inconsistent with the underlying principles of copyright. But the scope and limitations of copyright are determined by statute, and a legislative change might create an 'opt-out' mechanism even if a court considering approval of a class action settlement cannot.
18. Under the 'work-for-hire' doctrine, the employer is deemed to be the owner of the copyright from the moment of creation if the work is prepared by a full-time employee acting in the course of his or her employment. There are other circumstances in which a work may become a 'work-for-hire'. The party commissioning the creation of the work can in some cases (such as, for example, in the case of a contribution to a collective work) become the copyright owner under the work-for-hire doctrine by contract, which may apply to some forms of contributor agreements.
19. In countries that have a moral rights regime, copyrights are often regarded as primarily economic rights, and moral rights protect the creator's non-commercial interest in his work. Moral rights typically include at a minimum rights of attribution (the right to be identified as the author) and integrity (the right to object to any distortion, mutilation or modification of the work that is prejudicial to the author's honour or reputation). See, Berne Convention, *supra* at footnote 8, Article 6*bis*.
20. More information about COPE, including guidelines and useful flowcharts, can be found at http://www.publicationethics.org/.
21. Because government employees sometimes prepare research articles, journal article agreements do, however, sometimes have to address specific questions about public domain works or government-owned rights that less commonly arise in book publishing agreements.
22. More details on tenders and bid processes, and on the variety of issues that third-party publishing can involve, can be found in Page *et al.* (1997).

23. http://creativecommons.org/. A summary of the various types of Creative Commons licences, with links to the actual language of the licences, can be found at http://creativecommons.org/licenses/
24. For use with works for which the creator wishes to make a dedication to the public domain and waive all copyrights, Creative Commons provide a separate tool, the 'CC0 Public Domain Dedication'. Information about CC0 can be found at http://wiki.creativecommons.org/CC0.
25. Additional information about those groups can be found at their web sites: for the Free Software Foundation at http://www.fsf.org/; for the Open Software Initiative at http://www.opensource.org/. The CC0 Public Domain Dedication (mentioned above at footnote 24) is intended for use with software as well as with other types of works.
26. To enhance the likelihood that its licences will be enforceable, Creative Commons offers both generally applicable versions of the licences and 'ported' versions that can be used by creators in certain specified jurisdictions and have been tailored to the laws of those jurisdictions.
27. Creative Commons offers a variation or more accurately an addition to its basic licences, called 'CC+' that is designed to facilitate the granting of permissions to users wishing to go beyond those uses permitted by the relevant Creative Commons licence. Additional information is available at http://wiki.creativecommons.org/CCPlus#Simple_Explanation.
28. The question of whether an assignment or 'mandate' of rights to an RRO interferes with the use of the Creative Commons licences for some works may exist in a number of European countries (including Finland, France, Germany, Luxembourg, Spain and the Netherlands) as well as in Australia and Taiwan. Copyright owners in those countries would be well advised to do more specific analysis on this issue and contact their individual RROs.
29. For purposes of this chapter, we use the word 'piracy' to refer to concerted practices of providing unauthorised copies or access to copyright works, without authorisation of or compensation to the copyright owner or rights manager, for a commercial purpose. Not all unauthorised use or copying is done for a commercial reason, and non-commercial unauthorised copying, while not technically 'piracy', may nevertheless be infringing if it does not fall within a defined copyright exception or limitation.
30. US copyright law was substantially amended in the late 1970s to eliminate most of the 'formalities' that had previously part of US law (i.e. registration and notice requirements; the requirement that the copyright be 'renewed' after a fixed period of years). This brought US copyright law in line with copyright law elsewhere and permitted the US to become a party to the Berne Convention. Notwithstanding subsequent US accession to the Berne Convention and its prohibition of copyright formalities, the requirement that a work be registered for copyright in the US prior to the institution of an infringement lawsuit and as a pre-condition to the availability of statutory damages has remained a part of US law. See 17 U.S.C. §§411, 412.
31. ONIX for Publications Licenses (ONIX-PL): http://www.editeur.org/21/ONIX-PL/

32. The long-awaited lower court decision in the case brought by publishers against Georgia State University, dealing with uses of copyright works in e-coursepacks or 'electronic reserves', was delivered in May 2012. Although the court accepted the principle that such uses can exceed fair use, the court's view on the method by which fair use is applied would expand the scope of the exception more than publishers would believe is appropriate. The decision will probably be appealed. For more information, see the AAP press release on the decision at http://www.publishers.org/press/66/.
33. American Geophysical Union v. Texaco, Inc., 60 F.3d 913 (2nd Cir. 1994).

References

Jones, H. and Benson, C. (2011) *Publishing Law*, 4th edn. London: Routledge (Taylor & Francis).

Page, G., Campbell, R. and Meadows, J. (1997) *Journal Publishing*. Cambridge: Cambridge University Press.

Relationship management

Caroline Black

Abstract: This chapter considers the factors that underpin a successful relationship between the publisher of a journal and its editor and editorial board, as well as that between publisher and journal owner. It first looks at the formal aspects of the relationship, explaining how they should be encapsulated in a contract and suggesting how responsibilities should be allocated or shared. The importance of shared strategic planning is emphasised in particular. The chapter advocates an account management approach to publishing relationships, proposes a number of tools to support this approach, and discusses techniques for managing interpersonal communications.

Key words: Relationship management, account management, publishing contract, strategic development, collaboration, communication.

Introduction

The relationship with a journal editor can range from a warm personal friendship between editor and journal publishing manager to a rather distant connection in which the association is more like that between a contractor (the publisher) and a supplier (the editor). At either of these extremes, the success of the relationship may be over reliant on individual personalities and even luck, whereas a more thoughtful and strategic approach to managing the relationship will bring benefits to both sides and will contribute to the success of the journal.

Similarly, a publishing contract with a society can amount to no more than an agreement between a contractor (in this case the society) and a supplier (the publisher). In a relationship like this, there is a risk that the publisher's services are merely a commodity where price (or financial return to the society) becomes the only factor when considering contract renewal. A collaborative partnership will be more likely to endure and will again ensure the success of the journal.

This chapter proposes some tools to ensure that publishing relationships become partnerships in which the parties work together to achieve a shared vision, with clarity about objectives, responsibilities and obligations. This clarity is achieved through the mechanism of a good formal contract, a collaborative approach to strategic planning and through adapting some of the approaches used in client relationship management in other industries.

Establishing a formal relationship: contracts, obligations and responsibilities

Why use a formal contract?

While most journals will have a formal contract, there are still, no doubt, a number of well-established journals in long-standing relationships that survive without watertight contracts between publisher or society owner and editor. At the most there may be a letter on file offering the editor the role but with little or no indication of the term of office or clarity about who does what. The majority of these relationships survive through informal commitment, but the risk of misunderstanding remains. For example, it may be difficult in such cases to ask an editor to step down and so his or her term may drag on for longer than may be appropriate. If a problem were to occur, for example with supply of copy for issues or with production times, it may be unclear what either side can demand of the other or what steps should be taken if the relationship were to break down.

Even the best publishing relationships, built on warmth and mutual understanding, can benefit from a formal contract with a clear and unambiguous delineation of the responsibilities and obligations of the parties to the contract, as well as clarification of legal issues such as ownership, warranties and conflict resolution.

Contract with the journal editor

The generally accepted principle of editorial independence should be enshrined in any contract or agreement with an editor. This principle asserts that the editor of a journal has responsibility for and is accountable for the content of that journal, and the journal's owner or publisher should not interfere with editorial decisions on specific content. However, it is also generally agreed that it is reasonable for the publisher or owner to direct overall strategy or direction or policies.

A useful ALPSP (Association of Learned and Professional Society Publishers, 2010) advice note summarises the purpose of the editor's contract as follows:

- to articulate, define and formalise the relationship;
- to clarify ownership of the journal;
- to set out publisher/society obligations;
- to set out editor obligations;
- to protect each party from legal issues; and
- to establish agreement for what happens if things go wrong.

Also worth adding to the list are these points:

- to set a date and agree arrangements for contract termination or renewal; and
- to set out arrangements for remuneration and their basis for review.

Clark's Publishing Agreements (Owen, 2010) provides a template publisher–editor contract with notes about the rationale behind each clause. Some editors may find the concept of a formal contract unnecessary or even rather daunting. It may be reassuring to explain to them that the contract is based on a standard template used by many journals, and that it is for their protection as much as the publisher's. The editor should be invited to make comments on the draft, so that he or she does not feel coerced in any way into signing the contract.

It is worth deciding in advance which clauses are essential and which could be subject to negotiation. In fact, it can be useful to demonstrate flexibility in some areas if there is a need to be inflexible in others. For example, an editor may be nervous about the legal terminology of the clauses relating to warranties and indemnities: an alternative would be to ensure that there is a robust agreed mechanism to obtain appropriately worded copyright assignment forms or licences from all contributors to the journal, including from the editor.

Building on the framework outlined above, it is important to cover the following salient points in an editor contract:

- *Clarifying ownership*. The contract should include a simple statement about who owns the journal, particularly if an editor is closely involved in the concept and development of a new journal, to avoid any possible lack of clarity or even dispute in the future.
- *Setting out obligations*. This part of the contract should both clarify responsibilities (i.e. make clear who does what where there might be doubt) and spell out obligations (what each party *must* do to fulfil the terms of the contract) necessary to ensuring the journal functions well. Some examples of areas to cover in the contract are suggested in Figure 16.1, although the allocation of responsibilities will vary from journal to journal.
- *When things go wrong*. In case anything were to go wrong in a publishing relationship (for example, if the editor failed to provide material for issues), the contract should state any grounds for early termination of the agreement and also provide for an arbitration process and state which jurisdiction the contract operates under.

	Publisher	Editor
Obligations	Timely publication Production quality Appropriate promotion/Sales activity	Timely supply of accepted papers Quality of content Efficient peer review
Responsibilities	Copyediting Production Technology (hosting, tools) Pricing Promotion Sales Fulfilment	Peer-review Accept/reject decisions Commissioning material Appointing editorial board

Figure 16.1 Possible allocation of obligations and responsibilities in a contract between publisher and journal editor

Of course, this condition can apply to both parties to provide balance in the relationship.

- *Length of contract.* It is advisable to set a fixed termination date: for example, the contract could be for five years with a potential single extension of a further three years, and any future extension to be mutually agreed. This makes it straightforward to end an association gracefully if the time has come for a fresh approach with a new editor. An automatic roll-over every year unless notice is given can make it uncomfortable for both sides to raise the topic of termination, with concerns that doing so might seem like an accusation of poor performance, rather than a reasonable acknowledgement that the time has come to move on.
- *Remuneration.* The contract should state whether fees are paid in advance or in arrears, and when payment will be made. It should be clear whether fees can be reviewed during the term of the contract and, if so, the basis for the review (e.g. an inflation index, changes in workload). A clause stating whether expenses will be reimbursed and if so on what basis is also advisable. If a fixed amount is not agreed per year for expenses, it is useful to state maximum amounts for, for example, travel or administrative expenses. If the remuneration includes a royalty element, the contract should state exactly how it is calculated and when. Without appropriate conditions, the remuneration costs could unwittingly mount up.
- *Variation.* Elements of the contract that might vary during the course of the editor's term of office should be presented as separate schedules attached to the contract. For example, the contract could allow for the number of pages to be published each year to grow or the size of the editor's fee to increase (subject to renegotiation): the principle would be expressed in the contract itself and the detailed arrangements for the first year in the attached schedules. This means that the contract itself does not need to be amended every time the arrangement is changed.
- *Multiple editors.* When a journal has more than one editor, it is good practice to have separate contracts with each editor, in case there are performance problems with one, or one needs to step down early. If there is a second tier of editors (e.g. associate editors, handling editors), it is unlikely to be necessary to issue formal contracts to them provided that the final responsibility for the content of the journal clearly lies with the editor(s) in chief. However, it would be good

practice to have some kind of letter of agreement, co-signed by the publisher and associate editor, confirming expectations, any remuneration and the term of office.

Contract with the society

A publishing contract between a publisher and a society covers some of the same ground as an editor's contract (particularly if the society is responsible for appointing the editor) but should provide full detail about ownership, publishing rights, finances, and termination arrangements. Again, there is a useful ALPSP advice note (ALPSP, 2002) and Owen (2010) provides a comprehensive, annotated template for such a contract.

Important clauses to include are the following:

- *Ownership.* The contract must specify who owns the content (the copyright), the physical stock, electronic files, title, design and subscription lists. This is particularly important should the society wish to consider transferring to another publisher in the future.
- *Publishing rights.* The contract must grant publishing rights to the publisher for the duration of the contract. Without this, the publisher does not legally have the right to sublicense the content (e.g. to aggregators) or grant permissions for re-use let alone publish the journal in print and online.
- *Editor's responsibilities.* If the society rather than the publisher appoints and contracts the editor, the publisher–society contract should also summarise the editor's responsibilities and obligations to the journal, and should spell out the society's responsibility for ensuring that the editor implements these.
- *Finances.* The section on finance should set out the nature of the business relationship (profit share, royalty to society, commission to publisher, etc.), with a clear, unambiguous explanation of the basis of the financial calculations and timing of payments. It is also good practice to give the society the right to audit the publisher's accounts in specific circumstances.
- *Starting the agreement.* The contract may include stipulations about the handover from a previous publisher and ask for warranties from the society about historical data on subscriptions and sales to ensure realistic business planning.

- *Warranties*. In publishing content, a publisher takes on a number of legal risks including infringement of copyright and other rights, and defamation. The publisher therefore normally requires certain warranties and indemnities from the provider of the content in order to protect itself and comply with insurance requirements. It is generally considered reasonable for the party providing the content – and which therefore knows most about its originality and provenance – to warrant the legality of the content. Warranties are therefore generally given by individual contributors, editors, the society itself and if relevant the publisher, about the nature of the material that each is contributing to the work. If the warranties are backed by an indemnity, the indemnifying party will have to pay the legal costs of the indemnified party in the event of a dispute, and will generally control the claim. Fortunately, litigation continues to be a rare event, in the UK at least.
- *Ending the contract*. The clauses on renewal and termination arrangements should specify precisely what happens upon termination of the contract. Ideally the contract would reflect the *Transfer Code of Practice* (UK Serials Group, 2008) but, whether or not it does so, it should spell out what happens to electronic back files and access to them by subscribers, as this is can be an area of confusion and opacity. The termination clause may also give the publisher the right to make a counter offer if the society is considering moving to another publisher.
- *Variation*. As with the editor contract, arrangements that may change during the course of the agreement (e.g. procedure for supplying and charging for member subscriptions) can be referred to in the main contract but detailed in an attached schedule.
- *Responsibility for decisions*. There are a number of areas that would normally be the publisher's responsibility in a publisher–editor relationship but could either be the society's or the publisher's responsibility, or be shared. Examples include decisions on pricing, business policies that might have an impact on the journal, appointment of editorial board members, house style, design and page budget. Even where the final decision-making is clearly the responsibility of either owner or publisher, there should be an agreed mechanism for discussion and collaboration on these issues.
- *Authorisation*. It is important to identify the legal status of the society before entering the contract. The society may have corporate status as a limited company, or company limited by guarantee, in which case it

has a separate legal personality and can enter contracts in accordance with company law. If the society is a charity trust, or an unincorporated association, then it will not have a separate legal personality and will generally only be able to enter into contracts in the names of its individual trustees or management committee members. This can on occasion lead to the requirement for a number of signatures, although charities legislation in the UK includes a provision for delegation of signing responsibilities to two or more members. It is important when entering contracts with trusts or unincorporated associations always to include an express provision that the entity has the capacity to enter the contract and is acting in accordance with its constitution.

Collaborative journal development

A publishing partnership

The formal contract provides a structure for the management of a publishing partnership and there will usually be other mechanisms for interaction such as an annual meeting, agreed reports or a publications committee on which both parties sit. However, these tools will not in themselves guarantee that the parties to the contract will work together to achieve success. A collaborative approach, shared objectives and mutual support are also needed.

Developing a business plan

A journal business plan based simply on the publisher's overall objectives with minimal or no input from editor or owner will not necessarily fail but may be no more than a set of short-term objectives based on profitability, citation and submission targets with possibly some standard promotion activities planned. For some journals, indeed, this will be entirely appropriate: not all journals are stars or have untapped potential. For these journals, the priority is simply to ensure that their performance is monitored, they play their part in a subject portfolio and they benefit from any relevant company-wide initiatives.

For those journals where there is opportunity to be tapped, it is important that strategic planning is collaborative, with active input from the publisher, the editorial team and the society owner. This is, firstly, to ensure that any tensions between objectives are acknowledged and managed, secondly to ensure that everyone is working to the same goals and finally to provide a framework for prioritising activities.

Recognising and addressing tensions between objectives is vital before any attempt is made to agree long-term aspirations. For example:

- For a publisher and society increasing profitability might be a high priority, but the editor might want to increase the number of articles and start a programme of professionally recorded videocasts.
- A UK-based society might vigorously encourage its members to submit their research to the journal but the editor would rather increase submissions from outside the UK.

Benefits of working together on a strategic business plan

- Commitment of all stakeholders
- Fits in with strategic priorities of all parties
- More chance of commercial and academic success
- Opportunity for publisher to demonstrate expertise and commitment

A formal day of strategic planning can be a good way to elicit any such tensions and it can be beneficial to acknowledge them. The day can also be used to acknowledge in a relatively non-confrontational way any weaknesses of the journal by using a SWOT analysis (strengths and weaknesses, external opportunities and threats) of both the journal itself and its competitors.

Ideally the day would end with a single statement of a shared vision for the journal and a brief, coherent statement of its mission, also agreed by all. Any long- or short-term objectives should be aligned with these statements, and any action plans developed should lead to achievement of the objectives. The incidental benefit of such a strategic plan is that it can be a useful tool to manage unrealistic expectations from either the editor or the society.

The structure of a strategic planning session depends very much on the personalities involved and it is highly advisable to take these into account. Some editors and officers are entirely at home with the concepts of business plans, USPs (unique selling propositions), SWOT and PEST (political, economic, social and technological) analyses, whereas others will find the terminology so off-putting that they will not participate with enthusiasm and will therefore not be committed to the concept or the outcome. For the latter, it is a question of managing the vocabulary used: instead of agreeing a USP, for example, one could initiate discussion about what distinguishes or could distinguish the journal from its competitors. Instead of participating in a SWOT analysis, individuals could simply be invited to say what they think the journal does well and what it could work on.

A successful strategy day can bring additional benefits such as the development of a team spirit and the generation of vigour, energy and commitment to the objectives. However, these benefits will soon be lost if there is no outcome in the form of an agreed strategic business plan or if the actions that were agreed so enthusiastically are not implemented. It is advisable to set a date in the near future (no more than three months away) to review the commitments made and ensure that there has been progress.

Suggested approach to a collaborative strategy meeting

- Involve all stakeholders who are likely to contribute actively (e.g. from the publishing team, society officers, editorial board, editorial office staff)
- Review (ideally through reports circulated in advance) the current position of the journal and its competitors (readership, submissions, citations, downloads, pricing, publication times)
- Review the goals of the society owner, editor and publisher
- SWOT: analyse strengths and weaknesses of the journal (and its competitors), opportunities and threats in the subject field and journal market
- Agree vision, mission and long-term objectives
- Draw up short- to medium-term action plan
- Review at regular agreed intervals

Working together on ethical and legal issues

There are some important areas where collaboration is valuable but which cannot be enshrined in a formal contract. It is worth considering how these will be handled and who will take the lead. Ethical and legal infringements are an example.

Although an editor may be well positioned to judge whether a paper plagiarises another researcher's work, is an example of duplicate publication or appears to be fabricated, it can be daunting for that editor to take action (although some will be happy to do so). The publisher can support the editor not only by helping with the correspondence and acceleration of actions in particular cases, but also by providing education, tools and action plans [such as the flowcharts from the Committee on Publication Ethics (COPE, 2012)]. A new editor may be unaware of potential ethical issues that may arise, let alone of best practice in dealing with them. One tool, for example, that is increasingly being adopted is plagiarism detection software: if a publisher encourages an editor to use this, or even provides it, it is important to explain how to handle suspected infringements and to provide some carefully worded template text that will achieve a desirable outcome for all parties, avoiding any unpleasant situations such as the risk of libel.

Similarly, it is good practice to ensure that journal editors understand copyright. Editors have been known to believe that there is no need to obtain copyright assignment or publishing rights for short articles, such as editorials or commentaries, or have given misleading advice about permission to reproduce illustrations or obtaining patient consent for publication.

Many editors will welcome proactive support and even handholding on issues such as these. Even those who are confident in tackling these issues may benefit from guidance and education about best practice. Needs will vary, but this could include an induction pack for new editors with briefing documents on dealing with ethical and legal issues, encouraging or paying for the editor to join COPE, or reviewing the journal's ethics policies and advising the editor or society of any changes that might be appropriate.

Working together on editorial management

Although the contract will have stated that the editor is responsible for soliciting, assessing and making decisions on the journal's content, there are numerous ways in which the publisher can contribute to the successful performance of the journal by providing support for the editor in these areas.

For example, providing metrics on article processing times, and on citations and downloads of different article types, and benchmarking these against other similar journals, will help the editor to set targets for improvement. Providing a forum where editors can share ideas and best practice is another way that publishers can add value to their relationships. If a journal's budget can afford it, it may be worth paying for editors to attend relevant courses or conferences. It could also be helpful to send journal editors and editorial assistants copies of industry surveys and reports about peer review or editorial office management, to increase their understanding of their role and give them ideas for development.

If the publisher and editor together agree that changes to the journal are needed (for example, commissioning more reviews, improving wording of template emails, speeding up decision times) it is advisable to check whether the editor has the time, experience and resources to implement the changes. If it has been agreed that a journal will benefit from specific improvements, it may be in the publisher's interest to invest its own resources into the plans rather than relying on an overworked editor.

Adopting an account management approach

Rationale and overview of relationship management tools

In many service industries (e.g. management consultants, legal firms, financial services organisations, software providers), account management is the approach used to retain clients and make the most of client relationships. The account manager is the main contact with the client, although there is also a wider team of experts who provide the different elements of the service, and are responsible for identifying needs and ensuring that they are met, so that the client does not move its business elsewhere.

The account manager often uses a number of formal tools to manage the relationship, including contact plans, a strategy to make the most of meetings, networking and ensuring that any promises made are kept. A number of publications on account management can be found in any large bookshop: many claim to offer a unique approach or programme, but broadly they all propose the principles suggested in this section.

The general aim of taking a formal approach to managing important accounts is to identify opportunities for collaboration and business growth, and to ensure that the provider is seen as delivering more than a basic service (which others might be able to provide more cheaply) and is in fact adding value to the relationship.

Relationship audits or health checks

If you were persuading someone to take on the editorship of a journal, do you know what they would learn about you if they spoke to the editors of your highest-profile journals? Would you be happy for any of your society partners to stand as referees in a bid and do you know what they would say about you? When you are going into a publications committee or editorial board meeting do you know exactly what issues might be raised and how the group you are to meet rate the publishing team's performance? Would you have any worries at all if you heard that your managing director was about to meet one of your contacts?

For all these reasons (and more), it is prudent to review your working relationships regularly. There are a number of benefits to carrying out a periodic formal relationship audit or health check:

- It serves to identify unsolved issues and worries that may otherwise not be raised or communicated, allowing them to be resolved before they become threats to the relationship.
- It provides an opportunity to review the needs, priorities and expectations of both parties.
- It demonstrates the commitment of the publisher to the relationship.
- It increases the chance that the relationship will be long-lasting and productive.

Sometimes – ironically often when personal one-to-one relationships are good – an editor may be reluctant to raise issues because of the risk of damaging the relationship. However, those issues may become a source of increasing frustration. A formal, scripted meeting to review the relationship can appear a less confrontational way for the editor to raise and review problems.

It is useful to carry out the audit with all those who are stakeholders in the relationship: in other words, not just the journal editor but also the managing editor or publications manager, society officers, society secretariat staff and so on. A possible script for an audit meeting could look at the following areas, with two or three open questions under each heading:

- Whether the publisher demonstrates understanding of the editor and/or society's priorities
- The quality of the relationship between specific individuals
- The accessibility and responsiveness of the publishing team
- Specific areas of the publisher's service in detail (e.g. production, technology, marketing)
- Confidence in the publisher's strategic expertise.

The interview could end with an invitation to recommend any ways in which the publisher could work differently: this should elicit any issues not raised so far.

Conducting an audit interview

- Before starting, ask the interviewee(s) if they have any specific issues that they want to cover
- Ask open questions (that require more than a simple 'yes' or 'no' answer)
- Pause from the script after each topic to ask if the interviewee has anything else to add
- Ensure that the interviewee has time to think and respond before moving on
- Thank the interviewee occasionally for their comments
- Do not use the interview to defend actions or give explanations: simply express understanding (e.g. '*That must have been so embarrassing for you*' or '*I'm sorry you were disappointed by that outcome*')

Clearly, time and resources will mean that it will not be possible to carry out formal audits with all stakeholders in all relationships. In practice it will be necessary to prioritise the most important journals and contracts. However, the principle of audit can be used in all interactions. For example, if a new development is introduced, assess the impact on the journal, ask for feedback, make changes if necessary and keep checking until stakeholders are happy. A brief meeting or telephone call on any topic is an opportunity to devote five minutes to probing for outstanding issues that need to be resolved.

Issues and promises log

Having a mechanism to keep track of issues noted and promises made by all members of the publishing team is a way of minimising surprises during an audit meeting and also of ensuring that any problems are dealt with efficiently and promptly, and promises are kept (Figures 16.2 and 16.3).

Issue Second quarter statement late and inaccurate	
Date raised	4 August 2011
Who by	Treasurer
Who to lead	KB
Date resolved	15 October 2011
Notes 4 August 2011: KB confirmed receipt of email and apologised. 6 August 2011: KB explained our timetable and guaranteed to check next quarter personally 15 October 2011: KB called treasurer to check he had received Q3 report and was satisfied. He was happy about her personal involvement.	
Issue In conversation, passed on general feeling of officers that website out of date and seemed not a priority for us	
Date raised	2 December 2011
Who by	Editor
Who to lead	KB
Date resolved	Not yet resolved
Notes 3 December 2011: KB met JS to discuss whether justified and if so what low-cost enhancements could be done – concluded that journal had been low priority	

Figure 16.2 Sample template for issues log

Date	Occasion	Promised	By whom	Done
02 Sep 2011	Ed board meeting	Usage stats analysis	KB	
02 Sep 2011	Ed board meeting	Review cover design	KB	
02 Sep 2011	Ed board meeting	Reduce colour fees	KB	
19 Sep 2011	Phone call with TP	Monthly accepted papers report	JL	

Figure 16.3 Sample template for promises log

For example:

- A casual offer to review the price being charged for colour to authors might slide down the journal manager's priority list but it might be something that the editor is really excited about.
- A conference stand manager might receive a number of queries from members about missing issues.
- A society officer might ask a journal manager whether staff are overworked because the accounts were late again.

These issues need to be collated and recorded along with action points that arise from meetings with the journal editor or the society. Action points arising from meetings, even if not formally minuted, should be circulated immediately by email to all participants; within the publishing team, responsibility for each action should be assigned to the appropriate person, along with clear communication of any commitments made.

Communications management

Some relationships are more demanding than others, and, unfortunately, sometimes the less demanding editors or clients do not receive the attention that they are due.

To avoid falling into the trap of a purely reactive approach to communication it is good practice to monitor all interactions with key individuals, whether by email, by telephone or in person, to ensure that

2011	Target frequency	Jan	Feb	Mar	Apr
Society X	President: every 2 months Council: twice a year Editor: monthly	Called editor to sugest appointing book review editor	Sent annual report to council Sat in on production conference call with editor		Dinner with edito at conference Sent impact facto article to all
Society Y	Hon Sec: quarterly Editor: monthly Board: twice a year			Sent annual report to editor and Secretary	Sent impact facto article to all
Society Z	Editor: monthly Pub committee: quarterly		Sent annual report to editor and publications committee		Called treasurer check financial statement OK Sent impact fa article to all

Figure 16.4 Sample template for a communication tracking spreadsheet

no one is forgotten. Although communications or contact management software is available, a simple spreadsheet or page per person in a notebook or card index is all that is needed (Figure 16.4). The point is not to record every interaction but only those communications, meetings and emails that bring some value to the relationship.

These regular significant interactions need not be face-to-face meetings every month (and probably could not, given everyone's commitments), although meetings should be part of a communications strategy. The ideal is a balance of formal and more casual meetings, telephone calls, emails and letters. Editors enjoy being treated to lunch or dinner occasionally, but meals should be a good use of time and ideally expenditure should be matched to the journal's budget and the editor's expectations. Some editors will be shocked rather than flattered by the expense of a Michelin-starred restaurant.

If too much time has passed without contact, it will be necessary to create a reason for a meeting or telephone call. For example, maybe someone in the organisation has written an article on citation tracking: this can be circulated to a contact list with a suggestion about suitable actions to take.

Meetings management

To make good use of everyone's valuable time, it is good practice to have a valid reason for a meeting, so that all parties benefit from it.

For example, it might be a good use of the society treasurer's time to go through the annual accounts and to obtain clarification on certain points in order to be able to present them confidently to the council. This would form the main item on the agenda and would be the reason for the meeting. For the publisher, a secondary aim of the meeting might be to persuade the treasurer to support an increase in the membership subscription rate.

Every meeting should have an agenda, whether this is a formal document or two or three bullet points in an email. Before the meeting starts, it is good practice to confirm the agenda and to ask whether there are any additional points for discussion (see Figure 16.5 for a meeting checklist). This is a good relationship audit practice, as it can elicit a disappointment or frustration that would not otherwise be communicated.

Do I know how much time I have?
What information/documents do I need?
What information/documents ***might*** I need?
Have I checked with colleagues for issues raised or promises made that I might not know about?
For an important meeting, have I had a pre-meeting planning meeting?
What am I going to leave behind (e.g. reports, copies of publications)?
On the day: Do I know exactly how to get there? Do I have copies of maps and timetables? Do I have contact details in case of delays?

Figure 16.5 Sample meeting checklist

To manage expectations, every meeting or significant telephone call, however informal, should be followed with notes. These need not be formal minutes if the nature of the meeting does not require minutes, but a list of the action points agreed and promises made should be circulated to all participants. This not only manages expectations as there is a clear agreed record of the meeting but also is a useful document to provide evidence of commitments made and promises kept.

If a number of members of the publishing team attend a more formal meeting together, they should all have a reason for being there that is clear to the other party attending. For example, a journal manager may take a senior colleague, such as a director, to a meeting to demonstrate the importance of the relationship, but it is still advisable for the director to have a specific role at the meeting, such as to update the publications committee on the company's online strategy.

Managing expectations

During all interactions with editor or society partner, it is essential to manage expectations. Whether the publisher's contribution to the relationship has a positive or negative impact depends on a combination of how that contribution is perceived in relation to what was expected. In other words, success is achieved when perception of actions exceeds expectations (see Figure 16.6).

There are a number of practical ways to manage expectations:

- *Setting expectations*
  - Do not overpromise
  - Ensure that commitments made are expressed clearly and documented
  - Have shared objectives and an action plan
- *Monitoring expectations*
  - Understand the editor or society officer's priorities
  - Ask for their regular feedback
- *Influence perceptions*
  - Do not hide any possibly disappointing news: have a 'no-surprises' policy
  - Present regular reports about the state of the journals market
  - Benchmark the journal against other comparable journals

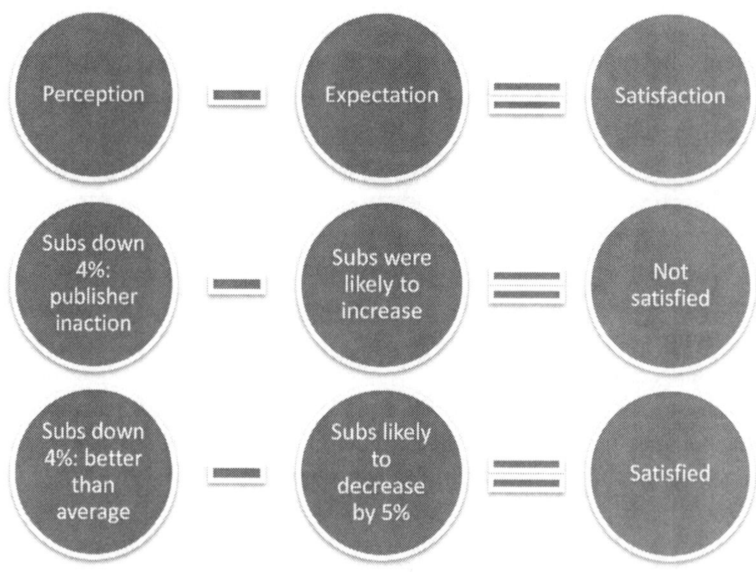

Figure 16.6 Satisfaction is achieved when perception exceeds expectations. If a journal's subscriptions decline by 4 per cent, the impact will depend on how the society or editor perceives this and what they expected

Managing the people in a relationship

Importance of peer-to-peer contact

The success of a publishing relationship is often over reliant on a single individual: a journal publishing manager, for example, who is particularly close to and respected by the journal editor and publications committee. The obvious risk is that if that person moves on the relationship may have to be rebuilt from scratch and important knowledge about the history of the relationship is lost, as the wider team may not be aware of issues. Moreover, no matter how experienced any one individual may be, they may not have the breadth of knowledge, experience or expertise that a broader team could bring or that a successful journal demands.

In managing a contract with a key society, it is good practice to develop peer-to-peer or mirror relationships between individuals with broadly equivalent functions. The benefit of this is that steps in communication are reduced, and the range of expertise and experience in the publishing team is available to both the editor and the society.

Of course, in practice this approach may have to be modified: it might be impractical, for example, for the society treasurer or managing editor to deal directly with the publisher's accounts department. However, it is worth identifying members of the core team who could work directly with appropriate counterparts at the society. In particular, it shows an appropriate level of respect and commitment if a senior member of the publishing staff, at director level if possible, is involved in any interactions involving senior figures at the society, such as the chief executive or the president.

Within this approach, it remains important to have a single lead contact person (the 'account manager') in the publishing team, such as the publishing manager. This individual (and indeed the whole team) must be accessible and responsive. He or she need not feel compelled to be on the end of a telephone at unsociable hours, but should give confidence that any messages will be responded to within 24 hours, either personally or by someone competent to handle the query or request. If it is not possible to respond fully, at the very least the issue raised should be acknowledged, with a commitment to following up by a specific time. This reassures the editor that the matter is being dealt with. It is inadvisable to use pressure of workload as an excuse for a slow response, as that might simply imply either inefficiency or that other relationships have a higher priority.

Finally, it is reassuring for the society or journal editor to know how to escalate any problems: who they would approach at a more senior level if necessary.

Working with the editor

A relationship that feels like a partnership will be more productive than one that seems like a contractor (the publisher) working with a supplier (the editor): this will be achieved by keeping the editor informed and, wherever possible, asking for his or her advice.

Hames (2011) proposes a seven part approach to a relationship with a journal editor or editorial board, as summarised here:

- *Provide support and back-up.* Make sure all the support and back-up the editors were promised is provided consistently and reliably.
- *Avoid work overload.* Monitor the editor's workload and take steps to acknowledge and resolve any cases of overload (the editor probably wants more than sympathy!).
- *Keep editors well informed.* Provide regular reports (and periodically check what information they would like to see and how they would like it to be presented).

- *Treat editors as individuals.* Get to know their strengths and weaknesses so you can take advantage of the former and compensate for the latter. Inspire trust and confidence so that they will let you know about any problems they are having and any mistakes or errors of judgement they may have made.
- *Create a feeling of community.* Work to achieve a sense of community, both within the editorial board and within the field the journal serves.
- *Discuss proposed policy changes.* Involve the editors fully in discussions on possible policy changes and take their comments into account.
- *Make things fun.* Introduce a lighter note and form good relationships. Make the editorial meetings enjoyable as well as useful and constructive. Help the editors with their travel and accommodation arrangements. Be understanding.

As in any relationship, being open about bad news is good practice, not only because it demonstrates honesty and helps build trust, but also because the editor can be involved in finding a solution rather than being annoyed when it is too late to do anything. For example, if an author is angry about how the production of a paper has been handled, inviting the editor to help pacify the author not only helps create that sense of partnership but also could be a good solution to the issue.

The approach to the editor relationship may need to be adapted depending on needs. For example, it is easy to underestimate how much hand-holding a first-time editor might need, but might be reluctant to ask for. An experienced editor might be willing to act as a mentor and to be available to give advice. If possible, it would be a good investment to pay for the new editor to attend relevant courses and seminars.

In the case of co-editors who do not know each other well, it cannot be assumed that they will take the initiative to build a relationship or to find ways of working together. It may be advisable for the first few months not only to suggest regular telephone catch-ups (depending on paper flow, perhaps every two weeks or so) but also for the publisher to set up these calls and to take part in them, in order to give direction as needed and to monitor how well they work together.

Working with the editorial board

Editorial boards are a valuable asset. Board members may serve a number of journals, and will have a sense of loyalty to some more than others. In order to win this loyalty, the relationship with the journal needs to amount to more than requests to referee papers and the annual invitation to an editorial board meeting. Keeping in touch with the editorial board should be part of the communication plan for a journal: for example, they could be sent emails with news about the journal (a change in impact factor, a successful press release); those members who cannot attend an editorial board meeting should be sent copies of the papers that were handed out; they could also be encouraged to distribute information about the journal in their institution and at seminars they attend.

To keep an editorial board lively and active, it is advisable to have a mechanism for appointing members and refreshing membership. Although most editorial boards comprise a combination of active contributors and figureheads, on some the proportion of active members can decline with time, and even those who were figureheads can be long retired. If members are appointed for a fixed term (e.g. three years plus maybe a single year extension) with overlapping termination dates, it should be possible to refresh a portion of the board every year. When appointed, board members could be sent a letter or information pack explaining how they are expected to contribute (how many papers they are expected to review, whether they are expected to commission reviews, attend board meetings, or write editorials, and so on).

Editorial board meetings are an opportunity to make the most of the board's expertise and to make individual members feel involved in and committed to the journal. Part of the meeting will almost certainly comprise the presentation of a number of reports, but it can be worthwhile and interesting to devote specific agenda items to topics inviting input from the board. Ideally brief discussion papers should be circulated in advance so that board members arrive ready to contribute. The most interesting and valuable editorial board meetings are those where the reporting is kept to a minimum and the discussion and generation of new ideas is lively.

It can be a challenge to hold a meeting of an international editorial board, particularly if there is no single conference that most of the members attend and if the journal cannot fund travel expenses. One alternative might be for the editor or the publisher to meet smaller groups at two or three conferences, with broadly similar agendas for discussion. Alternatively, rather than formal editorial board meetings, regular short online meetings using webinar technology could be held to present reports in slide format and then discuss progress and debate ideas using the chat facility.

Reviewers

A number of surveys have demonstrated consistently that peer-reviewers value both feedback on their work and recognition of their contribution. Feedback on decisions made not only gives the reviewer guidance about the expectations and standards of the journal but also helps demonstrate that their input was valued and respect for the time that the referee has spent on a paper.

Hames (2007) offers excellent advice on building relationships with reviewers and demonstrating how much they are valued. As well as emphasising the importance of thanking them and giving feedback, she discusses the benefits of training, suggests a number of ways to recompense reviewers, and gives a checklist of ways to develop and maintain reviewer loyalty, as summarised below:

- Treat reviewers well and with courtesy
- Ensure you do not overload reviewers: remember that they are reviewing for other journals as well as their day job
- Respond to queries and solve problems as quickly as possible
- Ensure that manuscripts sent to reviewers are relevant to the journal
- Provide feedback on manuscripts that they have reviewed
- Give them your time in return if they need help or advice.

Valuing referees

- Have a mechanism to let referees know what the final decision was on papers that they reviewed and what any other referees said
- List referees' names at the end of the year in the journal or on the home page with a thank you note
- Send Christmas cards (or similar)
- Send a certificate or letter once a year stating how many papers they have reviewed
- Consider rewarding referees who have done the most papers with a bottle of wine or an Amazon token
- Add a core list of regular referees to your mailing list for news items and announcements to make them feel part of the club

Winning and retaining publishing contracts

Winning through relationship building

This section is not a comprehensive guide about how to win new business but addresses some good practice in building valuable relationships that may increase the chances of winning a publishing contract.

As Ware (2008) has written:

> 'The problem for the society is distinguishing a good short-term deal (say, an attractive financial offer) from the partnership that will actually be in the better long-term interests of the journal... Underlying the performance of the best publisher partners are a good understanding of the needs of societies and their journals; a strong service orientation; and an ability to plan strategically for each journal on the basis of facts and data.'

Most major publishers are able to demonstrate convincingly that they are able to meet these criteria; so the challenge in tendering for business remains to find some differentiating factors – some way of demonstrating a solution that is the best match to the society's needs and an understanding of and sympathy with their objectives.

To achieve this requires building up relationships with all those who might influence the decision before the request for a proposal (RFP) arrives, bearing in mind that each individual may have a different view of the society's needs and objectives and how the best deal for the journal might be framed, and also may hold different personal motivations. This, of course, requires the knowledge of when contract renewals are likely to fall due and the application of a relatively formal approach to prospecting (there are a number of books on complex selling or strategic selling which describe tools for managing pipelines of prospects that can easily be adapted to bidding for and winning society contracts).

As the date for an expected RFP approaches, it is well worth reviewing whether any of those likely to be involved in the decision are also involved in other publications: are those publications and relationships running smoothly?

It is also likely that references from similar organisations will be required as part of the bid process. If there is any doubt about what one of the references might say, there is nothing to be lost in having an open discussion with the society in question. However, a programme of regular audits should make this unnecessary.

Examples of personal motivations and their implications

- The journal editor wants to ensure that his or her editorial assistant keeps their job, so a bid that offers editorial office management at the publisher's office would not appeal.
- Some publications committee members are uncomfortable about pharmaceutical company sponsorship, so would be nervous about a bid describing this at great length.
- The new chief executive of the society does not have a publishing background and so views the journal simply as a source of income to be maximised.

Retaining and renewing a contract

Handling contract renewals ideally involves a similar approach, i.e. one of establishing the priorities and motivations of all those who might have an impact on the decision. As an example, the president of the society might be in office for just a year or two and feel compelled to make an impact during that time. Negotiating a contract with a new publisher might appear to be a way of making such an impact. Working with him or her so that contract renewal can be presented as a significant success might appeal in such a case.

In general, it is wise to avoid relying on relationships with one or two individuals, especially if these are particularly warm and close. This can lead to complacency and a lack of understanding of what and who will have an impact on the final decision. Networking beyond one's comfort zone is the only way to ensure full understanding of all those with influence.

Other organisations tendering for the contract will no doubt present innovations and new ideas in their bid, which may or may not be realistic. If expectations have been appropriately managed, and a strategic business plan has been agreed and is being implemented, the society is more likely to be able to make a reasonable, well-informed assessment of the offers on the table.

Summary

A successful relationship is a partnership, in which all involved have shared goals and interests and in which the collaboration itself contributes to success, clearly generating value for all those involved. In a publishing relationship, the challenge is to create this sense of partnership, rather than a supplier–contractor relationship (publisher–society) or contractor–supplier relationship (publisher–editor). This requires not only working together collaboratively to agree priorities and develop shared objectives but also, on the publisher's part, taking a proactive approach to managing and building personal relationships. This will result in productive partnerships and successful publishing contracts.

References

ALPSP (2010) *Advice Note 8. The Journal Editor's Contract.* Available from http://www.alpsp.org/Ebusiness/Research/Publications/AdviceNoteGuidelines.aspx

ALPSP (2002) *Advice Note 9. The Society–Publisher Contract.* Available from http://www.alpsp.org/Ebusiness/Research/Publications/AdviceNoteGuidelines.aspx

Committee on Publication Ethics (2012) *Flowcharts.* Available from http://publicationethics.org/resources/flowcharts

Hames, I. (2011) Editorial boards: realizing their potential. *Learned Publishing*, 14: 247–56.

Hames, I. (2007) 'Reviewers – a precious resource', in *Peer Review and Manuscript Management in Scientific Journals – Guidelines for Good Practice.* Oxford: Blackwell Publishing, pp. 139–145.

Owen, L. (ed.) (2010) *Clark's Publishing Agreements*, 8th edn. London: Bloomsbury Professional.

UK Serials Group (2008) *Transfer Code of Practice Version 2.0.* Available from http://www.uksg.org/Transfer/Code

Ware, M. (2008) Choosing a publishing partner: advice for societies and associations. *Learned Publishing* 21: 22–8.

Other useful resources

ALPSP (2009). *ALPSP Advice Note 18. When a Society Journal Changes Publisher. Guidelines for Good Practice.* Available from http://www.alpsp.org/Ebusiness/Research/Publications/AdviceNoteGuidelines.aspx

Ashman, P. (2009) What societies want from a publishing partner. *Learned Publishing*, 22: 209–19.

Bammel, J. (1999) The publisher – author relationship. Principles of good practice in scholarly journal publishing. *Learned Publishing*, 12: 75–8.

17

Does journal publishing have a future?

Michael Mabe

Abstract: The demise of the peer-reviewed journal has been often predicted especially since the advent of digital publishing. This chapter examines what forces might impinge on journal publishing to precipitate such a collapse and whether they might succeed.

Key words: Journals, journal functions, author and reader needs, communication ecology, open access, business models, digital transition.

Introduction

Publishing and information science conferences over the last four decades have regularly debated whether the journal has a future. Originally these speculative sessions were predicated on the imminence of the electronic transition. With this rapidly receding into history, the speculation continues but now has other engines. This chapter examines what forces might undermine the journal and looks at whether they are likely to succeed.

To merely pose the question 'Does journal publishing have a future?' does not help answer it; to do so we must deconstruct what a functioning journal system does, and for whom, to be able to analyse how and where it might collapse. A standard business tool for strategic market analysis, the political, economic, sociological and technological (PEST) approach (Aguilar, 1967), can be very helpful here in breaking down our Big Question into Four Key Questions. When this is done there are four domains, each with its own question:

- *Research behaviour*: will researchers still communicate and be evaluated by journal publication?
- *Technology*: will tools develop that make the current journal obsolete?
- *Business models*: will there be any viable business models to sustain publishing operations with net returns?
- *Political zeitgeist*: will public (political) attitudes regarding the Internet make publishing impossible?

Answering each of these in turn should provide a good snapshot of how close to collapse we might be, where it may be expected to occur first and what are the forces that might cause it.

Key Question 1: Research behaviour: will researchers still communicate and be evaluated by journal publication?

Framing the question

Many analyses of the scholarly communication system focus on the *what* and the *how* of communication but rarely the *why*. Understanding the *why* is locked up in the sociology and psychology of human discovery: how can I establish that I discovered something first, how sure can I be that my claims will be accepted, and how do I prevent others stealing my ideas and passing them off as their own? These issues lie at the heart of answering our first question. But aspects of this sit even deeper, embedded in the DNA of what it means to say something is knowledge.

In Plato's epistemological formulation, knowledge is justified true belief, that is to say, I can only assert that a belief (an observation if you will) is knowledge if it can be justified and it turns out to be true. In philosophy of science, experimental results are observed (the collection of beliefs), they are put together to create theories that might explain them (justification) and are subsequently tested by further observation to see if they are true. In this context the scientific method is an epistemological engine generating knowledge out of observation.

This philosophical structure is also embedded in the evolved system of scholarly communication. An investigator reports on his or her observations (beliefs), relates them to the existing literature and the tests he or she conducts (the justification) and has them tested by external critical comment by peer reviewers (the test of truth). Of course this is only partially correct as the truth of the hypothesis is rarely contained or proved by a single experiment or paper reporting it. For the whole body of work in a field, however, the analogy is apt and I believe goes some way to explaining the essential conservatism of how academic work is reported. Albeit dimly, investigators know they have to demonstrate that what they saw once in their apparatus on a wet Wednesday is true everywhere for everyone for all time. For science, the status of knowledge is insufficient: that knowledge must be objective, seen by all. In Ziman's phrase, science is public knowledge (Ziman, 1968).

Researcher needs and the functions of the journal

The fundamental needs of researchers have been well studied over the last twenty or so years (Tenopir and King, 2000; Mabe and Amin, 2002; Mabe, 2003, 2009; Mabe and Mulligan, 2011). One of the key conclusions of this work is that what researchers want of their communication system very much depends on their role. What they want as the producers of research is very different from what they want when they are a consumer. We can sum up the findings of these studies as follows:

Needs in author (producer) mode:

- To be *seen* to report an idea *first*
- To feel *secure* in communicating that idea
- [For empirical subjects] To *persuade* readers that their results are general and arise from enactment of a canonical (scientific) method
- To have their claim *accepted* by peers
- To *report* their idea to the *right audience*
- To get *recognition* for their idea
- To have a permanent *public record* of their work

Needs in reader (consumer) mode:

- To *identify* relevant content
- To *select* based on *trust* and *authority*
- To *locate* and *consume* it

- To *cite* it
- To be sure it is *final* and *permanent*

The journal as a method of organising and communicating knowledge serves all these needs through the information functions it possesses. These functions were established right at the creation of the journal by its inventor, the diplomat and administrator Henry Oldenburg (1619–77), who introduced them when he conceived the world's first scientific journal *Philosophical Transactions* in 1665. The functions of the journal à la Oldenburg (Zuckerman and Merton, 1971; Merton, 1973), which deliver the author and reader needs outlined above, are:

- Date stamping or priority via registration
- Quality stamping (certification) through peer review
- Recording the final, definitive, authorised versions of papers and archiving them
- Dissemination to targeted scholarly audience

And these functions are all achieved via creation and then management of the 'journal brand': the type of material and range of authors published, the rigour of the peer review process, and the attitude of the community the journal serves to its quality and importance.

Oldenburg created the world's first research journal as first Joint Secretary of the newly founded Royal Society of London. He did this to solve a number of challenges faced by early scientists. Principal among these was the desire to establish precedence: the first authors of a phenomenon or result wanted their priority as discoverer to be publicly acknowledged and secured before they were prepared to share their results with their colleagues. Oldenburg realised that a periodical publication run by an independent third party could resolve this dilemma for the pioneering scientists of his age by faithfully recording the name of a discoverer, the date he or she submitted the paper as well as his or her description of the discovery. We can see this clearly in the letters that survive from Oldenburg to his patron Sir Robert Boyle (Hall and Hall, 1965–86), one of the founders of the Royal Society, and in the surviving records of the Royal Society:

- The idea of registration

> [We must be] very careful of registring as well the person and time of any new matter.., as the matter itselfe; whereby the honor of the invention will be inviolably preserved to all posterity. [Oldenburg to Boyle, 24 November 1664]

- The idea of dissemination

  [By setting up such a system] all Ingenious men will be thereby incouraged to impart their knowledge and discoveryes. [Oldenburg to Boyle, 3 December 1664]

- The idea of a permanent record or archive

  [I should not] neglect the opportunity of having some of my Memoirs preserv'd, by being incorporated into a Collection, that is like to be as lasting as usefull. [Boyle to Oldenburg, 1665]

- The idea of certification (peer review)

  [*Phil. Trans.* should be] licensed under the charter by the Council of the Society, being first reviewed by some of the members of the same. [Royal Society Order in Council 1 March 1665]

Launched on 6 March 1665, *Philosophical Transactions* did exactly this. In its monthly issues, it registered the name of the authors and date that they sent their manuscripts to Oldenburg as well as recording their discoveries in their own words. This simple act secured the priority for first authors and encouraged them to share their results with others, safe in the knowledge that their 'rights' as 'first discoverers' were protected by so doing.

Philosophical Transactions from the outset did not publish all the material it received; the Council of the Royal Society reviewed the contributions sent to Oldenburg before approving a selection of them for publication. Albeit primitive, this is the first recorded instance of 'peer review'. It was quickly realised by Oldenburg's contemporaries that the accumulating monthly issues of the journal also represented a record of the transactions of science of archival value.

The four functions of Oldenburg's journal, registration, dissemination, peer review and archival record, are so fundamental to the way scientists behave and how science is carried out that all subsequent journals, even those published electronically in the 21st century, have conformed to Oldenburg's model. All modern journals carry out the same functions as Oldenburg's and all journal publishers are Oldenburg's heirs.

The growth in the size of the literature since Oldenburg's day, with at the time of writing over 25 000 active peer-reviewed journals in existence, has made finding individual articles increasingly difficult for readers. This need to locate and retrieve has sometimes been called the 'fifth function': navigation. Fifty years after the creation of the journal, the first abstracting journals appeared with the role of helping readers navigate through the expanding number of papers. Price showed in the 1960s how the growth of this *secondary* publishing kept pace with primary; he estimates a ratio of about 300:1 between primary and secondary journal numbers (Price, 1963). Journals also developed their own indexes (subject and author) and published them on a regular basis.

All of this navigation apparatus has of course been swept away by the introduction of abstracting and indexing databases, firstly in paper and now electronically. These have drawn upon a key feature required in registration and dissemination: constant bibliographic citation. The journal system has since spawned a unique digital identifier for each article, the DOI (digital object identifier) which can be a pointer and link too. Citation has taken on a life of its own as a result of citation indices [originally developed by Garfield (1955) to help identify the core literature] being expanded and often misused to form a 'brownie point' system to identify top journals, scholars and their institutions. Such quality metrics have become incredibly important for the government agencies that fund research and have to justify their expenditure of public money, and in turn have begun to drive institutional macro-level behaviour and policy. This important topic is dealt with elsewhere in this book (see Chapter 10).

Evidence of the way researcher needs are served by the journal functions can be found in the literature. Probably the biggest continuous survey of author attitudes to publishing has been that carried out by Elsevier, reported by Mulligan and Mabe (2011). A summary of one whole year of responses from 63 384 authors is illustrated in Figure 17.1. This shows that the concerns about publication speed and therefore priority (the registration function in effect) remain paramount alongside those of quality (peer review, the certification function).

Despite considerable changes in the economic, sociological and technical environments within which academic authors publish over the last 300 years, their needs and therefore the journal functions remain unchanged. We can see this in the physical form of journal articles. Figures 17.2–17.4 show the opening pages of scientific articles published in 1672 in *Philosophical Transactions* (Newton's famous report about the spectrum of white light), in 1985 in *Nature* (Nobelists Kroto, Smalley *et al.* announcing the discovery of Buckminsterfullerene) and in 2009, an article in the online edition of *Tetrahedron Letters*. In all three cases, the same structural features can be found. The title of the article and the name and affiliation of its author(s); the date the paper was received by the journal, and in the later examples, when it was accepted for

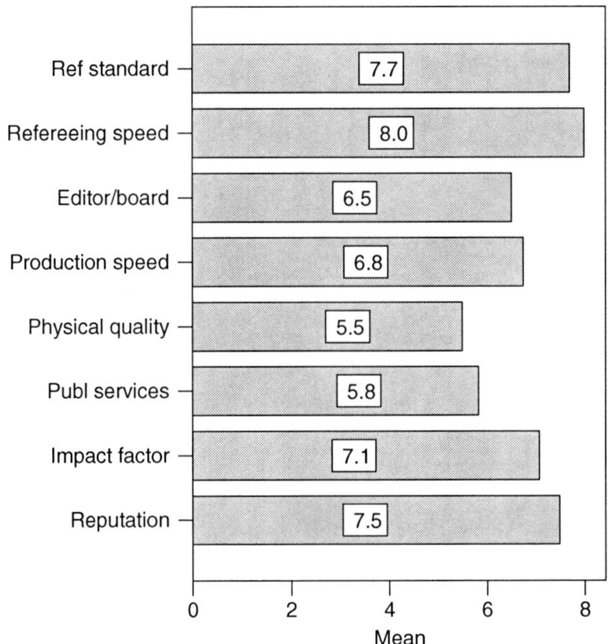

Figure 17.1 Eight most important factors for authors in 2009

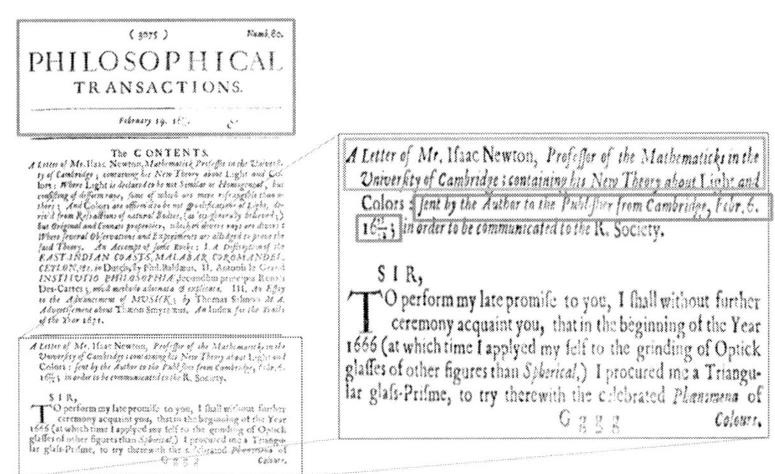

(3075) Numb. 80.

PHILOSOPHICAL TRANSACTIONS.

The CONTENTS.

A Letter of Mr. Iſaac Newton, *Profeſſor of the Mathematicks in the Univerſity of Cambridge; containing his New Theory about Light and* Colors: *ſent by the Author to the Publiſher from Cambridge, Febr. 6.* 16$\frac{71}{72}$; *in order to be communicated to the* R. Society.

SIR,

To perform my late promiſe to you, I ſhall without further ceremony acquaint you, that in the beginning of the Year 1666 (at which time I applyed my ſelf to the grinding of Optick glaſſes of other figures than *Spherical*,) I procured me a Triangular glaſs-Priſme, to try therewith the celebrated *Phænomena* of *Colours*.

Figure 17.2 Report of Newton's prism experiments

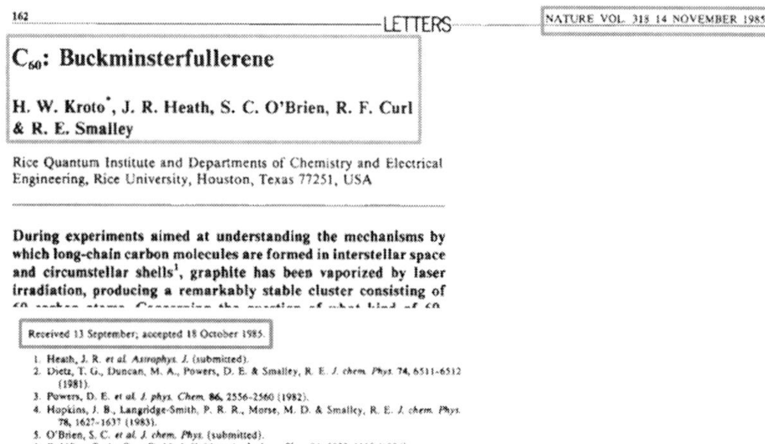

162 LETTERS NATURE VOL. 318 14 NOVEMBER 1985

C_{60}: Buckminsterfullerene

H. W. Kroto*, J. R. Heath, S. C. O'Brien, R. F. Curl & R. E. Smalley

Rice Quantum Institute and Departments of Chemistry and Electrical Engineering, Rice University, Houston, Texas 77251, USA

During experiments aimed at understanding the mechanisms by which long-chain carbon molecules are formed in interstellar space and circumstellar shells[1], graphite has been vaporized by laser irradiation, producing a remarkably stable cluster consisting of

Received 13 September; accepted 18 October 1985.

1. Heath, J. R. *et al. Astrophys. J.* (submitted).
2. Dietz, T. G., Duncan, M. A., Powers, D. E. & Smalley, R. E. *J. chem. Phys.* **74**, 6511-6512 (1981).
3. Powers, D. E. *et al. J. phys. Chem.* **86**, 2556-2560 (1982).
4. Hopkins, J. B., Langridge-Smith, P. R. R., Morse, M. D. & Smalley, R. E. *J. chem. Phys.* **78**, 1627-1637 (1983).
5. O'Brien, S. C. *et al. J. chem. Phys.* (submitted).
6. Rohlfing, E. A., Cox, D. M. & Kaldor, A. *J. chem. Phys.* **81**, 3322-3330 (1984).
7. Marks, R. W. *The Dymaxion World of Buckminster Fuller* (Reinhold, New York, 1960).
8. Heath, J. R. *et al. J. Am. chem. Soc.* (in the press).
9. Herbig, E. *Astrophys. J.* **196**, 129-160 (1975).

Figure 17.3 Discovery of Buckministerfullerene

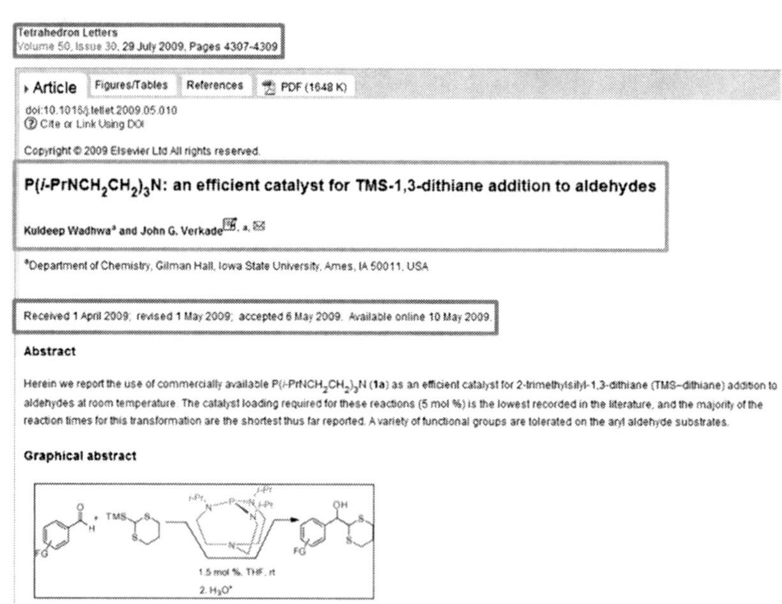

Tetrahedron Letters
Volume 50, Issue 30, 29 July 2009, Pages 4307-4309

Article | Figures/Tables | References | PDF (1648 K)

doi:10.1016/j.tetlet.2009.05.010
Cite or Link Using DOI

Copyright © 2009 Elsevier Ltd All rights reserved.

P(*i*-PrNCH$_2$CH$_2$)$_3$N: an efficient catalyst for TMS-1,3-dithiane addition to aldehydes

Kuldeep Wadhwa[a] and John G. Verkade[a]

[a]Department of Chemistry, Gilman Hall, Iowa State University, Ames, IA 50011, USA

Received 1 April 2009; revised 1 May 2009; accepted 6 May 2009. Available online 10 May 2009.

Abstract

Herein we report the use of commercially available P(*i*-PrNCH$_2$CH$_2$)$_3$N (**1a**) as an efficient catalyst for 2-trimethylsilyl-1,3-dithiane (TMS–dithiane) addition to aldehydes at room temperature. The catalyst loading required for these reactions (5 mol %) is the lowest recorded in the literature, and the majority of the reaction times for this transformation are the shortest thus far reported. A variety of functional groups are tolerated on the aryl aldehyde substrates.

Graphical abstract

Figure 17.4 A recent paper from the online edition of *Tetrahedron Letters*

publication; the date of publication. Together these instance the registration function (who, what, when) and the certification function (date of acceptance after peer review and publication). The presence of the journal title (with bibliographic citation metadata fulfilling the navigation function) in each case also illustrates the importance of that branding to the status of the article and can be viewed as an example of the dissemination function.

Could these functions be delivered in another way or by a different type of publication vehicle? It is clear that despite considerable evolution in many other spheres, the mechanisms for delivering author and reader needs seem to be largely in a state of stasis. If we were to view this as an evolutionary path we might conclude that natural selection had forced the manner in which scholarly material is published down a largely single route. The new major selective pressure, however, is the introduction of digital publishing via the Internet. So far this has not had the effect that many have predicted but clearly with only 20 years under its belt the World Wide Web may yet surprise us: that is a topic for the next Key Question. Nevertheless there have been some novel approaches to scholarly publishing inspired by digital developments and these should be examined in the light of the functional model discussed above.

Assessing alternatives to journals

Discussions about whether the cardinal four functions could be delivered separately have been around for some time (Smith, 1999; Crow, 2002; Van de Sompel *et al.*, 2004) and have been amplified by the growth of institutional repositories for digital material at scholarly institutions. There have also been subject-based repositories developed by associations or funding bodies. Could these replace the journal?

Figure 17.5 shows a cross comparison of various publishing vehicles and whether they are able to deliver the functions needed by academics. Unless documents have been already registered and certified by the journal process they will have the same uncertain status of any material that can be found on the Internet. The only vehicle that delivers all the functions simultaneously in one place as part of a unitary act of publication, distancing the interests of the author from those of the certifier, is the scholarly journal. Those who favour repositories either have to accept that journals are needed to give the documents status or have to find novel mechanisms that can work within a repository framework.

	Global	Community based/run	Registration	Certification	Dissemination	Archive
Web pages			0	0	X	?
Institutional repositories			0	0	X	X
Subject repositories	?	?	0	0	X	X
Journal	X	X	X	X	X	X

0 = done by document NOT vehicle
X = done by vehicle

Figure 17.5 Comparison of publishing vehicles

One suggestion has been to create 'peer review panels' that would sample the papers uploaded to repositories around the world, select the best and provide the certification function. It is assumed by adherents of this approach that the repositories are able to register, disseminate and archive. While the latter two functions could be achieved by repositories (although dissemination is about much more than simply placing stuff online and involves the brand value of the collecting entity as well as active dissemination tools), it is far from clear that an institutional repository could function as an independent, community-run, international collection and act as a registration centre, as these repositories are located in, funded by and intended to serve specific universities in specific nations. This might be possible with a subject-based repository, but even here issues of national politics (such repositories tend to be run and funded by nationally based and government-funded institutions) come to the fore. One cannot imagine a repository run by an agency of the former US Bush administration being too keen on publishing stem cell research.

I also believe that the idea of 'peer review panels' floating around and singling papers out for stardom from the morass of non-peer-reviewed content is organisationally flawed. Under the current journal system, authors (who have a clear self-interest in the matter) seek out journals that are appropriate for their needs and hope they are successful through the journal's peer review system. Under the proposed 'overlay journal system' the peer review panels would have to read everything on all repositories worldwide before deciding which to thoroughly review and give status. In the current system authors are motivated to seek out a brand which 'pulls' them towards it and which thereby re-establishes and enhances its identity. In the alternate system, the peer review panel have to find the papers they want in the haystack of un-refereed material on the web and 'push' to give them status. What if the author doesn't like the overlay journal panels standards, does he or she have a choice in their selection? This is also leaving aside the motivating factors for the 'overlay journal team'. In the case of the traditional journal the editor-in-chief evaluates what he or she receives and sends it on to appropriate peers for review. The editor can exercise control over what is received and who (and how often) an academic is asked to peer review. In a very real sense the publication is publicly recognised as 'his/her' journal, a reputational reward in addition to any honorarium or expenses they receive. In the case of the panel of reviewers it unclear why they would comb the whole literature and then peer review what they select, especially if the authors then say they don't want to appear there. Human factors are important in publishing and contribute to its success or failure.

What might cause the journal functions to breakdown?

A much bigger issue is whether the canonical journal function system will be affected by changes in demographics or by the singular nature of the practice in some disciplines. To examine this possibility, let's look at what would cause each of the functions to cease to work.

Registration is about establishing priority and ownership of an idea. Clearly, one's attitude to the ownership of the ideas presented in a paper will depend in part on how many authors that article has. So one factor that would contribute to a lessening of the desire to be registered would be a significant growth in co-authorship levels.

Certification is principally about peer review. Peer review practice will tend to vary by discipline, reflecting the nature of the research undertaken. The need for peer review will also be affected by the size of the discipline and whether practitioners could reasonably be familiar with most of the others working in their field. In areas where collaboration levels are high, the examination of the paper by co-authors may be so extensive that the additional review by referees appointed by a journal may not be seen to add much.

Dissemination is about public active disclosure. This will depend upon the levels of access to the journal by readers and the visibility to search of the content. While a situation could be envisaged where access levels (via subscription-related models) would be too low to sustain the interest of authors in publishing in a journal – a situation that was being approached in the paper-only publishing era – the growth of electronic delivery to usage levels in excess of that achieved even at the peak of paper circulation suggests this function is unlikely to break down, despite vociferous claims to the contrary. Indeed, recent studies show that academic satisfaction levels concerning access to research articles is very high and higher than other types of content, especially data (Publishing Research Consortium, 2010). The archival function is about ensuring permanence, and this depends upon the organisations involved and the technology applied. Currently, archive arrangements for articles are well thought through and do not raise undue concerns, although the situation for data is very different (Smit and Gruttermeier, 2011).

So, where could function breakdown occur? Figure 17.6 (from Mabe and Amin, 2002) shows the growth in co-authorship over the last 50 years. The average paper in 1950 had about 1.75 authors; in 2000 this had grown to just under 4. This does not suggest that the strength of the registration function would be significantly undermined by 2050, when, assuming a similar growth in collaboration, the average paper will possibly have eight co-authors. Each author may care a little less than if

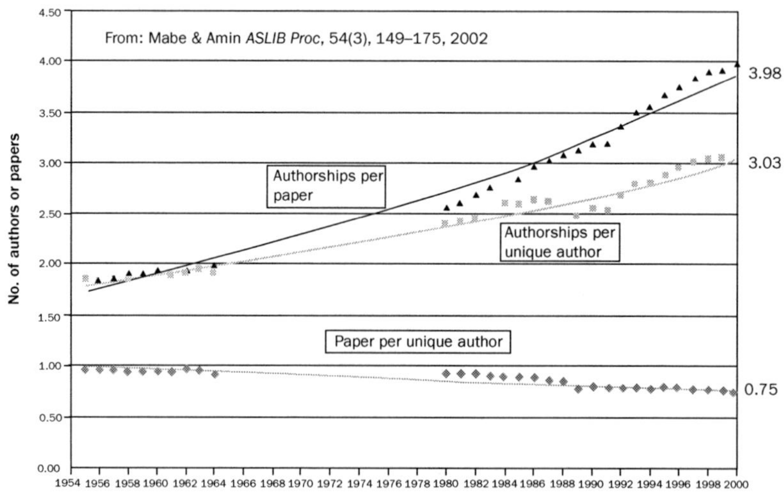

Figure 17.6 Growth in co-authorship levels

the paper was theirs alone, but they will still care. The exception here, as in many cases, can be found in the field of high-energy physics; where there are few but very large research groups and papers with over 100 co-authors (even over 200) are not uncommon. In this case, the idea that each of these myriad co-authors cares enough for registration to matter becomes a moot point. It is not uncommon for such papers to appear first on pre-print servers such ArXiv, and one can posit that the diminished need for registration contributes to this. This does not just affect registration, however, because as noted above, if a hundred or more co-authors have collectively corrected a draft paper it is difficult to see how a further two anonymous referees are going to help much. As co-authorship grows, then, certification also becomes less important.

The nature of the discipline also affects the degree to which the certification function is important. Those subjects where the number of practitioners is small and the personnel of research groups known widely throughout the discipline will have less need of an independent anonymous check to enhance trust and authority. If I know the researchers well I can probably judge how much I trust their work. These conditions would be fulfilled in smaller subdisciplines where each researcher knows the others, such as theoretical physics for example. Equally, if the nature of the research work is *sui generis*, that is, if it is contained within the paper without any need for external experiment, such as mathematics, theoretical physics and economics, or describes or actually operates a model, such as the programs of computer science, the reader may intuit what he or she believes about the trustworthiness of the paper without any need for independent reviewers. On the other hand, for most other subjects where the number of research groups is large, their members are not known personally to each other, and where the work is of an experimental nature, trust and authority can only be enhanced by the act of peer review.

In 2005 I directed a major survey study to test some of these hypotheses (see Figure 17.7 and Mulligan and Mabe, 2011). The vast majority of respondents to the survey gave answers that emphasised the continued importance of the four functions to the work of the journal even in the Internet age. However, a number of questions related to the decoupling of the article from the journal had statistically significant deviations from the majority view in particular subject areas. These were high-energy physics, mathematics, computer science and economics, exactly as predicted by the functional model.

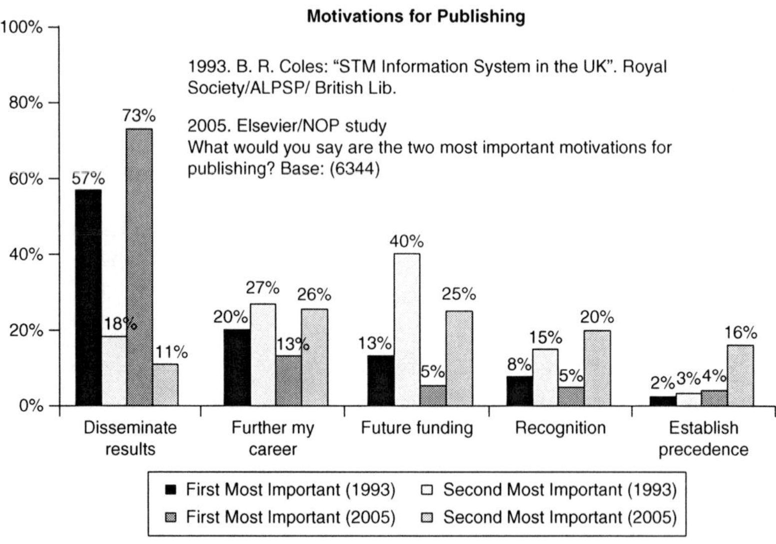

Figure 17.7 **Results of the Core Trends study**

Answering Key Question 1

So where does this leaves us in answering our first Key Question? From a philosophical perspective, the journal model is well designed to fit with the requirements for knowledge generation. It also fits well with the generalised needs of authors and readers, and this has not been unduly affected by the rise of digital publishing or so-called alternative systems such as the repository landscape. That said there are a minority of subjects where the canonical offering of the journal model does not sit well with their practice, and here we are seeing differences. While the vast majority of scientific disciplines adhere to the model, a minority do not. In most cases these deviations are due to intrinsic factors in specific disciplines rather than more general issues of growth in co-authorship. I think we can safely say that at least for the foreseeable future and with the noted exceptions of high-energy physics, economics, mathematics and computer science, most researchers will continue to want to communicate and be evaluated by journal publication.

Key Question 2: Technology: will tools develop that make the current journal obsolete?

The rise of the Internet

The late 1990s, the era of the first Internet bubble, were a heady time. Many observers were convinced that the introduction of the Internet and the web would fundamentally overthrow almost all existing practice. Two quotations catch the zeitgeist rather well:

> 'Here, on the edge of the twenty-first century, a fundamental new rule of business is that the Internet changes everything.' Bill Gates *Business @ The Speed of Thought*, 1999.
>
> ' "The Internet changes everything!" They say.' *New York Times* 14 December 1998, digital commerce article.

It is sometimes difficult to remember that most of the Internet tools we have become familiar with and use virtually every day are barely 20 years old. In scholarly publishing the key landmarks have been

- 6 August 1991 – World Wide Web goes live
- 1992 – first www journal, *Online Journal of Current Clinical Trials*
- 22 April 1993 – Mosaic browser launched
- 13 October 1994 – Netscape browser launched
- August 1995 – Internet Explorer browser launched
- 1996 onwards – e journal platforms: Ideal, ScienceDirect, Synergy, Interscience, etc.

At the time of writing, the web is about to celebrate 20 years, web journals are just 19 and the multi-journal electronic platforms from which most content is browsed are teenagers.

Assessing the Internet's impact on journals publishing

So, has the Internet changed everything? Since over a generation has now passed with electronic content and services as the norm, it is difficult to argue that the observed lack of change is due to users only just getting used to the new medium. We are at the early stage of maturity in terms of technology adoption. The results of recent studies on motivations for publishing by researchers seem to show that less has changed than we might hope or fear (University of California, 2007; RIN, 2009; Harley *et al.*, 2010; Mulligan and Mabe, 2011).

The Core Trends Survey (Mulligan and Mabe, 2011) was organised and funded by Elsevier with the collaboration of the CIBER research unit at UCL and the NOP polling organisation. It was inspired by an earlier survey conducted at the very end of the paper publishing era (Coles, 1993), and with over 6000 respondents, Core Trends is one of the largest surveys of its kind to date. In the Coles study, a number of motivations were identified and respondents invited to indicate which two were the most important. Figure 17.7 shows the results from this study in comparison with the results from the later one.

Dissemination is the most important motivation in the Coles study, with 57 per cent of the respondents indicating this is the reason why they publish. However, first stated motivations can be misleading; respondents often choose a response that is 'top of mind', which can conveniently convey a more altruistic position than might truly exist, especially when the respondents are sophisticated and know that their answers are likely to be seen by their peers. Analysis of secondary motivations can get beyond this somewhat 'obvious' response to reveal the 'covert' motivations that are more likely to be influential in driving behaviour. In the Core Trends study, respondents were also invited to indicate which two motivations were the most important for them. The most important motivation was again 'dissemination' (73 per cent); 'furthering my career' and 'future funding' were the key secondary motivations.

By comparing the two studies we can determine whether there has been motivational shift in the intervening 12 years between the surveys and whether the Internet has had an effect on researcher motivations. In terms of change to secondary motivations, 'recognition' and 'establishing precedent' have clearly increased, especially the latter, but in general there has been no substantive shift in secondary motivations (which are more likely to represent the covert or 'underlying' motivators and relate directly to the canonical journal functions) as the research community moved from a fully paper-based environment to a virtually fully electronic one.

Yet clearly some things have changed. At the obvious level virtually all journals are now online and online has become the definitive edition with paper as the add-on. There are new communication possibilities, especially in the earlier informal interactions that precede formal public publication:

- Internet relay chat – used for informal research collaborations
- Internet forums – used for semi-formal sharing of information and practice
- Blogs – used for opinion leaders engaging debate
- Wikis – used for collaborative authoring

With the exception of wikis (which create the entirely new functionality of many-to-many written interaction), these are new tools but they are new tools for old purposes. They make communicative acts that were already happening more efficient through the application of technology. The challenge for the publisher, though, is how such enhancements might be monetised, and so far there is no clear answer.

We can think of this as a communication ecology (Altheide, 1994) with each communication type occupying a particular niche. In almost all cases, the addition of a technology component does not change the communication instance but merely enhances it. Table 17.1 shows the dimensions that a communication instance may adopt. Table 17.2 gives

Table 17.1 **Communication dimensions**

Dimensions	Options			
Mode	1:1	1:many		many:many
Directionality	Unidirectional		Interactive	
Delivery regime	Oral		Written	
Temporality	Live		Recorded	
Register	Private	Public	Informal	Formal
Enhancement	Local		At a distance	

Table 17.2 **An example of an oral lecture**

Dimension	Option
Mode	1:many
Directionality	Unidirectional (except for Q&A)
Delivery regime	Oral
Temporality	Live
Register	Public, formal
Enhancement	None (in the lecture hall) but technology allows development to 'at a distance' and 'recorded' broadcast, but reduced directionality webcast, no reduced directionality

an example of how this works, looking at the instance of a live lecture and the consequences of technological enhancement.

Thus an enhanced lecture which becomes a television broadcast or a webcast is *still* a lecture although much more useful for distance and time-shifted applications. Similarly, a one-to-one interactive communication between two people is at its simplest either an in-person conversation or an exchange of letters, or else a telephone conversation or an exchange of emails, or else a VoIP conversation or an exchange of instant messages. These are all the same communicative act but with slightly different enhancements that can both add and detract from the utility of the communicative act, but they are *not* something entirely new. Looking at the current publishing technology landscape with communications ecology glasses on reveals why so little appears to have changed in the fundamentals.

Answering Key Question 2

The biggest imponderable for this Key Question is whether a killer application could arise that would sweep all away. Based on the analysis here, it seems unlikely given that all the communication ecological niches appear to be occupied, but it cannot be ruled out entirely. So the Internet has not changed everything yet – but there still remains a remote possibility that it might, and it certainly has changed attitudes, as we shall see later.

Key Question 3: Business models: will there be any viable business models to sustain publishing operations with net returns?

The landscape of journals publishing business models

There are a wide variety of business models which publishers can adopt singly or jointly for the journal. These range from supply-side models involving author payments, to demand-side reader payments, and to tolls and tariffs of various sorts. The most familiar approaches have been user-based models where either the reader pays directly, or the readers' agents (in an academic context, libraries) pay, or national authorities pay through national site licences or their equivalent.

Supply-side payment models have been introduced over the last decade or so. These, commonly called 'open access' models, involve authors paying directly to publish, or their institution paying for them to be able to publish, or, in the case of funded research, their funders paying. Third-party tolls and tariffs have existed for some time and largely comprise advertising or telecommunication access charges. Experience has shown that in the academic marketplace there is a fairly limited applicability for advertising models except in broad-spectrum journals with a magazine component (*Nature*, *Science*, *BMJ*, etc.).

Sponsorship of publications by charities, foundations, companies or government has also existed for some time, long before this approach was subsumed under the open access heading (a significant proportion of journals listed in the Directory of Open Access Journals are actually using a sponsorship model). The most recent business model arrival has been the time-share or rental approach of the new start-up DeepDyve in which online access only (without being able to print) is granted for a limited amount of time for a micropayment (usually a few dollars).

Currently, the majority business model remains a subscription or electronic licensing one, with about 95 per cent of the market by article share. Pay to publish models have roughly a 2–5 per cent share. Overlapping with both these is advertising, also with about 5 per cent, but being used as a model jointly with subscriptions or another approach. The biggest challenge to sustainable business models in the future has been the enthusiasm for a variety of approaches clustered under the moniker 'open access' which unlike any other business model variant have vocal advocacy from the 'open access movement'. So what are these varieties of open access and do they challenge future sustainability?

The development of open access publishing models

A rough working definition of open access would be 'a combination of philosophy and business models allowing all readers (not just those within institutions) free online access to scholarly research literature without payment at point of use'. Increasingly, the terms of access and use granted to the user are assuming a greater importance, with unrestricted re-use being termed by advocate Peter Suber 'libre open access' and that with restrictions, such as non commercial re-use, being termed 'gratis open access'. The details of such doctrinal niceties are beyond this chapter but are becoming important and could easily affect the viability of the models proposed.

Open access comes in a number of variants dependent upon *what* is made open, *when* it is made open and *how* it is made open. The *what* question is itself a derivative of the progressive smearing out of the published/unpublished dichotomy which, while once a stark binary choice in the paper world, now digitally allows varying degrees of 'published'.

Three *what* stages may be distinguished:

- stage one – author's un-refereed draft manuscript for consideration by a journal, often called (especially in physics) a preprint (Authors Version in the NISO nomenclature, see NISO, 2008);
- stage two – author's final refereed manuscript accepted for publication by a journal and containing all changes required as a result of peer review but without copy-editing or any of the sophisticated digital enhancements possessed by the final article on a platform (Accepted Manuscript in the NISO nomenclature); and
- stage three – final published citable article available from the journal's website (Version of Record in the NISO nomenclature).

In terms of *when* it is made open, there are two possibilities: immediately upon publication or at some time period after it, often called an embargo period. The *how* question is largely one of business model, if there is one. Using these definitions it is possible to disentangle the often complex mix of open access variants currently practised and these are shown in Table 17.3.

Assessing the role of open access publishing models

Each of the four types of open access described in Table 17.3 has advantages and disadvantages. In the case of 'Gold' open access and 'Delayed' open access the final peer-reviewed published version of the article is made freely available via two different but sustainable business models. In the case of 'Gold', this is a pay-to-publish model, which has the potential advantage that because it involves the use of research funds to pay for publication, money to publish increases in line with the growth in funded research, thereby avoiding one of the biggest causes of

Table 17.3 **Open access (OA) types**

PAY TO PUBLISH OA '**GOLD**'	▪ *what* – final published articles (stage 3) ▪ *when* – free upon publication on publisher's website ▪ *how* – pay-to-publish model
DELAYED OA '**DELAYED**'	▪ *what* – final published articles (stage 3) ▪ *when* – free some time after publication on publisher's website ▪ *how* – existing model
SELF-ARCHIVING OA '**GREEN**'	▪ *what* – peer-reviewed author mss (stage 2) ▪ *when* – systematic/self-archiving with a variable delay or embargo on institutional or subject repositories ▪ *how* – no model
PRE-PRINT SERVERS	▪ *what* – pre-prints (stage 1) ▪ *when* – free upon deposit on pre-print server ▪ *how* – no model

the serials crisis (the inability of library funding to keep pace with the volume of research published) in the subscription or licensing system. It also makes the article available online immediately upon publication. The downside is that unless care is taken with the choice of the re-use rights environment, about 20 per cent of journal income arising from corporate subscribers (who read but do not author) gets lost.

The 'Delayed' approach has the advantage that no new business model is required, but it is based on the hypothesis that free availability of content does not affect the business model. For short embargos under a subscription model, this assumption seems counterintuitive, and much heat has been expended in arguing whether free availability undermines sales. The risk is clearly visible in data made available by Elsevier and their ScienceDirect platform, shown in Figure 17.8. Even the most fast-moving disciplines (life sciences and medicine) potentially give up a significant proportion of their saleable downloads if content is made free at an embargo period of six months from publication. For slower moving fields such as chemistry only half of lifetime downloads have occurred after 18 months and the social sciences does not even reach half this mark.

The self-archiving or 'Green' approach has a variety of flavours depending upon whether the author is simply spontaneously depositing the accepted manuscript version of his or her paper in the institution's digital repository or whether a more systematic deposit is occurring

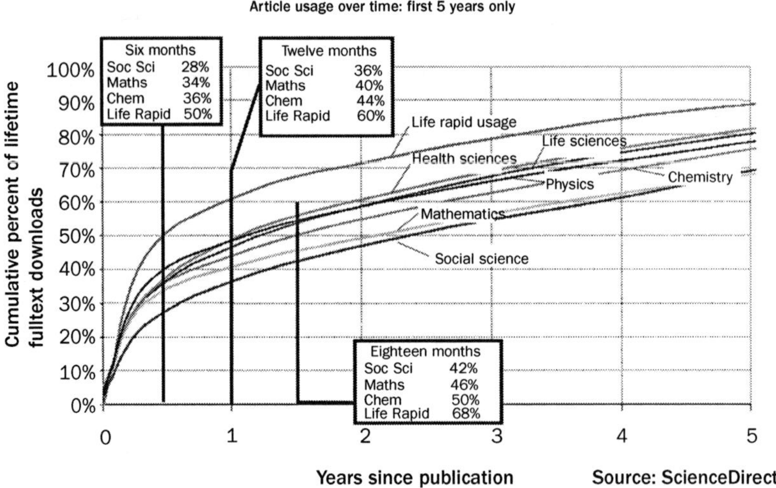

Figure 17.8 Proportion of downloads at 6, 12 and 18 months

under a funding body (or other) mandate. While the haphazard deposit of these intermediate but peer-reviewed items probably will have little effect on the journals from which they come, the systematic variation not only starts to resemble an earlier version of the 'Delayed' approach but has no business model at all. Apparently free, it is a 'nobody-pays' model, parasitic on the status, authority and critical honing provided to an article by the journal system. At the time of writing, the European Commission-funded PEER Project has been trying to gather data to help resolve what the effect of a European-wide embargo mandate might be, and look at the wider viability at the practical level of 'Green' open access. The results are expected during 2012 (www.peerproject.eu).

Preprint servers have existed for a long time, right from the onset of digital publishing in 1991 with the creation of the high-energy physics preprint server ArXiv at Los Alamos National Labs by Paul Ginsparg (Ginsparg, 1994). At the time it was claimed that it was 'publishing for free' but since then it has become clear that it is neither publishing nor free. Nevertheless, as a clearing-house for draft papers providing an early-warning system for particular research communities it has proved popular and successful. The idea has not really spread very far from its home in physics. It has been embraced by mathematics, economics in places and computer science, but isn't preferred in the life sciences and is positively deprecated in chemistry, where the prior appearance of an un-refereed manuscript is still treated as first publication and bars the author from submitting the public preprint to any journal.

As these early, draft non-peer-reviewed manuscripts come directly from their authors and have no journal investment in them, their widespread availability causes none of the potential parasitism of 'Green'. However, they are just un-refereed drafts and most researchers still want to see the final paper and have the reassurance that it was accepted and published by a journal that they value.

Answering Key Question 3

It is clear that open access models are here to stay but it is far from clear whether they are yet truly sustainable. There are considerable question marks over 'Green' and 'Delayed' and the preprints do not really deliver the sort of authoritative content users demand. 'Gold' has the potential to be a viable alternative to existing model mixes, as a recent study confirms (RIN CEPA, 2011), but the issues of re-use of material, cannibalisation of corporate revenue, and questions about whether article processing charges high enough to sustain a fully 100 per cent 'Gold' universe would be acceptable to the market remain to be answered. Net returns will be possible but might involve considerable curtailing of services to do so.

We are already seeing experiments with minimalist 'Gold' open access journals: those where editorial intervention and any peer review involving more than basic methodological checks have been abandoned. *PLoS ONE* was the forerunner of this new type of 'no-frills' high-volume, low-cost journal publishing. Trading on the branding of PLOS and a perception (not always borne out in reality) of extreme speed of publishing, it has become a run-away success, publishing thousands of papers at a modest but certainly far from zero publishing fee. This has enabled PLOS to cross-subsidise its very expensive, high-quality titles that were not breaking even at article processing fees in the order of $3000. Many other publishers have jumped on this bandwagon, launching look-alikes in various disciplines. If successful, these initiatives could change the market significantly.

Given the considerations above, the answer to this Key Question clearly has to be: 'perhaps'.

Key Question 4: Political zeitgeist: will public (political) attitudes regarding the Internet make publishing impossible?

Public perception and digital publishing

In the section on technology I remarked that surprisingly little had changed in terms of the fundamentals. However, the broader socio-political ramifications of the digital revolution have been considerable. It is in establishing a very challenging environment for political and public discourse that the effects of the Internet on values and attitudes to information have been profound.

The key factor in this is simple and obvious: Digital *is* Different! Digital documents can be reproduced infinitely and are, despite the best intentions of software producers, infinitely changeable. This has profound consequences for all players in the chain, in terms of business models, copyright, issues of authority and trust, and public attitudes. If one copy can serve the world, then concerns about access controls or perhaps a move to avoiding any access issues at all become important. If each document can be altered, how can we trust that we really are looking at the final version? If documents are decoupled from the organisations that issue them, how can we be sure that they carry the authority of that organisation with them?

Some of these issues are resolvable through branding and watermarking (such as the CrossRef project CrossMark which will certify with a logo the Versions of Record of articles). Issues of business models and copyright are much less tractable. The biggest problems of all, however, are those created by the attitudes which digital operation throws up. Some of these arise from the culture of the Internet but others are *sui generis*.

Assessing public attitudes to digital and the politics of 'free'

The political environment can be summed up by four powerful slogans:

- 'e = free'. Here the non-tangibility of digital objects ('e' standing for electronic) prejudices the consumer into thinking that the non-physical must be free or at lower cost (a debate already happening over the pricing of e-books). It has been estimated that for STM journal publishing a fully digital chain with no paper products at all would potentially reduce prices by about 10–20 per cent but certainly not to zero (Ware and Mabe, 2009).

- 'yours = mine'. Here the ethos of the 1960s hippy counterculture meets the expectation of the Internet generation. This follows quite naturally from the first bullet. If electronic objects are 'free' then why should they not be copied and shared? The recording industry has already discovered the consequences of this phenomenon (napsterisation etc.) and the motion picture industry is having similar problems. E-books are regularly being pirated and the market cannot understand why an e-book isn't substantially cheaper than any other edition (or free). Much of the radical wings of the open source and open access movements are influenced by this supposition.
- '(intellectual) property = theft'. There have always been those who disagree in principle with the concept of copyright (perhaps notoriously the science fiction writer Cory Doctorow, who views it as a threat to democracy!). In the past the physical difficulty of making copies of a work worked to support the legal notions of intellectual property (IP). Now the tables are turned and the digital universe pulls seductively in the opposite direction to copyright law leading to calls to 'update' IP, to bring copyright out of the 'quill pens and paper' era into the sunlit digital uplands. The habits of the mass market and the lure of 'free' attract politicians into supporting such measures.
- 'public funding = public access'. This is probably the most dangerous, pernicious and erroneous slogan for the journal publishing community. Although it is true that a majority of research worldwide is funded by government (the public purse), publication is not. It could be argued that the outputs of the research funding are the data collected and the preprints (if there are any). As I pointed out above (within the limits imposed by various subjects whose views differ on the acceptability of preprints appearing in public), making preprints fully available is possible and would have no effect on journals whatsoever. But this is not what the politicians want. They want something (the peer-reviewed final published paper with all the investment in it made by the publisher) for nothing, and this slogan has underlain most political discussions of 'Green' open access mandates, especially in the USA and the EU.

Answering Key Question 4

So, to answer the last Key Question, can publishing still be successful in such a hostile political environment? The jury is out on this, but providing a copyright framework is maintained and politicians can be persuaded that what is apparently 'free' may turn out to be expensive for their economies in the long run, there is some hope.

Conclusions

So, can we now answer the question posed at the outset: 'Does journal publishing have a future?' I hope I have shown that scholarly behaviour is remarkably unchanged, and while technology has provided new tools, these are new tools for the same old purposes.

Based on these conclusions, the answer to our Big Question would be 'Yes, probably ...'. And yet. It is clear that profound behaviour shifts have been observed in a few, largely predictable, subject areas. It is also clear that while we do not yet have the killer application, the memes of the Internet world are leaking out to affect attitudes to information across the board. Where these attitudes feed public and political positions they threaten to undermine the basic evidence-based approaches we have lived with for many years. Some business models will work in the future but this all depends on continuing respect for copyright, a sympathetic IP law regime and business conditions that make publishing economic.

Predicting the future is a difficult game. Gottlieb Daimler, inventor of the petrol-powered car, said in 1889: 'There will never be a mass market for motor cars – about 1,000 in Europe – because that is the limit on the number of chauffeurs available!' I hope this chapter's conclusions may fare better in the future than his.

References

Aguilar, F.J. (1967) *Scanning the Business Environment*. New York, Macmillan.

Altheide, D.L. (1994) An ecology of communication: toward a mapping of the effective environment. *The Sociological Quarterly* 35(4): 665–83.

Coles, B.R. (1993) The *Scientific, Technical and Medical Information System in the UK*. Royal Society, British Library, ALPSP [British Library R&D Report No. 6123].

Crow, R. (2002) *The case for institutional repositories: a SPARC position paper*. SPARC. Available at: http://www.arl.org/sparc/bm~doc/ir_final_release_102.pdf

Garfield, E. (1955) Citation indexes to science: a new dimension in documentation through association of ideas. *Science* 122: 108–11.

Ginsparg, P. (1994) First steps towards electronic research communication *Computers in Physics* 8(4): 390–6.

Hall, A.R. & Hall, M.B. (1965–86) *Correspondence of Henry Oldenburg*. Madison, WI: University of Wisconsin Press.

Harley, D., Krzys, S., Earl-Novell, S., Lawrence, S. and King, C.J. (2010) *Final Report: Assessing the Future Landscape of Scholarly Communication: An Exploration of Faculty Values and Needs in Seven Disciplines* CSHE 1.10 Centre for Studies in Higher Education, UC Berkeley. Available at: http://cshe.berkeley.edu/publications/publications.php?id=351

Mabe, M.A. (2003) What do authors really care about? Presentation made at the *Fiesole Collection Development Retreat* 2003. Available at: http://digital.casalini.it/retreat/2003_docs/Mabe.ppt

Mabe, M. (2009) Scholarly publishing. *European Review* 17(1): 3–22.

Mabe, M.A. and Amin, M. (2002) Dr Jekyll and Dr Hyde: author–reader asymmetries in scholarly publishing. *ASLIB Proceedings* 54(3): 149–57.

Mabe, M.A. and Mulligan, A. (2011) What authors want. *New Review of Information Networking* 16(1): 71–89.

Merton, R.K. (1973) *The Sociology of Science*. Chicago, University of Chicago Press.

Mulligan, A. and Mabe, M.A. (2011) The effect of the Internet on researcher motivations, behaviour and attitudes. *Journal of Documentation* 67(2): 290–311.

NISO (2008) *Journal Article Versions*. Available at http://www.niso.org/publications/rp/RP-8-2008.pdf

Price, D. da Sollar (1963) *Little Science, Big Science*. New York: Columbia University Press.

Publishing Research Consortium (2010) *Access versus importance*. Available at: http://www.publishingresearch.net/documents/PRCAccessvsImportanceGlobalNov2010_000.pdf

RIN (2009) *Communicating Knowledge: How and Why UK Researchers Publish and Disseminate their Findings*. London Research Information Network. Available at: http://www.rin.ac.uk/communicating-knowledge

RIN CEPA (2011) *Heading for the open road: costs and benefits of transitions in scholarly communication*. London Research Information Network. Available at: http://www.rin.ac.uk/system/files/attachments/Dynamics_of_transition_report_for_screen.pdf

Smit, E. and Gruttermeier, H. (2011) Are scholarly publications ready for the data era? *New Review of Information Networking* 16(1): 54–70.

Smith, J.W.T. (1999) The deconstructed journal – a new model for academic publishing. *Learned Publishing* 12: 79–91.

Tenopir, C. and King, D.W. (2000) *Towards Electronic Journals*. Washington, DC: Special Libraries Association.

University of California (2007) *Faculty Attitudes and Behaviors Regarding Scholarly Communication: Survey Findings from the University Of California*. Available at: http://osc.universityofcalifornia.edu/responses/materials/OSC-survey-full-20070828.pdf

Van de Sompel, H., *et al.* (2004) Re-thinking scholarly communication. *D-Lib Magazine* 10(9).

Ware, M. and Mabe, M.A. (2009) *The stm report: An overview of scientific and scholarly journals publishing*. Oxford: International Association of Scientific, Technical and Medical Publishers. Available at: www.stm-assoc.org/2009_10_13_MWC_STM_Report.pdf

Ziman, J. (1968) *Public Knowledge: The Social Dimension of Science*. Cambridge: Cambridge University Press.

Zuckerman, H. and Merton, R.K. (1971) Patterns of evaluation in science: institutionalization, structure and functions of the referee system. *Minerva* 9(1): 66–100.

18

External forces and their impacts on academic and professional publishing

Kent Anderson

Abstract: This chapter discusses the long-term implications facing scholarly publishers and other stakeholders in academic information services owing to the fact that the Internet has made scholarly communications available to anyone with a web connection. The chapter covers emerging user expectations, issues of trust and authority, implications of social sharing, pressures on business models, the expansion of information publishing outputs, and sources of stability within the tumult of change.

Key words: Disruptive change, trust networks, social media, business models.

Introduction

Of all the changes the Internet has introduced for scholarly publishers, authors and information specialists, perhaps the most fundamental is that scholarly communications are now on full display to the outside world.

Scholarly publishing was relatively cloistered for much of its history. Barriers included remoteness, gatekeepers such as admissions officers and librarians, specialised language and jargon, and difficulty discovering academic resources. Now, all of this has been changed by a networked information infrastructure that is vast, integrated, open, highly engineered and always on. It's very unlike the world in which scholarly communications and academic cultures evolved, and the pressures this basic change has unleashed are being felt in publishing now, but there is sufficient momentum to believe this is only the beginning of a whole suite of changes.

Physicians now routinely face patients who have pre-diagnosed themselves via Google (Bird *et al.*, 2010). Experts outside the academic sphere frequently comment on, and even force corrections to, scholarly articles. Attempts at humor in the literature can no longer be assumed to be 'inside jokes', and are quickly, sometimes painfully, exposed to ridicule themselves (Anon., 2011). Questions about who the audience now is have the potential to reset our basic quality thresholds.

The simplistic approach of 'dumbing down' scientific information for the public is fraught with risks for scholarly publishers, who often don't know quite how to do it, can't do it systematically enough or simply can't invest the millions of dollars it takes to do it right. And it's not clear whether the public wants more of it than current providers can offer – providers (such as WebMD) that are well funded, established and capable of taking on interlopers.

While the public is drifting into the scholarly realm, scientists and researchers are using publicly available tools more and more. Specialist tools such as PubMed are being subsumed by general tools (e.g. Google and Google Scholar) that have greater scope, better engineering and often more useful information presentations. Pieces of privately held information are moving online, with laboratory data captured in genomic databases, for instance. And hallway conversations, once only possible synchronously and face-to-face, can now occur asynchronously in online forums or at a distance through services such as WebEx.

Accordingly, scholarly publishers have had to expand their repertoire and tool sets. Now, experts in search engine optimisation (SEO), user experience and user interface design, analytics, and social marketing are part of most major publishing organisations, and appear here and there even at the smallest publishers. Editorial pace has quickened everywhere as the news cycle has become more important to authors, funders and consequently publishers. What used to be competition for authors and funds – which could be achieved largely by specialised market positioning – is increasingly predicated on competition for time and attention. Traffic, usage and prominence all depend on these.

In short, scholarly publishers are now integrated with the broader communication sphere. No longer is the deliberate, self-defined pace of academia the primary factor driving knowledge generation and cultural attenuation within science. No longer is the audience for scholarly research a closed system. And no longer is competition for supremacy based only on securing the best content. But while change has come and more is coming, predicting where we are headed is difficult. It can come suddenly or slowly, and sometimes in unpredictable ways.

Abundance and absorption: the reality of a 'flat' information world

Thomas Friedman famously titled a book *The World Is Flat*. While a provocative title, the world is much more complicated than that, and the information space has peculiarities all its own. Perhaps a more useful starting point is Clay Shirky's statement that 'abundance changes everything' (Shirky, 2010). This simple statement reflects a profound change in the assumptions of our information world. When print resources were scarce, pricing was simpler, functions such as preservation and duplication were clearly necessary and comparatively straightforward, and the information world that had evolved within scarcity was stable and familiar. Incremental changes – moving from lead type to phototypesetting, shifting from sheet-fed to web offset printing – occurred within a world of information scarcity, where setting a price and counting copies aligned.

The world of scarcity for scholarly publishers also meant that libraries, academic departments, personal subscriptions and specialty bookstores generally defined the information distribution system. It would be rare for a patient, a non-professional or a non-expert to read specialist literature, and even harder for them to secure copies for personal use. The scholarly world was remote and had a semi-permeable barrier around it, one that permitted information flows at a slow, sporadic rate.

With everything shoveled onto the Internet, a surprising change occurred quickly and irrevocably – the 'university without walls' (Kassirer, 1999) became a reality, with some uncomfortable consequences. Suddenly, scholarly publishers found themselves subject to additional scrutiny from the media and the public; user interfaces and online feature sets were naturally compared with those of major online players; and new dimensions of information management emerged almost overnight.

Scholarly publishers found themselves in a 'flat' information world. But while the world was flat from an information standpoint, the terrain for making it work for various customer constituents while generating a sustainable commercial model remained uncertain and certainly not flat.

In fact, it has proven to be full of daunting new peaks to scale and ravines to bridge. These are the complexities beyond Friedman's meme.

Information competition and publishing competencies

The vaccine and autism story provides one of the most poignant stories from the first decade of online publishing. Due largely to the newfound exposure to scientific information the public was experiencing, and their ability to use the Internet to publish their own thinking, a breakdown in a scholarly publishing competency – the publication of a flawed study – was exacerbated by inadequate competitive know-how in the information world.

The paper in question (Wakefield *et al.*, 1998) suggested a link between vaccines containing thimerasol and a supposed increase in autism. The paper was ultimately retracted years after publication, and its author banned from medicine, but why this flawed study caused problems is instructive. In a prior era, it would have been unlikely to light a wildfire.

Scott Karp, formerly of the *Atlantic* and now running Publish2, followed this story closely. Soon after the vaccine–autism connection was suggested and began to take hold in the public imagination, the American Academy of Pediatrics, among others, published studies showing that the connection was non-existent, and ultimately issued practice guidelines and policy statements underlining the lack of evidence, all in the hope of swaying public opinion with scientific findings. Unfortunately, while the Academy was doing excellent scientific and policy work, it was doing a poor job of SEO. Meanwhile, celebrity bloggers like Jenny McCarthy, whose child is autistic, became major sources of information for anyone searching on these issues on Google and other search engines. Resources from the American Academy of Pediatrics, not geared for search engine indexing, could only be found deep in search engine listings, making them virtually invisible to the majority of searchers.

The controversy lasted far too long, and was extended to no small extent by the inability of scientific organisations to make important content prominent in the modern information world. In the age of information abundance, rising to the top is vital. The information world may be flat, but it's not two-dimensional. Achieving that third dimension – prominence – requires knowledge of the tools of online discovery, the ability to utilise a powerful brand online, and the skill to render trust proxies in the digital realm. The public is watching now.

Commercial hopes and realities

The outside world served as a model for publishers moving online. Consequently, advertising sales was one of the first big hopes for the new world of online publishing. Projecting the broader information landscape inward, it was imagined in some circles that scholarly publishers might finally be able to use their affluent, highly educated audience in ways print never had allowed. However, there were two major barriers – first, the commercial space wasn't prepared to spend large amounts of money online; and second, the same audience was spending 90 per cent and more of its time online elsewhere because of the low engagement offered by narrow, archive-like specialist publishing sites. Clearly, more work needed to occur before scholarly publishers could compete effectively online for audience engagement. Only then would advertising, subscription dollars and other commercial opportunities arise.

Today, some scholarly publishers are doing well with online advertising, but these tend to be those with major audience segments, larger and more experienced sales forces and sophisticated offerings. In short, those with advertising programs resembling mass media advertising programs are doing better. Yet, online advertising remains relatively undervalued compared with radio, print, television or outdoor (Meeker, 2010), suggesting that those succeeding now in these areas might do even better when ad rates rise to reflect audience engagement. The Matthew Effect – in which the rich get richer and the poor get poorer – is clearly at play.

Fortunately for scholarly publishers, one commercial opportunity arose quickly and right in front of them – namely, the institutional site license. For many publishers, these content licenses became the bread-and-butter of their online revenues. However, there were opportunity costs below the surface – a lack of a direct customer relationship with the end-user, and susceptibility to fluctuations in university funding.

In 2008, the macro-economic downturn around the world set off alarm bells in many publishing houses. Academic libraries were being asked to reduce their expenditures as part of general belt-tightening, while at the same time publishers were seeing usage through site licenses increase significantly. That is, there was more value flowing through site licenses at the same time libraries had to consider paying less. This mini-crisis is mainly playing out quietly. In some cases (Anderson, 2010), the crisis has played out in full view.

Publishers continue to serve the institutional library market, but they are also slowly diversifying their revenue streams through new products aimed at other parts of academic budgets (e.g. open access initiatives aimed at research funding bodies and academic publication funds, data products aimed at department and personal budgets, and integrated products aimed at academic IT budgets). As this diversification proceeds, the information available through traditional site licenses will probably become less and less interesting to the practicing researcher or practitioner. The modern products that require investments to build and market will follow the money elsewhere.

Pricing practices have also been shaped by referencing outside sources, most notably successful online file retailers such as Apple and its iTunes store. The $0.99 pricing originated by Apple for individual songs has been cited by Geoff Bilder with his iPub idea (Bilder, 2008), and extended commercially by Deep Dyve (DeepDyve, 2009), which added a Netflix-inspired model of renting articles in order to approach both publishers and the market with something novel. It seems unrealistic to expect success by modeling pricing approaches for a popular commodity like music. After all, scholarly content is niche, keepsake and generates a low volume of sales. However, the fact that leaders in the field are advocating and experimenting with models like this reveals the extent to which publishers and entrepreneurs in the scholarly space are looking outside for inspiration.

Integration into meta-architectures

One way that publishers are coping with the Internet is through better integration into larger architectures. For major publishers, this means things such as Science Direct and the 'Big Deal'. For smaller publishers, this means syndication, aggregation, SEO, partnerships, presence on common technology platforms and the like. In the era of abundance, being in more than one place is a good strategic option. Also, selling a package that allows buyers to get more for their money and approach the nirvana of one-stop shopping is often advantageous.

Yet these larger architectures teeter on the edge of being 'black boxes', with opaque rules for prominence, payment or both. Google's algorithm is routinely adjusted, sometimes harshly, making SEO as much an act of monitoring and adjusting as strategising and tagging. Aggregators are large, impersonal and employ formulae for royalties that are often hard to pin down, but are often too good to give up in the short run (which inertia often extends into the long run). The lack of individual user data within institutional licenses may prove to be a problem in the long term, for all involved.

The information world may be flat, but there are still intersections such as Google, Ovid, EBSCO, Science Direct and conglomerate sales. Maintaining publishing prominence now means managing your presence through multiple layers and systems.

Customer demands and preferences

Because the customers we find on the Internet have expectations derived from the larger information realm, their demands and preferences deviate somewhat from the traditional journal or book consumer. Nevertheless, the PDF has retained its value as the content container of choice – for now. Pressures from multimedia publishing, data publishing and visualisation publishing are impinging on the article economy, where the PDF dominates. Better portable solutions are also eroding its dominance. Browser plug-ins like Readability allow users to send web pages directly to e-reading devices like the Kindle, removing the need to print and providing a satisfactory, portable and disposable reading experience.

Search engines effectively eliminated print indices and other traditional content access products, but it is only over the past 5–7 years that Google has emerged as the dominant search tool for many academic disciplines, supplanting even PubMed and its ilk.

From a browsing perspective, the flat information world has made faster editorial production around selected content a priority for many publishers, so that news sites, social sharing and email alerting can occur and drive traffic and awareness, while also satisfying authors. Interpretive editorial features are also more common now, as the Internet rewards some degree of repetitive content linking and layering, while the wider audience benefits from synthesised content.

Editorial impacts

For editors, faster publication has meant everything from publishing raw manuscripts online as soon as they are accepted (*Journal of Biological Chemistry* and others) to creating fast-track peer-review systems. This usually requires faster peer review either generally or selectively; less or faster copy editing and formatting in order to publish the information first; and tighter coordination with authors' institutions for public and media relations, especially around big meetings.

Product and brand impacts

Given the increased importance of branding in a flat information world, many publishers are engaged in brand management and rebranding initiatives. Although not entirely new, the pace of these changes and the stakes around them are both higher. Products and brands have been stretched to accommodate new Internet-inspired initiatives. Blogs, brand embellishment for fast-track articles, new article types, new journal siblings and some non-journal initiatives have been launched over the past decade. As these brand extensions and enhancements have proliferated, concerns have been raised about brand confusion and brand over-extension. In some cases, it is no longer clear what the brand promise is, as the brand supports initiatives of various quality, based on various authorship and review models, and geared to non-traditional user groups.

Value equation impacts

While products and brands have been stuffed full of interesting and useful new initiatives, deriving new revenues from these has proven more difficult. Concentrated purchasing power, a fragmented and often modest-sized core audience, users who are accustomed to having information appear to be free and sizeable competing outlets (aggregators, proxy access and the like) all make it more difficult to directly commercialise new offerings. Many publishers are seeking new purchasing outlets, reshaping or integrating products to appeal to different user groups (and, hence, different budgets) and investing in new product launches. Many publishers now have a significant percentage of revenues coming from recent product development initiatives.

As Simon Waldman discusses in his book *Creative Disruption*, experimentation and innovation can be driven by economic necessity, an often overlooked factor in market evolutions. The economic downturn of 2008–09 led many publishers to begin diversification efforts, which are now beginning to bear fruit. In short, the pace of change has accelerated because of macro-economic pressures.

Devices and mobility

The mobile networked information device lurked on the outskirts of user adoption for years, slowly gaining adherents, then rapidly achieved market power with devices like Amazon's Kindle, Apple's iPhone and iPad, and various Google Android devices. It's now fair to say that non-mobile information consumption is on its way to becoming the exception rather than the rule. As Kevin Kelly has asserted in *What Technology Wants* (his final paper book, he says), we are in a screen-centric culture, and these screens are replacing paper as the substrate of choice. Becoming 'people of the screen' means that distinctions between mobile and deskbound are less useful than distinctions between screen-based and paper-based or connected and disconnected.

Journals were among the first print-based scholarly publications to move online, closely shadowed by catalogs and indices. This was partly because the articles within journals were easily separated from the issue batch, and were short enough for users to print on their own. Books, on the other hand, took much longer to become susceptible to the sway of new technologies, primarily because print-on-demand technologies are taking longer to become mainstream and because other options for individual consumption of very longform texts had not emerged. However, as soon as viable e-books emerged with the likes of the Kindle and the Nook, the book market changed rapidly and fundamentally, with more independent authors, new price points, new power centers and bankrupted bookstore chains.

This was not due to a shift from immobile to mobile – books were as mobile as e-books. It was a shift from paper to screen, the implications of which are not only user preference, but also price, market dynamics, manufacturing processes and sales channels. E-books often sell for less, but also can be shorter than traditional books, or even constituted out of pieces taken from separate titles as some publishers, such as O'Reilly and the National Academies, have shown.

As users become more screen-centric, more change will come. A recent pilot of the Amazon Kindle DX at various universities showed that while the DX had several flaws, users wanted it to be more like their computer, not more like their printed materials. The direction of change is clear.

Business model pressures

Sustainability is a clear goal that publishers, authors, librarians, institutions and readers all share. It's not just a code word for financial stability, but has many facets in the scholarly world. However, while elements such as prestige, reputation, impact factor and career have been affected to some degree by the changes in scholarly publishing, the underlying business model has been directly attacked by some as unfair and unsustainable, with options offered that aren't clearly superior from a cost–benefit standpoint. Part of these claims has been the notion that the public now has a stake in research output, drawing a straight line from taxpayer to published paper. Because this could never have been contemplated in the print era, such pressures to make papers based on government-funded research reports freely available are clearly due to the availability the Internet has created.

The end of the subscription panacea

The print model of scarcity was solved by the subscription, a form of sales that matched print nearly perfectly – it allowed publishers a steady flow of income, allowed readers and publishers to share content batches of mixed quality, and created a long-term relationship for stable cashflows on the publisher side and high brand affinity on the reader side. This panacea ended with the Internet, as the print bundle fell apart under the pressure of search engines; as sales moved from the individual to the aggregator (whether that aggregator is an institution or one like Ovid); and as brand loyalty could be fulfilled without direct interaction with the publisher.

The dilemma of customer contact has hit publishers and librarians in a number of ways, from reduced or anemic subscription data to less foot traffic at library facilities. For publishers, some solutions have included creating services only available to identified users, selling products through non-traditional channels such as sponsorships, and launching products geared for personal devices (e.g. smartphones and iPads). Because partners like Apple and Amazon withhold customer data, this latter approach has proven problematic in a new way. For libraries, efforts to bring patrons into facilities through new amenities, training courses and rented space have not turned the tide. Worse, such trends may be nothing more than a slippery slope to library brand devaluation as the library becomes about square footage rather than about expertise and knowledge. The direct relationship with either patrons or readers has been difficult to retain, redefine or re-establish.

A major alternative to the subscription model has been open access publishing. This model, which is financed up-front from authors instead of spreading the costs of publishing across multiple papers and an entire audience, has proven successful in two main ways: for selective journals, it has not created a barrier to success while providing a partial revenue solution; for less selective journals, it has provided a full revenue solution while not seriously impacting the prestige of the journal genre. Because author–reader overlap is large in many fields, open access can work in many places with little downside.

Many traditional publishers are launching open access journal programs or standalone open access journals, partly as a way to fend off competition and partly as a way to garner revenues from the open access funds many institutions and charitable bodies have established. How well this works long term has yet to be seen. Market dynamics seem destined to hold these service-based prices back to a common mean, making differential pricing unlikely for publishers accustomed to these practices in the subscription market.

Trust networks and anchoring communities

The publishing business model online depends on traffic – from usage statistics to advertising impressions, if users aren't visiting a site, the business model suffers to some extent. Journals, in particular, create value by filtering content and aggregating an audience with a high affinity around that content. So when something attempts to replicate those traits, publishers should pay attention.

The emergence of social media has created new ways to drive traffic via Facebook and Twitter, but has also created new filtering and affinity mechanisms for users. Nick Bilton, in his book *I Live In the Future & Here's How It Works*, talks about two of these new filtering and affinity trends, which he names 'trust networks' and 'anchoring communities'.

Trust networks are new to the online world. Instead of anonymous editors, fellow readers and distant authors – the trust network typically offered by a journal, for instance – Facebook and Twitter offer trust networks consisting of your friends and favorite colleagues. Publishers have realised they need to be in these trust networks, so have launched their own Twitter feeds and Facebook pages, all in hopes of being 'liked' in Facebook and 'followed' in Twitter. Again, new tasks have emerged because of external technological and social developments.

Anchoring communities are a slight variant on the trust network. It's where people go to orient themselves in whatever mode they're currently in. If you're in a news acquisition mode, your anchoring community may be the *New York Times*, CNN, Twitter or Facebook. If you're in a literature surveillance mode, your anchoring community may be Google,

PubMed, Facebook or a journal portal site. Understanding modes of functioning and then creating the proper starting point for users takes user-centered design in new directions, away from the archival journal site and toward something that is more dynamic, broad-based and timely. Users are expecting a rich launch pad from any online property. Providing something less can set you back.

Publishers are playing with integrating social tools into their sites, from sharing buttons to commenting features to article ranking devices. But the question of community management goes deeper than technology solutions, and editorial groups are not inherently community organisers. There has not yet been an effective community effort in academic publishing, but the possibility seems to exist. Efforts such as the American Institute of Physics' UniPHY offer hope in this area.

Efforts like the Open Researcher & Contributor ID (ORCID) have been launched to deal with the ambiguity of author names, partially in response to the increased pace of publication and contribution emerging from the social Web.

Workflows and use-cases

A natural consequence of external forces reshaping scholarly publishing is that user workflows are a central question now. When information devices are on hand everywhere, how people use information becomes ever more important. This begs the question, 'Which people?' And this is where I believe we are heading into some fraught areas.

One of the most common distinctions that has haunted the emergence of digital publishing has been the myth of young versus old, also known as the digital native versus digital immigrant distinction. This myth has largely been disproven, especially in light of many indications that culture trumps technology. That is, middle-aged and older academics and scientists are more prone to adopt new tools for expressing their results and opinions than younger colleagues simply because they are safer in doing so. Younger scientists and academics are gun-shy, carefully avoiding missteps online that could derail their careers. Designing for the young researcher or young academic is very likely designing for the most hesitant user of new technologies.

But there is a reason to look at the young, because the older academics and scientists are actively modeling some of their young colleagues' most obvious behaviors, such as device adoption, social media use and communication preferences. There is a virtuous cycle here, with cautious younger members of the community inadvertently showing some of what they prefer but not using it professionally, and older colleagues adopting what is apparent and more confidently turning it to professional ends. But even for older academics, the culture of 'publish or perish' and the follow-on demands for legitimate, citable publications in prestigious branded journals has led to relatively unimpressive efforts in new media.

Metrics and meaning

The digital revolution has promised increased transparency into customer behavior, yet after more than a decade, many analytics initiatives seem to generate more heat than light. Part of the challenge is the openness of online, which makes usage and the definition of the user less predictable. Also, transparency has proved somewhat challenging for both institutional and advertising sales, laying bare some of the mismatches in expectations between constituents on either side of the buyer–seller paradigm. There is no doubt that our sites and initiatives throw off more data than print ever did, but deciding what matters, what it means and how one set of data compares with another has in some ways returned us to clearing houses of measurement and third-party data sources. The notion of the self-sufficient data warehouse has proven to have dramatic limitations.

Source of stability

Many things have remained stable throughout these turbulent times. First, the 'publish or perish' culture has not only been stable, it has become more demanding as more academics and scientists compete for grants, publication and reputation. Second, despite a torrent of legitimate criticism, the impact factor has become even more ingrained and powerful in many scientific cultures, especially in Asia and Europe, with financial rewards or tenure tied directly to impact numbers. Third, brands have retained their power, if not increased their sway. Readers need clear ways to cut through search results and save time, and brands provide reliable guidance in many cases. Authors need efficient paths to publication, and brands are a guide for submissions. Finally, the behavior of academics and scientists at various career stages seems as predictable as ever. Scientific culture has not changed as dramatically as information distribution technologies, and in some ways may have become more rigid because of what these changes have enabled.

Trends worth watching

In *The Clock of the Long Now*, Stewart Brand articulates the layers of change as concentric circles. The outermost, which he labels 'Fashion', changes erratically and often. Subsequent layers, such as 'Infrastructure' and 'Culture', change much more slowly. We have experienced many changes in the fashion of information distribution and acquisition, from print to simple print-like websites to fully realised digital authoring and distribution platforms. Throughout this, however, the one piece of information fashion that has not changed is the authoring toolset, which mostly relies on Microsoft Word. Because of this, and because the infrastructure has also begun to change to the point where video and still cameras are everywhere, geolocation is commonplace, and other sensors can be strapped onto cheap mobile computers, I would watch for changes in the fashion of authorship. We are already seeing this with video abstracts in some journals, and papers that rely more on visualisation than on text presentation.

Culture will change more slowly, but it will change. In the past few years, I have seen more and more researchers and practitioners willing to admit they use tools like Google and Wikipedia over the presumably superior sources like PubMed and textbooks. Speed and comprehensiveness are competing effectively with other dimensions of value and driving some new choices. Prohibitions on citing outside the accepted literature are being relaxed here and there. The first culture tremors kicked off the acquisition of the Eigenfactor by Thomson-Reuters and new developments at PubMed, just to name two. I think some of the major providers of infrastructure will be redeveloping their offerings over the next decade, in response to larger cultural tremors. And financial tremors in academia will continue, especially as the 'higher education bubble' is examined. No matter whether it withstands scrutiny, pops or slowly deflates, caution will creep into planning and budgeting, further depleting the inventory of available options. Hard choices in a world of 'satisficing' (Simon, 1956), free tools and options may drive fundamental behavioral and economic change. What is now 'dabbling' in the electronic world with these new computer displays, apps and tools may become hard-core and irreversible reliance on them.

Conclusion

When scholarship moved onto the Internet, it opened itself to new external forces. Now, in fact, it may be claimed the tide has turned, and that it is the Internet that is beginning to invade academic research and study. The action is coming from outside, the external world is dictating terms and we are responding as the Internet moves into our realms. Efforts to take the lead often ring hollow, as new commercial players and laser-focused upstarts often seem to have the upper hand over slower-moving and established information providers.

The movement from scarcity to abundance has paved many new roads for users – patients, consumers, practitioners and scientists from other disciplines – while adding new devices, new capabilities and new expectations. As scientists and academics find success using these new tools and balancing these new information collaborators and competitors, the pressures publishers and librarians have been experiencing will ultimately intertwine with the cultures of science and academia. And that's when we may be able to say we've truly witnessed a revolution.

References

Anderson, K. (2010) Available at: http://scholarlykitchen.sspnet.org/2010/06/14/the-latest-library-as-purchaser-crisis-are-we-fighting-the-wrong-battle/ [Accessed 2011].

Anon. (2011) *Retraction Watch*. Available at: http://retractionwatch.wordpress.com/2011/04/06/forget-chocolate-on-valentines-day-try-semen-says-surgery-news-editor-retraction-resignation-follow/ [Accessed 2011].

Bilder, G. (2008) Available at: http://sspnet.org/documents/300_geoffrey%20bilder_ssp_2008_iPub.pdf [Accessed 25 June 2011].

Bird, C.E., Conrad, P., Fremont, A.M. and Timmermans, S. (2010) *Handbook of Medical Sociology*. Nashville, TN: Vanderbilt University Press.

DeepDyve (2009) Available at: http://blog.deepdyve.com/2009/11/03/a-new-market-opportunity/ [Accessed 25 June 2011].

Kassirer, J. (1999) Goodbye for now. *New England Journal of Medicine* 341: 686–7.

Meeker, M. (2010) Available at: http://www.slideshare.net/marketingfacts/mary-meekers-internet-trends-2010 [Accessed 2011].

Shirky, C. (2010) *Cognitive Surplus*. Penguin Press.

Simon, H. (1956) Rational choice and the structure of the environment. *Psychological Review* 63(2): 129–38.

Wakefield, A.J., Murch, S.H., Anthony, A., *et al.* (1998) Ileal lymphoid nodular hyperplasia, non-specific colitis, and pervasive developmental disorder in children [retracted]. *Lancet* 351: 637–41.

19

Career development in academic and professional publishing

Nicholas Canty and Anthony Watkinson

Abstract: This chapter sets out the options available to entrants into this publishing sector and considers subsequent career development. There are now various professional qualifications and training courses available both for those entering the sector and for those at various levels within it. The academic and professional publishing industry increasingly seeks people who have digital skills whether they are in editorial or marketing: knowledge of and preferably experience of technology is now considered vital. This chapter was written following a survey and interviews conducted by the authors with individuals working across academic and professional publishing in the UK, Germany and North America. Other recent surveys are also used.

Key words: Career, qualifications, courses, training.

Introduction

Adding value to, marketing and dissemination of academic and professional information is a dynamic sector of the publishing industry. This sector was early to embrace the Internet and now transacts the majority of its business online, making it highly attractive to those with a strong interest in technology. Moreover, although it is seemingly in constant change as it faces new challenges and responds to developments it has so far been able to maintain its profitability and represents a relatively safe career progression for those who value stability. It could also be argued that the nature of what is published, books and journals that are obviously valuable for the specialists who use them, can attract entrants who want to facilitate the increase of knowledge or skills. As publishing is constantly evolving, so new opportunities arise for those seeking to enter the sector and for those already established in their careers.

Entry routes

There has traditionally been no agreed route into publishing, and academic and professional publishing is no exception to this. People have entered the sector through various means, not least through networking and responding to job adverts. Jobs are usually advertised and although a position may ask for subject knowledge and/or publishing experience, these are rarely requirements and certainly a degree in publishing is never necessary – but see below. Entry jobs are usually as assistants in sales, marketing, editorial and production (for example) but academic experience, library qualifications and other special skills may lead to entry at a higher level. Oxford Brookes University commissioned an excellent report on recruitment into the industry as a whole – see Resources under the title *Finding the Candidate* – which is probably relevant to our sector. It also has international relevance.

Subject expertise and skills

It is often assumed that to work in academic or professional publishing it is necessary to have an academic background in the subject (as is the preference in educational publishing) or to have worked in the sector, perhaps as an academic or researcher or as a lawyer for example. However, possession of deep subject knowledge could be considered a handicap as it could result in someone becoming engrossed in the content and blind to the commercial opportunities. There is a perceived danger that by being 'too close to the subject' products could be over-engineered for market needs. Being able to quickly get to grips with a market and understand its dynamics is what is sought by most publishers. The exceptions to this generalisation are mostly companies in the USA and Germany where those with an academic background in the relevant subject (chemistry, mechanical engineering and so on) are perceived to have an advantage, particularly for more senior positions. In addition, most learned society publishers employ specialists in internal editorial positions where work usually done by those in academic life (e.g. managing peer review) is done by them in house.

Our survey shows that publishers overwhelmingly seek individuals with enthusiasm, confidence and excellent communication skills combined in this sector with an ability to work methodically and consistently. To break this down, this covers people skills (ability to interact with people internally and externally, especially with authors and societies), written skills whether in electronic or paper format, and decent numerical skills needed to understand spreadsheets and work on business models. It is worth nothing here that even in the electronic age a good covering letter to an application for an appointment is still important as evidence of good communication skills. This is a personal advertisement and should look professional. A willingness to learn, decent organisation skills (time management, multitasking, etc.) and business or commercial acumen are highly valued.

Marketing professionals in publishing value a relevant qualification from a recognised industry body, such as the Chartered Institute of Marketing in the UK.

Although this did not come out particularly in our survey, other evidence is that if a candidate for a publishing job seeks to improve their potential acceptability and cannot afford either to take a publishing MA or go into a series of unpaid internships, it is sensible to seek employment in a skills position in a different industry or profession. For example, there are obvious crossover skills in marketing. Any business experience is likely to be useful.

Qualifications

In the UK, results from the 2010 Labour Force Survey show that 51 per cent of the entire publishing workforce is a graduate compared with 37 per cent in the wider economy. When analysed further these figures reveal that in book publishing 70 per cent are graduates, and in journals and periodicals the figure is 63 per cent. If it was possible to separate learned journals from periodicals the 63 per cent would be recognised as an understatement. The vast majority of these graduates do not hold degrees in publishing or media studies, however, with the majority studying languages, literature and culture (36 per cent), according to Skillset's 2010 Creative Media Workforce Survey.

The value of a publishing qualification

Publishers have traditionally entered the industry with a non-specialist qualification and have gone on to learn their skills 'on the job' working alongside a more senior colleague and serving a period of time deemed appropriate before promotion. In recent years higher education has attempted to engage with business to provide highly focused, relevant and practical courses that provide students with the skills needed by the modern publishing industry. Unfortunately almost all these courses treat trade publishing as the norm and academic/professional publishing as 'specialist'. Compulsory modules covering editorial and marketing skills are useful to some extent in all sectors but only one course treats (for example) journal publishing in this way – this is the University College London (UCL) course. Unfortunately it is also the case that even when the publishing course is run alongside a library (Library and Information Science) MA there is a lack of recognition by the teaching staff and the students alike that both courses essentially are concerned with the needs of the same academic researchers or teachers. Ideas for joint courses projected by some international bodies have not got off the ground. It could be argued that the emphasis of these courses reflects the interests of the students mostly aiming for trade publishing, but on the other hand these students often come to recognise during their study that most of the jobs are in academic, professional and other non-trade sectors. In addition, for some courses, there are significant numbers of students who are post-experience or perhaps working part-time in a publishing job. In some cases modules are offered to people in post through their companies.

Internationally, the UK scores well with publishing education. The British publishing industry is highly regarded and courses attract high numbers of students from overseas. There is a list of institutions offering courses in publishing to be found in The Publishers Association Guide (see Resources). The largest number of students attend the Oxford International Centre for Publishing Studies at Oxford Brookes followed by the UCL Centre for Publishing MA.

Publishing courses in North America are relatively speaking thin on the ground and there are no courses at all with a serious component of modules intended to prepare for entry into academic and professional publishing. Degree programmes are offered at several universities predominantly on the East coast, including New York University, George Washington and Yale. There are similar opportunities in Canada, of which the course at Simon Fraser is probably the most relevant. As in the

UK, North American publishers recognise these programmes and value applicants with publishing training.

The courses offered at university level aim to provide the skills that are required by the modern publishing industry. The teaching is often practical and students are encouraged to engage in group work and participate in presentations and practical projects. External speakers from industry give first-hand experience of the real world. All courses recognise the importance of acquiring digital skills and these are often embedded in teaching materials and learning outcomes. Part of a course is often a full-time attachment to a publishing company for an extended period, typically five weeks, although some institutions require students to work a couple of days a week in industry throughout their course. Either way, students gain insight into the workings of a publisher and gain valuable experience. Quite a number of students also do internships during their courses arranged privately. These are usually unpaid. In academic and professional publishers such openings are not as common as they are in trade publishing. Awareness of the range of courses available is now high and a publishing qualification is seen as a positive addition to the CV, one that is likely to at least get a candidate an interview. A relevant publishing qualification demonstrates a genuine commitment to the industry and a career in publishing; it is an investment in a future career.

Internal and external training courses for publishing staff: learning on the job

Publishing professionals responsible for hiring and managing staff use both internal and externally run courses to train and develop individuals. Often, the budget for external courses is held in the operational department rather than with a central HR department. It is often not ring-fenced and unfortunately staff development tends to be the first casualty of any cutbacks in a harsh economic environment. Internal courses not surprisingly tend to concentrate on company-specific systems or workflow procedures, together with general computer skills such as MS Office and more general management training issues such as team building and time management. The larger publishers have established courses which are run regularly for new starters and those wishing to refresh their skills in specific areas.

With publishing changing at bewildering speed and with new technologies, formats and evolving business models to understand, companies have to look outside their organisation to acquire new skills swiftly. In the UK, external courses are run by several providers including industry groups (see below), together with workshops and seminars run by commercial companies in the field, often specialising in an area such as copyright, marketing and increasingly social media. It is worth noting again that staff in marketing departments sought out marketing-specific courses such as those run by the Chartered Institute of Management.

Table 19.1 lists the most common areas of training undertaken within the total publishing industry and specifically within books and journals in 2010. Computer skills across a variety of software packages is not surprisingly the most popular area for the workforce and reflects the need to have a broad working knowledge of digital developments and confidence using the latest technologies. When considering training in social media the journals sector has been the most active part of the publishing industry to

Table 19.1 **Most common areas (per cent) of learning or development undertaken in the past 12 months**

Subject of training	Total publishing	Book publishing	Journals and periodicals	Other publishing
Computer skills – specific software packages	17	21	16	26
Writing or copyediting	16	15	23	16
Management and leadership skills	15	21	20	7
Technical or craft skills	11	12	8	20
Rules, regulations, legal	10	3	1	4
Business development, commercial awareness	9	16	10	4
Online and social media publishing	7	2	13	9
Sales & marketing skills	5	5	8	7
Copyright and intellectual property	4	2	8	0
Design and creation of digital content for individual platforms	4	0	1	0

Source: Creative Media Workforce Survey (2010) cited in *Publishing – Labour Market Intelligence Profile*. Skillset 2011

train employees in these platforms, perhaps reflecting the importance of digital distribution to this sector. Furthermore, training in writing and copyediting is seen as a key area and 23 per cent of employees received some training in these skills, significantly higher than the rest of the industry.

Most publishers recognise the importance of letting staff attend industry events and conferences, although some of the biggest have a somewhat ambivalent attitude to this. Policies within a company also vary from one office/country to another. Courses can be seen as vital to gain knowledge, learn about the competition and to keep people motivated and outward looking, hugely important when so much is changing. The networking opportunities were similarly viewed positively. Events mentioned in this connection include annual conferences and fairs including in particular the London and Frankfurt Book Fairs – not strictly training. The annual meetings of the organisations mentioned below are also regarded as training opportunities.

At higher management levels staff in the larger companies will be sent on courses where they mix with others at the same level outside the publishing field. It is said that fewer staff are encouraged to enrol for an MBA programme than was once the case.

In the UK the Publishers Association provides statistics on the industry and a guide which includes course information (see above). The Academic and Professional Division (APD) in particular offer content relevant to this book but no training as such.

The heavyweight courses for the sector are provided by the International Association of Science, Technical and Medical Publishers (STM) with their STM Master Classes and Intensive Journals Courses. These courses are held in Europe, the USA and Asia. Their website (see Resources) explains the level of experience required. These are four- or five-day residential events and are suitable for publishers in the social sciences and the humanities as well as those in science and medicine. Students are mostly from the larger houses.

The Publishers Training Centre (PTC) provides training across all sectors but at a national level. The majority of the courses are short and tend to provide a thorough grounding on specialist topics, often taught by consultants with educational or trade publishing backgrounds. They do, however, make available three-day courses on journal publishing. Some of the courses are online and the PTC works with companies to produce in-house training.

The Association of Learned and Professional Society Publishers (ALPSP) run an extensive range of training courses, mostly one day and some two days in length, all of which are appropriate for the academic sector. They are mostly held in the UK and they tend to be attended by smaller companies and societies. Three courses are now available online for self-study.

In the USA the equivalent to the APD is the Professional and Scholarly (PSP) Division of the Association of American Publishers (AAP), although unlike the APD the PSP does run an educational programme which includes 'boot camps' (not unlike the STM Intensive Journals Course) with books and journals in alternate years. The PSP works alongside the STM in this part of their programme. Other one-day courses are not unlike some of those provided by the ALPSP (already mentioned).

Another relevant organisation in North America, for individual members and mainly for publishers, is the Society for Scholarly Publishing (SSP). They have a site for professional development and do hold training seminars. A significant section of their membership is from the university presses, an important part of the US publishing scene mainly concerned with humanities publishing. These university presses have their own organisation, the Association of American University Presses (AAUP), which holds workshops and webinars sometimes in collaboration with the SSP.

In addition in the US a number of prestigious universities run short summer courses which are aimed at publishers in post as well as students looking for a job. Well-known examples are run by the University of Denver and Yale University. Probably the best known of these courses at Stanford closed in 2009. Unfortunately, none of these courses emphasizes academic and professional publishing.

There are publishing courses at a degree or postgraduate level in Germany but they are often associated with media studies and the content relevant to academic and professional publishing is minimal.

Occupational standards

The UK has a series of National Occupational Standards for the publishing industry. There are currently 39 Standards covering all aspects of the publishing process from commissioning, managing editorial projects to controlling reprints. The UK National Occupational Standards are managed by Skillset, the Sector Skills Council for the Creative Industries. The Standards are developed in consultation with industry and provide a clear description of what is needed to enable someone to perform their job competently. Each Standard consists of a detailed breakdown of the tasks, knowledge and skills needed for effective performance within a job role, including any statutory or legal responsibilities.

The Standards can be used to help plan career progression, develop job descriptions, recruit skilled staff, and design training courses and development schemes. The Standards are being reviewed in 2011 to bring them up to date with digital developments and will include journals publishing.

Career development in post

Within a particular function such as editorial, marketing or production there are quite clear progressions from assistant to managerial and indeed to directorial roles. There is some chance of moving from one function to another within the first year and again at senior level where directors of departments or divisions not infrequently have been moved from a different function as well as a different discipline. Unfortunately, most companies admit to a tendency to functional specialisation which is widely seen as unhelpful but is actually becoming more noticeable. For example, those in editorial are no longer able to calculate detailed production or marketing costs for a product. They come from a black box, a program provided by the relevant department. Some external courses, such as the STM Intensive Journals course, attempt to provide a holistic view. Equally concerning is the growing complexity of ways of making content available digitally. Some digital jobs need special knowledge and skills (see below) but all publishing staff need some level of understanding of what is possible and cost-effective.

Case study: The graduate publishing programme at a professional institution

A major UK-based professional institution has run a graduate recruitment programme for a number of years. The scheme was set up to attract highly skilled individuals to join its sizeable publishing operation. The institution has an active publishing programme which includes monograph books, scholarly journals, several advertising-supported magazines, various member publications and technical databases used by scientists and researchers.

The institution uses external assessment centres to undertake the recruitment process, although activities are all held at the organisation's main administrative site not far from London. A one-day assessment event is run four to five times a year and the focus is on various team-working activities, problem-solving tests, interviews followed by a tour of the building and introductions to key staff. Successful applications are offered a 12-month contract in the journals division, either in journals development or editorial and production. A well-established mentoring scheme ensures new starters are given the chance to learn from experienced colleagues and gain a thorough overview of all aspects of the publishing process.

What do they look for when hiring?

Candidates are required to hold a relevant degree in a science subject but the institution does not expect prior publishing knowledge or skills. Individuals with an awareness of the academic research process and subject knowledge, the ability to work in teams, an open mind and a willingness to learn are highly valued.

There are various online learning resources available as well as internally run courses on a variety of management issues and external courses are offered when appropriate.

The career ladder

Editors go on to a variety of positions in the publishing department. The typical path would be from junior (assistant) editor, to development editor, deputy editor and then managing editor of a journal. The choices are broad, however, and some choose to work with books or to become writers on the institution's member magazines.

Current and future skills

Publishers need to employ people who can deliver their products across a variety of print and digital media, including mobile, social media, apps, blogs and downloads. The digital transition and the arrival of new media have forced publishers to reassess the skills they need to ensure they can deliver content across a variety of channels to different customer bases. These skills are fluid and extend across the publishing process from editorial through to sales and marketing. Indeed, as publishing technology and business models evolve it is vital that publishing staff have a solid grasp of the digital world and should be comfortable moving between print and online.

Research conducted in 2011 by the UK sector skills council for the creative industries, Skillset (*Publishing Digital Futures*, 2011), identified two key areas where skills are most need in the publishing industry.

1. *Digital skills*. These are required across the publishing process and include:
   a. Product and brand development skills. This includes the ability to identify commercial opportunities and package content across platforms.
   b. Multimedia production skills.
   c. Being able to understand and interpret data, such as sales figures, website analytics and marketing campaign results.
   d. The ability to price and sell in the digital environment.
   e. Digital marketing and customer relationship management. Editors as well as marketers should be comfortable using social media platforms.
2. *Leadership and management skills*. Managers with these skills are required to deliver change, impart a vision and strategic direction to an organisation and be able to take products and market them using digital tools and platforms.

In 2010 Skillset carried out a survey asking employers in publishing to identify the skills they thought their organisations would need in the future (see Table 19.2).

It would appear that at present staff do not always have the knowledge base enabling a transition to the more technical roles now essential and new staff without publishing backgrounds have to be brought in, which

Table 19.2 **Future skills gaps in publishing**

Future skills gap	%
Sales & marketing	37
Specific software packages	32
Technical skills	21
Multi-skilling	21
Business skills	21
Content development across platforms	21

Source: Skillset Creative Media Employer Survey 2010.

is not necessarily ideal. This problem is also picked up by section 5 of the report *Finding the Candidate* (see Resources). The research further revealed that more experienced managers and professionals lacked an awareness of the opportunities presented through new technologies such as social media. There is scope here for new types of training courses and management development and for books like this one!

Resources

Some of the existing introductions to publishing have useful sections on, for example, how to enter and progress in the industry but they neglect the special needs of the academic and professional sector. The three most up-to-date ones are listed below followed by other recent publications describing how the industry works. Other older books are omitted except the general survey of our industry by Thompson (2005), which is so impressive and far-sighted that most of its analysis is still highly relevant:

- Davies, G. and Balkwill, R. (2011) *The Professionals' Guide to Publishing*. London: Kogan Page.
- Clark, G. and Phillips, A. (2008) *Inside Book Publishing*, 4th edn. London: Routledge.
- Baverstock, A., Carey, S. and Bowen, S. (2008) *How to Get a Job in Publishing: A Really Practical Guide to Careers in Books and Magazines*. London: A&C Black.

- Cope, B. and Phillips, A. (2005) *The Future of the Academic Journal*. Oxford: Chandos.
- Thompson, J.B. (2005) *Books in the Digital Age*. London: Polity.
- Maisonneueve, H., *et al. Science Editors' Handbook*. EASE, Ongoing.
- Barnas, E., LaFrenier, D., Morris, S. and Reich, M. (2012) *Handbook of Journal Publishing*. Cambridge: Cambridge University Press.
- Richardson, P. and Taylor, G. (2010) *PA Guide to the UK Publishing Industry*, 2nd edn. The Publishers Association.
- PSP Consulting (2010) *Finding the Candidate: Recruitment Processes in the Publishing Industry.* Oxford International Centre for Publishing Studies.
- *Learned Publishing*. ALPSP, ongoing.
- *Journal of Scholarly Publishing*. University of Toronto Press, ongoing.

More useful are the sites of the main professional and representative organizations listed above in the discussion on training:

- Association of American University Presses (AAUP), USA: http://www.aaupnet.org
- Association of Learned and Professional Society Publishers (ALPSP), UK: http://www.alpsp.org
- Chartered Institute of Marketing, UK: http://www.cim.co.uk
- International Association of Scientific, Technical & Medical Publishers (STM): http://www.stm-assoc.org
- Professional & Scholarly Publishing Division of Association of American Publishers (AAP-PSP), USA: http://www.pspcentral.org
- Creative Skillset, the Sector Skills Council (SSC) for the Creative Industries, UK: http://www.creativeskillset.org/
- Society for Scholarly Publishing (SSP), USA: http://www.sspnet.org
- The Publishers Training Centre, UK: http://www.train4publishing.co.uk
- UK Publishers Association: http://www.publishers.org.uk

Further information on the university courses mentioned in the text above can also be found online:

- George Washington University, USA: http://cps.gwu.edu/publishing.html
- New York University, USA: http://www.scps.nyu.edu

- Oxford International Centre for Publishing Studies at Oxford Brookes, UK: http://publishing.brookes.ac.uk
- Simon Fraser University, Canada: http://tkbr.ccsp.sfu.ca
- University College London (UCL) Centre for Publishing, UK: http://www.ucl.ac.uk/publishing
- University of Denver, USA: http://www.du.edu/pi
- Yale University, USA: http://publishing-course.yale.edu

Other sites that may be of interest to those interested in careers in academic and professional publishing include:

- Association for Publishing Education (APE), UK: http://www.publishingeducation.org
- Council of Science Editors (CSE), USA: http://www.councilscienceeditors.org
- German Society for Information Science and Practice (DGI), Germany: http://www.dgi-info.de
- European Association of Science Editors (EASE): http://www.ease.org.uk
- Frankfurt Book Fair, Germany: http://www.buchmesse.de/en/fbf/
- Independent Publishers Guild (IPG), UK: http://www.ipg.uk.com
- International Society for Managing and Technical Editors (ISTME): http://www.istme.org
- London Book Fair, UK: http://www.londonbookfair.co.uk
- Open Access Scholarly Publishers Association (OASPA): http://www.oaspa.org
- Society for Editors and Proofreaders (SfEP), UK: http://www.sfep.org.uk
- Society of Young Publishers (SYP), UK: http://www.thesyp.org.uk
- United Kingdom Serials Group (UKSG), UK: http://www.uksg.org

Acknowledgements

We wish to thank all those who we have consulted in preparing this chapter. There is not enough room to list them all by name but special thanks to those who answered the UCL questionnaire or who agreed to be interviewed in confidence.

20

Epilogue: trust in academic and professional publishing

Ed Pentz

Abstract: This chapter highlights the core message provided by the book's contributions: the central role of trust in academic and professional publishing. Publishing is undergoing rapid changes in technology, business models, production processes, delivery channels and user expectations, and so the chapter reviews what publishers need to understand about how trust was established and maintained in the print era and what needs to change, and what doesn't, now that digital publishing dominates. Publishers need to establish and maintain trust in the online world if the enduring values established over hundreds of years are to last, but they can only do so by understanding the online world, adapting to change and continuing to add value to scholarly communications.

Key words: Trust, scholarly communications, digital publishing, online content.

Introduction

As outlined in this book, academic and professional publishers have managed the move to publishing online very well and have, at least so far, adapted effectively and avoided serious disruption to their business models. Scholarly publishers have certainly done well compared with the music and newspaper industries, which have both seen huge disruption and declining revenues.[1]

Nevertheless, as Clarke (Chapter 4) notes, we are just 'emerging from the incunabula period of digital publishing' where digital mimics print.

Change will only accelerate going forward and scholarly publishers will need to continue to work hard and innovate effectively and efficiently to stay relevant in a changing scholarly communications landscape. So although it is true, as Campbell points out (Chapter 1), that selling to institutions and having a niche product has helped publishers adapt, there remain dark clouds. In addition, while most of the tasks currently performed by publishers will continue to be necessary there is no guarantee that in the future it will be the existing publishers who do them.

One issue is that technology companies are increasingly driving the changes that will have the most impact on scholarly communications over the next few years. In particular, Google, Amazon, Apple, Twitter and Facebook are setting researchers' expectations about how online services should work and, while scholarly communications is but a small blip on the radar for these technology companies, they are starting services specifically aimed at the scholarly research community. Anderson (Chapter 18) captures this when he says:

> '... scholarly publishers are now integrated with the broader communication sphere. No longer is the deliberate, self-defined pace of academia the primary factor driving knowledge generation and cultural attenuation within science. No longer is the audience for scholarly research a closed system.'

So, even though scholarly publishers may have so far adapted to change better than some other content industries, scholarly publishers certainly cannot be complacent. How research is conducted and disseminated is changing rapidly and therefore research funders, authors, readers, librarians and even the general public have changing expectations about what content and services they need from publishers. As Canty and Watkinson (Chapter 19) outline, this constant evolution means the need for education and training to enhance digital skills is more critical than ever. In addition, with change being so rapid, 'on the job training' and attending conferences and workshops on current topics is an effective means for publishers to keep up to date with the latest developments.

The contributions in this book highlight the wide range of roles and responsibilities that publishers adopt to produce original, useful and high-quality content. One over-arching theme that runs through all the chapters of this book, either explicitly or implicitly, is that of trust as the foundation of academic and professional publishing.

Trust in scholarly publishing

Trust is a critical aspect of scholarly publishing, but the many things that publishers do to establish and maintain trust are often taken for granted or not promoted well by publishers themselves. Over more than four centuries publishers have developed a wide range of practices and conventions to ensure that scholarly content is original and of high quality. At a conceptual level these practices are the same for print and online content.

Scholarly publishers have been very successful at transferring the trust in their print products to the online versions of the content, but they have to do more by emphasising to their readers that, in their role as publishers, they work to high ethical standards and take on the responsibility of ongoing stewardship of content after publication. This is the solution to the problem of the proliferation of authors' versions as a result of Green open access (OA) highlighted by Campbell (Chapter 1). Considering the importance of trust it is useful to take a step back and ask: What is trust?

In his book *Digital Identity* Phil Windley defines trust as 'a firm belief in the veracity, good faith, and honesty of another party, with respect to a transaction that involves some risk' (Windley, 2005, p. 16). This is a useful definition in relation to scholarly publishing where researchers read content and act on it in some way – to move forward with their own research, to replicate techniques or to perform a medical procedure. The risks are that the researcher might waste time on useless information or act on incorrect or fraudulent information, thereby damaging his or her reputation or even worse, in the case of medical information, causing harm to someone.

Windley also makes the important point that 'Trustworthiness cannot be self-declared. This is so self-evident that the phrase "trust me" has become a cliché sure to get a laugh'. (Windley, 2005, p. 17). This means that trust has to be earned and maintained. In the print era, publishers became very adept at dealing with issues of trust and have been working to transfer trust metrics from the print to the online world and to establish new ones as well.

How do publishers establish trust?

To answer the question of how scholarly publishers establish trust we need to go back to 1665. Mabe (Chapter 17) highlights how, with *Philosophical Transactions* in 1665, Henry Oldenburg established the key aspects of trust for journals:

- Date stamping or priority via *registration*
- Quality stamping (*certification*) through peer review
- Recording the final, definitive, authorised versions of papers and *archiving* them
- *Dissemination* to targeted scholarly audience.

What is interesting is that the journal developed in an environment that was devoid of trust in many areas. Adrian Johns in *The Nature of the Book* describes how, as experimental science started to develop in the second half of the 17th century, the exchange of private letters amongst a small circle of 'natural philosophers' who knew each other personally developed into a system of wider dissemination around Europe amongst people who didn't know each other (Johns, 2000, pp. 514–515). *Philosophical Transactions* was created as a way of establishing rules of the road for communicating information about experiments, establishing priority and ensuring appropriate authorial credit. This was essential because, as Johns points out of the early experimentalists, 'Theirs was a world of plagiarism, of usurpation' (Johns, 2000, p. 541) but, with *Philosophical Transactions* playing a critical role, 'this age of piracy created a fierce reaction in favor of truth' (Johns, 2000, p. 541). Establishing the protocols for publication wasn't easy and involved many fierce disputes but over time a very successful system of scholarly communications was established. The success of science itself was inextricably linked to the journal and this has continued to the present day.

Looking back at this history is important for scholarly publishing today because the Internet can also be seen as a world of plagiarism and usurpation where establishing authority is very difficult. In an article in *Scientific American* (Shadbolt and Berners-Lee, 2008) discussing the new discipline of 'Web Science', and echoing what Johns says was the tenor of the times when *Philosophical Transactions* was founded, Tim Berners Lee and Nigel Shadbolt point out that:

> 'The Web was originally conceived as a tool for researchers who trusted one another implicitly; strong models of security were not built in. We have been living with the consequences ever since.' (Shadbolt and Berners-Lee, 2008, p. 35)

As a solution they call for 'layers of trust and provenance' to be developed for the Web.

Scholarly publishers need to understand the part that they can play in this process of establishing provenance and trust and what not to lose from the print world. This will involve more transparency about the pre-publication processes publishers undertake to ensure the originality and quality of content. Hames (Chapter 2) outlines why peer review is so critical to scholarly communications and how it is changing and adapting but not becoming any less important. Publishers also need to highlight their ongoing role in actively maintaining content, or acting as stewards of the content, over the long term. Wager (Chapter 14) highlights how publishers play a vital role in establishing ethics and integrity in pre-publication processes but also how the publisher has an important role post-publication. Seeley and Wasoff (Chapter 15) describe the legal aspects of this and why copyright and author agreements are so important but also how a company like Google can potentially set the agenda with the Google library digitisation project. This project raises fundamental issues about copyright and has required publishers, librarians, authors and others to stake out positions and push back or be consigned to irrelevance.

Another critical area where publishers establish trust and foster efficient and effective scholarly communications systems is in the area of relationship management, as outlined by Black (Chapter 16). Something that is often not well understood by non-publishers is the complex set of relationships that publishers establish and maintain with editors, editorial boards and societies. The value of peer review is widely recognised as a key part of the scholarly communications system but Black highlights an area that is critical, but often overlooked, for scholarly communications.

Stewards of content

The idea of scholarly publishers as stewards of content is something that needs to be more widely recognised. There is a general impression that there is a static, 'final' version of content and that once the publication is printed or available online the publisher's role is over. If you look at the role of the journal established by Oldenburg, one of the four functions is 'archiving'. This is too limited and static a vision of what role publishers must play with scholarly content on the Web.

In 2008 a National Information Standards Organisation/Association of Learned and Professional Society Publishers working group published some recommendations on Journal Article Versions, which characterized the 'final' version as the Version of Record as established and declared by the publisher. The definition of Version of Record says it is a 'fixed version of a journal article that has been made available by any organization that acts as a publisher by formally and exclusively declaring the article "published".' This is a useful definition but it is not complete. The recommendations also describe a 'Corrected Version of Record' and an 'Enhanced Version of Record' but only briefly. This is a big issue that is critical to the future of scholarly publishing: it is publishers that certify the Version of Record of content (this is more commonly associated with journal articles but can and should apply to books, reference works and other types of content). It is also the publisher that maintains the content and is responsible for making corrections, retractions and withdrawals and disseminating the information about these events, which occur after publication. This will, of course, be no surprise to publishers who have long had this role, but it is something that is often overlooked in the Web environment. Publishers need more consciously and publicly to adopt the role of both certifying content via peer review and other editorial and production processes and maintaining the content by certifying and disseminating any corrections or enhancements to the content. In addition, all this should be done in a very transparent manner so the user can check and verify what has happened to the content.

Trust is also established by having commonly agreed metrics for assessing quality and impact. Finch (Chapter 10) outlines how existing metrics are being questioned and new ones being developed and tested and some of the difficulties of finding consensus on what certain metrics mean and what they should be used for. Whatever the merits of the various metrics, publishers play a vital role in this area.

Another aspect of trust is that of standards. Carpenter (Chapter 9) highlights the importance of standards for publishers. Echoing Anderson's statement that scholarly research is no longer a 'closed system', Carpenter covers international, national and sector-specific standards that all have an impact on scholarly communications and give publishers valuable tools in addressing the challenges of digital publishing.

Publishers must never forget that librarians are key partners of publishers in the scholarly communications system and Webster (Chapter 13) writes about the changing landscape of digital publishing from the library point of view.

What about business models and costs?

Of course scholarly publishers, commercial and non-profit alike, can only do what they do if they generate revenue or if someone is willing to cover their costs because they add value. Both commercial and non-profit publishers have to operate efficiently and have funds to invest in new developments. Haynes (Chapter 6) gives an overview of this critical area for scholarly publishing and highlights the creativity and adaptability of the industry and Clarke (Chapter 4) outlines the many experiments with new modes of publishing that publishers are investing in. There is currently an active debate about how much more business models will need to change and whether scholarly publishing will be disrupted as the music and newspaper industries have been.

With respect to journals, Green and Cookson (Chapter 5) cite physicist's Michael Nielsen's blog post 'Is scientific publishing about to be disrupted,[2] which argues that scientific research is undergoing fundamental change that will result in massive changes to how the results of research are disseminated and that existing publishers are likely to be left out of the new way of doing things. Along these lines, Jubb (Chapter 3) highlights the many changes occurring in research, research funding and the expectations of research funders. In particular he cites 'a new "fourth paradigm" for research: following the moves from empirical to theoretical to computational science, it is suggested that we now need to think in terms of data-intensive science.' Publishers need to track these changes and stay close to the communities they serve or they will be in danger of being disrupted.

Publishers have not been standing still in the face of all this change. Green and Cookson counter Nielsen's argument by highlighting 'the incredibly complex set of services, activities and products that publishers bring to the material output of the academic and research worlds.' They also cite the statistic that the journals industry has invested over £2 billion since 2000 'in areas such as editorial systems, author tools, production workflow, plagiarism checking, content management, online content platforms, global sales management and many more elements.' Clarke (Chapter 4), Böing (Chapter 8) and van Baren (Chapter 11) all highlight areas where publishers have invested significant sums to develop new products and processes. Böing and van Baren, in particular, highlight that it requires significant investment in new processes to be an efficient and effective digital publisher. Pinter (Chapter 7) points out many of the specific issues facing book, reference and textbook publishers with changing formats and business models and the explosion of eBooks, which are subject to very different forces from journals.

A critical aspect in the development of a publisher's business model is understanding customers, including the needs of authors and readers, libraries and funders, as O'Rourke highlights (Chapter 12). In the highly competitive marketplace of academic and professional publishing and with increasing constraints on funding, publishers must look to differentiate a product or service by quality and coverage to suit the needs of the community on the one hand, and on the other hand to maximize access through intelligent pricing models.

What about small publishers?

Achieving and maintaining an adequate level of investment, particularly in technology, does present challenges for smaller publishers. Can the smaller publishers keep up with the larger ones? It is a challenge but there are positive signs that smaller publishers can do well in the new environment.

Larger publishers invest huge sums in developing their own publishing platforms and it is unclear whether this is money well spent as more and more researchers are using tools like Google and link into publisher sites at the journal article or book chapter level. The Research Information Network report *E-journals: their use, value and impact* (RIN, 2011) found that top rated researchers 'do not use many of the online facilities provided on the publishers' platform' (RIN, 2011, p. 4) and 'are much more likely to enter via gateway sites' (RIN, 2011, p. 4) such as PubMed, Web of Science and Google. In fact, users may spend only a few seconds on the publisher platform – just enough time to look at an abstract or click to download the full-text PDF article. The report quotes one young life science researcher: 'I go to PubMed – always. I ... don't really notice the publisher page at the end. (RIN, 2011, p. 13). So general gateway services have a levelling effect whereby content from small publishers can be just as discoverable as that from larger publishers.

Smaller publishers have options for hosting content with many vendors and aggregators offering commodity services. Many scholarly societies partner with commercial publishers, or even larger societies with dedicated publishing divisions, to outsource their publications while still maintaining ownership of the content and brand (journal titles, book series and the society name). In addition, as Pinter (Chapter 7) outlines, with eBooks there are more options than ever with Amazon,

Google and Apple competing fiercely in the eBook space but also having a big say in business models and pricing given that they control the distribution and the sales platform. Additional options for scholarly eBooks are also arising, from Project MUSE partnering with the University Press e-Book Consortium (UPeC) to launch University Press Content Consortium (UPCC) e-Book Collections,[3] and JSTOR launching Books at JSTOR,[4] to Oxford University Press expanding Oxford Scholarship Online to launch University Press Scholarship Online (UPSO).[5] For journals there is also the option of the Open Journal System (OJS),[6] which is a free, open source journal management and publishing system from the non-profit Public Knowledge Project. OJS is being used by over 7000 journals on six continents.

Identification of content and people

In the last decade there have been two major areas, digital linking and author disambiguation, where publishers have addressed market developments by creating systems built on trust between stakeholders in scholarly communications. In the first case publishers collaborated to set up a cross-publisher reference linking system, the CrossRef System,[7] using DOIs (Digital Object Identifiers). Founded in 2000, CrossRef enables the identification and linking of over 52 million scholarly content items (as of January 2012) including journal and conference proceedings articles and books and book chapters. CrossRef expanded its services to plagiarism detection with CrossCheck and is developing more collaborative services, including CrossFund, which will link funders and grant numbers with the resulting publications.

The second and more recent development is the founding of ORCID (Open Researcher and Contributor ID)[8] in August 2010. ORCID is a non-profit organisation made up of publishers, universities, researchers and private and government research funders from around the world. ORCID has been set up to solve the name ambiguity problem in scholarly communications by creating an open, global registry of unique identifiers for researchers. There are many existing author identifier systems but ORCID is unique in that it is global, cross-disciplinary and is governed by universities, publishers, research funders (private and government) and the researchers themselves. A registry of unique identifiers for researchers coupled with unique scholarly content identifiers and permanent links will add a huge amount of value to scholarly communications.

Both CrossRef and ORCID are very valuable to researchers because they facilitate content discovery and the appropriate crediting of researchers for their work and new services will be built around these two systems. Publishers also benefit from these projects by doing things collectively that cannot be done individually and by creating the conditions for the development of new services that build off from CrossRef and ORCID.

Conclusion and outlook

All the investment by publishers into quality content doesn't guarantee the continuing success or even the continued existence of the current set of scholarly publishers in all their diversity. To survive, publishers will need to learn the right lessons from what happened to the newspaper and music industries, be flexible and take calculated risks. What is required is a clear understanding of how to add value to the process of scholarly communications however it changes in the future and the flexibility and intelligence to experiment with new ways of doing things without letting go of core values. On one side of the equation, it is critical for publishers to stay close to researchers and academics and keep abreast of the changes in research and research funding. And on the other side, it is critical for publishers to have a deep understanding of the online world – both technology and services – and how they can be applied in the most effective way in scholarly and academic publishing. The creation of both CrossRef and ORCID are positive signs that the industry can collaborate in the spirit of enlightened self-interest.

This book has captured the important aspects of both the rapid changes occurring in academic and professional publishing as well as the enduring values of the industry. Of course, publishers cannot afford to be complacent because the industry is still in the middle of the maelstrom of change. What it comes down to in the end is whether academic and professional publishers add value to scholarly communications. If they do, then they will survive. The trick is figuring out how to add value in a period of rapid change. Publishers have gone through periods of change before – adopting new technology, business models and editorial and production processes, and developing new products and services – so although there are certainly dark clouds there are also patches of blue sky to head towards. It won't be easy for publishers to adapt and change, but it will definitely be interesting and a lot of fun.

Notes

1. For a sobering look at the financial impact of disruption see these charts available for the music (http://theunderstatement.com/post/3362645556/the-real-death-of-the-music-industry) and newspaper industries (http://theunderstatement.com/post/3890398012/the-newspaper-business-implodes)
2. http://michaelnielsen.org/blog/is-scientific-publishing-about-to-be-disrupted/
3. UPCC e-books; http://muse.jhu.edu/about/new/ebook_collections.html
4. Books at JSTOR; http://about.jstor.org/books
5. University Press Scholarship Online; http://www.universitypressscholarship.com/
6. Public Knowledge Project's Open Journal System; http://pkp.sfu.ca/?q=ojs
7. http://www.crossref.org/
8. http://www.orcid.org/

References

Johns, A. (2000) *The Nature of the Book*. Chicago: The University of Chicago Press.

RIN (2011) *E-journals: their use, value and impact – final report*; http://www.rin.ac.uk/our-work/communicating-and-disseminating-research/e-journals-their-use-value-and-impact

Shadbolt, N. and Berners-Lee, T. (2008) Web Science emerges. *Scientific American* October: 32–7. http://webscience.org/publications/ws_emerges.pdf. [This article also provides a very succinct description of Google PageRank and the Semantic Web.]

Windley, P. (2005) *Digital Identity*. Sebastopol, CA: O'Reilly Media.

Index

CPSIA information can be obtained at www.ICGtesting.com
Printed in the USA
LVOW071346270912

300476LV00003B/2/P